ROUGH NOTES TO ERASURE

BEFORE YOU START TO READ THIS BOOK, take this moment to think about making a donation to punctum books, an independent non-profit press,

@ https://punctumbooks.com/support/

If you're reading the e-book, you can click on the image below to go directly to our donations site. Any amount, no matter the size, is appreciated and will help us to keep our ship of fools afloat. Contributions from dedicated readers will also help us to keep our commons open and to cultivate new work that can't find a welcoming port elsewhere. Our adventure is not possible without your support.

Vive la Open Access.

Fig. 1. Hieronymus Bosch, *Ship of Fools* (1490–1500)

First published in 2020 by punctum books, Earth, Milky Way.
https://punctumbooks.com

ISBN-13: 978-1-950192-79-3 (print)
ISBN-13: 978-1-950192-80-9 (ePDF)

DOI: 10.21983/P3.0287.1.00

LCCN: 2020936034
Library of Congress Cataloging Data is available from the Library of Congress

Book design: Vincent W.J. van Gerven Oei
Cover image: Lisa Goren, *Whalebones, Abandoned Whaling Station, Antarctica
#41.* http://www.lisagorenpaintings.com; info@lisagorenpaintings.com.

HIC SVNT MONSTRA

Dolsy Smith

Rough Notes to Erasure
White Male Privilege, My Senses, and the Story I Cannot Tell

Contents

for Natalie

Remember, turn not away thine eyes from thine own
FLESH.

— Abiezer Coppe, *Selected Writings*

*The moment I disappear into the woodwork for good
will be the exact moment of all my work is fully realized.*

*This has very little to do with other people's recog-
nition of it. I do not have the time or energy to spend
on that. I am talking to you. You are part of the work
I am making by writing this. You are no more or less
invisible than I am.*

— Adrian Piper, *Escape to Berlin*

*This is why we stay with poetry. And despite our con-
senting to all the indisputable technologies; despite
seeing the political leap that must be managed, the
horror of hunger and ignorance, torture and massa-
cre to be conquered, the full load of knowledge to be
tamed, the weight of every piece of machinery that we
shall finally control, and the exhausting flashes as we
pass from one era to another – from forest to city, from
story to computer – at the bow there is still something
we now share: this murmur, cloud or rain or peaceful
smoke. We know ourselves as part and as crowd, in an
unknown that does not terrify. We cry our cry of poetry. Our boats are open, and we sail them for everyone.*

— Édouard Glissant, *Poetics of Relation*

Introduction

In writing this para-academic work, I wrestled for a long time with a false problem. Without the academic credentials appropriate to the kind of book that I wanted to write (a monograph in the humanities), I imagined that writing such a book had to be a solitary, even a solipsistic, act. For my lack of credentials seemed to imply a lack of expertise. And that, in turn, suggested an absence of legitimate purpose and, therefore, of a community of readers to which I could address my work. Stuck on this dilemma, I dwelt on my fear that my career in letters up to this point (the point of this writing) amounted to failure. And as I wrote, I became invested in that failure. Or perhaps it's fair to say that I was already invested: that I had learned to inhabit failure as a structure of feeling that can be self-imposed. My writing had become the tortuous space of that inhabitation, a tangle of fear and desire, pride and envy. Writing sentences that didn't want to resolve themselves, writing paragraphs that refused to stay focused, writing pieces that I never knew how to wrap up, that I didn't dare consider finished. The conviction of failure didn't stop me from writing, but it kept me from sharing what I wrote — which is the wager without which a talent may be a measure of possession but will hardly become a gift. Having invested, moreover, in the idea of failure as the inevitable condition of the sorts of texts that I sought to produce, I strove to align my work in progress with an intellectual tradition that celebrates writing, not to mention thought itself, as an exercise in negativity and erasure (from Hegel to Blanchot, the early Foucault, and Derrida). I imagined myself in that "labyrinth" invoked by Foucault to describe the "trouble" and the "pleasure" of writing, where fascination, in the folds of anonymity, becomes freedom:

> I am no doubt not the only one who writes in order to have no face. Do not ask who I am and do not ask me to remain the same: leave it to our bureaucrats and our police to see that our papers are in order. At least spare us their morality when we write.[1]

Here Foucault is Theseus on the trail of the Minotaur, and also the Minotaur himself, and also Daedalus. Hero, monster, and architect merge in the avowed facelessness of the European intellectual — white, male, and a member of the professional elite — whose papers are already, for the most part, in order. And I am the child poring over *D'Aulaires' Book of Greek Myths,* with its star-struck Phaethon on the cover.

But I am hardly faceless when, over drinks one night with colleagues, these flesh-and-blood readers want to know, *Who is your audience?* I wish the beer bottle's lip could hide the answer that I will botch. *That's just it: that's my problem.* I try to explain how I've been writing an academic book from a position of deep ambivalence about academic writing. Feeling as though the suit doesn't fit, though at the same time refusing to leave off this prolongation of the sartorial No. Finally, I confess: I'm afraid that no one will want to read it, that in fact I'm writing for nobody. My colleagues assure me that they get my ambivalence; they've felt it, too. And they would, indeed, read such a book. But somebody there wants to know, *What are you trying*

---

1   Michel Foucault, *The Archaeology of Knowledge: And the Discourse on Language,* trans. A.M. Sheridan Smith (New York: Vintage, 1982), 17.

to say in this book? That I don't know *what* I want *explicitly* to say; that I am writing in fidelity to that ignorance, as well as out of resistance to the demand, normative in academic writing, for maximal explicitness, and for critical explication as the function (at least in the humanities) of formally sanctioned expertise: none of that answers the question. Somebody who was there before, but without my seeing them, lets me know, I'm not writing for them. Generous and brave, their question broaches a truth that, up to now, I have managed to dodge, both in my writing and in my thinking. And that is my investment in the dominant subject-position of academic writing and expertise. The fact remains that as a white cishet man, I always already enjoy the privilege of understanding — even when I disclaim it. I encounter nearly everywhere, if not the satisfaction of my desires, then their legibility, their endorsement. *Look at you looking at you,* the TV chirps and the billboard booms, *Looking good!* And in academia, too: *You,* says the library in its susurrus of dead white male voices, *This is you.*

I made him turn red! she said with a laugh. I blamed it on the beer, which was, of course, a lie. What makes the white man show his true colors? Shame, of course. Shame and anger. Or like the cover of a book of myths, my baffled face declared my investment in the ruses of patriarchal white supremacy. The great waffler Thomas Jefferson — as Tavia Nyong'o reminds us — adduced as evidence for the superiority of whites their "capacity to blush."[2] But racialized shame, as Nyong'o argues, refuses to stay put. If shame appears in the performances of moral refinement that can signify belonging to the white bourgeoisie, its weaponized deployment bears down on those marked by their exclusion from whiteness's folds.[3] And as I explore in

2 Tavia Nyong'o, *The Amalgamation Waltz: Race, Performance, and the Ruses of Memory* (Minneapolis: University of Minnesota Press, 2009), 86–87. Provocatively, Nyong'o claims that "race emerges in its modern form only when it becomes possible to be ashamed of it" (90).

3 Jefferson's remarks contributed to an intellectual arsenal aimed at justifying, for an "enlightened" European audience, the perpetuation of

a later chapter, anger, too, runs deeply through the embodied textures of racialized and gendered status, hierarchy, and power. In Jefferson's racist imagination, a blush, testifying to a capacity for shame, justifies the white subject's possession of liberty and fraternal citizenship.[4] You might say that as a political emotion, shame indexes the susceptibility of the subject to the demand for justification. (As a writer, I blushed at having to justify myself to hypothetical readers. As a white man, I blushed at being asked to explain my motives to somebody who is not white.) By *justification,* I mean an act of making explicit how the self measures up within hierarchical orders of value. *What are you trying to say?* The question can shame, because while the value judgments at play are frequently rendered as totalizing abstractions, with an appeal to categories like "a good scholar" or "a good person," any possible response begins and ends with the flesh, flush and perplexed and lousy with partiality. Likewise, these orders of value matter because they rest on material supports. They recruit and organize, even as they are disrupted by, forms of labor, violence, and power. Often an agent of the state compels such a performance, bringing down the hammer of grammar on the stake of one's indexical self. *Hey, you!* shouts the cop in the Althusserian scene. But the important point is that the police don't hail everyone the same. Despite explicit

chattel slavery. After Emancipation, racialized shame remained part of the "burdened individuality" imposed on an emancipated but still politically and socially subordinate population. See Saidiya V. Hartman, *Scenes of Subjection: Terror, Slavery, and Self-Making in Nineteenth-Century America* (New York: Oxford University Press, 2010). Nyong'o's work demonstrates how the rhetoric of shame was deployed by abolitionists like David Walker as an ambivalent tool in the counter-discourse against white supremacy (*The Amalgamation Waltz*, 89–91).

4   In a different but closely linked register, "the language of Indian savagery," as Robert A. Williams, Jr. notes, has "helped organize the West's will to empire on a global scale, and its deep imprints on the American racial imagination are even more profound" (*Like a Loaded Weapon: The Rehnquist Court, Indian Rights, and the Legal History of Racism in America* [Minneapolis: University of Minnesota Press, 2005], 34).

commitments to equality, the institutions of North American society continue to insist that white people — especially white cishet men who have normative bodies and own (or could own) property — are worth more than everyone else. The obligation to say what we're up to and to know what we're saying, with or without credentials, falls more lightly on people who look like me. Where the cop might hail me with words, for many others his baton performs this office, or his gun. And a great many are those whom our institutions conspire in telling, time and again, that they have nothing worthwhile to say at all.

The lightness of the world's demands on me has everything to do with my idea of failure as a personal possession, as something that I have freely, if foolishly, chosen. The white man is at liberty to be a fool. Part of the folly he enjoys consists in his conviction that everything about him is of his own doing. (Only as long as it suits him, of course. He's also generally allowed to blame others for any shortcomings in himself.) The social and political dominance of whiteness, and especially of white cishet masculinity, depends on the sanctity of this optical illusion: that the figure cut by these properties is at once distinct by virtue of its superiority to all others and at the same time boundless, universal, and hence no figure at all.[5] Inspired by feminist and anti-racist traditions, for decades scholarship in the humanities has sought to correct this illusion, making explicit our complicity in structures of domination. As an heir to these hopes, this book represents my own efforts to reckon with my composition as a subject of white male privilege and power. Its writing has offered me the chance of coming to terms with my own complicity. However, if such a reckoning is to take root in active dispositions — dispositions that can prepare me to resist the ways that I

---

5   As Nahum Dimitri Chandler argues, white supremacy entails "a narrative of purity, of the self-repleteness and historical becoming of a white subject, a historical and social being supposedly arising of its own initiative, unmarked by any sign of difference" ("Originary Displacement," *boundary 2* 27, no. 3 [2000]: 273). See also Harryette Mullen, "Optic White: Blackness and the Production of Whiteness," *Diacritics* 24, nos. 2–3 (1994): 71–89.

aid and abet patriarchal white supremacy, in order that I might become a better ally in the resistance to structural violence and oppression — then it must, this reckoning, be both critical and therapeutic. I use therapeutic in Wittgenstein's sense: as a kind of counterpoint to the explicit. The philosopher's healing gesture is not about coddling the self. Rather, it responds to the limits of critique as understood in the Kantian tradition. Or of the limits of explication as a practice by which subjects come to understand the conditions of their own subjectivity. It is not enough, for Wittgenstein, to rest our understanding on a set of propositions: propositions that supposedly translate private experience into public discourse. Such propositions may parade the virtues of clarity, precision, and apodictic certainty. But their inadequacy lies in hiding from us just how much those virtues eclipse. For Wittgenstein, we have to tarry with our language-games. In doing so, we prepare ourselves, not for the moment when doubt turns to insight, but for what the philosopher calls the "dawning" of a new aspect. As when the drawing you took at first for a rabbit now, suddenly, discloses a duck.[6] It's critical to the idea of aspect that the rabbit doesn't disappear, even if it's not possible to see (i.e., to identify) both figures at the same time. In other words, when a new aspect dawns, it doesn't transform the viewer, unlocking some heretofore latent capacity or converting passive receptivity into active, reflective thought. Nor is it a matter of replacing a set of false beliefs with a true and justified set, thereby qualifying me for my status as the subject of knowledge.[7] I'm not trying to say that now I *know* better.

6   The discussion of aspect can be found in Part II, Section xi of Ludwig Wittgenstein, *Philosophical Investigations,* trans. G.E.M. Anscombe, 3rd edn. (Malden: Wiley-Blackwell, 1991). On the duck-rabbit, see especially 165–71.

7   The example of the duck-rabbit confounds classical philosophical treatments of the relation between knowledge and belief, according to which knowledge is a belief that is both true and justifiable. (By definition, such knowledge must be capable of being made explicit.) In the case of the aspect-shift, my knowledge of what the picture represents (once I know that it depicts both animals) can never be commensurate to my moment-

I'm drawing on Wittgenstein's discussion of aspect in the service of a more relational approach to social structure, power, and domination. Here I'm following Alexander Weheliye's move (which follows the lead of Black feminist theorists) to think about how the categories of race and gender, through their mutual inflection, trace the shifting contours "that apportion and delimit which humans can lay claim to full human status and which humans cannot."[8] Whiteness or white cishet masculinity does not stand on its own as a thing, though as we shall see, defending against the threat of one's own thinghood remains central to the subject-positions of those who identify as white men. For now, it bears repeating that *whiteness* refers to one side of an interface between domination and subordination, possession and dispossession. In an effort to think it, I imagine the chalk outline at the scene of a crime, or the cartographic lines that

to-moment experience of it. This is unlike, for instance, learning that you have misidentified the animal in the backyard. In that case, perhaps it suffices to say that the warrant of empirical knowledge — gleaned by going up to the window for a closer look — banishes your mistaken belief to the bestiary of analogy. You might say, having corrected yourself, that the duck appears very rabbit-like, etc. When confronted with the duck-rabbit, on the other hand, it would sound odd or nonsensical to say of the rabbit, when you're attending to the latter aspect, that you might almost believe it was a duck.

8   Alexander G. Weheliye, *Habeas Viscus: Racializing Assemblages, Biopolitics, and Black Feminist Theories of the Human* (Durham: Duke University Press, 2014), 3. Fred Moten recruits Wittgensteinian aspect to different, albeit related, ends in his book *In the Break: The Aesthetics of the Black Radical Tradition* (Minneapolis: University of Minnesota Press, 2003), 88–93. For Moten, the idea of seeing (or hearing) aspect gestures toward a theory of the ensemble in its excess of what can explicitly be said about it: "Perhaps it is the supplement of description that allows description; for description of the phenomenon or experience of ensemble is only adequate if it is also itself the phenomenon or experience of ensemble" (92). For Moten, the ensemble offers a way of opening Western philosophy to an aesthetics of Blackness whose lessons that philosophical tradition has repeatedly foreclosed (thereby mistaking the direction of the debt). Occurring, you might say, only in that special, fugitive light of the dawning of an aspect, the ensemble's phantom fullness has also something "to do with utopian aspiration and political despair" (90).

designate, with sovereign but arbitrary precision, the boundaries of a territory. And yet, these metaphors suggest something more fixed and indifferent than the fluid practices by which the body identified as white, and *a fortiori* as white and male, moves through its milieu. This body apportions space as the medium of its inalienable rights of possession. It unspools its thoughts in time as the unbroken line of development toward the promise of a future in which personal, national, and civilizational achievement coincide. But this is a development anchored in the world that stolen labor built, and which terror, neglect, and discrimination sustain, upon stolen lands.[9] It is hardly sufficient to the projects of racial justice that this body should become conscious of its privilege. Not so long as consciousness remains

---

9   My argument is indebted to Shannon Sullivan's "transactional" account of whiteness in *Revealing Whiteness: The Unconscious Habits of Racial Privilege* (Bloomington: Indiana University Press, 2006). See also Mike King, "Aggrieved Whiteness: White Identity Politics and Modern American Racial Formation," *Abolition,* May 4, 2017, https://abolitionjournal.org/aggrieved-whiteness-white-identity-politics-and-modern-american-racial-formation/; Charles W. Mills, *The Racial Contract* (Ithaca: Cornell University Press, 1999); Alexis Shotwell, *Knowing Otherwise: Race, Gender, and Implicit Understanding* (University Park: Pennsylvania State University Press, 2011); George Yancy, *Black Bodies, White Gazes: The Continuing Significance of Race in America,* 2nd edn. (Lanham: Rowman & Littlefield, 2016); and George Yancy, *Look, a White! Philosophical Essays on Whiteness* (Philadelphia: Temple University Press, 2012).

On whiteness and the occupation of space, see Sullivan, *Revealing Whiteness,* 143–66. Andrea Smith addresses the temporality of settler colonialism, in which Native peoples seem "to have no future," in "Queer Theory and Native Studies: The Heteronormativity of Settler Colonialism," GLQ: *A Journal of Lesbian and Gay Studies* 16, nos. 1–2 (2010): 41–68, quotation at 48. Aileen Moreton-Robinson's important work addresses the erasure or marginalization of Native and Indigenous perspectives and histories in whiteness studies, reminding us that "the existence of white supremacy as hegemony, ideology, epistemology, and ontology requires the possession of Indigenous lands as its proprietary anchor within capitalist economies such as the United States" (*The White Possessive: Property, Power, and Indigenous Sovereignty* [Minneapolis: University of Minnesota Press, 2015], xix).

synonymous with the entertainment of propositions or intentional representations whose meanings can be made explicit. This model enshrines the Western prejudice against the flesh, seeking through moral reason to break the lease of its contingency, to consecrate a kingdom on its parcel of earth.[10] In other words, the explication of privilege remains bound up with the conditions that privilege explication as a vehicle for what Sylvia Wynter calls the "overrepresentation" of the white Western subject, by which "Man" becomes a universal figure for the human being.[11] By this catachresis, which the white Western subject defends as his unique entitlement, the latter figures himself as transcendent to his body and its milieu, including the racialized and gendered signifiers that determine which bodies are entitled to indulge in such fantasies, forgetting shared history and collective destiny.[12] On the other hand, and because of this history, as Denise Ferreira da Silva argues, it does not suffice to insist on the *particularity* of whiteness or white masculinity.[13] Whiteness is not one ethnicity among others, as some strains of multiculturalism, desperate to placate a deeply American hypocrisy, maintain. Permitted to ignore the particular ways in which my race and gender entitle me to lands, goods, opportunities, and protections denied to others, I may regard myself as one of the "good white people" of whom Shannon Sullivan

---

10 As Saba Mahmood observes, Western moral philosophy has a tendency to suppose "that a moral act could be moral only to the extent that is was not a result of habituated virtue but a product of the critical faculty of reason. The latter requires that one act in spite of one's inclinations, habits, and dispositions" (*Politics of Piety: The Islamic Revival and the Feminist Subject* [Princeton: Princeton University Press, 2005], 25).

11 Sylvia Wynter, "Unsettling the Coloniality of Being/Power/Truth/Freedom: Towards the Human, After Man, Its Overrepresentation—An Argument," *CR: The New Centennial Review* 3, no. 3 (2003): 257–337.

12 In *Black and Blur* (Durham: Duke University Press, 2017), Fred Moten writes that "blackness isn't a people problem. It's the problematization of the people" (202). And whiteness is the "solution" in which the people disappear, leaving only oblivious individuals.

13 Denise Ferreira da Silva, *Toward a Global Idea of Race* (Minneapolis: University of Minnesota Press, 2007).

writes: while *consciously* attending to the effort not to let racial prejudice seep into their thoughts, they shunt onto others the demanding emotional, intellectual and physical labor of standing up for racial justice. They can do so because forms of violence like police brutality, as well as more structural harms like lead in the water, don't infringe on their mundane white worlds. These worlds are populated by good white people like themselves (and perhaps a few people of color for good measure).[14] Though living on stolen land and stolen time, the closure of these worlds under conditions of white supremacy and settler colonialism appears to ratify their distance from the latter. It's as if those things only occurred where white people weren't. As if one could sever, by force of will or practice of neglect, the rabbit from the duck. My point is that this closure is compatible with the entertainment of explicit propositions that denounce racism. It is compatible even with those propositions that describe racism in institutional and structural terms.[15]

Once it occurs, of course, the aspect-shift that Wittgenstein describes remains easy to reverse. As we look at the image, duck and rabbit lap and displace each other endlessly. But I need a notion of aspect that involves all the senses, including the affects. A sort of deep aspect, if you will. The dawning of deep aspect, if durable, will represent a long and arduous process. Perhaps

14   Shannon Sullivan, *Good White People: The Problem with Middle-Class White Anti-Racism* (Albany: State University of New York Press, 2014). Indeed, as Sullivan suggests, the limited cognitive and emotional labor that "good white people" do to temper the racism in themselves yields its own psychological wage, in the form of a feeling of superiority vis-à-vis those "other" white people who are explicitly racist, and who appear, in the middle-class white imaginary, uniformly working-class, i.e., "white trash."

15   In his trenchant critique of liberal strategies as applied to the political struggles of trans and gender nonconforming people, Dean Spade notes that "the anti-discrimination/hate crime law strategy relies on the belief that if we change what the law says about a particular group to make it say 'good things' […] and not 'bad things' […] then those people's lives will improve" (*Normal Life: Administrative Violence, Critical Trans Politics, and the Limits of Law* [Brooklyn: South End Press, 2011], 29).

an interminable one. And this process implies a pedagogy, one addressed to the senses as the terrain of those sociogenic forces by which race and gender cement themselves in the modern psyche.[16] George Yancy argues for the utility of "a form of writing that is not meant to be simply cerebral, but to impact the body and to weave a narrative that captures something that is profoundly familiar and intensely mundane."[17] The deep aspect of my privilege lies in what it means, for me as a white cishet

16 On sociogeny, see Frantz Fanon, *Black Skin, White Masks,* trans. Richard Philcox, rev. ed. (New York: Grove Press, 2008): xv. In what follows, I draw on Sylvia Wynter's reading of Fanon in "Towards the Sociogenic Principle: Fanon, Identity, the Puzzle of Conscious Experience, and What It Is Like to Be 'Black,'" in *National Identities and Sociopolitical Changes in Latin America,* eds. Mercedes F. Durán-Cogan and Antonio Gómez-Moriana (New York: Routledge, 2001), 30–66, as well as the discussion in Weheliye, *Habeas Viscus,* 25–27.

17 Yancy, *Black Bodies, White Gazes,* 17. Yancy's treatment of "the elevator effect" — his phenomenologically rich description of his encounter, as a Black man, with a white woman on an elevator — offers a model for academic writing that moves beyond the "cerebral" in order to elicit an awareness of racism in its deep aspects. Yancy's attention to "the white *bodily* repertoire" conveys a sense of how the infra-personal force of prejudice disfigures Yancy himself: feeling this woman's reaction to his proximity, he feels simultaneously reduced to his existence as a racialized body (a "Black presence"), and somehow atomized or aerosolized ("omnipresent within that space, ready to attack from all sides") (21, emphasis in the original). The white woman's perhaps unconscious, but nonetheless performative, bias weaponizes Yancy's body against them both. And yet, as his essay recounts, many white readers identify with the woman. Although she is a figure of argument, rather than an actual, named person, they feel compelled to come to her defense. This visceral identification breeds discomfort, and as a white reader sympathetic to Yancy's argument, I find that this discomfort is not easily absorbed by the good fit between the argument's propositional content and what I already know about race and white supremacy. There remains a kernel, a nub, that proves difficult to digest. A figure that disturbs what I am content to see. That I am not entirely comfortable with Yancy's depiction of the woman in the elevator, that I want to think that he's exaggerating, maybe just a bit, alerts me to a reserve of defensiveness within myself, confronting me with my own desire to be a "good white" and with the work that I have to do on my own dispositions.

25

man, to have a body and to regard it as my inalienable possession. It lies in my embodiment of those "possessive logics" that,
as Aileen Moreton-Robinson writes, are "underpinned by an
excessive desire to invest in reproducing and reaffirming the
nation-state's ownership, control, and domination."[18] A deep aspect, because the excessiveness of this summons to investment,
rising with a flush to the cheeks, might be felt only in certain
instances. Such as when those whose presence or experience I
have learned to deny, neglect, or misrecognize refuse, in Sylvia Wynter's words, to "make [themselves] into a fact of negation." For it is the social and political erasure of people of color
"which alone enables the experience of being white."[19] Just as
the objectification of women, white or otherwise, enables the
experience of the white cishet masculine subject.[20] But the erasure of subjects as a means of subject-formation remains rough
work. (You can't very well rub out the rabbit without deleting
the duck.) Taking a cue from Hortense Spillers, let's say that
these "hieroglyphics of the flesh," by which political relations
make physiology signify, always operate in excess of what the
subject can avow or the body can bear.[21] For Spillers, "before

---

18 Moreton-Robinson, *The White Possessive,* xii. As Moreton-Robinson
    explains, "to be able to assert 'this is mine' requires a subject to internalize
    the idea that one has property rights that are part of normative behavior,
    rules of interaction, and social engagement" (114). Situating the "normative
    behavior" of the possessive in the context of the settler-colonial seizure
    of Native and Indigenous lands serves to unnerve, perhaps, some of its
    self-evident and unexceptional naturalness, reminding us how "property
    rights" (over lands, over other people) have been the prime vehicle for
    the violence of modern empires, carving out the Western nation-state as
    the state of exception and of the exceptional (the subject who produces
    himself out of what he takes from others).
19 Wynter, "Towards the Sociogenic Principle," 42.
20 These processes are not to be understood as analogous, but as
    complementary: in the cut of their complementarity, they trace the seam
    or suture of the dominant subject. On the suture of whiteness, see Yancy,
    Black Bodies, White Gazes, 256–58. On "the cut," see Moten, *In the Break.*
21 Hortense J. Spillers, "Mama's Baby, Papa's Maybe: An American Grammar
    Book," in *Black, White, and in Color: Essays on American Literature and*

the 'body' there is the 'flesh,' that zero degree of social conceptualization that does not escape concealment under the brush of discourse or the reflexes of iconography."[22] A reason to think about the trouble with the explicit starts from a consideration of all those "impossible people" (in Dean Spade's powerful phrase) who have lived through and have to live through the ruptures in the explicit — the abrogation of treaties, the lies and misprision woven into the official histories, the false promises of legal and social equality, the myriad bureaucratic mechanisms by which the liberal state distributes vastly "unequal life chances" to the populations under its control.[23] For them, the "zero degree" sits like a live charge beneath the surface of liberal discourse and legal iconography, waiting to be triggered by the varieties of state-sponsored and state-tolerated violence that sustain patriarchal white supremacy. On the other hand, whiteness (and *a fortiori* white cishet masculinity) are grammars for making the flesh signify as a body that, to different degrees (depending on a host of other social inflections), escapes vulnerability. And these grammars are the grain within or against which I think and feel. I blush not only at being the unmarked subject suddenly "marked," but also because certain kinds of anger and shame decline the self in its ascension to whiteness and masculinity. They suture my flesh to performances of domination.[24] The

Culture (Chicago: University of Chicago Press, 2003). The phrase is Alexander Weheliye's (*Habeas Viscus,* 40).

22 Spillers, "Mama's Baby, Papa's Maybe," 206. Spillers anchors this distinction in the facts of circum-Atlantic captivity and enslavement: the enslaved, being brutally cut off from the modern state's guarantees of bodily autonomy and integrity, were condemned to this "zero degree" as the living hell on top of which global capitalism rose to its Babelian heights. She writes: "If we think of the 'flesh' as a primary narrative, then we mean its seared, divided, ripped-apartness, riveted to the ship's hole, fallen, or 'escaped' overboard" (ibid).

23 Spade, *Normal Life,* 41.

24 On the affects of white cishet male subjects in the face of challenges to the hegemony of their experience, see Sally Robinson, *Marked Men: White Masculinity in Crisis* (New York: Columbia University Press, 2000); Robyn

durability of this suture suggests that critical explication alone cannot prepare us for the improvisatory work that freedom and justice require. As James Baldwin and Patricia Hill Collins would remind us, the experience of being Black, or of being a Black woman, carries and transmits a knowledge of whiteness that whites themselves cannot possess. The attachment to acts of possession renders us as whites incapable of such knowledge, which is more like an intimate praxis of resistance and survival, of surviving this world by making another, than the knowledge you carry like cash in your wallet, ready to present it as the price of entry to where you believe you belong. This other knowledge requires immeasurably more courage, fortitude, and intellectual intensity than that.[25]

Along with this introduction, the three chapters in this book sketch failures of explication with respect to deep aspects of privilege and domination.[26] The first chapter, "The Promise of

Wiegman, *American Anatomies: Theorizing Race and Gender* (Durham: Duke University Press, 2002).

25 James Baldwin, "The Devil Finds Work," in *Collected Essays,* ed. Toni Morrison (New York: Library of America, 1998), 477–576; Patricia Hill Collins, *Black Feminist Thought: Knowledge, Consciousness, and the Politics of Empowerment,* 2nd edn. (New York: Routledge, 2009). As Collins argues, the specific contours of Black women's knowledge about whiteness derive, in part, from the vantage point of the kinds of labor that Black women have historically been required to do in the US: "Domestic work allowed African-American women to see White elites, both actual and aspiring, from perspectives largely obscured from Black men and from these groups themselves" (13).

26 These pieces do not offer anything like a concrete program of practices with which to supplement those of explicit critique. This failure on my part may disappoint readers committed to institutional and public pedagogies for dismantling the white supremacist patriarchy. And their disappointment will be well founded: the development of these pedagogies is among our most urgent tasks, and we desperately need good recipes for them. The recipe is a genre in which explicit statements convey what has become for others tacit knowledge, i.e., a matter of habit and reflex, a durable part of the body's perceptual and dispositional field. This book aims less at recipe than at experiment, an activity without guarantee, suspending epistemic certainty, opening the field. In these pieces, I have

Composition," explores the optimistic pedagogy of liberalism,

wanted to see how one might write *against* the grain of explication in a genre that prizes the explicit as both method and end, the academic critical essay. Undertaking this project, I drew inspiration from the epistemic modesty and the close attention to the implicative side of language cultivated by the "ordinary language" philosophers (chiefly J.L. Austin, Wittgenstein, Gilbert Ryle, and Stanley Cavell). I found myself gravitating toward those moments in their work that suggest a forsaking of professional abstraction for the itinerant richness of the concrete and the amateur, the by-ways along which the speaking and acting body of anybody travels in the course of its liaisons with the world. At the same time, this body of work tends to fall short in its chronic inattention to the social position of the body that, in the guise of the philosopher, is actually speaking (i.e., white, middle-class, cishet, male). More attentive to these matters is a rich vein of recent scholarship on affect, which challenges — thematically, if not always formally — the priority given to discursive reason in academic critical theory. These writers seek to trace across time and space the unpredictable career of affects, which spread from person to person through a rich culture of practices, swarming, transforming, and multiplying. And like many of these same scholars, I draw inspiration and borrow insights from robust traditions of feminist, queer, anti-racist, decolonial, and feminist/queer of color writing from within, outside, and on the margins of the academy, a daring literature that dislodges the "juridical machine" of form, genre, and discipline in order to make room for what Alexander Weheliye calls "the plenitude of our world" (*Habeas Viscus*, 131).

For scholarship on the affects, see Elisabeth R. Anker, *Orgies of Feeling: Melodrama and the Politics of Freedom* (Durham: Duke University Press, 2014); Lauren Berlant, *The Female Complaint: The Unfinished Business of Sentimentality in American Culture* (Durham: Duke University Press, 2008); Berlant, *Cruel Optimism* (Durham: Duke University Press, 2011); Ann Cvetkovich, *Depression: A Public Feeling* (Durham: Duke University Press, 2012); Shoshana Felman, *The Scandal of the Speaking Body: Don Juan with J.L. Austin, or Seduction in Two Languages*, trans. Catherine Porter (Stanford: Stanford University Press, 2003); José Esteban Muñoz, *Cruising Utopia: The Then and There of Queer Futurity* (New York: New York University Press, 2009); Sianne Ngai, *Ugly Feelings* (Cambridge: Harvard University Press, 2007); Donovan O. Schaefer, *Religious Affects: Animality, Evolution, and Power* (Durham: Duke University Press, 2015); Eve Kosofsky Sedgwick, *Touching Feeling: Affect, Pedagogy, Performativity* (Durham: Duke University Press, 2003); and Kathleen Stewart, *Ordinary Affects* (Durham: Duke University Press, 2008). Schaeffer, *Religious Affects,* offers a thorough review of "affect theory" and its vicissitudes.

which vests hope in the composition of good citizens and ethical subjects through critical self-reflection. Such subjects appear in the liberal imaginary with the trappings of middle-class whiteness, and the reflection that composes them is imagined as

And sampling from the plenitude, I would refer the reader to the following (in addition to those sources cited elsewhere in this chapter): M. Jacqui Alexander, *Pedagogies of Crossing: Meditations on Feminism, Sexual Politics, Memory, and the Sacred* (Durham: Duke University Press, 2005); Hilton Als, *White Girls* (San Francisco: McSweeney's, 2014); James Baldwin, "The Fire Next Time," in *Collected Essays,* ed. Toni Morrison (New York: Library of America, 1998), 291–348; Hazel V. Carby, *Reconstructing Womanhood: The Emergence of the Afro-American Woman Novelist* (New York: Oxford University Press, 1987); Barbara Christian, "The Race for Theory," *Cultural Critique* 6 (1987): 51–63; Kimberlé Crenshaw, *On Intersectionality: Essential Writings* (New York: New Press, 2019); Angela Y. Davis, *The Angela Y. Davis Reader,* ed. Joy James (Malden: Blackwell Publishing, 1998); Roderick A. Ferguson, *Aberrations in Black: Toward a Queer of Color Critique* (Minneapolis: University of Minnesota Press, 2004); Alexis Pauline Gumbs, *Spill: Scenes of Black Feminist Fugitivity* (Durham: Duke University Press, 2016); Gumbs, *M Archive: After the End of the World* (Durham: Duke University Press, 2018); Evelynn Hammonds, "Black (W)Holes and the Geometry of Black Female Sexuality," *differences: A Journal of Feminist Cultural Studies* 6, no. 2/3 (1994): 126–45; bell hooks, *Ain't I a Woman: Black Women and Feminism,* 2nd edn. (New York: Routledge, 2014); Audre Lorde, *Sister Outsider: Essays and Speeches* (rpt. Berkeley: Crossing Press, 2007); Marisa Parham, ".break. dance," *sx archipelagos,* no. 3 (July 2019), http://smallaxe.net/sxarchipelagos/issue03/parham/parham.html; M. NourbeSe Philip, *A Genealogy of Resistance: And Other Essays* (Toronto: Mercury Press, 1997); Christina Sharpe, *Monstrous Intimacies: Making Post-Slavery Subjects* (Durham: Duke University Press, 2010); Valerie Smith, "Black Feminist Theory and the Representation of the 'Other,'" in *Changing Our Own Words: Essays on Criticism, Theory, and Writing by Black Women,* ed. Cheryl A. Wall (New Brunswick: Rutgers University Press, 1989), 38–57; Claudia Tate, *Domestic Allegories of Political Desire: The Black Heroine's Text at the Turn of the Century* (New York: Oxford University Press, 1992); Keeanga-Yamahtta Taylor, ed., *How We Get Free: Black Feminism and the Combahee River Collective* (Chicago: Haymarket Books, 2017); Rinaldo Walcott, *Queer Returns: Essays on Multiculturalism, Diaspora, and Black Studies* (London, Ontario: Insomniac Press, 2016); and Ida B. Wells, *The Light of Truth: Writings of an Anti-Lynching Crusader,* eds. Mia Bay and Henry Louis Gates, Jr. (New York: Penguin Books, 2014).

an explicating practice, as bringing features of the self and the world into consciousness through the rehearsal and production of propositional content. This practice, in turn, is supposed to reveal the sovereign agency latent in the subject, their power (as university marketing departments everywhere put it) to change the world. But these subjects occupy a place marked by an irreconcilable tension. For the agency of the subject is supposed to derive from its capacity for a certain kind of interiority; the self is sovereign (on this view) because it follows the dictates of moral reason, which are transparent to introspection and unclouded by material conditions or external circumstances. And yet, the economic, political, and cultural hierarchies of liberal, capitalist societies recognize as agents only atomic individuals identified by their possession of, or dispossession from, the explicit signs of privilege (money, whiteness, pedigree, etc.). Moreover, the sovereignty of the liberal subject, like that of the modern nation-state, remains an artifact of settler-colonial occupation and expropriation.[27] Or as Denise Ferreira da Silva puts it, the commitment to transparent interiority that appears to justify the white Western subject's dominance requires the violence that sustains its global "others" in affectable exteriority — i.e., in a vulnerability to the force of circumstance that strands them on "the horizon of death."[28] Thinking about how the global reach of neoliberalism and empire sends ripples through the ordinary moments of a privileged pedagogical scene, my essay stages a distension of that privileged ordinary in both space and time. For those ripples have shaped a distinctly modern pedagogy, the sentimental. The genres of the sentimental express the friction between the abstract summons to become a citizen-subject

27 For important critiques of the liberal concept of sovereignty, see Moreton-Robinson, *The White Possessive*; Sandy Grande, *Red Pedagogy: Native American Social and Political Thought* (Lanham: Rowman & Littlefield, 2004); and Scott Richard Lyons, "Rhetorical Sovereignty: What Do American Indians Want from Writing?" *College Composition and Communication* 51, no. 3 (2000): 447–68.

28 Ferreira da Silva, *Toward a Global Idea of Race*, 25.

and the embodied, relational facts of being (as mother, sister, worker, lover, teacher, student, etc.). Such facts reveal our vulnerability to forces that are anything but transparent in operation or effect. Forces at play upon the flesh itself, which inure us to domination and orient our desires toward the commodity-form. Like the blush that is one of its hallmark performances, the sentimental suggests an excessive investment, but in this investment, it lies perilously close to another genre — the critical — that is supposed to remedy those excesses. My essay explores the aspect-shift between the critical and the sentimental, treating both as vexed modes of agency that the modernity of capital and empire bequeaths its subjects.

In my second chapter, "Composition as White/Mansplanation," I explore the more desperate side of this patrimony. Here the animating tensions are the same, but the polarity is reversed. Taking as its occasion instances of anonymous hate-speech, this essay argues that the extreme violence of white cishet male rage and resentment — far from being the rot of a few bad apples, or the cry of those left behind by social and economic progress — proliferates in the soil prepared for it by the transparent rule of reason associated with bureaucratic capitalism. A pedagogy of oppression, bureaucratic capitalism organizes relations of domination and subordination in order to harness the energies that these relations produce. Explication furnishes the ruse of this exploitation, as in the wage that makes explicit the worker's worth on the market, while masking the surplus value that their labor produces.[29] But explication is a kind of labor,

29 I am using *explication* here in a sense close to that of *reification* in the Marxist tradition, so perhaps a word or two is in order to explain my unorthodox choice. Like explication, reification presents a slice or aspect of the world as though it were a whole and complete picture, thereby blocking access to those aspects that refuse the transformation. Thus, the "dead labor" of the worker, congealed in the commodity, obscures the "living labor" of the production process. The vital and creative energies of the worker drop out of our experience of the value of the commodity qua thing, so that we don't stop to consider how other human beings have benumbed their senses and exhausted their bodies for the sake (to use

too. Those privileged to hold positions of bureaucratic authority take credit for the work that their subordinates do, just as those privileged in virtue of their assigned race and/or gender reap benefits from the labor of feeling and imagination that marginalized bodies and voices regularly perform. In both cases, those in dominant positions stand exempt from the work of explication on which their dominance depends. The boss isn't bound to explain himself to those he employs, or at least not with the same degree of coercion that his employees face. And this asymmetry lends support to a possessive model of meaning, i.e., a possessive attitude toward the bodies and labors of others, mediating a possessive model of the self. This "narrative self" is "solipsistic," as Hortense Spillers notes, because on this model, the occupant of a dominant role — the expert, the executive, the white American cishet man, etc. — enjoys a monopoly on the meaning of his role.[30] He is not liable to be called to account. Enshrined in

Ruskin's example) of some glass beads. But as a term of critical discourse, *reification* may belie the kinship of this process, so fundamental to capitalist accumulation, with the wider array of explicative practices by which the modern Western episteme constitutes itself. Indeed, it may seem as though making *explicit* reification's remainder should form the aim and goal of critique itself. But if what is ordinarily tacit and implicit in our experience, or some portion thereof, escapes between the slats of discourse (including what remains implicit in discourse itself); and if our concern is specifically with that not-to-be-specified, fugitive portion, or with its "singular and unverifiable" trace; and if, in relation to this trace, we cannot avoid the choice of a necessarily dis-figuring figure (being obliged to name either the rabbit or the duck, knowing that the name allows the other to slip away) — if this knot of conditionals, themselves unverifiable, amounts to something like an ethic, disclosing the possibility of re-training our desires, then perhaps we have less to learn from the patent power of language to surface, unravel, organize, and analyze, than from the power of language to plunge us into that very gap. (On the humanities as an ethic of "learn[ing] from the singular and unverifiable," see Gayatri Chakravorty Spivak, "Terror: A Speech After 9–11," *boundary 2* 31, no. 2 [Summer 2004]: 109.)

30 Spillers, "Mama's Baby, Papa's Maybe," 211. The monopoly in question is not universal, insofar as everyone in a position of dominance is (or can become) the subordinate in a different setting. The boss, of course,

modernist theories of information and bureaucratic rationality, this model forgets the mutual implication of self and other in acts of becoming. That is, it forgets (to follow the trail blazed by Spillers) the flesh. Taking cues from what Fred Moten calls "the black radical tradition," this chapter reads and listens to a handful of literary and musical texts — by Claudia Rankine, Dionne Brand, Tracie Morris, and Julius Eastman — that offer ways of re-training our senses to attend to the present's dense layering of multiple histories and destinies. Texts that encode and care for traditions of resistance to the possessive model of meaning as well as to the violence of white supremacy. Texts that usher us toward a view of the senses as both personal and social, and of discourse as the involution of language into the flesh. My interest here lies less in overturning or undoing the so-called linguistic turn than in following it through, following it out, bringing it back around to the flesh that "speaks, conjures, intones, and concocts sumptuous universes" (the resonant cavity, the importunate hands, the clamoring tongue) in concert with others, in suffering and pleasure, beginning with the breath.[31]

In these chapters, my analysis aims to unsettle the equation of white cishet male privilege and power with a certain "dominant fiction" of interiority.[32] A consequence of this equation, which denies full humanity to others, is to refer the search for the sources of racism, misogyny, homophobia, transphobia, etc., to the crypt of the self. We white cishet men tend to demand respect for our beliefs and desires as inalienably private posses-

typically has a boss of their own, or else shareholders to answer to, etc., and the dominance enjoyed by white men in virtue of their race and gender does not exempt them from subordination to others (especially other white men) in virtue of other social characteristics. A generalized asymmetry produces local and specific monopolies on meaning, which necessarily come into conflict, rendering the whole system unstable and in need of constant defense.

31 Weheliye, *Habeas Viscus,* 121.
32 For the "dominant fiction" as the vehicle by which ideology secures our attachments, see Kaja Silverman, *Male Subjectivity at the Margins* (New York: Routledge, 2016), 15–17.

sions, even as we routinely fail to grant others the same respect. In the book's third and final chapter, "Confusions of a White Man/qué," I imagine the cryptic self as the site of a haunting, of sensation's haunting by the otherness that it tactically excludes. This piece is the inside-out sleeve of the preceding essays. Here I use critical, philosophical, and psychoanalytic discourse to frame an intimate narrative of my own embodiment of whiteness and cishet masculinity. But what is the story I have to tell? To acknowledge that the story does not belong to me means listening to the stories of others, stories that the terms of my embodiment would silence or efface. It means acknowledging that I should amplify those voices that I tend to appropriate instead as citational supports for my own white melancholy. It means taking seriously the idea that this work, the work of acknowledgment, demands the undoing of my own seriousness and its wages in the seriality of an erasure that can claim no purpose (at least, not in the way that purposiveness is conscripted to the cause of enclosure). My turn to personal narrative in the book's final chapter is intended to resist the enclosure of the scholarly essay. I offer it as way, not of owning the story, but of exposing the teller, outside the refuge of critical distance and control. For these things, in the hands of the white male critic, no matter how smart his analysis, tend to bracket or defer the question of the writer's flesh.

The story of this book is, in a way, about my failure to tell a story. Beyond the see-saw between explication's push and implication's pull, writing has meant, for me, a commitment to deferring the question. Refusing to show my work, I have opted instead to write my own writing, i.e., the fact of my having written, into erasure.[33] This program testifies to how I have

---

33 The first part of my book's title — "Rough Notes to Erasure" — is a quotation, under partial erasure, from Alan Turing's seminal essay on computability, which furnishes part of the theoretical foundation for the digital and computational revolution of the twentieth century. Turing's eponymous machine, as described in that essay, represents an apotheosis of Enlightenment models of the mind, a "universal" machine that can

sought to "earn" my own privilege (including the opportunity that a white man with a middle-class upbringing and education enjoys to land jobs that don't leave him too poor or exhausted for unremunerated pursuits, like writing this book, in the off-hours). Or it testifies to my desire to earn an exemption from the subordination to waged work that is even the white man's lot. At any rate, though never quickly enough to stop time's passage through the flesh, I've sought to earn something that I both do and do not have, seeking to prove myself exceptional in one domain (as a writer). And I've preferred to keep that effort private rather than expose myself to the risk of failure. But this failure, the failure that I have been afraid to risk, is really the failure of the project or promise itself. I mean the promise that one's whiteness or white masculinity can mean more than the violent pursuit of possession through the erasure of others' potential,

perform an infinite set of possible operations, provided that the steps involved in each of these operations (the machine's "instructions") can be made explicit. Turing's machine is also a machine that works by *writing*, by literally inscribing symbols, drawn from a fixed set, on a length of tape. In fact, the machine generalizes the labor of the human beings who performed the extensive calculations required by modern science and industry before the advent of the digital computer. These were often white woman and women of color with high levels of mathematical ability but denied professional status. It is their "rough notes" that are "liable to erasure" in Turing's description, intermediate steps in the calculation that do not appear in the final output, like the rough edges of the laboring flesh that vanish behind the products of mechanical production ("On Computable Numbers, with an Application to the *Entscheidungsproblem*," in *The Essential Turing: Seminal Writings in Computing, Logic, Philosophy, Artificial Intelligence, and Artificial Life: Plus the Secrets of Enigma,* ed. B. Jack Copeland [New York: Oxford University Press, 2004], 60). *Explication,* for my purposes, is this scriptural process that erases as it produces, erasing the trace of its own process. And it does violence in order to reveal, like the social inscription of the categories of race, gender, sexuality, class, etc., which makes bodies more manageable, visible, divisible, and disposable. The asymmetry of this process sustains the unequal distribution of wealth, power, and security in modern liberal societies. Much like the power enjoyed by the men in charge of the "human computers" in the background of Turing's proof: men who did not, presumably, have to show *their* work, in rough notes or otherwise.

more than one's complicity in the erasure of one's own potential for the sake of another's profits. The fiction of interiority
expresses a desire to close off the self from those histories, personal, national, and global, that challenge one's claims to such
potential. But this attempt to escape from the folds of history is
bound to fail, fracturing one's relations to others and to oneself.
And yet, far from being a cause for reckoning, such failure can
become something that the subject clamps down on, as if failure
could serve as its own justification, assuming mythic proportions in the stories we tell ourselves, stories about the minotaur
we harbor in our breast. In this way, the white man is manqué:
like the poet manqué, for whom the profession of failure, internalized, becomes a vocation in itself.

But through every piece of writing, you can trace threads that
are the gifts of others. And while the academy increasingly plays
host to a discourse that links practices of citation to the regime
of private property, we might imagine citation's kinship with
other traditions, other ways of thinking through, rather than
deferring or effacing, the commons. One might think about,
for instance, the "black Atlantic" compositional traditions of
the mix, the sample, and the improvisational text or score.[34]
I'm on the terrain here of a debt that I cannot hope to acquit,
even as I must acknowledge, following Stefano Harney and Fred
Moten, that "the black aesthetic is not about technique, is not a
technique."[35] It's a way of folding space and time. Of seeing what
happens when one aspect gets articulated through the grain of
another, in a texture that pulls against itself, neither one being
the shadow or reflection of the other, but together displacing
form even as they produce it. Failure or not, my writing exposes
my debt to those, living and dead, in the grain of whose works
and days I become what I am, and whose aspect my selfhood

34 On the "black Atlantic" and the aesthetic practices, vital to modernity, that
    we owe to it, see Paul Gilroy, *The Black Atlantic: Modernity and Double
    Consciousness* (London: Verso, 2007).
35 Stefano Harney and Fred Moten, *The Undercommons: Fugitive Planning &
    Black Study* (Wivenhoe: Minor Compositions, 2013), 48.

numbs me to. In writing this book, I've tried to quicken my senses to that debt, without making a sideshow of the modern world's profound reserves of suffering and pain. And I've come back, again and again, to the grain of the sentence and the phrase, trying to improvise with (not improve upon) the brilliance of those whom I cite. For as Moten suggests, "phrasing, where form — grammar, sound — cuts and augments meaning in the production of content, is where implication most properly resides."[36] Phrasing is the spool whereby, fool that I have been, I can find my way back to you.

At times, no doubt, I've entangled my tongue in nonsense, or given vent to enthusiasms that a composed scholarly voice is supposed to disavow. But what would it take to entertain the leporine leap of blood into the cheeks as something other or more than a loss of composure? Or to welcome that loss as the advent of a new rhythm, a syncopation that, instead of putting the present to flight, brings it closer? To pursue my own acts of composition into the moments where composure falters? To falter is not to fail as final, irreducible act.[37] Faltering, rather, can mean the price of admission into ways of working and being that prize openness, vulnerability, and improvisation. It can trace an opening onto what Moten calls "the ensemble." The members of an ensemble collaborate; they riff off one another; they renew their sense of the possible in fresh configurations of the sensible. Their art flourishes in that zone of indetermination where what waddles or hops might burst into a run or flight, quickening us in its wake. Moten deploys the ensemble as a dis/figure for forms of experience that court the disruption — what he calls, following Nathaniel Mackey, "the cut" — out of which meanings emerge.[38] The cut interrupts the chiastic structure (or suture) of the same with itself, parsing it out into space or spac-

---

36 Moten, *Black and Blur,* 10.
37 For a generative account of failure, see Jack Halberstam, *The Queer Art of Failure* (Durham: Duke University Press, 2011).
38 Moten, *In the Break,* 6.

ing it out into time. Like the white space between words, or the wet and buzzing points of friction in the mouth and throat that produce phonemes, or the rests between musical tones that constitute rhythm. But Moten's work tarries with the cut in a deeper sense (a deeper aspect) than that abstract vantage point from which critical thought glimpses its dispersal behind a deceptively univocal meaning.[39] The cut evokes the eruption, within the dominant practices of modernity, of the matter of the flesh and its history, which is the matter of spirit. And in particular, the spirit of the Black radical aesthetic, including Black feminist theory and poetics, embodying creative resilience in an unredeemed time of terror and pain. To exploit this aesthetic, as in to capitalize on it, is not the same as to draw strength from it. To write within a history of privileged appropriation, as a subject identified with that privilege, is perhaps necessarily to fail or fall short before Moten's invitation. I announce this fact at the outset: not in order to absolve myself of responsibility, but in the hopes of tracing the cut of it through what is to come.

In the remainder of this introduction, I propose a partial theory of racialized and gendered privilege, hoping to show its participation in what Jacques Rancière calls "the explicative order."[40] As a way of phrasing in theoretical, historiographic terms the questions and concerns that motivate this book, this introduc-

39 You might think of "the cut" as what traces the contours of aspect, cutting what is sensed into what makes sense, where that making leaves a remainder whose aporetic and atopic play we only gesture toward in talking about the tacit, the implicit, the dispositional, etc. In a phenomenological vein, we might liken it to what Maurice Merleau-Ponty describes as the infra-personal process of sensation, which is a field saturated by absence and opacity: "Between my sensation and myself, there is always the thickness of an *originary acquisition* that prevents my experience from being clear for itself" (*Phenomenology of Perception,* trans. Donald A. Landes [Abingdon: Routledge, 2013], 224, emphasis in the original).

40 Jacques Rancière, *The Ignorant Schoolmaster: Five Lessons in Intellectual Emancipation,* trans. Kristin Ross (Stanford: Stanford University Press, 1999), 4.

tion situates dispositional approaches to the dismantling of patriarchal white supremacy alongside critiques that attend to the latter's articulation in and through the dominant Western episteme. But why *privilege*? If we acknowledge the role that ordinary performances of whiteness/white cishet masculinity play in structures of domination — structures, moreover, with an unprecedented capacity for causing harm on a global scale — can't we dispense with the more genteel term *privilege* altogether? Has it not exhausted its productivity for feminist and anti-racist critique? Hasn't it lost its critical edge on migrating into the dominant idioms of corporate-mediated mass culture, where "wokeness" becomes yet another bespoke commodity, along with pour-over coffee and a hot-towel shave, for good white dudes? Doesn't the term's overuse in fact dampen our feeling for the violence, mundane, ongoing, and terrible, that props up the prevailing order of things? *Patriarchy* and *white supremacy* are ugly words. They look and sound as though they leaked from some petty bureaucrat's pen or burst, with phlegm and spittle, from the maw of a demagogue. *Privilege,* however, has a sheen on which we're still soft. We say, "it's a privilege to have known him," etc. We love *Downton Abbey* and, shame-facedly, *Real Housewives.* But I would argue that our ambivalence toward the idea of privilege derives from its role as the suture between identity and hierarchy. Not only do the interwoven hierarchies of race, gender, sexuality, class, national origin, and physical ability identify subject-positions as relatively dominant or subordinate. Not only do those hierarchies mark some bodies as valuable and others as disposable. But hierarchy also operates, in ways both tacit and explicit, within the enclosure of identification itself. In other words, some good white dudes have more power, prestige, wealth, and opportunity than others. And this fact, as W.E.B. Du Bois recognized, is not devoid of consequences for the tenacity of patriarchal white supremacy in an aggressively capitalist society.[41] A form of subject-formation that precedes the liberal social contract, privilege ramifies through the ravages of capitalism and colonialism, multiplying the hierarchical, perturbing the modernity of those who consider themselves to have left the past behind. But we hold its vile edge close.

Privi-lege: the etymology suggests a privatization of the legible, or the legibility of the private. The oxymoronic nature of this suggestion (as Wittgenstein wants to know, can a "private language" be considered a language at all?) reveals, in fact, a double entitlement, like the recto and verso of a text. On one side, which is legible only by the interior, private light of what has been called reason, the text blazons its universality in terms that elevate the soul. On the other side — the public side — it spells out, in print no less indelible for being fine, the invidious terms of corporeal difference as the signifiers of social worth. Both sides, having the apparent finality of law, divide the senses from their openness to difference and to the richness of multiple futures that such openness, which is the radical destiny of the flesh, implies. But the fixity of the text is an illusion. In modernity — where the resources available for composing selves and inventing communities proliferate at a speed that mirrors the growth of capital itself — the legibility of privilege blots and bleeds under pressures from within and without. As a name for these pressures that suggests their kinship with practices of verbal composition, I have lit on the term *enthusiasm*. Enthusiasm designates the drive to express or make explicit what lies buried within. But it designates, too, explication's remainder: what escapes the grip of a logic that deals only with what is, or can be made, explicit. Enthusiasm might serve as a figure for the

41 See especially W.E.B. Du Bois, *Black Reconstruction in America: An Essay toward a History of the Part Which Black Folk Played in the Attempt to Reconstruct Democracy in America, 1860–1880* (New York: Atheneum, 1977); and Du Bois, "The Souls of White Folk," in *Writings: The Suppression of the African Slave-Trade; The Souls of Black Folk; Dusk of Dawn; Essays and Articles* (New York: Literary Classics of the United States, 1986), 923–38.

fate of the senses and the affects under capitalist, settler-colonial modernity, but it is a disfiguring figure. It hearkens to a way of embodying the forces of estrangement, disruption, and devastation, forces that everywhere attend modernity itself. The sections that follow trace enthusiasm's career within and against the ruses of privilege, gesturing toward a history whose resonance I am, strummed by what I struggle to hold a stranger to myself.[42]

private property and the sense(s) of privilege

At the root of the many crises of modernity lies a crisis of the senses. In the *Economic and Philosophic Manuscripts,* Marx registers this crisis with great clarity:

> Private property has made us so stupid and one-sided that an object is only ours when we have it — when it exists for us as capital, or when it is directly possessed, eaten, drunk, worn, inhabited, etc. — in short, when it is *used* by us. Although private property itself again conceives all these direct realizations of possessions as *means of life,* and the life which they serve as means is the *life of private property* — labour and conversion into capital.
>
> In place of the physical and mental senses there has therefore come the sheer estrangement of *all* these senses — the sense of *having*.[43]

---

42 My aim in this introduction is not to produce a coherent historical narrative. Rather, with Alexander Weheliye, I propose to follow certain "folds" or "hiccups" in "historicist" time, with an ear for "singularities" that disrupt the seemingly inevitable succession of moments that inscribes the future as the replication of the present and the erasure of the past. See *Phonographies: Grooves in Sonic Afro-Modernity* (Durham: Duke University Press, 2005), 79–80.

43 Karl Marx, *Economic and Philosophic Manuscripts of 1844,* trans. Martin Milligan (Moscow: Progress Publishers, 1932), 87 (emphasis in the original).

I return to Marx because he reminds us (he reminds me) of the stakes of having privilege. It means more than the moral inconvenience of having to check my knapsack at the door. More, indeed, than the shame of not knowing that I had a knapsack to begin with. Rather, the stakes are stultification; a numbing of the senses, moral and physical; a kind of chronic anesthesia. Of course, Marx does not use the word *privilege*. In this passage, he locates the sources of alienation in the conflation of what is *for us* with what is *for our use*.[44] Utility appears inseparable from those "possessive logics" that characterize the dominant modalities of social and political life in the modern nation-state.[45] These logics estrange our senses and affects, collapsing the multiple vital destinies that bind us to the world into a single sense, the "sense of *having*." By contrast, what Marx calls the "emancipated" senses would "relate themselves to the thing for the sake of the thing, but the thing itself is an objective human relation to itself and to man, and vice-versa."[46] Under the regime of private property, our lives are dominated by a unitary and exclusive relation, one in which I, as an owner, construe an object's po-

---

44 This analysis remains orthogonal to Marx's treatment of the commodity fetish in *Capital,* where value or exchange-value is said to mystify our relations to the object, i.e., to the labor that produced the object, and thus to each other and ourselves. The focus in that later work is, of course, the social relations from which we are alienated by capitalism. But certain passages in *Capital* give the impression that the object's use-value — as opposed to its value in and for exchange — is grounded in its "physical properties": "The usefulness of a thing makes it a use-value. But this usefulness does not dangle in mid-air. It is conditioned by the physical properties of the commodity, and has no existence apart from the latter. It is therefore the physical body of the commodity itself, for instance iron, corn, a diamond, which is the use-value or useful thing" (Karl Marx and Friedrich Engels, *Capital: A Critique of Political Economy,* trans. Ben Fowkes and David Fernbach, vol. 1 [London: Penguin Books, 1990], 126). This analysis makes of use-value something natural, (uncritically) normative, and inert. But in Marx's early work, it is the very concept of utility that deadens the life of the thing, paving the way for labor-power's "conversion into capital."
45 Moreton-Robinson, *The White Possessive,* xii.
46 Marx, *Economic and Philosophic Manuscripts,* 87–88.

tential as exhausted by my use. This relation displaces an openness crossed by a multiplicity of paths to others by way of things (e.g., in which things serve as signs, projects, provocations, adventures, gifts), where each object serves as a sort of nexus of nature, a place where nature meets itself in the complex sensory and affective traffic of human (and non-human) beings.[47]

You might say that the stultification of which Marx writes begins in practices not of use, but of domination. His mention of the "emancipated" senses both evokes and forgets the circum-Atlantic trade in stolen life underwriting nineteenth-century capitalism, just as the phrase "the life of private property" conceals capital's undead aspects, beginning with the afterlife of plunder and genocide that constitutes the haunted existence of both the settler-colonial and the modern European nation-state. The concept of race, as well as the modern categories of gender and sexuality that racializing logics saturate, carries the trace of this violence, but refracted, as Katherine McKittrick observes, through "multiscalar discourses of ownership." These discourses, McKittrick argues, "are, in part, narratives of displacement that reward and value particular forms of conquest."[48] What Alexander Weheliye calls "the restricted idiom of personhood-as-ownership" solidifies the self through the displacement of

47 On the moral, political, and epistemic roles of the gift in Native and
    Indigenous communities, which remain irreducible to the concept
    of reciprocity as understood by Western anthropologists, see Rauna
    Kuokkanen, *Reshaping the University: Responsibility, Indigenous Epistemes,
    and the Logic of the Gift* (Vancouver: UBC Press, 2007), 74–96.
48 Katherine McKittrick, *Demonic Grounds: Black Women and the
    Cartographies of Struggle* (Minneapolis: University of Minnesota Press,
    2006), 3. As Hortense Spillers movingly writes, "The European males
    who laded and captained these galleys and who policed and corralled
    these human beings, in hundreds of vessels from Liverpool to Elmina, to
    Jamaica; from the Cayenne Islands, to the ports at Charleston and Salem,
    and for three centuries of human life, were not curious about this 'cargo'
    that bled, packed like so many live sardines among the immovable objects.
    Such inveterate obscene blindness might be denied, point blank, as a
    possibility for *anyone,* except that we know it happened" ("Mama's Baby,
    Papa's Maybe," 210, emphasis in the original).

others (from their lands, from their homes, from the enjoyment of self-determination in relation to their own bodies).[49]
Property remains the index of an unequal struggle in which the
rules are written by the winners, and where the application of
disparate force displaces the "means of life" onto the "life of private property."[50] And the life of property not only feeds on living labor, but it also needs and sustains those institutions that,
targeting subjugated populations, enforce real and social death.
Following Moten, Weheliye, and Spillers, we might posit the
commodity as a category haunted by the flesh.

Private property haunts our bodies. Its charge accumulates in
loins, limbs, and tongue. The senses are their own ghosts. Consider again the closed worlds of middle-class, majority-white
suburban America: the leafy streets, clean and quiet; the large
and well-appointed and air-conditioned houses; the neighbors'
encountering each other on a morning jog, in line at Starbucks,
or in the aisles of the grocery store, where plump local produce
vies with more exotic varieties, conducive to a cosmopolitan
palate and a body kept both sated and at the peak of health. Such
a world has not banished pain, but what pain there is presides
over the private dominion of home, car, and cubicle. The public
spaces, meanwhile, seem designed to reproduce a vision of communal life as aggressively docile and polite (if sorely attenuated
by the pressure of private obligations). But this is America, and
pain sponsors such places: the pain of broken bodies, broken
families, stolen wages, stolen chances. The sense of docility and

49 Weheliye, *Habeas Viscus,* 4.
50 It's important to note, however, that the "sense of having" is inflected by
    race, gender, sexuality, class, and disability in ways irreducible to one
    another. McKittrick reminds us that "black geographic ownership is
    coupled with repossession and displacement rather than easy, fulfilled
    acquisitions" (*Demonic Grounds,* 151, emphasis in the original). And
    Aileen Moreton-Robinson points to the vastly different "ontological
    relationship" that land ownership entails for many Native and Indigenous
    peoples, involving "the intersubstantiation of ancestral beings, humans,
    and land," such that belonging to the land becomes not only a means of life
    but "a form of embodiment" (*The White Possessive,* 12).

politeness rests on the greed that buttresses such a place and the racist aggression that serves as a rampart against a guilty conscience. In one of the vignettes in her book *Citizen: An American Lyric,* Claudia Rankine describes a scene where a couple, having asked a friend to babysit, comes home to find that their neighbor has called the police on their friend, who had been talking on the phone outside while Black:

> Your friend is speaking to your neighbor when you arrive home. The four police cars are gone. Your neighbor has apologized to your friend [for calling the police] and is now apologizing to you. Feeling somewhat responsible for the actions of your neighbor, you clumsily tell your friend that the next time he wants to talk on the phone he should just go in the backyard. He looks at you a long minute before saying he can speak on the phone wherever he wants. Yes, of course, you say. Yes, of course.[51]

Rankine's prose has a powerful way of ratcheting up tension through the very flatness of its reportage. The threat of violence in this scene remains implicit; the friend's encounter with the police is not described. But the hovering potential of that threat, ominous as the sound of planes in wartime, constant as cicadas in the summer heat, is, I take it, Rankine's point. Nor does she instruct us how to picture the neighborhood in which this scene occurs, though "common sense" all too readily furnishes something not unlike the description above. But here common sense betrays its production by the dominant arrangements of race and property, time and place. The "long minute" in which "your friend" registers the compounded injustice of the situation and formulates his response, like his claiming the right to talk on the phone "wherever he wants," attests to the long history of what McKittrick calls "black spatial struggles." As does the second-

---

51 Claudia Rankine, *Citizen: An American Lyric* (Minneapolis: Graywolf Press, 2014), 15.

person narrator's response, if we imagine the narrator, too, as Black: inhabiting the double-consciousness of how whiteness structures, even as it undermines, the social contract; how it divides good intentions against themselves. Wanting both to acknowledge the wrong done to their friend, and to protect him from further harm, the narrator is forced to embody that division, even if they themselves, as a person of color, remain beyond the pale of what whiteness protects. But in fact, Rankine doesn't specify whether "you" are white or not. In its ambiguity, the pronoun highlights the work of what Alexander Weheliye calls "racializing assemblages," because Rankine's work both provokes and frustrates our desire to map the boundaries of race onto the narrative and figurative terrain of her text.[52] Rather, race appears there as the unstable force of macro- and micro-aggressions that mark the flesh for mistreatment in ways that are at once predictable and, at the same time, powerfully violent because of their capacity to rattle the frame of sense.[53] (In this scene, it might be the case that the narrator's position as property owner momentarily locates the narrator and their friend on opposite sides of the blue line. Then again, perhaps not.)

The fragile cage of what makes sense in a predominantly white, middle-class (or aspiringly white and middle-class) community speaks to the ways in which social privilege accumulates across generations. It accumulates through habits and tastes, opportunities and prospects, property and possessions. While its career may appear as tidy and inevitable as the fall of dominoes, it spreads with the tenacity of kudzu.[54] At the same time, the

52 With a nod to Marx, Weheliye writes, "race is a mysterious thing in that the social character of racializing assemblages appears as an objective character stamped upon humans, which is presented not in the form of sociopolitical relations between humans, but as hierarchically structured races" (*Habeas Viscus,* 51).

53 As McKittrick notes, "black geographies, ostensibly, do not make sense in a world that validates spatial processes and progress through domination and social disavowal" (*Demonic Grounds,* 8–9).

54 For an account of how whiteness multiplies political and economic advantages over time, see George Lipsitz, *The Possessive Investment in*

vital field of propinquity between world and flesh remains enclosed. Beyond the enclosure, traditions of solidarity and collective resistance sustain communities for which political neglect,
economic exploitation, social segregation, and aggressive policing reproduce the conditions that make life in public a daily
struggle. When Fred Moten insists that "black art neither sutures nor is sutured to trauma," his insistence addresses the cut
of an aesthetics and an episteme that refuse, openly or surrep-
titiously, the bargains demanding estrangement from every alternative as the conditions of existence.[55] Refusing that bargain,
these alternatives have been invented by "the Others within the
nation" time and again.[56] But in the Faustian bargain basement
of white bourgeois culture (which, it's worth repeating, exists
both everywhere and nowhere, being more a phantasmic attachment and a project of emulation than an achievement held
in common), it proves too easy to reiterate these truths without
feeling them. *Not feeling them* enacts a flight from my debt to
others, a flight whereby I know myself as a subject. But I ought
to demand a reckoning of myself and the dominant culture. I
ought to demand to know why these forms of knowing and feeling, of sensing and sustaining the commons, do not count as
worth understanding to those of us privileged by our identification with whiteness. Which is not to say that they are not worth
something to the dominant culture, for they are worth consuming by imitation and appropriation, but in deracinated fashion,
pulled from the grounds of reciprocity and entanglement that

Whiteness: How White People Profit from Identity Politics, rev. and exp.
edn. (Philadelphia: Temple University Press, 2006). As one example,
Lipsitz notes that "the suburbs helped turn Euro-Americans into 'whites'
who could live near each other and intermarry with relatively little
difficulty. But this 'white' unity rested on residential segregation, on shared
access to housing and life chances largely unavailable to communities of
color" (7).

55 Moten, *Black and Blur,* ix.
56 Michelle M. Wright, *Becoming Black: Creating Identity in the African
    Diaspora* (Durham: Duke University Press, 2004), 38.

are the only foundations of an ethical life. Must we remain so stupid and one-sided?

privilege and the paradoxes of explication

Like the predominance of the property relation, the privileging of explication over other forms of knowledge and understanding distorts sense. Unequal access to the means to make the truths of experience explicit allows those who benefit most from histories of conquest and domination to treat their particular experiences as universally valid. And the compact between explicitness and power requires this distortion as the condition, in modernity, of truth itself. If the modern subject can be said to be the sole proprietor of their body and its labor — "this," as John Locke wrote, "nobody has any right to but himself" — then experience becomes the subject's private property.[57] Participation in civil society depends on the subject's willingness and ability to make some socially necessary portion of that experience explicit, i.e., available for introspection by others. But this nobody remains nobody if they cannot command a price for their labor sufficient to convert it into the ownership of other things. Or if they are denied even the modicum of dignity involved in disposing of their body as they see fit. Vine Deloria, Jr. argues that "the lack of property […] makes the individual person completely defenseless and vulnerable" on the unspoken terms of the modern social contract.[58] Locke's "nobody" marks the spot where the explicit terms hide what has been erased from the account that

57   Quoted in Vine Deloria, Jr., "Minorities and the Social Contract," *Georgia Law Review* 20 (1986): 923. For a classic critique of this thesis, see C.B. MacPherson, *The Political Theory of Possessive Individualism: Hobbes to Locke* (Don Mills: Oxford University Press Canada, 2011). On the ambiguities of the contract relation vis-à-vis the (in)alienability of one's property in oneself, see Carole Pateman, *The Sexual Contract* (Stanford: Stanford University Press, 2009), 39–76.
58   Deloria, "Minorities and the Social Contract," 924.

common sense gives of itself. One can, and one routinely does, assert a right to lands and to their fruits that was never formally ceded by the original owners and inhabitants. One could, and under certain conditions (e.g., if one is the state) one still can, assert a right to another's living body. And in the lacunae of the law's text, where its violence operates, one finds the "burdened individuality" endured by members of those populations that have been remanded to a state of excessive vulnerability, a vulnerability that proves politically and economically advantageous to the governing elite.[59] In this way, self-proprietorship is the optical illusion at the center of the social contract, flickering into view precisely at the point where the excessive investment in private property overflows the narrow bed of liberal rights and responsibilities, and the individual with rights vanishes into a population that can be managed, manhandled, and, as necessary, disposed of.[60]

On the side of the ones and the one percent, common sense has the job of justifying this excess. In her account of the modern idea of race, Colette Guillaumin argues that the European bourgeoisie, starting in the seventeenth and eighteenth centu-

---

59 On "burdened individuality," see Hartman, *Scenes of Subjection,* 115–25. In his reading of Justice Rehnquist's majority opinion in *Oliphant v. Suquamish Indian Tribe,* Robert A. Williams provides a strikingly literal illustration of how the law relies on complex strategies of explicitness and erasure in the production of common sense. In *Oliphant,* "one of the most important Indian law decisions issued by the Supreme Court in the post-*Brown* era," Rehnquist employs a tissue of citation and elision that allows him and his colleagues to invoke as valid precedent, "in color-clueless fashion," the overtly racist logic of nineteenth-century US Supreme Court cases in order to perpetuate "the inherent limitations on Indian rights imposed on tribes under the doctrine of discovery" (*Like a Loaded Weapon,* 97, 110). Through a clever use of ellipses, Rehnquist quotes a key passage from *Ex parte Crow Dog,* a passage full of the tropes of "Indian savagery," and presents it as an enduring model of judicial restraint and common sense.

60 As Dean Spade puts it, "at the population level [...] power works differently and individual behavior is not the target of intervention, nor can it prevent vulnerability" (*Normal Life,* 121).

ries, sought to deck out their political and social ambitions in the mantle of moral and intellectual distinction. "In the absence of coats of arms, titles, and great houses," she writes, the bourgeoisie "invented ability, aptitude, merit."[61] These new symbols for the "sense of having," albeit abstract, need their anchors in the world of bodies, land, and things. As the linchpin of "an auto-referential system, centered on the Self," the feudal aristocracy described by Guillaumin lived in a world where acts of power, condensed into spectacle, clung to a web of familial bonds and intimate relations of dependence.[62] Their "coats of arms, titles, and great houses" served as lures for love and fealty, fear and envy. And race, in this system, designated the purity of the aristocratic bloodline, as sustained by the rites of marriage and the inheritance of title and real property. It's not as though our lives are no longer governed by the suture between race, property ownership, and heteronormative genealogy. If anything, the suture is only tighter.[63] But the tightness alerts us to a basic instability. An instability at the root of modernity, defining new relations to the flesh. As Spillers writes,

> "family," as we practice and understand it "in the West" — the vertical transfer of a bloodline, of a patronymic, of titles and entitlements, of real estate and the prerogatives of "cold cash," from fathers to sons and in the supposedly free exchange of affectional ties between a male and a female of his choice — becomes the mythically revered privilege of a free and freed community.[64]

61 Colette Guillaumin, *Racism, Sexism, Power and Ideology* (London: Routledge, 2005), 55.

62 Ibid., 50.

63 On the link between heterosexuality and patriarchal white supremacy, see Richard Dyer, *White: Essays on Race and Culture* (New York: Routledge, 2017), 132–42; Mason Stokes, *The Color of Sex: Whiteness, Heterosexuality, and the Fictions of White Supremacy* (Durham: Duke University Press, 2001).

64 Spillers, "Mama's Baby, Papa's Maybe," 218.

The white, middle-class, and heteronormative concept of family, for Spillers, names the site of a rupture barely contained by its scare quotes, a scarred terrain divided between those who are "free" and those who are not, who bear unfreedom's stain. In other words, Guillaumin's bourgeoisie could do without titles and great houses because they could count on a seemingly endless supply of land for the taking and a maximally subjugated, disposable labor force. As for the peoples displaced from that land and/or disappeared into that labor force, *their* abilities and aptitudes could be exploited without considerations of merit so long they could be excluded from the emerging imaginary circle of national or ethnic belonging. As Sylvia Wynter has shown, the rhetorics of European science and philosophy, seeking to explicate the essence of human nature, came to the aid of the colonial enterprise by relegating these dispossessed bodies to a discursive space outside the human altogether.[65] "Natural Reason" displaced "Noble Blood" as the fictive attribute that could justify material and social privilege and the sanguinary crimes necessary to shore it up.[66]

"Mythically revered," the privilege of the European bourgeoisie and their etiolated descendants requires excessive investments in part because it is detached from the body's intimate mutual figuration with peers and kin. The abstractions of "ability, aptitude, merit" mean something only insofar as they

---

65 Or as Andrea Smith puts it, "the project of aspiring to 'humanity' is always already a racial project" ("Queer Theory and Native Studies," 42).

66 Sylvia Wynter, "The Ceremony Must Be Found: After Humanism," *boundary 2* 12/13, nos. 3/1 (1984): 35. Wynter's work is foundational for my analysis (as for the work of many other scholars). In addition to the sources cited elsewhere in this introduction, see Sylvia Wynter, "1492: A New World View," in *Race, Discourse, and the Origin of the Americas: A New World View,* eds. Vera Lawrence Hyatt and Rex M. Nettleford (Washington: Smithsonian Institution Press, 1995), 5–57; "Beyond the Word of Man: Glissant and the New Discourse of the Antilles," *World Literature Today* 63, no. 4 (1989): 637–48; Weheliye, *Habeas Viscus,* 17–32; and Katherine McKittrick, ed., *Sylvia Wynter: On Being Human as Praxis* (Durham: Duke University Press, 2015).

can be embodied by bureaucratic documents of certification, and what's more important, by money and monetary forms of credit. The latter allow social value and social power to travel through far-flung, impersonal networks. And yet, as Spillers puts it, "the social mechanism at work here is *difference in, and as, hierarchy,* although 'race' remains one of its most venerable master signs."[67] Access to social power requires explicit signs of success. While wealth and capital function as such signs, the very dependence of hierarchy on the flows of capital exposes the elite to "antagonisms and power relationships which disturb the [...] organization of society."[68] The instability of privilege under capitalism is a problem *partially* addressed by the projection of one set of abstractions — the aforementioned "ability, aptitude, merit" — onto another: the "master signs" of race, gender, sexuality, class, and physical ability. And these signs mutually inflect one another.[69] Race and gender, in particular, represent the patrimony of modern privilege, its link to the feudal past. Unlike the virtues that they come to symbolize, these signs admit of being assessed at a glance. Or you might say, to be so assessed is their function. To borrow a term from Jacques Rancière, these categories partition the sensible.[70] By forming salient divisions within the field of the human being, they mark subjects for their differential share of what is held in common. In this respect, the somatic markers of privilege represent the fine print underneath the promises of the liberal public sphere. They allow Guillaumin's "new elite" to designate a priori the particular bodies that can gain entry — just as, per Spillers, these markers allow those in power to designate which bodies matter *as bodies,* deserv-

67 Hortense J. Spillers, "'All the Things You Could Be by Now, If Sigmund Freud's Wife Was Your Mother': Psychoanalysis and Race," in *Black, White, and in Color,* 380 (emphasis in the original).

68 Guillaumin, *Racism, Sexism, Power and Ideology,* 72.

69 See Michael Omi and Howard Winant, *Racial Formation in the United States,* 3rd edn. (New York: Routledge, 2015), 53–76.

70 Jacques Rancière, *Disagreement: Politics and Philosophy,* trans. Julia Rose (Minneapolis: University of Minnesota Press, 2008).

ing the basic rights of bodily integrity and self-determination.[71] This exclusion, even when practiced tacitly, encloses a field. Within the enclosure, those admitted cultivate more explicit judgments — judgments of ability, aptitude, and merit — which become the vocation of those so admitted, and the explicit sign of their right to belong. What sounds at first like an epochal break — between titles and talents, coats of arms and letters of credit — is better described as a complex fold.

The modern sense of racialized privilege, according to Guillaumin, involves an "occultation of the Self [...]; there is no sense of belonging to a specific group, so the group itself always remains outside the frame of reference, is never referred to as a group."[72] While the rhetorical and narrative canons of white supremacy belie this assertion, it is true that as a child, I learned to see race by reading it off the bodies of others, others who were not white. Whiteness, you might say, remains inseparable from certain habits of vigilance about the flesh, about the otherness of the flesh. It is the enclosure that projects the other as a threat. Hence the "spurt of psychic energy" that accompanies the white subject's reading of race, which becomes a thing that is, as it were, *too* explicit.[73] Perhaps the white subject's self-possession

---

71 Spillers, "Mama's Baby, Papa's Maybe." As Patricia Hill Collins, *Black Feminist Thought,* reminds us, "This larger system of oppression works to suppress the ideas of Black women intellectuals and to protect White male interests and worldviews. Denying African-American women the credentials to become literate certainly excluded most African-American women from positions as scholars, teachers, authors, poets, and critics. Moreover, while Black women historians, writers, and social scientists have long existed, until recently these women have not held leadership positions in universities, professional associations, publishing concerns, broadcast media, and other institutions of knowledge validation" (7).

72 Guillaumin, *Racism, Sexism, Power and Ideology,* 50. In her analysis of acts of white supremacist terror, Robyn Wiegman provides a striking reminder of how this occultation occurs: "the perpetrators of dismemberment and murder were ritually veiled and acted not in the service of a lone sovereign but for a now-homogenized, known-but-never-individuated, power" (*American Anatomies,* 39).

73 Spillers, "Psychoanalysis and Race," 379.

requires the "occultation of the Self" because the selfhood it entails is never more than a dangerous supplement to a social position established by violence that both founds and rends the terms of the modern social contract. You might say that racialized privilege needs explication as the resource for forgetting its own foldedness, its implication in practices of othering that signal an "already fatal internal differentiation."[74] Interiority, as a resource for the coherence of the self, can be sustained only by the violent production of an exterior. This exterior is occupied by those who, by definition, lack a proper interiority. As Ferreira da Silva explains,

> the knowledge arsenal, which now governs the global (juridic, economic, and moral) configuration, institutes racial subjection as it presupposes and postulates that the elimination of its "others" is necessary for the realization of the subject's exclusive ethical attribute, namely, self-determination.[75]

The "proper" subject, enclosed by the limits of human reason, enjoys the capacity for coherent representation of what is exterior to itself, where representation glides perilously close to ownership. Kant gives the subject of private property its most concise gloss: "The 'I think' must be able to accompany all my representations."[76] Unlike the Cartesian motto, which melds subjectivity and being in the solvent of grammar, Kant's formula insists on the mutual exclusivity of centers of experience as the condition of understanding. (You might even say, it demands their violent displacement.) My thoughts must be mine and mine alone, not another's. It follows that understanding others and ourselves requires that we interrupt the ensemble of the senses, and the dispositions that improvise there, in order to

---

74 Fred Moten, "Preface for a Solo by Miles Davis," *Women & Performance: A Journal of Feminist Theory* 17, no. 2 (July 2007): 224.

75 Ferreira da Silva, *Toward a Global Idea of Race,* xiii.

76 Immanuel Kant, *Critique of Pure Reason,* trans. Paul Guyer and Allen W. Wood (Cambridge: Cambridge University Press, 1998), 246.

consider — with the precision of the surveyor's art, or the navigator's, or the ballistician's — each subject's singular perspective, the sight-lines that human reason, lacking an omniscient perspective, traces through an exterior, lifeless, and fundamentally irrational matter. That we account for, as Hume puts it, each subject's "peculiar point of view."[77] This nobody has a right to but himself. And to make explicit to oneself, either at moments of crisis or in the thrashing of fancy and desire, that others occupy vectors of perspective, hence centers of experience, different from one's own: that appears to the modern subject as its "peculiar" burden. In return, the liberal episteme allocates to the individual qua individual his *peculium* (Latin: "private property") as his privileged access to himself, unique and inviolate, which serves as his token of inclusion in a universal human nature.[78]

When it comes to representations of the human body, the *explicit* describes the objectification in the other's flesh of the subject's desire. The subject makes a bid for their integrity as a subject via the device of another's objectification. But this process becomes the site of a fundamental failure — a failure that founds the subject — through the latter's encounter with what Moten calls the "resistance of the object."[79] The Atlantic crucible of modernity — the genocide practiced against Native peoples and the transoceanic, transcontinental trade in stolen life — intensified, if it did not in fact unleash, relational energies that Europe's customary modes of knowledge and belief could not contain.[80] They beat the hedges, and flocks darkened the skies.

77 David Hume, *A Treatise of Human Nature,* ed. Ernest Campbell Mossner (Harmondsworth: Penguin Books, 1984), 626.
78 The phrase "privileged access" comes from Gilbert Ryle, *The Concept of Mind* (Chicago: University of Chicago Press, 1984), 14.
79 Moten, *In the Break.* In a similar vein, Rizvana Bradley describes Black femininity as "a fold of that outside" ("Living in the Absence of a Body: The (Sus)Stain of Black Female (W)holeness," *Rhizomes: Cultural Studies in Emerging Knowledge* 29 [2016]: para. 10).
80 As Paul Gilroy writes, "Modernity might itself be thought to begin in the constitutive relationships with outsiders that both found and temper a self-conscious sense of western civilization" (*The Black Atlantic,* 17). We

At the level of abstraction pursued by liberal social theory and moral philosophy, it appears that only private property — what Cheryl I. Harris calls the "unfettered right to exclude" — can vitiate this relational excess.[81] And yet, to imagine the world without the constraints of private property is not necessarily to imagine a state of war. Or perhaps that imagination is made possible precisely because the bellicose state of nature already lurks in the stock exchange and the coffee-house and the book-seller's stall. In the belly of Leviathan, every man is a wannabe leviathan if, as Hobbes wrote, "Every man is in the market for power."[82] If the property relation, as transformed by the liquid-ity of capital, can "engulf" (Ferreira da Silva's term) the violent intimacy of physical and sexual enslavement, rendering the en-slaved equivalent to any other commodity — that is, rendering the enslaved not just a "thing," but a thing potentially *equivalent to any other thing,* which is how the commodity functions for capital — then the property relation cannot partition the human being (as a thing indelibly self-sovereign) from the rest of the natural and material world (which stands open to the exercise of that sovereignty). Just as such putative sovereignty, located in a property claim to land already belonging to others, can-not secure the subject from future incursions upon "his" land or person. This problem engenders a supplement. That supplement is the modern "fact" of racialized difference (projected along the axes of gender, sexuality, and social class). As Ferreira da Silva writes, this supplement "produces [...] the affectable (subaltern)

might complicate this argument with Silvia Federici's claim that the new European elite defined itself *also* in relation to the outsiders in its midst, i.e., the European peasant and urban working-class populations, and especially peasant and working-class women, from whom this elite sought to differentiate itself even as it developed new intimacies of domination and exploitation (*Caliban and the Witch* [New York: Autonomedia, 2014]).

81 Cheryl I. Harris, "Whiteness as Property," *Harvard Law Review* 106, no. 8 (1993): 1715.

82 Quoted in MacPherson, *The Political Theory of Possessive Individualism,* 38.

subjects that can be excluded from juridical universality without unleashing an ethical crisis."[83]

As the possessive that is supposed to render one self-possessed, privilege negotiates an uneasy compromise:

> If property is nothing more than what it evokes on the most intimate and subjective levels, then the inherence of its object is denied; the separateness of the thing that is property must be actively obliterated in order to maintain the privately sensational pleasantry of the mirror image. A habituated, acculturated blindness to the inherent quality of the people and things around us grows up, based on our safety from having to see. Our interrelationships with these things are not seen; their reasons for being are rendered invisible.[84]

Rather than "stultification," the subordination of our senses to the single sense of having might be better described as *involution* or *implication*. I use the latter term in its more literal acceptation, signifying an entwining or entanglement. For the property relation is supposed to abet our interiority under the figure of our radical, absolute separateness from the external world of things that have properties and that can be possessed. And yet, as Patricia Williams suggests, separateness itself "must be actively obliterated" in the act of enjoyment. Profit and pleasure

---

83 Ferreira da Silva, *Toward a Global Idea of Race,* 35. For understanding intersectional vectors of oppression, Kimberlé Crenshaw's work remains indispensable; see especially Crenshaw, "Demarginalizing the Intersection of Race and Sex: A Black Feminist Critique of Antidiscrimination Doctrine, Feminist Theory and Antiracist Politics," *The University of Chicago Legal Forum* 140, no. 1 (1989): 139–67. In her essay "Wicked Problems and Intersectionality Telephone," in *Antiracism, Inc.: Why the Way We Talk about Racial Justice Matters,* eds. Felice Blake, Paula Ioanide, and Alison Reed (Earth: punctum books, 2019), 161–87, Barbara Tomlinson provides an interesting account of the uses and misuses of Crenshaw's work in feminist and anti-racist scholarship.

84 Patricia J. Williams, *The Alchemy of Race and Rights* (Cambridge: Harvard University Press, 1991), 40.

cross in a cut that, obscuring the material and mutually con-
stituting character of our "interrelationships" with other people
and things, torques the senses into a narcissism that feels its
entanglement with others and otherness as interiority itself.[85]
Thus, the (non)sense of having privilege becomes an instrument
of extreme sensitivity. The modern subject is taught to measure
his position vis-à-vis other subjects according to their relative
distance from a shared norm or ideal.[86] And on the streets of
major cities and college towns, on radio and television as well as
in the most isolated pockets of social media, in the grumbling of
sectors of a newly precarious middle class that harmonizes with
the rhetoric of those in the highest echelons of power, we find
ourselves in the midst of a virulently renewed enthusiasm for
the explicit location of privilege in visible anatomy. This enthusiasm centers on whiteness and masculinity, not just as marks of
privilege, but as marks bearing the significance of a reason, a ra-
tionale. This enthusiasm suggests that the sense of privilege is a
kind of negative subjective energy, an (occulted) self-knowledge
that knows only its innate superiority. Or only the desire thereof.[87] It is not only a fragile, stupid, and one-sided knowledge,

85 Spillers, linking the sexual violation of enslaved Black women to the
    dominant imaginary's continued displacement of Black paternity (and the
    degradation, in that same gesture, of Black maternity), quotes Frederick
    Douglass on the slaveholders' project to "make a gratification of their
    wicked desires profitable as well as pleasurable" ("Mama's Baby, Papa's
    Maybe," 221).
86 I have borrowed (albeit liberally) this image of the modern subject from
    René Girard, *Deceit, Desire, and the Novel: Self and Other in Literary
    Structure* (Baltimore: Johns Hopkins University Press, 2010); and Eve
    Kosofsky Sedgwick, *Between Men: English Literature and Male Homosocial
    Desire* (New York: Columbia University Press, 2016). Robyn Wiegman,
    American Anatomies, describes modernity's project of "locating in the
    body an epistemological framework for justifying inequality" (2).
87 A renewed enthusiasm, but by no means a new one. The violent
    mobilization of an explicit ideology of patriarchal white supremacy to
    buttress the latter's tacit power has been a feature of modern Western
    societies for a very long time. For a survey of how this strategy has shaped
    American history, see Ibram X. Kendi, *Stamped from the Beginning: The*

but also a dangerous one. It is a knowledge estranged from the senses that gave birth to it, searching for the conditions of conviction, tirelessly expanding, even as it plumbs, the vacuum of itself.

enthusiasm, or the labor of breath

The sense of privilege demands of others an explicitness to which it does not submit itself. The institution's or the culture's sanctioned explicators stand ready to silence a challenge to their privilege by condemning another to that very gap over which their own words glide. Heresy, hysteria, nonsense, madness, sedition, the noise of brutes: the other must be spoken for or barred from speaking altogether. Even when she tries to justify herself on their terms, the explicators, like the Puritan elders confronting Anne Hutchinson, can shut down her efforts by fiat. For the circuit that links them runs only one way:

Definitive History of Racist Ideas in America (New York: Nation Books, 2017). The strategy forms a significant part of the "psychological wage of whiteness" (and white manhood) noted by W.E.B. Du Bois, *Black Reconstruction in America.* As Dana D. Nelson succinctly observes, "The advantage of whiteness for men […] perhaps more immediately than the cultural capital it entailed in the marketplace of democracy, was the disavowal and projection of internal fragmentation that it allowed" (*National Manhood: Capitalist Citizenship and the Imagined Fraternity of White Men* [Durham: Duke University Press, 1998], 100). On the recent history of white power movements as a paramilitary force operating in the United States with relative impunity, see Kathleen Belew, *Bring the War Home: The White Power Movement and Paramilitary America* (Cambridge: Harvard University Press, 2018). In a sentence that powerfully invokes these currents, Fred Moten writes, "the sociopaths who call themselves the mainstream have produced an image of themselves as a thing in and for itself manifest as trained and regulated plenitude when what they are, in fact, is nothing but an always already transgressed boundary, or limit, both instantiated, finally, but also figured as (white) skin" (*Black and Blur,* 260).

Mrs. H. [...] —Do you think it not lawful for me to teach women and why do you call me to teach the court?

Gov. We do not call you to teach the court but to lay open yourself.

Mrs. H. I desire that you would then set down a rule by which I may put them away that come unto me and so have peace in so doing.

Gov. You must shew your rule to receive them.

Mrs. H. I have done it.

Gov. I deny it because I have brought more arguments than you have.[88]

The elders compel Hutchinson to "show" the "rule" that justifies her practice (of practicing theology as a woman, usurping the ministers' authority). They demand that she ground her knowing-how on a knowing-that. But only they, the elders, know how, i.e., possess the institutional power, to judge whether her explication is sufficient. Being a function of power, *this* know-how *cannot* be made explicit. Its ultimate justification lies in what Jacques Rancière calls the "material aggregation of consent."[89] That aggregation appears in the physical, political, and economic power of the men confronting Hutchinson as a united body. A body in which divergent or even opposed personal interests, filtered through the commitment to a hierarchy that situates Hutchinson beneath them all, require them to close ranks. They act against her individual body in order to suppress the inspiration in her flesh. The Governor says, "I have brought more arguments than you have," but what he has really brought are more bodies, more power. No amount of explication can prevail against them, for the elders have decided that they already know what Hutchinson's testimony is supposed to reveal. Onto her ap-

88 David D. Hall, ed., "The Examination of the Mrs. Anne Hutchinson at the Court at Newtown," in *The Antinomian Controversy, 1636–1638: A Documentary History, Edited, with Introduction and Notes* (Middletown: Wesleyan University Press, 1968), 315.

89 Rancière, *Ignorant Schoolmaster*, 82.

peals to fairness and justice, they project their own image of her interiority: "her Judgment is one Thinge and her Expression is another."[90] And yet, as a pedigreed Englishwoman who became a spiritual leader in her settler-colonial community, Hutchinson is granted — rhetorically, at least — what most women in such situations would have been denied: the capacity for judgment. Unlike, for instance, those accused of witchcraft, Hutchinson's community service and spiritual practice do not mark her as an empty vessel of the flesh, a vessel whose imagined violation by the devil authorizes her real violation by upright Christian men. Nonetheless, when the Governor locates Hutchinson's sin in the discord between interiority ("her Judgment") and exteriority ("her Expression"), he shows us what her "sin" signifies: the social discord threatened by a woman's having claimed the mantle of political and theological authority for herself. And so, Hutchinson's recantation, performed during her trial, fails. For her crime *is* expression: her giving voice to an inwardness that only "Man" (the trousers of the capital letter hitched high) is supposed to possess.

Silvia Federici describes various forms of femicide in the seventeenth and eighteenth centuries as a circum-Atlantic phenomenon, one gathering steam in exchanges between Old World and New, reflecting the very resistance that provoked it. But as Sylvia Wynter admonishes, we must be mindful of the differential terrain of this resistance, of how "the partial liberation of Miranda's hitherto stifled speech" rests on the "new [...] silenced ground" of "the majority population-groups of the globe — all signified now as the 'natives' (Caliban's) to the 'men' of Prospero and Fernando."[91] As the shifting grounds of

---

90 Hall, "A Report of the Trial of Mrs. Anne Hutchinson before the Church in Boston," in *The Antinomian Controversy,* 386.

91 Federici, *Caliban and the Witch*; Sylvia Wynter, "Beyond Miranda's Meanings: Un/Silencing the 'Demonic Ground' of Caliban's 'Woman,'" in *Out of the Kumbla: Caribbean Women and Literature,* eds. Carole Boyce Davies and Elaine Savory Fido (Trenton: Africa World Press, 1990), 363. Shakespeare's Miranda, on Wynter's reading, becomes "the beneficiary of a

subject-positions that refuse to stay put, resistance and subjugation get mixed up in what Tavia Nyong'o calls the "circum-Atlantic fold," a metaphor that complicates our understanding of these exchanges, even as it deepens our conception of exchange itself.[92] I have quoted from the record of Hutchinson's trial in part because of how this fragment might evoke, through the silences that populate it, the vast field of expression — verbal, gestural, postural, musical, rhythmic, haptic — that has never left its trace in print. Or perhaps the traces of such expression cut the text, between the lines of interrogation and response. Even the question, perfectly legitimate from an editorial point of view, as to whether this particular text constitutes Hutchinson's "own words" is cut by other questions: What does it mean to own words? How can acts of ex-pression possibly requite the possessive impulse, and at who's ex-pense?

mode of privilege unique to her, that of being the metaphysically invested and 'idealized' object of desire," in relation to which European *cum* white men triangulate their own desires as evidence of inwardness, subjectivity, or spirit. I say triangulate because they do so only in relation to the place occupied by a third party. In this context, that third party is the colonial Other, the racialized man (Caliban) and/or the racialized woman. For Wynter, the latter's absence from the Shakespearean text further testifies to her role in the structure as a figure accumulating catachresis, excess, and displacement. But Zakiyyah Iman Jackson notes how "Wynter's term 'Caliban's woman' runs her right into the problem of heteronormativity [that] her discussion of a particular 'ontological absence' wants to trouble, particularly as this 'ontological absence' functions in the eugenic production of gender, desire, and reproduction" ("'Theorizing in a Void': Sublimity, Matter, and Physics in Black Feminist Poetics," *South Atlantic Quarterly* 117, no. 3 [July 2018]: 639).

92 Nyong'o, *The Amalgamation Waltz,* 19. On the connections between political and religious dissenters in Europe and the New World, sailors and other transient free laborers, indentured servants, and the enslaved, see Peter Linebaugh, "All the Atlantic Mountains Shook," *Labour / Le Travail* 10 (1982): 87–121. Linebaugh argues that these exchanges provided the crucible in which the abolition movements in England and North America were formed, writing of "the oceanic generalization of the theory and practice of antinomian democracy" (113).

We might imagine this field in terms of a circum-Atlantic circulation of the breath, of the desire for breath.[93] Among prophecy; rebellion; mutiny; the manifold practices and rituals of healing and council otherwise labeled *witchcraft*; a million mundane forms of insurrection, including the endlessly repeated resistance to bondage, forced labor, torture, harassment, and rape; ranting and raving; vagrancy and vagabondage; frauds, dodges, close cuts, and narrow escapes; strikes and boycotts; utopian visions, plans, fictions, and otherwise unspoken convictions carried in at the base the spine; and what Saidiya Hartman refers to as the fugitive forms of redress pursued by the enslaved…among these things, I am asserting not a genealogy, but a certain family resemblance.[94] One marked by disjunctions, cuts, and the fugitivity of origins. A field of exchange not founded on equivalence, but productive of singular and collective strategies for survival and flourishing in the face of the violence of equivalence and its enclosure of the world and the flesh. A spacing of the breath. Of prophetic breath, which is the lungs working before and beyond profit.[95] If I call it *enthusiasm,*

---

93 In a book that I did not discover until late in the process of preparing this manuscript for publication, that is to say, belatedly, breathlessly, I read Ashon T. Crawley's claim that

   "Blackpentecostalism belongs to all who would so live into the fact of the flesh, live into this fact as a critique of the violence of modernity, the violence of the Middle Passage and enslavement, the violence of enslavement and its ongoing afterlife, live into the flesh as a critique of the ongoing attempt to interdict the capacity to breathe. The aesthetic practices cannot be owned but only collectively produced, cannot be property but must be given away in order to constitute community. Blackpentecostalism—and those that would come to describe themselves as such—is sent into the world; it is an aesthetic practice that was sent and is about being sent: 'to be sent, to be transported out of yourself, it's an ecstatic experience, it's not an experience of interiority, it's an experience of *exteriority,* it's an *exteriorization*'" (*Blackpentecostal Breath: The Aesthetics of Possibility* [New York: Fordham University Press, 2017], 4, emphasis in the original).

94 Hartman, *Scenes of Subjection,* 76–78.

95 On prophecy, see Harney and Moten, *The Undercommons,* 42.

I do so in order to invoke the history of the affects themselves as modes of politics, *emotion* (in English) having originally been a term meaning "political agitation, civil unrest."[96]

In the improvisation of life beyond the closed domains of elite reason and debate, enthusiasm refers us to "the possible survival of […] autonomy […] outside the head."[97] Derrida's figure suggests the unsettling, indeterminate spread of expression beyond the judgment that is supposed to have produced it. It echoes, too, the topos according to which sovereignty resides in the head of the social body, while the limbs execute the head's commands. And it returns us to Marx, whose critique of the "phantom-like objectivity" of value depicts tables and chairs as conversing, dancing, and testifying on their own behalf. In their phantasmic guises, these commodities have bewitched the economists, who fail to understand value as a figure for the relations among men, mistaking it for a concrete property of the things themselves.[98] But the commodified, dispossessed flesh — marked as less than "man," but on whose labor the achievements of modernity rest — did, and does, speak. This testimony, per Moten, demands that we

> think the possibility of an (exchange-)value that is prior to exchange, and […] think the reproductive and incantatory assertion of that possibility as the objection to exchange that is exchange's condition of possibility.[99]

96 *Oxford English Dictionary,* s.v. "emotion," https://www.oed.com. As a term of opprobrium during the Reformation and its aftermath, enthusiasm, as Jon Mee explains, signifies "the dangers facing the self-authenticating subject" (*Romanticism, Enthusiasm, and Regulation: Poetics and the Policing of Culture in the Romantic Period* [Oxford: Oxford University Press, 2003], 6).

97 Jacques Derrida, *Specters of Marx: The State of the Debt, the Work of Mourning and the New International,* trans. Peggy Kamuf (New York: Routledge, 2011), 216.

98 Marx and Engels, *Capital,* 1:128.

99 Moten, *In the Break,* 10–11.

This exchange-ability without measure I read as the voice or motion of affectability itself. Or the fold thereof, where matter encounters itself as at once continuous and different, in an intimate or impossibly proximal otherness that spells both resistance and vulnerability at the same time.[100] The flesh feels, it suffers. In the throes of prophecy, it dreams of other worlds, and this conviction of the possible runs to seed. It sheds spores that in their dispersal, through songs, rumors, gossip, arguments, and daydreams; whispered from mouth to ear or written down and passed from hand to pocket; in the corners of the marketplace and factory, around a fire at the wooded margins of the fields, and wherever else the wind howls, ruffling the owl's feathers with the summons to flight, can engender the dawning of a new aspect, and turn estranged senses newly strange. "[I]t stands on its head, and evolves out of its wooden brain grotesque ideas."[101] As Saidiya Hartman writes, "the dispossessed body of the enslaved is surrogate for the master's body since it guarantees his disembodied universality and acts as the sign of his power and dominion."[102] Autonomy's "survival [...] outside the head" would include how the limbs of the social body communicate ideas and practices to one another, speak up for themselves and for one another, and lend each other a hand.

Troubling differences between the autonomous, the autonomic, and the antinomian, enthusiasm is a labor of breath. The breath that impassions song; the breath that incarnates prophecy and jeremiad; the breath that powers the pen of critique.

See Mr. Caldwell's intended blessings for us, O! my Lord!!
"No," said he, "if they must remain in their present situation,

---

100 Glossing Moten here, too, who writes of choreography that "[o]penness to the embrace moves against the backdrop of exclusion and the history of exclusion, which is a series of incorporative operations. This is how openness to being affected is inseparable from the resistance to being affected" (*Black and Blur*, 175).
101 Marx and Engels, *Capital*, 1:163–64.
102 Hartman, *Scenes of Subjection*, 21.

keep them in the *lowest state of degradation and ignorance.* The nearer you bring them to the condition of brutes, the better chance do you give them of possessing their *apathy*." Here I pause to get breath, having labored to extract the above clause of this gentleman's speech, at that colonizing meeting. I presume that everybody knows the meaning of the word "*apathy*," […] I solicit the attention of the world, to the foregoing part of Mr. Caldwell's speech, that they may see what man will do with his fellow men, when he has them under his feet. To what length will not man go in iniquity when given up to a hard heart, and reprobate mind, in consequence of blood and oppression?[103]

David Walker's *Appeal* became a crucial anti-slavery tract and "for a time, the most notorious publication in North America."[104] Walker's tract is also a profound critique of the ruses by which patriarchal white supremacy seeks to justify itself. In his impassioned text, prophetic speech ("O! my Lord!!") and critical explication ("that they may see what man will do with his fellow men") interanimate one another. Dissecting Elias Caldwell's address to the American Colonization Society, Walker exposes the perverse irony by which "this benevolent man" offers, as a crumb of redress to the enslaved, the very apathy that buttresses the greed and sadism of the slave-holding classes. The ruses of capitalism justify exploitation by denying the capacity for autonomy to those whose autonomy capitalism would remove by force. Locked into the status of affectable things, the exploited are then denied even the capacity for feeling; they are denied, that is, the minimal right *to be affected* by what affects them, in order that feeling, and the inwardness that it appears to signify, may remain the sole privilege and property of their exploiters.

---

103 David Walker, *Walker's Appeal, in Four Articles: Together with a Preamble, to the Coloured Citizens of the World, but in Particular, and Very Expressly, to Those of the United States of America* (Chapel Hill: University of North Carolina Press, 2011), 52.
104 Sean Wilentz, introduction to ibid., vii.

In a society where humanity is galvanized by performances of ownership, Caldwell's discourse suggests that the dispossessed are so utterly dispossessed that the sole hope left for them is to possess "their apathy," i.e., their non-being, the systematic erasure of their humanity.

Turning the tables on this logic, Walker's text flings the charge of apathy back upon white society. And unlike much of the abolitionist literature by white authors, which appealed to the virtues of that very society to redress of the plight of the enslaved, Walker's text is addressed to "the Coloured Citizens […] of the United States of America." Beginning with its title, his tract performs its revolutionary, emancipatory intent. If, as Michelle Wright puts it, "whiteness […] signifies an ability to transform words into deeds," Walker's tract claims this ability for its primary audience no less than for itself.[105] And we can easily imagine the threat that it posed to the antebellum body politic. Not only does it agitate for the immediate (and therefore violent) overthrow of slave-holders by the enslaved. Not only does it predict, by appeal to divine warrant, the imminence of this overthrow, citing the hypocrisy of those who profess to reconcile slavery with Christian morality: "I tell you that God will dash tyrants, in combination with devils, into atoms, and will bring you out from your wretchedness and miseries under these *Christian People!!!!!!*"[106] Beyond all this, Walker's text cultivates a conviction in the improvisatory power of the speaking (and writing) and suffering flesh. Communicating its power to others, the flesh channels grief and anger into a force that unsettles the sense of what can and will be.

Rhetorically and orthographically, Walker's *Appeal* registers the radical force of the flesh. Interjections and exclamation points pile up with an energy that the regulatory circuits of grammar and rhetoric cannot contain. This is affect that exceeds the sayable, affect battened down by the condition of

---

105 Wright, *Becoming Black,* 64.
106 Walker, *David Walker's Appeal,* 71.

enslavement itself.[107] In the same breath, Walker's painstaking critique of Caldwell's speech strains the writer's composure, as the author struggles to wrest from the knowledge of "blood and oppression," and from the grip of the oppressor's hypocrisy, the stamina to write: "I pause to get breath, having labored to extract the above clause of this gentleman's speech." The *Appeal* is a complex text, and I cannot do justice to it here.[108] But I appeal to its affinity with traditions of enthusiasm because much of what received that label during the early modern period was the work of men and women who dared lay claim to the authority to interpret and contest divine and secular discourse without the sanction of privilege or (what would come to be called) expertise.[109] And though many, perhaps, did so in pursuit of those

107 As Saidiya Hartman points out, any form of self-expression was extremely dangerous for the enslaved (*Scenes of Subjection,* 54–56).

108 Tavia Nyong'o, for instance, reads Walker's *Appeal* as performing a kind of masculine shame: as exhorting his Black male readers to "vindicat[e] their race" in the face of the degradation of slavery and the insults of white supremacist thinkers like Thomas Jefferson (*The Amalgamation Waltz,* 90–95). Following this reading, and quoting Denise Ferreira da Silva, we might say that Walker "occupies the affectable (outer-determined) position in the racial text and the transparent (self-determined) one in the patriarchal text" ("Hacking the Subject: Black Feminism and Refusal beyond the Limits of Critique," *PhiloSOPHIA* 8, no. 1 [2018]: 24).

109 I would like to think that Walker's spirit might keep company in the circum-Atlantic fold with all sorts of troublemakers, among them Ranters like Abiezer Coppe. Coppe's seventeenth-century pamphlets championed the cause of "poor creeples, lazars, […] rogues, thieves, whores and cut-purses," advocating for a truly radical revolution that would cast down the "Great Ones" and liberate the oppressed. Coppe's texts target both the hereditary nobility and the Puritan middle classes eager to replace them in their pursuit of "Honor, Nobility, Gentility, Propriety, Superfluity," which (writes Coppe) "hath (without contradiction) been […] the cause of all the blood that ever hath been shed, from the blood of righteous Abell, to the blood of the last Levellers that were shot to death" (*Selected Writings* [London: Aporia Press, 1987], 24). Coppe is a hymnist of the flesh, and he imagines his own compositional practice in visceral terms:
    "And behold I writ, and lo a hand was sent to me, and a roll of a book was therein, which this fleshly hand would have put wings to, before the time. Whereupon it was snatch out of my hand, & the Roll thrust into my

bloodless idols, "ability, aptitude, merit," many also did it out of fidelity to that collective compact between the senses and the imagination by which alone we might learn, coming to know it together, what it means to live.

The labor for breath, tracing its cut through interlocking yokes (chattel slavery, indentured servitude, debt-peonage, lynching, low-wage labor, incarceration, prostitution, military conscription, segregation, discrimination, isolation, deprivation, sexual and domestic violence, etc.) in search of other modes of being and becoming, gave and gives vent to what Marx calls "the sensuous outburst of […] life activity."[110] This ventilation sustains the creativity of social and collective life. It can be found, at the turn of the twentieth century, in the close, crowded quarters of the slums where young Black women embarked on "beautiful experiments" in desiring freedom, as chronicled by Saidiya Hartman. Queer or otherwise living outside the enclosure of middle-class gender roles, poor, and frequently crimi-

---

mouth; and I eat it up, and filled my bowels with it […] where it was as bitter as wormwood; and it lay broiling, and burning in my stomack, till I brought it forth in this forme" (18).

Coppe testifies to a gestation in the bowels that proves necessary before he can transmute into words what he has seen and felt. Nor is the voice that commands Coppe to write any sort of Kantian weighing and accounting of perspectives. If the voice of conscience, then conscience is a harrowing of the senses and a revolt in the gut. In the folds of this affective history, voices like Walker's and Coppe's hook up with those whom Harney and Moten celebrate in *The Undercommons*:

"These other ones carry bags of newspaper clippings, or sit at the end of the bar, or stand at the stove cooking, or sit on a box at the newsstand, or speak through the bars, or speak in tongues. These other ones have a passion to tell you what they have found, and they are surprised you want to listen, even though they've been expecting you. Sometimes the story is not clear, or it starts in a whisper. It goes around again but listen, it is funny again, every time" (68).

110 Marx, *Economic and Political Manuscripts*, 77. Moten writes of a "spirit manifest in its material expense or aspiration" (*In the Break*, 18), and Christina Sharpe takes up the theme of "aspiration" in her consideration of the "wake work" of Black ethical and aesthetic practices (*In the Wake: On Blackness and Being* [Durham: Duke University Press, 2016], 112–13).

nalized, these unsung women sang themselves in pursuit of what the dominant order told them, time and again, could not be theirs. And which they knew could not belong to them, but for a different reason from what those with so much more than their share of everything else could understand. For beauty does not belong to you. Only in giving yourself, can you, in moments of longing and drift, belong to it:

> It's hard to explain what's beautiful about a rather ordinary colored girl of no exceptional talents, a face difficult to discern in the crowd, an average chorine not destined to be a star, or even the heroine of a feminist plot. In some regard, it is to recognize the obvious, but that which is reluctantly ceded: the beauty of black ordinary, the beauty that resides in and animates the determination to live free, the beauty that propels the experiments in living otherwise. […] Beauty is not a luxury; rather it is a way of creating possibility in the space of enclosure, a radical art of subsistence, an embrace of our terribleness, a transfiguration of the given. It is a will to adorn, a proclivity for the baroque, and the love of *too much*.[111]

Of these young Black women, we might say, as Fred Moten writes, "they renovate sequestration."[112] Just as Hartman renovates what has too often been the sequestration of social history by writing beautifully, boldly, and with great care of what escapes the archive. Of what cuts the archive with the rawness of an exposed site, from which the healing, desiring, and flourishing powers of the flesh have long since fled. But if the social history of Black lives too often resembles an overexposed photograph, where nuance and detail are lost in the obliterating whiteness of the image itself, Hartman attends to how flight

---

111 Saidiya Hartman, *Wayward Lives, Beautiful Experiments: Intimate Histories of Social Upheaval* (New York: W.W. Norton & Company, 2019), 33.
112 Moten, *Black and Blur,* 161.

haunts these sites with the "glimmer of possibility […] the ache of what might be."[113] Writing "a love letter to all those who had been harmed," she writes waywardly, and this waywardness expresses a double movement, a doubled becoming that, in overcoming the confinement of the urban "wards" where her subjects fought to thrive, confounds the difference between interior and exterior (like all the plans concocted, the loves pursued, and the knowledge of life, at times beautiful, at times terrible, consecrated in the hallways, in the embrace of a vestibularity that most middle-class social critics and reformers, Black and white, could only read as signs of a moral and cultural deficit that the white world both had the right to impose and the duty, somehow, to remedy).[114]

Beyond the shallow paradigms of uplift that reflect only patriarchal white supremacy's exhausting search to recover its own good intentions, Hartman's book — and the currents of Black feminist and Black queer thought that nourish it and that it nourishes — renovate my own white man's sense, morally, aesthetically, and intellectually, of the possible. Including my sense of what language, as an instrument of longing and struggle, yes, but also mutual comfort and pleasure, might make room for. For obsessively policing the boundaries of its fantasized superiority (which is a thin film glossing the realities of hierarchy and exploitation that harm white lives, too), whiteness fears the breath that animates language. Fears it as a source of contagion. Breath roots us in our commonality with others *as* flesh; as such, it expresses the radical capacity for feeling together that we might call *compassion*.[115] But sutured to the labor of its own sep-

---

113 Hartman, *Wayward Lives*, 30.

114 Ibid., 31, 22. For "vestibularity," see Spillers, "Mama's Baby, Papa's Maybe," 207.

115 See Crawley, *Blackpentecostal Breath,* who writes of the "breathed critique" of Black aesthetic and religious practices in their opposition to the "totalizing force" that encloses Black lives; these practices "mak[e] evident the incompleteness, the incompletion, of the project of white supremacy" (46). Crawley also notes that "[s]hortness of breath from thinking the very

arateness-as-self-possession, whiteness names an intimacy with *failures* of compassion. Like that of the white middle-school teachers in Kiese Laymon's memoir *Heavy,* who take their Black students to task for what the teachers perceive as the students' inattention to proper hygiene:

> Worse than any cuss word we could imagine, "gross" existed on the other side of what we considered abundant. And in the world we lived in and loved, everyone black was in some way abundant. We'd all listened to grown-folk spade sessions on Friday. We'd all dressed in damn near our Easter best to watch the pregame, the game, and, mostly, the halftime show of Jackson State vs. Valley, Valley vs. Alcorn, Alcorn vs. Southern, or Grambling vs. Jackson State on Saturday. Saturday night, we'd all driven back home in the backseats of cars, listening to folk theorize about the game, Mississippi politics, or why somebody's auntie and uncle were trying to sell their child's World's Finest Chocolates in the parking lot after the game. Sunday morning, we'd all been dragged into some black church by our parents and grandparents. And every Sunday, we hoped to watch some older black folk fan that black heathen in tennis shoes who caught the Holy Spirit. But outside of stadiums and churches, and outside of weekends, we were most abundant. While that abundance dictated the shape and movement of bodies, the taste and texture of our food, it was most apparent in the way we dissembled and assembled words, word sounds, and sentences.[116]

I quote this passage at length because Laymon's figure of "abundance" traces the ethical and aesthetic dimensions of what I have tried to summon, in its fugitive resistance to modernity's

capacity of Others breathing the same air, it seems, was a vivifying force of racial mob and lynching violence" (68).

116 Kiese Laymon, Heavy: *An American Memoir* (New York: Scribner, 2018), 76.

violent reconfiguration of social privilege, under the heading of enthusiasm. And because the abundance Laymon describes breathes through his prose, too, fanning the contours of what we might call ordinary lives. Except that *ordinariness* suggests an ordering, an enclosure the violence of which this abundance troubles with its heathen holiness, its non-stop pursuit of renovation and invention. In its un-ordinal seriality, *abundance* refers us to a multitude of insurgent sites where messages pass to and fro, on frequencies outside the narrow range of a racialized visibility, elliptically, conspiratorially, compassionately, with the radiance of possible worlds.[117]

acknowledgments

Prurient interest, scholarly or otherwise, would penetrate such sites in order to exploit what they shelter from the metrics of exchange. And guilt is only the other side of prurience. But *gratitude,* by which I try to name the impropriety of a response that always exceeds and falls short of its object, gratitude is felt as excessive in the moment of falling short. Perhaps because through it, this feeling, you are brought up short on the incompletion of your flesh, radical and pre-possessive. Or perhaps because gratitude is fugitive, and the feeling too soon goes away. At any rate, gratitude gathers the rest of what I have to say, by way of introduction and acknowledgment. I'm after a manner of reaching for trust in the body and the body's buried knowledge: the search, determined or desperate, for time's tackle coiled in the flesh, which modern discipline has unraveled, tallied up, and translated into an inventory of formal rules, procedures, and mechanisms. To live estranged from this trust is to suffer that

117 In addition to the work of Fred Moten, I am thinking here of Laura Harris's deployment of the concept of the "sociality of blackness" in "What Happened to the Motley Crew? C.L.R. James, Hélio Oiticica, and the Aesthetic Sociality of Blackness," *Social Text* 30, no. 3 (2012): 49–75.

alienation that so many writers have attributed to modernity. But to cling to that estrangement, in the name of one's own "ability, aptitude, merit," is to double down on alienation as though it were the very ground of trust. James Baldwin writes, "The person who distrusts himself has no touchstone for reality — for this touchstone can be only oneself."[118] Baldwin suggests that the habits and emotions by which white people defend their privilege — especially their fear, anger, and indifference toward those who have borne and continue to bear the consequences of the white greed for land and cheap labor — have severely enclosed whites' ability to know, hence to trust, themselves. "Such a person," Baldwin writes, "interposes between himself and reality nothing less than a labyrinth of attitudes." Baldwin's metaphor beautifully describes the persistence of privileged dispositions in history and their role in the construction of subjectivity and intersubjective life. They are not imaginary, these attitudes, at least not like vapors that can be brushed away. For they govern the movement of bodies as well as the arrangement of physical space. To picture it precisely, we would have to imagine multiple labyrinths, layered one on the other in N dimensions. Each of us has such a labyrinth, and we invite others into our labyrinth by how we treat them: how we try to love them or refuse them love; how we envy or despise them; how we nurture the good in them or goad them toward the terror in themselves. My sense of having privilege consists, perhaps, in a feverish enjoyment of such powers of bondage and refusal. Seduced by them, I aspire to a petty architecture of Babelian proportions, following and reinforcing the endless turns of invidious contrasts (dark and light, weak and strong, dirty and clean, dumb and smart, brutish and sensitive, ugly and beautiful, fat and thin, poor and rich, foreign and native, mad and sane, ill and hale, stranger and friend (one passage leading only into another, where the walls are flesh and blood (as Saidiya Hartman writes, "the denigrated and deprecated, those castigated and saddled by varied corpo-

118 Baldwin, "The Fire Next Time," 312.

real maledictions, are the fleshy substance that enable the universal to achieve its ethereal splendor"), and the monster at the center, only what, in the course of my pursuit, I have become (only myself))).[119]

As Baldwin says, these attitudes "do not relate to the present" in that they substitute relations fixed in the past for an openness to the achievement of solidarity that is the present's unending gift.[120] To turn away from the flesh we share, and to substitute the shuffle of value judgments, as though the senses were so many sliding panels we might rearrange in order to construct clear passage to the freedom we have been promised…weaving in and out of one another's path…striving to distinguish ourselves as individuals by the actions that we collectively invent… refusing to feel how, beneath us, the ice grows thin and is already breaking up. This is an image of society as the aggregation of self-possessive individuals. An image of society as haunted by that "impartial spectator" each person patches together out of the value judgments that they have learned to attribute to others, feeling desperate to measure up.[121] My description is not meant to elicit sympathy for the fragility of such a figure, nor in any way to excuse this figure from a reckoning with the history that their attitudes reproduce. For if attitudes, habits, and dispositions lend a person's acts, moment to moment, that always

---

119 Hartman, *Scenes of Subjection,* 122.

120 Baldwin, "The Fire Next Time," 312.

121 Adam Smith, *The Theory of Moral Sentiments* (Indianapolis: Liberty Classics, 1982), 110. But the impartial spectator is really an imp of partiality. For the logic of invidious distinction demands that the judgments of another (of any particular other) confer value only insofar as that value retains its deferred and promissory power. In other words, the other's judgment matters as a measure of what I *might* be worth. It's my potential that's at stake, vis-à-vis a generalized market of exchange, rather than my actual entanglement with this other person. Therefore, as Merleau-Ponty puts it, "at the moment my value is recognized by the other's desire, the other person is no longer the person by whom I wanted to be recognized: he is now a fascinated being, without freedom, and who as such no longer counts for me" (*The Phenomenology of Perception,* 170).

partial consistency we call a self, then in pursuit of such consistency, the privileged subject relies on the emotional, imaginative, and critical labor of others. Thus, men, especially cishet men, lean on the enthusiasm for them shown by the women in their lives. And white lives would be barren without the inventions of Black, immigrant, and Native/Indigenous cultures, just as heteronormative society needs the creative energies of queerness to renovate its tunnel vision of the future. My sense of having privilege has the shape of a series of cuts against the matter of the world, cuts that part the self from others. Deep cuts felt as anger, fear, and shame. But if I hope not to explicate my subject (cutting off the reader at the pass with my expertise), but to do something else, something other (something that others myself), how do I name it? And how do I know when I have attained it? What does it look like, sound like, feel like?

Perhaps what I am after might be called *exposure*. Exposure can certainly feel different from, even if it resembles, explication. If the latter is a means of possessing one's subject (matter), the former suggests a loss of possession, a losing it or having lost it. We usually apply the term to what befalls someone (as in, being exposed to a bad turn of fortune). And in the moral domain, exposure signifies an unwilled unveiling, like what undoes the liar, the hypocrite, or the fraud. In what might exposure consist, as an ethical condition purposely sought (if not exactly an intentional act)? I behave toward others, each of whom is never merely *an*other but none other than *this* other, whose becoming otherwise frustrates the compass of my knowledge, in ways that do not fail to expose the shape of me. They expose not only what I know, but also what I believe and desire, what I have been and what I might become. For your being someone worth my concern and care (i.e., your being a *someone* for me) is not a property that it lies in your power to disclose, as if I might demand it of you. Rather, you have the right to demand it *of me*. This demand exposes me, one way or the other. In my refusal, as Stanley Cavell would say, I stand exposed as someone who lacks the motive, or has lost the capacity, to care.[122] But in such a reckoning, I feel the rub within myself between the singularity or particularity of my attitudes or dispositions, and their generality or commonality. I mean the idea that these things are, in the same breath, mine and not mine. Mine, in that these things do not just happen to me, but they commit me to who I am vis-à-vis others, and their performance yields my most salient internal trace. Not mine, in that the presence within me of these attitudes or dispositions registers my implication in orders outside of myself. I am exposed because I stand liable for the consequences of my actions, feelings, and judgments, and because those consequences are something I must own up to but that I do not possess. They may lie beyond my power to control, but they are not beyond my responsibility. If, as Cavell suggests, "acknowledgment goes beyond knowledge," it is because acknowledgment engages the limited positive freedom with which dispositions are endowed, the freedom to syncopate, to pivot, to dwell in a pause, to pick up or drop a thread, a beat, etc., in the interest of introducing a new drift into the pattern itself.[123] To quote Stefano Harney and Fred Moten, "a way of feeling through others, a feel for feeling others feeling you," acknowledgment returns us to our affectable being.[124] It entails a feeling for the other's being affected by me, which is also my being affected *through* the other's feeling and suffering. Even when I am not (when I affect not to be) affected

---

122 My thinking about exposure, like my use of the term "acknowledgment," draws heavily on Stanley Cavell, *The Claim of Reason: Wittgenstein, Skepticism, Morality, and Tragedy* (New York: Oxford University Press, 2009). There Cavell argues that "Being exposed to my concept of the other is being exposed to my assurance in applying it, I mean to the fact that this assurance is mine, comes only from me. The other can present me with no mark or feature on the basis of which I can settle my attitude. I have to acknowledge humanity in the other, and the basis of it seems to lie in me" (433).

123 Ibid., 428. As Saba Mahmood writes, "the outward behavior of the body constitutes both the potentiality and the means through which interiority is realized" (*Politics of Piety*, 159).

124 Harney and Moten, *The Undercommons*, 98.

by it. Acknowledgment exposes me, not when I explain myself to you, but when I attend to my lapses in attention to the cut of our commonality, which constitutes our mutual separateness (the separateness of our flesh) as what we share, what we have in common. In that cut, wayward ever, we might improvise a new embodiment together, without any sort of guarantee.

Acknowledgments: a book strums the writer's debt to those, living or dead, whose intimacy vibrates across those dispositions on which the writer draws. The range of vibration is indefinite, and manifold are the opportunities for distortion. Or as Rauna Kuokkanen observes, "to recognize someone is always to misrecognize others and render them and their works invisible."[125] The privileges I have enjoyed in writing this book, including the leisure time and institutional support, not to mention the material comforts in which I was ensconced and access to the land on which I wrote, rest on the lives and labor of others, and yet, the work's pretention to success as a work implies their erasure. To call the work a failure cannot repair the rift, no more than my own (shamefaced) desire for anonymity can mitigate the misrecognition I prolong. But the least I can do, groping my way through the labyrinth of false equivalences, is to acknowledge that this work does not stand (or fall) on its own merits (merely in consequence of the writer's aptitude or talent). The least I can do is to expose, however partially, the network of support on which it rests. (Randi Kristensen, whose friendship and conversation over the past decade have been a kind of tutelary genius for this piece. And Zak Wolfe and the rest of the fellowship of ranters gathered at the sign of the Fox and Hounds). Might such exposure prepare me for the work of acknowledgment? (Rachel Riedner, who first encouraged my ideas for this book, refusing to hear the excuses I made about not having the expertise.) Might my lack of expertise make room for a more capacious sense of my senses? Our parity begins there, where the senses, yours and mine and theirs, bring it forth. (The pa-

---

125 Kuokkanen, *Reshaping the University,* 91.

tient readers in the "works in progress" group of the GW University Writing Program, including Sandie Friedman, Shonda Goward, Kathy Larsen, Derek Malone-France, Gordon Mantler, Danika Myers, Pam Presser, Michael Svoboda, and Phil Troutman, who talked me through early versions of this project. And Bro Adams, Debra Bergoffen, Jane Flax, Gayle Salamon, and Gail Weiss, who welcomed me into their Merleau-Ponty reading group, where I enjoyed conversations that have left traces throughout this text.) Can we compare acknowledgment to enthusiasm? Are they not both ways, however hedged round by dangers, of projecting ourselves into an "improvisation in the disorders of desire"?[126] (Cathy Eisenhower and Ken Jacobs, dear friends whose improvisatory gusto in art and life never fails to inspire me.) Under their tutelage, might writing become the raveling of deep aspect, threading the world's lures with their scriptural trace? (Brian Casemore, a fellow critical traveler along the by-ways of white southern masculinity, whose scholarship and conversation breathed new life into my sense of what this book might do.) As the indisposition of my dispositions, the shear of composing against composure? (Bob Mondello, Carlos Schröder, and the rest of the folks around Bob and Carlos's table for the monthly night of ñoquis, a haven for conviviality and wit.) Writing, I have to hope, has more to offer than a mere figure for the ineffable, like the picture of a kettle boiling that we would not say is itself boiling, or a coat as a vessel for the value of some linen that is not in the coat. (Those whose teaching and mentorship motivate me still, especially Brad Richard, Pam Alexander, Tim Scholl, and Carl Phillips.) Or if a figure, then of the sort that Wittgenstein evokes when he claims that "the human body is the best picture of the human soul," or when he writes that "my soul, with its passions, as it were with its flesh

---

126 Stanley Cavell, *Philosophy the Day after Tomorrow* (Cambridge: Harvard University Press, 2008), 185.

and blood, must be redeemed, not my abstract mind."[127] (Garth Greenwell, whose practice of art and friendship has been my best picture of what those things might be.) Perhaps writing, in moments of what I could describe as erasing your expectations, offers a figure for how our bodies themselves breach the envelope of self-possession; how they thresh us into a space and time in which the flesh ceases to belong to your or me. (Leah Richardson, whose enthusiasm for this project helped sustain it in the home stretch. And Keturah Solomon, whose compassion as a reader and a friend reminded me what this is all about.) A liminal zone, rife with trauma and strife but also transformation, where our beliefs *about* the other can yield to our belief *in* them. (Hannah Sommers and Peter Cohn, who, believing in me, made the professional space for me to finish this project.) A space and time of entanglement, of mutual indebtedness, which can, under the right conditions, give birth to our belief in us, or maybe I just mean love, though never without the risk of failure. (Eileen Fradenburg Joy and Vincent W.J. van Gerven Oei, whose agreement to take on this book and its risks remains a gift that exceeds my powers of gratitude; and whose commitment to the creation of new publics — critical, utopian, enthusiastic, and necessary — is matched by their belief in the productive errancy of writing, its eccentric paths toward truth.) It goes without saying that, for all the companionship I have enjoyed, the errors in this book are my responsibility. And yet, they are hardly mine to own. Writing about the soul in despair, Kierkegaard likens it to an "error [that] slipped into an author's writing and […] became conscious of itself."[128] The error seeks to expose its author: "I refused to be erased; I will stand as a witness against you, a witness that you are a second-rate author." One cannot be a first-rate au-

---

127 Wittgenstein, *Philosophical Investigations,* 178, and quoted in Alessandra Tanesini, *Wittgenstein: A Feminist Interpretation* (Cambridge: Polity Press, 2004), 40.

128 Søren Kierkegaard, *The Sickness unto Death: A Christian Psychological Exposition for Upbuilding and Awakening,* eds. and trans. Edna H. Hong and Howard V. Hong (Princeton: Princeton University Press, 2006), 74.

thor as long as the error stands. Yet erasing the error would ruin the "whole production." What if error, resisting its own erasure, might yield an errancy that works against (authorial) privilege? What if the exposed failures of thought might become the joists to support other structures of feeling? (My mother, Marguerite Hoffpauir, whose love and wisdom have never failed me. My younger brother, Kant Smith, whose creative partnership I cherish no less than his generous and steadfast friendship.) It is not the invisible activity of thought that provides the warrant for the work's truth, but the hidden labor, coiled within it, of parents, children, teachers, students, editors, colleagues, neighbors, friends, and lovers. (My father, Ashton Smith, who did not live to see this project come to fruition, but whose fierce belief in me is a bequest I have yet to learn the right way to use.) These attachments represent the braid of artistry, experience, and care (and occasionally, enmity and sabotage) that have brought a work, sometimes in spite of itself, to fruition. (And Natalie Prosin, who — it goes without saying, only because I cannot find the right words — has nurtured this book and its writer in ways that I could not have imagined, that I cannot hope to deserve. But with whom every day I learn more deeply how to love.) Cryptic co-authors, their presence in the work rehearses its life among those strangers who, as its readers in the wide world, are the work's co-authors to come.

1

The Promise of Composition:
Liberalism, Sentimentality, and Critique

(the hope of/for) composition
— Fred Moten, *In the Break*

His need to set himself up as a model of taste, piety, and
sensibility before an appropriately enthralled female
spectator is so intense as to make his pedagogy suspect.
— Ann Douglas, *The Feminization of American Culture*

There's something wrong with judgment itself in writing classrooms.
— Asao B. Inoue, *Antiracist Writing Assessment Ecologies*

The semester began under the impress of a new logo (a notable occasion in the seasons of university life). Some will even have said that they preferred the old George Washington, who resembled his oil portraits (his face, in three-quarters view, with that soft, rouged look of the elder statesman and slave-holder at home, familiar as the dollar bill). Now George sports a profile fit for empire — forehead high, chin chiseled, all business — rendered in a kind of high-gloss grisaille. From website and letterhead (where rules prescribe his position) his gaze surveys abstract vistas, a sphinx poised between the nostalgia for Anglo-

American cultural hegemony and a techno-bureaucratic optimism trained on East and South Asia; or a cyborg, part anime superhero, part postage stamp. His facelift suits the university's neoliberal rhetoric, celebrating the retrenchment by corporate and financial elites as "innovation" (at home) and "development" (abroad), terms that lend a new visage to the perennial appetites of capital and empire. As for this university's students, those who by privilege or pluck leave college for the orbits of the elite preside over an increasingly immiserated precariat. Those not so positioned join the ranks of a clerical class whose economic and political power is being drained to the dregs by the upward flow of capital to the one percent, or the one-tenth of the one percent, or the one-tenth of that tenth again. Along with its logo, the university unleashed a new slogan: "We Make History." In such times, how should we regard the promise to "make history" with which an expensive private university markets itself?

I have been writing and revising this essay, which was the germ of this book, for close to a decade. I feel at once too close to the subject matter and not close enough, my subject being the role of composition pedagogy in the contemporary neoliberal university, and the place of white masculinity in that pedagogy. Not close enough, because I am not a composition scholar, nor do I teach composition. But as a librarian, I have spent a lot of time in first-year writing classes over the years, working with teaching faculty to introduce students to the dispositions of research in the academy. The generosity of these teachers in welcoming me as a partner and collaborator has given me occasion to think about how such pedagogy participates in the traffic of affect and the senses, as dispositions are composed and recomposed in acts of thinking aloud and writing things down, in the classroom and on the page. In part, this essay draws on my experiences working with my good friend and colleague Randi Kristensen, a brilliant teacher whose critical praxis has taught me a great deal, as has her refusal to shy away from questions of race, class, and American imperialism. Questions that might otherwise remain only marginally visible in the frequently all- or majority-white classrooms at our university. But this essay is not about Randi's course and its pedagogy; that is her story to tell.[1] Rather, following M. Jacqui Alexander and many others, this essay proposes to trace the pedagogical, as a set of discourses *about* teaching as well as practices *of* teaching, in its implication with the production of citizens and subjects of the modern liberal state. Which is also, of course, the capitalist, patriarchal, white supremacist, settler-colonial, imperialist, carceral state. A state run by the moment's boardroom buffoon, our racist- and misogynist-in-chief. In the historical present of empire, pedagogy might become an occasion for learning to feel oneself caught up in a certain texture, or a certain fold of space and time, which links the local to other localities that disappear within what we call "the global." This texture makes the present moment a palimpsest or multiple exposure of occasions that do not fit neatly into the kind of narrative that sells tuition or textbooks.[2] In turn, this essay is a palimpsest of the writer's efforts to come to terms with (to grapple with, morally and intellectually, but also to find words for) how that learning might transpire in writing, however errant and halting its path. And with what it might mean for the writer's flesh — freighted with habits that he cannot, by fiat of self-reflection, cast off — to adopt what, following Hortense Spillers, one might call a "critical posture."[3]

1   See Randi Gray Kristensen, "From *Things Fall Apart* to *Freedom Dreams*: Black Studies and Cultural Studies in the Composition Classroom," in *Writing against the Curriculum: Anti-Disciplinarity in the Writing and Cultural Studies Classroom,* eds. Randi Gray Kristensen and Ryan M. Claycomb (Lanham: Lexington Books, 2010), 171–82.

2   This chapter owes a methodological debt to Lauren Berlant's concept of "the historical present" as articulated in *Cruel Optimism* (Durham: Duke University Press, 2011), 12–17. On the "palimpsest" as a decolonial temporality, see M. Jacqui Alexander, *Pedagogies of Crossing: Meditations on Feminism, Sexual Politics, Memory, and the Sacred* (Durham: Duke University Press, 2005).

3   UWaterlooEnglish, "Hortense Spillers: The Idea of Black Culture," *YouTube,* November 24, 2013, https://www.youtube.com/watch?v=P1PTHFCN4Gc.

This chapter is about the promise of composition. Which is the promise tendered to students who arrive at the university in pursuit of fulfilling professional and civic lives, hoping to make their mark on the world. And the promise guiding the labor of many of us who, in teaching these students, hope to make our own mark, cultivating through our pedagogy a cohort of informed citizens.[4] In this, the promise of the university (of my university, where as of this writing, the administration continues to neglect calls to abandon its offensive mascot, "the Colonials") remains of a piece with that of European enlightenment, which has been a promise complicit with the wholesale theft of land and the murder or displacement of its inhabitants, in conjunction with the circum-Atlantic trade in stolen life. A promise protected by an arsenal of erasure and neglect that keeps pristine the conviction that the human being qua white cishet man is the author of his own destiny. The university wields this arsenal through its preference for making history as opposed to reckoning with it. (Although by *history* the university's leadership often means little more than increased revenue and a bet-

4   As I have said, my own practice as a teacher is occasional, a matter of leading one-off sessions and workshops, rather than developing and teaching entire courses. But I am interested, too, in how the call to teach might appear occasional in the etymological sense, as what *befalls* one. For this essay, the etymological kinship between "occasion" and "occident" proves suggestive. As denizens of the Eurocentric West, "we" — that is, many of us in my imagined audience — have been taught to imagine our positions relative to racialized and class privilege and the settler-colonialist state as something that has befallen us, as a matter of history and destiny, rather than an ongoing work of implication and complicity. This destiny, however, furnishes our "orientation" (or vocation), a figure of intentional agency against the ground of the global, which appears in its under-description as a field of untapped potential out of which we shall reap our future good. In modernity, the subject's oscillation between intentional agency and inherited or conventional dispositions (or occasion and orientation) generates charged feelings. The effort to resolve to them, as I shall propose, generates the competing modes of the sentimental and the critical.

ter reputation according to the market-based metrics by which even non-profit institutions live and die.)

I say that this promise guides our labor at the university, not wanting to collapse the nuance and complexity of approaches to teaching that remain diverse in their means and ends, nor to efface the work of those (like my friend Randi) committed to more radical anti-racist, anti-capitalist, decolonial, queer, or feminist visions for how the classroom can become a space of solidarity and critique. Likewise, my characterization neglects the important organizing by students, faculty, staff, and some administrators on behalf of making the university as a whole a more inclusive, equitable, and socially just place.[5] But there is, all the same, a liberal template embedded in most university curricula and in much university discourse. And this template enforces a set of dispositions that one must, whatever one's ideological commitments, at least occasionally adopt and perform. I call that template *liberal* because it remains deeply wedded to the idea that individuals, by pursuing rational goals and acting with self-awareness, can harmonize with the actions and pursuits of others, jointly and freely producing a common good. As a pedagogy, liberalism frames ways of imagining the future as the progressive explication of a potential that inheres in the here-and-now. A potential, however, that remains centered on the self. This promise links liberalism, citizenship, and the various modalities of modern privilege. For embodiment of the privileged terms (whiteness, cishet masculinity, etc.) seems to disclose a promise that the self is destined for a certain status, a

---

5   Within the last two years, a new administration at my university has taken small but salutary steps toward making diversity and inclusion, at least among the student body, a substantive priority. Whether the promise of this work comes to fruition in structural change, or peters out in empty slogans and spectacular gestures, remains to be seen. But my neglectful characterization hews to the character of the promise as our liberal institutions insist upon tendering it: as the largesse of corporate persons, Hobbesian sovereigns with whom we are supposed to identify, investing our emotional, sensuous, critical labor in sustaining the precarious felicity of the promise itself.

certain level of achievement, and certain kinds of success. And this promise, in the liberal imaginary, represents both the universal destiny of subjects in the abstract, and the just reward for a merit conceived as particular to the concrete person and his accomplishments.

More and more, that promise participates in the brand of optimism that Lauren Berlant, writing of the cultural logic of our neoliberal moment, calls "cruel." "Cruel optimism" signifies an attachment to forms of life whose pursuit perennially disappoints us, indeed hurts us, without our being able to abandon them. Cruel optimism obtains because we have learned to love the pursuit itself, and because we can fathom no alternative: nothing else to do, nowhere else to turn.[6] But Berlant's analy-

---

6   For Berlant, an optimistic structure includes "a sustaining inclination to return to the scene of fantasy that enables you to expect that this time, nearness to *this* thing will help you or a world to become different in just the right way" (*Cruel Optimism,* 2, emphasis in the original). Like Freud's *fort-da,* optimism depends on both the repetitive or habitual, and the deictic aspects of desire. But its habituation betrays, behind the apparent deixis of "this thing, here and now," an inductive structure, the attempt to reach from the particulars of site and situation to something that transcends particularity. In this sought-after (and for Freud, always fantastic) transcendence, desire at last sheds habit, as repetition gives way to enduring presence (the universal claim, the general rule). Cruel optimism, then, partakes of the affective and cognitive economy that Freud assigns to trauma, where repetition turns to compulsion, suturing the self to a bad scene or thing such that the desire for avoidance rehearses the harm itself. Berlant, however, distances her work from trauma theory; for her, the latter's focus on the singularity of the event forecloses attention to the extended temporality of what she refers to as "crisis ordinariness" (9–10), where prolonged exigency calls for a variety of strategies for management and survival in the world.

At the same time, I think Berlant's work can be productively aligned with much work that theorizes Black lives — and Black women's lives in particular — with reference to the traumatic afterlife of slavery, where what motivates the analysis is precisely the violent "ordinariness," the ongoing-ness, of oppression. Where trauma is not only the shrapnel of past violence, enclosed in the compelled, suffering body, but also present in the interface with structures that compel the flesh (as a term for collective, social, interstitial embodiment) to suffer over and over again.

sis of cruel optimism doesn't make us out to be dupes of the system. Her work, as I read it, practices a form of therapy (à la Wittgenstein). For at stake is a picture of agency, of intentional consciousness, that insists on personal autonomy as its grounding condition. This is the liberal sense of sovereignty, for which freedom is bound to the postulate of an interiority that, as Denise Ferreira da Silva maintains, cannot escape haunting by its dependence on what that postulation excludes.[7] Modeled on the idea of an exclusive right to property, such sovereignty can achieve coherence only through systematic forms of ignorance and neglect, beginning, as Sandy Grande notes, with "the fail-

In the recovery of histories and present histories of creative resistance, much of this work tends also to strive against an optimism that would fail to recognize itself as cruel. See, for example, Kimberly Juanita Brown, *The Repeating Body: Slavery's Visual Resonance in the Contemporary* (Durham: Duke University Press, 2015); Patricia Hill Collins, *Black Feminist Thought: Knowledge, Consciousness, and the Politics of Empowerment,* 2nd edn. (New York: Routledge, 2009); Marisa J. Fuentes, *Dispossessed Lives: Enslaved Women, Violence, and the Archive* (Philadelphia: University of Pennsylvania Press, 2016); Saidiya V. Hartman, *Scenes of Subjection: Terror, Slavery, and Self-Making in Nineteenth-Century America* (New York: Oxford University Press, 2010); Hartman, *Wayward Lives, Beautiful Experiments: Intimate Histories of Social Upheaval* (New York: W.W. Norton & Company, 2019); bell hooks, *Ain't I a Woman: Black Women and Feminism,* 2nd edn. (New York: Routledge, 2014); Katherine McKittrick, *Demonic Grounds: Black Women and the Cartographies of Struggle* (Minneapolis: University of Minnesota Press, 2006); Fred Moten, *Black and Blur* (Durham: Duke University Press, 2017); Moten, *In the Break: The Aesthetics of the Black Radical Tradition* (Minneapolis: University of Minnesota Press, 2003); M. NourbeSe Philip, *A Genealogy of Resistance: And Other Essays* (Toronto: Mercury Press, 1997); Christina Sharpe, *In the Wake: On Blackness and Being* (Durham: Duke University Press, 2016); Hortense J. Spillers, *Black, White, and in Color: Essays on American Literature and Culture* (Chicago: University of Chicago Press, 2003); and Michelle M. Wright, *Becoming Black: Creating Identity in the African Diaspora* (Durham: Duke University Press, 2004).

7   Denise Ferreira da Silva, *Toward a Global Idea of Race* (Minneapolis: University of Minnesota Press, 2007). Berlant refers to the "mimetic concept of sovereignty," which "legitimates as something objective the individual's affective *sense* of autonomy" (*Cruel Optimism,* 96, emphasis in the original).

ure to problematize the issue of (colonized) land."[8] You might say that cruel optimism abounds in this moment because the doctrines and customs of neoliberalism (rational choice theory, hyper-consumerism, the attenuation of solidarity) have rendered such performances of personal sovereignty profoundly lonely, a matter of solitary agents seizing what pleasures and scrambling for what gains they can.[9] But if the liberal sense of sovereignty has always been, behind the scenes, a messy affair, involving the machinery of multiple kinds of state-sponsored and state-sanctioned violence — i.e., settler-colonial theft, murder, and domination; kidnapping, torture, and enslavement; land enclosure; wage exploitation; and then the partial transformation of those techniques into the mechanisms of biopolitical management and control — then it may be that the loneliness of neoliberal subjects surfaces that messiness. Perhaps it exposes,

8   Sandy Grande, *Red Pedagogy: Native American Social and Political Thought* (Lanham: Rowman & Littlefield, 2004), 49. For liberalism, "human subjectivity — and therefore emancipation — is conceived of as inherently a rights-based as opposed to a land-based project" (116). But this conception is itself the product of a violent series of transformations, transformations that profoundly altered the relationship between the flesh and its worlds. For the conversion of lands held in common by Native and Indigenous peoples into the exclusive property of European settlers or a European sovereign (not unlike the enclosure of the commons in England and other parts of Europe) grounds a settler-colonial subjectivity in a regime of property rights that abstract from an embodied relationship to the land. Such property rights, as theorized by eighteenth-century bourgeois European men and canonized in the laws of modern nation-states, became the pretext for the violent subjugation of peoples and, ultimately, their conversion into a mass of individuals governed differentially by the reified categories of modern personhood.

9   For a critical history of rational choice theory as ideology, see S.M. Amadae, *Rationalizing Capitalist Democracy: The Cold War Origins of Rational Choice Liberalism* (Chicago: University of Chicago Press, 2003). Amadae notes that for rational-choice theorists like Kenneth Arrow, a guiding assumption is that the ideas of collective preferences, a collective will, and the collective good are meaningless. Society, on this theory, is nothing but the aggregation of individuals, whose preferences sometimes align but frequently do not (115–16).

as a perturbation in the sense of self, the fraught dependence on arrangements that the morally autonomous subject is at pains to disavow. And then the elastic dynamics of cruel optimism, in which gestures of egress or flight always seem to snap one back into the same spot, would have, as their spatial and temporal counterpart, the "intimacy" of which Lisa Lowe writes, describing how the "settler-imperial imaginary" produces itself through an entanglement with the others whom, both within and beyond the borders of the nation-state, it excludes from the social contract.[10]

The intimacies of empire are material, affective, and sensory. Nor does a moment of experience, on this view, represent a single node in a network (however vast). Rather, moments are better described, following M. Jacqui Alexander, as palimpsests, in which the most salient elements cover others whose trace persists, frustrating efforts at clarity that would demand a

---

10 Lisa Lowe, *The Intimacies of Four Continents* (Durham: Duke University Press, 2015), 8. These intimacies are both temporal and spatial, tracing the trajectory of the modern capitalist order in its gobbling up of the globe. For Denise Ferreira da Silva, the spatial has a tendency to slide under the temporal in the imaginary of modern liberalism; she writes of "the modern construction of distance as a temporal metaphor," which serves "to circumscribe the place of emergence of the colonized as a transparent I." This occultation of space is, to be precise, an occultation of the spatial *opposition* that obtains between Europe/colonized North America and its "globalized" others. This is an opposition forged by the forms of violence previously alluded to, and sustained today by, among other things, economic restructuring in the service of international debt, trade agreements that serve multinational corporate interests, racist immigration policies, and covert and overt military aggression under the guise of the "War on Terror." Occulted, the spatial opposition is smuggled into the teleological just-so story we call "civilization" or, more demurely, "development." What's at stake, then, is understanding how "the racial and the cultural write the others of Europe as an effect of signifiers of exteriority, of political-symbolic strategies to institute a particularity that does not belong to time, one that threatens history because it recuperates the relationship postponed in modern representation" (*The Global Idea of Race,* 168).

unitary interpretation.[11] Thus, the rich taste of fair-trade coffee rouses the subject of imperial privilege on their way to the office, where they are vexed by overwork and underpay, taking a brief but sustaining pleasure in their morning cup, which marketing has made to signify a benign image of transnational corporate hegemony. This image depicts hard-working but self-sufficient, *ergo* happy, coffee farmers in Nicaragua or Ethiopia as the counterparts to hard-working white-collar contract workers in the global North who enjoy the ergonomic freedom afforded by the erosion of more stable forms of employment. These imaginary intimacies eclipse others buried in the paper cup, which may have been produced by women and girls working 14-hour days in a *maquiladora* just south of the US border.[12] The *maquiladora,* owned by a transnational corporation headquartered in the United States, occupies lands whose original and rightful inhabitants were dispossessed by agents of the Spanish crown. And while the combined carbon footprint of this beverage contributes to droughts that threaten the coffee farmers' livelihood, the coffeeshop cultivates its lineage as a hub of bourgeois sociability, where the business of state and empire can be transacted on an intimate, informal scale. Where the low-wage staff are trained to smile, and the restrooms are for customers only. Yet a brand, a logo, a ritual gesture accomplish so much precisely because,

11 Alexander, *Pedagogies of Crossing,* 246. Lowe, in calling attention to liberalism's "linked genealogies," likewise cautions against a unitary interpretation of liberalism itself (*The Intimacies of Four Continents,* 10–11).

12 On transnational linkages of exploitation and solidarity, see Alexander, *Pedagogies of Crossing,* 104–5. The phrase "imperial privilege" comes from Piya Chatterjee and Sunaina Maira, "The Imperial University: Race, War, and the Nation-State," in *The Imperial University: Academic Repression and Scholarly Dissent,* eds. Piya Chatterjee and Sunaina Maira (Minneapolis: University of Minnesota Press, 2014), 9. And as Rauna Kuokkanen reminds us, "the global political economy is being fuelled by the accumulation of capital extracted from indigenous peoples' territories" (*Reshaping the University: Responsibility, Indigenous Epistemes, and the Logic of the Gift* [Vancouver: UBC Press, 2007], 115).

within the present's dense folds, a desire takes hold, a desire for the exemplar, for the symbol that condenses and binds the forces of sensation and affect into a form that feels thinkable. As a figure of moral reasoning, the example partakes of cruel optimism because the effort to smooth the wrinkles of experience only intensifies the unease of dwelling in the polyvalent present. (Some of those women and girls in the *maquiladora,* descendants of the land's rightful owners, are linked by ties of migration and solidarity to those who keep the restrooms clean at the imperial university.) Like a restless sleeper, tossing and turning in search of that elusive spot that would stay cool, but the warm night air only thickens instead.

The symbol, the simile, the example: these genres appear sentimental beside the rigor that is supposed to be the hallmark of the truly autonomous subject, the "transparent I" freely traversing the abstract, perfectly lawlike, and timeless transparency of universal reason itself.[13] In one sense, the transparency of this I belies its visibility in the dominant discourses of modernity. As the default subject-position, available only to certain kinds of bodies, its transparency requires the erasure of other subject-positions (non-white, non-cishet masculine, non-able-bodied). It is, you might say, the un-erased. But if every position is a palimpsest, then every erasure remains partial, just as the profoundly internalized, hierarchical logics of patriarchal white supremacy, in their support for capitalism, guarantee that nobody escapes some degree of subordination. This capture is what domination's capillary reach absolutely requires. To inhabit po-

---

13 On the "transparent I" see Ferreira da Silva, *Toward a Global Idea of Race.* It is the protagonist of what Gilbert Ryle calls the "Cartesian myth" of modern self-consciousness. In this myth, the being who can recognize his own thinking (*cogito*) as such claims the right to a self-assured existence in the world (*ergo sum*). Descartes cast the template for liberal moral (and political) agency in its most concise form: the sovereign subject "knows that there is nothing that truly pertains to him but [the] free disposition of the will." See Ryle, *The Concept of Mind* (Chicago: University of Chicago Press, 1984). The quote from Descartes appears in Charles Taylor, *A Secular Age* (Cambridge: Belknap Press of Harvard University, 2007), 134.

sitions of social privilege and power under these conditions is to live a dream, a dream of the body itself, on its privy ledge, cradling "the fragile 'as if equal' of liberal discourse" like an egg that holds the ego.[14] This performance of being somebody rather than nobody, caught between experiences of privilege and experiences of exploitation, might be described as involving modes of sentimental agency.[15] The sentimental presupposes a pedagogy, a training of the dispositions that promises to transform the gap between desire and deed, the gap that both constitutes and undermines the modern notion of free will, into "influence." Influence is a spatially and temporally fattened or thickened version of agency, compounded, paradoxically, of patience. Or it is an agency submerged in the murk of the affects, rather than tracing its meteoric course across the sky.[16]

14   Hartman, *Scenes of Subjection,* 116.
15   The language of "nobody" and "somebody" is borrowed from Alexis Pauline Gumbs, "Nobody Mean More: Black Feminist Pedagogy and Solidarity," in Chatterjee and Maira, eds., *The Imperial University,* 237–59.
16   I am indebted for this definition of sentimental agency, though not for the term itself, to Ann Douglas, *The Feminization of American Culture* (New York: Farrar, Straus and Giroux, 1998). As a set of dispositions wedded to the desire for reform, sentimental agency implicates itself in efforts to justify the alliance between bureaucratic capitalism and patriarchal white supremacy. Such agency is best described as being summoned by a structural position. Thus, while Douglas's study focuses on middle-class white women in the nineteenth century, an equally sentimental agent, in her telling, was the white male Congregational minister. Once dominant voices in their communities, men of deep learning with significant cultural and social authority, Congregational ministers faced a different world after disestablishment. Shorn of the lifelong tenure that establishment had conferred, such men could no longer expect to lead a scholar's life, fashioning a congregation in the image of their theology. Now that he was dependent on the financial support and goodwill of his congregants, the successful minister, according to Douglas, had to be an entrepreneur: "Fearful of openly challenging the economic forces of his society, compelled by unbeatable competition to abandon his former monopoly on culture [...], he was under a sometimes claustrophobic pressure from his fastidious and not always fervent congregation to be better trained, more skillful, and more versatile, while presenting a smaller number of topics

A pedagogy of sentimental agency is woven into the legacy of liberalism in its enduring compact with empire. Coeval with the rise of circum-Atlantic capitalism and the consolidation of the European nation-state, liberal humanism emerged under the aegis of the imperialist project. The latter established and sustains key institutional sites, including the modern academy, with the spoils of slave labor, colonial plunder, and other forms of primitive accumulation. As a result, this humanism depends on the racializing arsenal that defined the colonized and the enslaved as less than human, as the others of the Western European self (and that continues to define their descendants as such).[17]

and evoking a slighter intensity of feeling; he was asked to be more agile in an ever-shrinking space" (41).

    Douglas's minister faced the same commandment as the twenty-first-century academic: *Commodify thyself.* As Tony Scott, Nancy Welch, and others have pointed out, neoliberal retrenchment in the academy imposes the demand "to be more versatile" on increasingly vulnerable academic workers, who are compelled not only to do more with less, but also perpetually to demonstrate their worth. The demand falls hardest, of course, on those who have traditionally struggled for a voice in the institution: men and women of color; queer, trans, and non-binary people (especially queer, trans, and non-binary people of color); people with disabilities; and white women. And the demand expresses itself nowhere more clearly than in the generally unabashed dependence of universities on an adjunct labor force that qualifies for membership in the ranks of the global precariat. In fields like rhetoric and composition, the sense of a public and pedagogical vocation warps under the pressure, as Scott and Welch argue, to "embrace neoliberalism's privatizing and commodifying market pursuits as somehow compatible with the field's public ethos and mission" (Nancy Welch and Tony Scott, "Introduction," in *Composition in the Age of Austerity,* eds. Nancy Welch and Tony Scott [Logan: Utah State University Press, 2016], 6).

17 On the "arsenal of raciality," see Ferreira da Silva, *Toward a Global Idea of Race,* 34–35. On the relationship between "liberal humanism" and colonization, see Lowe, *The Intimacies of Four Continents,* as well as Sylvia Wynter, "The Ceremony Must Be Found: After Humanism," *boundary 2* 12/13, nos. 3–1 (1984): 19–70; Wynter, "1492: A New World View," in *Race, Discourse, and the Origin of the Americas: A New World View,* eds. Vera Lawrence Hyatt and Rex Nettleford (Washington: Smithsonian Institution Press, 1995), 5–57; Wynter, "Unsettling the Coloniality of Being/Power/Truth/Freedom: Towards the Human, After Man, Its Overrepresentation—

The liberal self is coded, in the first instance, as white, cishet, and masculine, but it relies on the disciplines of the sentimental for a crucial supplement. In the logic of this supplement, white bourgeois femininity frames the sovereign subject in his pursuit of economic and political domination. This frame includes the supposedly civilizing influence of the white cishet woman's voice and touch, which is required to soften and mitigate the violence of those pursuits. And it includes the seductive innocence of the white cishet woman's body, the presence of which appears to justify that very violence, summoning it against the hordes, foreign and domestic, that threaten to corrupt civilization itself.[18] Like an eggshell, the imagined fragility of the white feminine encloses what the white cishet masculine subject wants to forget: how the violence that he exerts also produces him.

The sentimental tenders a cruel promise to this subject, that his agency and autonomy are not exhausted by the competitive, acquisitive acts that underwrite his enjoyment of social privilege and power. In other words, the figures of the sentimental serve to contain the vulnerability that such a subject necessarily feels and that he has been taught to disavow. He can safely — with all the safety of dandling a loaded gun — deflect such feelings onto those marked as feminine, who become objects of his desire and protection, his tutelage and neglect, his tenderness and cruelty.

An Argument," CR: *The New Centennial Review* 3, no. 3 (2003): 257–337; Alexander G. Weheliye, *Habeas Viscus: Racializing Assemblages, Biopolitics, and Black Feminist Theories of the Human* (Durham: Duke University Press, 2014).

18 On femininity's "civilizing influence," see G.J. Barker-Benfield, *The Culture of Sensibility: Sex and Society in Eighteenth-Century Britain* (Chicago: The University of Chicago Press, 1996). Michelle Wright, citing Anne McClintock's work, notes that "since the eighteenth century, Western nations have relied on the image of the white female to justify, construct, and deploy the devastating campaigns of enslavement, colonization, exploitation, murder, and disenfranchisement against peoples of African descent" (*Becoming Black,* 126). See also Sylvia Wynter, "Beyond Miranda's Meanings: Un/Silencing the 'Demonic Ground' of Caliban's 'Woman,'" in *Out of the Kumbla: Caribbean Women and Literature,* eds. Carole Boyce Davies and Elaine Savory Fido (Trenton: Africa World Press, 1990), 355–72.

But as feminists of color have long argued, the discursive white-ness of the Eurocentric feminine — bound up with compulsory heterosexuality and a binary construction of gender — effaces the lives of Black women and other women of color, even as it moves violently to smooth out the folded complexities of any-one's experience of the flesh.[19] As María Lugones argues, colo-nial violence marks its targets as "less than" man or woman, hence as something less or other than gendered. Thinking about how this violence was and is "continually resisted," Lugones pro-poses that we regard such resistance as "the minimal sense of agency required" to think about the colonial relationship as "an active one" — without imposing the liberal sense of agency as the destiny of the colonized (and thereby recapitulating the very teleological gesture that, for the colonizer, justifies this violence to begin with).[20] I am also mindful of Saba Mahmood's critique of liberal feminism, that the conflation of agency and autonomy, and the elevation of that conflation to "the political ideal," dis-poses us to ignore how "agentival capacity is entailed not only in those acts that resist norms but also in the multiple ways in

19 In addition to the sources cited above, see Hortense J. Spillers, "Interstices: A Small Drama of Words," in *Black, White, and in Color,* 152–75. On the tradition of Black women's writing as resistance to the tropes of the sentimental, see Hazel V. Carby, *Reconstructing Womanhood: The Emergence of the Afro-American Woman Novelist* (New York: Oxford University Press, 1987). The nineteenth- and early twentieth-century texts studied by Carby offer alternatives to the white-femininized representation of agency as influence.

20 María Lugones, "Toward a Decolonial Feminism," *Hypatia* 25, no. 4 (October 2010): 746–48. Lugones's argument resonates with Hortense Spillers's tracing of the contours of racialized gender in "Mama's Baby, Papa's Maybe: An American Grammar Book," in *Black, White, and in Color,* 203–29. Likewise, Andrea Smith argues that "when colonists first came to the Americas, they saw the necessity of instilling patriarchy in Native communities because they realized that indigenous peoples would not accept colonial domination if their own indigenous societies were not structured on the basis of social hierarchy" ("Queer Theory and Native Studies: The Heteronormativity of Settler Colonialism," *GLQ: A Journal of Lesbian and Gay Studies* 16, nos. 1–2 [2010]: 61).

which one *inhabits* norms."[21] The intimacy of resistance and subjugation, of agency and habit, of individual acts and the forms of
solidarity that they compose or de-compose, disrupts the promised autonomy of the liberal self. At the same time, it's important
to emphasize that many kinds of practical autonomy — such as
the capacity to live without violent interference from the police
and other parts of the state's disciplinary apparatus; or to enjoy
shared spaces without fear of sexual harassment; or to perform
one's erotic choices or one's gender as one sees fit; or to navigate
public space without obstacles to one's mobility — remain tightly coupled to the possession of embodied norms of social privilege and power. Having privilege is a form of entangled agency.
And this entanglement frustrates the privileged subject's efforts
to reconcile their privilege with moral autonomy, a frustration
that may deflate the sense of agency required by the responsibility for change. In what follows, I focus on the sentimental subject of composition pedagogy in order to think about the critical
itself as a work of entanglement, and to think through how the
erasure of the liberal promise might make space for hopes of
another kind.

the cruel whiteness of composition

I focus on composition pedagogy because, as scholars like Robert McRuer and Alexis Pauline Gumbs have pointed out, it func-

---

21 Saba Mahmood, *Politics of Piety: The Islamic Revival and the Feminist
Subject* (Princeton: Princeton University Press, 2005), 15 (emphasis in
the original). I am not asserting that Mahmood's ethnographic approach
to understanding agency and Lugones's more abstract arguments are
compatible in their assumptions. Nor need they be. Lugones's work
theorizes gender in the transnational, transhistorical colonial encounter,
while Mahmood's seeks to render an adequate account of a particular
set of women's experiences in a particular time and place (women
participating in the "mosque movement" in contemporary Egypt). I cite
them together in order to specify further what's at stake in the liberal
picture of agency that both Mahmood's and Lugones's work resists.

tions as a site where teachers are conscripted "to teach the student population how to be composed, contained, and conformist in a society in transition."[22] More than etymology, the link between *composition* and *composure* suggests a kind of cultural, political, and economic metonymy, expressed in "the flexible body of the contingent, replaceable instructor" and "the flexible body of the student dutifully mastering marketable skills and producing clear, orderly, efficient prose."[23] At once marginal and central to the academy, composition pedagogy struggles under the demand for student-citizens capable of making themselves legible to our (neo)liberal institutions. Over time this demand has taken many forms.[24] In a current iteration, the demand calls for "critical thinking" as the (self-)possession of subjects adrift in a world riven by financial, institutional, and ecological crisis who must not (no matter what) give up their attachment to the idols of "measurement and marketability."[25] But I would argue that the disciplining of composition aims at subjects proficient in *explication,* which means more than the production of "clear, orderly, efficient prose." Explication refers here to the labor of disentangling human agency, recuperating reason's autonomy, within the circum-Atlantic fold. Given the geometrical progression of precariousness worldwide — through the tangled processes of economic inequality, political instability, and natural and human disasters — critical thought doubles down on that

22 Gumbs, "Nobody Mean More," 243. See also Robert McRuer, *Crip Theory: Cultural Signs of Queerness and Disability* (New York: New York University Press, 2006).

23 McRuer, *Crip Theory,* 148.

24 Including a focus on normative usage and grammar (which remains, for those who don't teach composition, a kind of default model); a revival of the canons of classical rhetoric as training in deliberative democratic citizenship; and a cultivation of the "true," authentic, therapeutically expressive self.

25 McRuer, *Crip Theory,* 148. This is the "critical thinking" bandied about by university administrators, accreditation bodies, business leaders, and perhaps especially, educational consultants and others peddling high-priced technological "solutions" to a captive academic market.

avoidance of the body's vulnerability, which McRuer locates in the fear of queerness and disability, and which Ferreira da Silva describes as the modern imperative "not to write the I as an affectable thing."[26] As autonomous, the "transparent I" would be self-a/effecting, "self-authenticating," a presence that writes itself in the erasure of that writing's trace.[27] But such composure, as Fred Moten reminds us, does not stand alone. For its

> sovereignty implies a kind of auto-positioning, a positioning of oneself in relation to oneself, an autocritical autopositioning that moves against what it is to be positioned, to be posed by another, to be rendered and, as such, to be rendered inhuman, to be placed in some kind of mutual apposition with the in/human and the animal (the black female servant; the lascivious little cat).[28]

In Moten's analysis, the posing of the white female figure in Manet's *Olympia* (or in Titian's *Venus of Urbino*) "render[s her] inhuman" by "apposition" with other figures in the composition whose inhumanity is taken for granted. Taken together, this ensemble projects the singular humanity of the artist–spectator, who stands before the arrangement in transparency (even if transparent only to himself). If Moten's argument can survive this violent (and perhaps lascivious) translation, we might conclude that the liberal pedagogue poses his students so that they might see themselves as falling short of fully human agency. This agency can be theirs once they learn how properly to see themselves. As if Olympia were both the model and the spectator of Manet's painting, a fantastic doubling that does nothing,

26 Ferreira da Silva, *Toward a Global Idea of Race,* 31.

27 The phrase "self-authenticating" comes from Jon Mee, *Romanticism, Enthusiasm, and Regulation: Poetics and the Policing of Culture in the Romantic Period* (Oxford: Oxford University Press, 2003), 6.

28 Fred Moten, "Preface for a Solo by Miles Davis," *Women & Performance: A Journal of Feminist Theory* 17, no. 2 (July 2007): 217–46, at 229.

of course, to unfix the figure of Black female labor that attends this scene of white feminine dis/composure.[29]

This pedagogical fantasy exists in tension with other hopes for the critical, which draw not only on traditions of scholarly critique in the humanities and social sciences, but also on radical veins of resistance outside the academy, including socialism and anarchism; various forms of avant-garde practice; feminism; anti-colonial struggles; the Civil Rights and Black Power movements; Black feminist theory and praxis; and queer, trans, and crip forms of resistance and organizing and survival.[30] Drawing on these veins, McRuer invokes a pedagogy of "critical de-composition," attuned to the energy of resistance that rustles around the body's and the writer's failures of composure, which is also a radiance born of their falling-short before the norm. Against the sentimental imperative to stretch and bend oneself to fit the present's ever-shrinking space, McRuer's vision of critical pedagogy aspires to recover another kind of futurity, which is founded on solidarity, and made more capacious by the embrace of corporeal difference in all its forms.[31] But how do

29 I'm suggesting that composition, as an intellectual and corporeal discipline, "at once articulates and disavows the human body" (Ferreira da Silva, *Toward a Global Idea of Race,* 42).

30 In their academic guise, such hopes often recruit the idea that by restoring to all discourses a sense of their partiality — their incompleteness vis-à-vis the actual world — we can avert what Ralph Cintron calls "the violence of fixation." See "'Gates Locked' and the Violence of Fixation," in *Towards a Rhetoric of Everyday Life: New Directions in Research on Writing, Text, and Discourse,* eds. Martin Nystrand and John Duffy (Madison: University of Wisconsin Press, 2003), 5–37. But if Cintron focuses on the partiality of discourse, Immanuel Kant inaugurates the critical tradition in a move that insists on the totality of the discursive, i.e., that there is nothing comprehensible outside of the discursive dimensions of human experience (or of human understanding in its synthesis of experience) (*Critique of Pure Reason,* trans. Paul Guyer and Allen W. Wood [Cambridge: Cambridge University Press, 1998], 205). A question oscillates between these two positions as to what quotient of our experience we can hope to make explicit, if explicitness is taken as the a priori condition of critique.

31 McRuer, *Crip Theory,* 146–70.

we make sense of such hopes for the critical in light of that liberal optimism circulating under the same name? Is there a way of being critical that lets us distinguish between true and false, spurious and authentic, "good" and "bad" versions of the critical itself? And if there is, how do we teach it? In other words, how does critique escape its own fixations, remain true to its own partiality?[32]

Phrased as such, these very questions appeal to an ideal of "autocritical" sovereign reason, which would, in virtue of its decisiveness, once and for all escape autonomy's vicious regress. To get beyond their reductive opposition and see up close the entanglement of the critical and the sentimental, I turn now to a perennial genre of (writing about) composition pedagogy: the case study of the student essay. This genre frames excerpts from student-authored texts with argument and commentary addressed to an audience of compositions scholars and teachers. The arguments are often of a practical nature, illustrating the application of a particular method or approach. Such studies tend to exhibit a familiar narrative arc. We see, in before-and-after panels, a pupil's progress from one kind of writing to another, exemplary of the passage toward an assumed norm of sophistication, academic literacy, etc. Such narratives evoke a form of sentimental agency, insofar as they enact the presence of the teacher's influence (however coded in terms of putatively objective standards, communal best practices, etc.) on scenes of striving for the promise of autonomy toward which liberal pedagogies tend. At the same time, the composition case study often highlights the teacher's and the student's critical agency in working together, the student on their writing, the teacher on their teaching, each striving to achieve, as the composition

32 Though sympathetic to the critical-pedagogic tradition, Sandy Grande argues that too often "critical pedagogies retain the deep structures of Western thought — that is, the belief in progress as change, in the universe as impersonal, in reason as the preferred mode of inquiry, and in human beings as separate from and superior to the rest of nature" (*Red Pedagogy*, 3).

scholar Joseph Harris puts is, a certain "reflectiveness about [their] own aims" in practice.[33]

On one view, a critical practice need not entail such reflectiveness. As Gilbert Ryle argues, one "applies criteria in performing critically, that is, in trying to get things right."[34] But liberal pedagogies, no less than their more radical kin, tend to invoke a more substantive sense of the critical. Here the critical refers to a special kind of striving, one that does not collapse into the effort to satisfy just any old norm. Indeed, such striving might be thought to take aim at the norm itself, opening the possibility of its contestation. But perhaps this distinction hinges on an ambiguity present in the idea of the *criterion* itself. On the one hand, to "apply criteria" might signify a quality of attention, attuned to the embodied (though not necessarily solitary) ways in which the performance of any act unfolds in time and space. Think of the toddler's struggle to put one foot in front of the other, or of the concert pianist's constant effort to balance precision and expression. Such forms of attention might be described as involute. They furl inward, along a trajectory of greater intimacy with disciplined capacities of the flesh. On the other hand, one may "apply criteria" in a far more explicit way, via acts specifically intended to result in corrections to another's (or one's own) performance. In the first case, the application of criteria, while effective and affective, is *not* transparent. Which is to say, it is not intended to be so. (Would we say that Glenn Gould's humming was meant to alert us to his feeling for Bach, as opposed to being itself part of that feeling, one of that feeling's restless, multiply articulated feelers, as it were?) And however normative or rule-governed such performances might seem, the dynamics of attention do not permit sustained reference to a static representation of the norm or rule. In the second case, however, one intends to affect the performance of the other or the self, often

---

33 Joseph Harris, "Revision as a Critical Practice," *College English* 65, no. 6 (2003): 575.
34 Ryle, *The Concept of Mind,* 29.

from a position that presumes and insists on (perhaps with a rap across the knuckles, or a red pen to the page) the transparency and self-evidence of the governing rule.

I don't mean to imply that these two meanings of the critical occupy stable positions. Rather, the hinge between them generates a friction, the irresolution of which resonates at the sites of pedagogy with a kind of sentimental background hum. Before attending to a contemporary example, I want to turn to a text where sentiment, critique, and the case study exist in sustained counterpoint: Kant's *Critique of the Power of Judgment.* Written as a supplement to the project of critical philosophy articulated in the *Critique of Pure Reason,* Kant's later text struggles to tame something that escapes the limits of this articulation, something fugitive that unsettles the foundations of that project. This fugitive something is feeling. In the first *Critique,* Kant answers skeptical challenges to Cartesian transparency by positing that all experience, the skeptic's included, arises within the confines of a subjectivity that produces or, let's say, composes the phenomenal world. This composition takes place through the application to sensation of the pure forms of intuition (space and time), according to the categorical rules laid down by the discursive understanding.[35] By relegating experience to the law-like operations of the human mind, Kant gives up Descartes's tight suture between thinking and being. Human reason, for Kant, has no access whatsoever to the world as it might exist outside of its mediation by human consciousness. But with this gesture, he manages to retain for consciousness the rights of an "auto-critical" agency (which becomes, in the strained logic of the *Critique of Practical Reason,* autonomous with respect even to the laws governing its own operation), thereby writing the *I* as "not [...] an affectable thing." Or he almost manages to do so. For although the awkward forwardness of the flesh remains on the margins of his critical philosophy, Kant does pose the question,

35 My reading of Kant tracks Ferriera da Silva's in *Toward a Global Idea of Race,* 59–62.

in the belatedly written third *Critique,* of why a feeling (that is to say, a mode of *being affected*) should appear essential to the application of certain criteria. "[A]n aesthetic judgment," writes Kant, "is that whose determining ground lies in a sensation that is immediately connected with the feeling of pleasure and displeasure."[36] The account hinges on the "disinterested pleasure" that, as Kant claims, we experience when making judgments of taste. The delicate poise of such judgments between the cog-like operations of cognition and the erratic pull of desire suggests, in turn, the presence of a kind of freedom, a "free play" of the faculties (sensation, imagination, and rational cognition) in their "mutual [...] correspondence."[37]

This freedom exists in a strange tension with the pleasure that occasions it. It is as though Kant will sanction play only if it can be made to express a pedagogical intent. The latter emerges from what the free play of the faculties teaches us about the subject:

> The consciousness of the merely formal purposiveness in the play of the cognitive powers of the subject in the case of a representation through which an object is given is the pleasure itself, because it contains a determining ground of

36 Kant locates this class of judgments midway between two extremes. On the one hand, a "cognitive judgment" (i.e., that this figure represents a rabbit or a duck) is objective, meaning, in Kant's critical lexicon, that the laws of the understanding fully determine its validity, because they alone allow the object to appear. On the other hand, there is the purely subjective case of our sensuous interest in the object, e.g., when we find, as Kant says, something "agreeable" in it. Such judgments are equally determinate, though they lay no claim to objective validity, being entirely the product of bodily needs or irrational whims. In either case, judgment serves at the behest of a higher faculty: cognition in the one case, desire in the other. But "the feeling of pleasure and displeasure," which provides the "determining ground" of aesthetic judgments, is not a faculty, nor is it strictly explicable in terms of the other two. See *Critique of the Power of Judgment,* trans. Paul Guyer and Eric Matthews (Cambridge: Cambridge University Press, 2009), 29, 64.

37 Ibid., 103.

the activity of the subject with regard to the animation of its cognitive powers, thus an internal causality (which is purposive) with regard to cognition in general, but without being restricted to a particular cognition, hence it contains a mere form of the subjective purposiveness of a representation in an aesthetic judgment.[38]

Through its harmony of form alone, the beautiful object broadcasts the presence of what feels like an animating intention. This *purposiveness* lies latent in the object, seeking its complement in the labor of our imagination. But on this other intention, the mind can get no determinate purchase. For pleasure, qua aesthetic, stems from the mind's own agency in contemplation, from its enjoyment of the dance in which it leads the world's given forms. Or, as Kant writes, from "an internal causality (which is purposive) with regard to cognition in general, but without being restricted to a particular cognition." The beautiful object, or the object of taste, seems to disclose a surplus of purpose, on which the beholder can capitalize. In truth, beauty only awakens the mind to its own reserves of intentionality. We find it pleasing, Kant suggests, to learn that our ordinary, determinate purposes and striving do not exhaust our capacity for experience.

Moreover, his discovery of this purposiveness at play bolsters his critical project because Kant makes the former the vehicle of a "subjective universal communicability."[39] It is "subjective" because, of course, no one can hope to prove that what appears beautiful to them appears so to everyone else. Nonetheless, in a curious modal chain, Kant insists that the subject of the judgment of taste must insist that it *should*.[40] And indeed, one might extend this claim to many varieties of critical argument. Without the requirement of either empirical warrant or formal logic, critique nonetheless adduces its own necessity. Sustained by

38 Ibid., 107.
39 Ibid., 103.
40 Ibid., 121.

their feeling for the relevance of the particular case to the general idea (or for the intimacy between the two), the critic expects the assent of others. The critic (including the critical philosopher) expects their own feeling to be communicable, and this communicability validates the feeling itself. Thus, the theory of aesthetic judgment discloses an optimism, which we might call the promise of a *felt transparency*.[41] For what affects the subject in aesthetic judgment is ultimately only the interior purposiveness of the subject itself, via a detour through the external object that provides the occasion for this judgment.[42]

Why should this detour furnish the narrative arc of so much thinking about the pedagogical? Consider, for instance, the case studies presented by Joseph Harris as "interchapters" in his influential book on composition pedagogy, *A Teaching Subject*. Harris, who elsewhere describes "discursive agency" as the hallmark of "critical practice," proposes to show how this agency emerges when "beginning college students" navigate "the paradoxical task of both forging their own voices and writing in a way that their teachers find interesting and familiar."[43] Here we meet Heather, author of a personal essay about her involvement in a high-school newspaper. Heather is a competent writer, capable of writing with "some real care and intelligence." Not without an aesthetic sensibility of her own, she is clearly "trying

41 Certainly, Hannah Arendt reads it that way, making the third *Critique* central to her analysis of Kant's political philosophy and to her definition of "critical thinking." For Arendt, the communicable purposiveness of aesthetic *cum* critical judgments means that in performing such a judgment, one "always reflects upon others and their taste, takes their possible judgments into account." The pedagogical function of aesthetic judgment allows one "to think with an enlarged mentality." It "trains one's imagination to go visiting" (*Lectures on Kant's Political Philosophy,* trans. Ronald Beiner [Chicago: University of Chicago Press, 1989], 43, 67).

42 My reading of the third *Critique* is indebted to Jacques Derrida, *The Truth in Painting,* trans. Geoff Bennington and Ian McLeod (Chicago: University of Chicago Press, 2001).

43 Harris, "Revision as a Critical Practice," 577; and Joseph Harris, *A Teaching Subject: Composition since 1966* (Upper Saddle River: Prentice Hall, 1997), 46.

[…] to give some lift to her prose."[44] Her first draft, however, fails to do "anything" with its source material. Anything, that is, other than make what Harris calls "the weakest possible" use of the assigned text, Mike Rose's *Lives on the Boundary.* Heather's draft merely poaches quotations to fill out a narrative that isn't critically attentive to Rose or his subject matter. Nor is Heather critically attentive to "her own experiences." In thrall to "one of the key narratives of American culture," her first draft presents both her own story and her source text in a kind of textual taxidermy, producing a tidy but glassy-eyed tableau, "a straightforward narrative of success." The narrative of Heather's first draft is straightforward in its bid to achieve transparency as a piece of prose — and indeed, in its bid to achieve a certain feeling that can signify the communicability of the subject's experience. (Heather writes, concluding her essay, "I believe my story, of my first front page article, would definitely be in Rose's book, because it shows how I struggled to overcome my obstacles to achieve what I wanted.")

But the student writer's desire to succeed at the assignment apparently blocks her ability to communicate (the validity of) her experience. Harris, her teacher, can discern there only the lineaments of that desire:

> [F]or all the work she seems to have put into this draft, Heather really only manages to give a sense of herself in it as a kind of typical good kid and good student, who has already taken to heart much of the advice about writing her high school teacher gave her, but who is still eager to learn more. What she hasn't come up with yet is anything […] that would mark what she has to say as distinctively her own.[45]

On the one hand, Harris represents Heather's draft as saturated with a certain kind of purpose ("to give a sense of herself […] as

44   Ibid., 48–49.
45   Ibid., 49.

a kind of typical good kid and good student"). At the same time, the draft lacks that discovery of purposiveness, that "discursive agency," that "would mark what she has to say as distinctively her own." For Harris, positioned here as the critical subject, seeking in the object a summons to transcend his own interests and enlarge his common sense into a feeling for human commonality, Heather's bid for agency fails by being *conventional*. As the performance of a "typical good kid," its striving bears the stamp of what Kant calls the "common human understanding," i.e., the rule-bound cognition that Kant associates with the "vulgar" sort, whose understanding is "merely healthy" but "not yet cultivated."[46]

Kant's elitism is at pains to distinguish the *sensus communis* that defines critical judgments from its vernacular version, the latter being "the least that can be expected of anyone who lays claim to the name of a human being."[47] Harris, of course, does not frame his narrative in such terms. For him, Heather's case demonstrates how the student writer's agency can emerge in revision. This means acknowledging how her experience — presumably white and middle-class — differs from those "lives on the boundary" of literacy and privilege represented in her source text.[48] And it means surpassing the tendency toward "ventriloquism" that characterizes her first draft. In her second draft, Heather

> draws on [Rose] not merely to support but to complicate what she has to say. Rather than simply suggest […] that she and Rose have had similar experiences with writing, Heather

---

46 Kant, *Critique of the Power of Judgment,* 173.

47 Ibid.

48 Lester Faigley trenchantly notes the preference in "expressivist" composition for "student selves […] that achieve rationality and unity by characterizing former selves as objects for analysis" ("Judging Writing, Judging Selves," *College Composition and Communication* 40, no. 4 [1989]: 411). Though avowedly not expressivist in his pedagogy, Harris's comments on Heather's draft and revision betray a similar preference.

now imagines herself as part of a scene he has described and shows how it would be different for her […]. Through this contrast between her own anxiety and the easy pride of the kids Rose talks about, she achieves a kind of distance and control over both her and his stories, which means she now has something to say about each.[49]

Like many composition theorists today, Harris is critical of "expressivist" theories that locate the "writer's voice" inside the writer, in some radically private store of experience to which the writer alone has access. Part of the problem with such theories, he argues, is that they make it difficult to specify, to be explicit about, what qualifies as truly (or "authentically") expressive writing. For what textual features can distinguish authentic expression from writing that merely reproduces the conventions of personal expression, which are exactly as generic as those guiding any other kind of discourse?[50]

In contrast to the Cartesian transparency promoted by expressivist pedagogies, "distance" and "control" appear as key terms in Harris's account. His praise for her revised draft takes pleasure in imagining Heather's imagination of herself vis-à-vis Rose's text. This positioning signals also that she has "achieved," via a detour through a newly disinterested feeling for the object of her critical judgment, a different kind of relation to herself. Kant might call it "cultivated." For Harris, Heather "now has something to say." Aesthetic–critical distance militates against attachments that cling too close. It teaches a pleasure disrup-

---

49 Harris, *A Teaching Subject,* 51–52.

50 Ibid., 33–34. Like the Cartesian myth at which ordinary-language philosophy tilts, expressivism refers judgments to the truth-content of a hypothetical set of propositions: what the writing subject *really* had to say. Not only does writing remain an insolubly solitary act (since the writer alone knows what she has to say), but it also involves an impossibly recursive series of translations into a private language. For how shall the writer (much less the reader) know when they have reached the *real* content, such that no further translations are necessary, unless by fiat of an intuition that cannot itself be expressed in discourse?

tive of those more conventional promises (like the desire to be a "typical good kid") that stunt one's potential to engage with others' judgments on one's *own* terms. It grants one possession of something intangible but crucial to liberal subjectivity: "something to say." A mode of self-possession, this composure heralds the subject's readiness to participate in those purposive relations among strangers mediated by objects of taste, i.e., commodities. But as a supplement to the pursuit of self-interest in the marketplace, the disinterested feeling of critical thinking entails a readiness to "put [one]self into the position of everyone else, merely by abstracting from the limitations that contingently attach to our own judging."[51] And this supplement ensures the transparent, autonomous communicability through which a collection of individuals, atomized by market relations, becomes a public, insofar as "everyone is willing and able to render an account of what he thinks and says."[52]

The public toward which aesthetic–critical judgment orients us remains a potential public, a public in abstraction (abstracted from the particular but also conventional judgments of the members of the vulgar crowd).[53] But what about those "lives on the boundary" who provide the occasion for Heather's writing and Harris's critique? In the latter, they barely figure, or they figure as a framing device, delineating the space in which Harris's pedagogical pleasure attaches to Heather's coming into her own. They are not the objects of pedagogy, for they do not receive the solicitation, the solicitous gaze, that invites them to be cultivated (to become subjects). And yet, not unlike the Black maid in Manet's painting, the explicitness of their bracketed presence is (somehow) required.[54] What, in other words, do composition's

---

51 Kant, *Critique of the Power of Judgment*, 174.
52 Arendt, *Lectures on Kant's Political Philosophy*, 41.
53 It is also a public of individuals whose conditions of being are grounded in the abstraction of property rights, which represents a kind of haunted privacy, a deracinated relation to history, land, labor, and the flesh.
54 On the idea of bracketing in the western philosophical tradition, see Sara Ahmed, *Queer Phenomenology: Orientations, Objects, Others* (Durham:

critical judgments have to do with racialized and class privilege? Writing about the hegemonic role of "Standardized Edited Academic English" (SEAE) in the North American classroom, Asao B. Inoue describes the performance of critical agency, the performance of having something to say, as follows:

> It is a self-reliant voice that is focused on itself as a cool, rational, thinking self in the writing and in its reading of [the] writer's own experiences or ideas. This isn't to say these are bad qualities in writing, only that they are linked to whiteness and this link often has uneven racist consequences in classroom writing assessments.[55]

Inoue argues that these "racist consequences" are "not usually produced by conscious intentions, purposes, or biases of people against others not like them."[56] Rather, as he puts it, it is quite possible that the demand for performances of SEAE, grounded in the "abstract liberal principle [...] to teach all students the same English," will have a racist "function" without its being articulated as part of a racist "purpose" on the part of the teacher.[57] Inoue's formulation suggests how aesthetic–critical judgments can serve as a supplement to the social power that white bodies accumulate in moving through the world. The whiteness of these bodies performs a certain function, as does the white person's insistence that performances intimately linked to whiteness, like performances of SEAE, represent universal norms of cultivated behavior, having nothing to do with the violence of white supremacy. Relative to these functions, the purpose and purposiveness appealed to by critical judgments promise to transform abstract liberal principles into felt possessions. They

---

Duke University Press, 2006), 32–35.

55 Asao B. Inoue, *Antiracist Writing Assessment Ecologies: Teaching and Assessing Writing for a Socially Just Future* (Fort Collins: The WAC Clearinghouse, 2015), 49–50.

56 Ibid., 53.

57 Ibid., 55–56.

promise to make one's composure as a subject of white privilege and power signify more than the social and political functions of whiteness itself.[58]

The critical and the sentimental encounter one another in the thoroughly hierarchical space or scene where the racializing and gendering structures of dominance *interest* the self, and where one accedes to the position of a subject by inhabiting one's place, performing one's function, vis-à-vis those structures. Explication's fraught work is to retrieve subjectivity, as an interiority that can be home to rational purpose in its transparency, from

58 As Michael McKeon argues, in the formulations of eighteenth-century European aesthetic theories, "the capacity for disinterestedness" exposes a side of objects that remains obscure to the multitudes, conferring on the privileged subject "a kind of 'possession' that improves upon the merely sensible grossness associated with the rude, uncultivated literality and interestedness of actually owning 'real' estate" (*The Secret History of Domesticity: Public, Private, and the Division of Knowledge* [Baltimore: Johns Hopkins University Press, 2009], 364). McKeon describes taste as "one of those quasi-somatic terms that was fashioned by eighteenth-century writers to replace, within a culture increasingly skeptical about the literal and bodily innateness of nobility but increasingly taken with arguments from the natural, the honor that traditionally distinguished those of noble birth" (359). Taste, in other words, sublimates the "innateness" of nobility, locating it in a faculty of the mind, rather than in a whole ensemble of dispositions more obviously linked to the circumstances of breeding and education.

   Paradoxically, this effort to transpose the justification for economic, social, and political privilege from the "literal" and the "bodily" to the "natural" doubles down on innateness, granting the latter a flexibility and power in direct proportion to its refusal to be specified. As the vehicle of the aesthetic, taste became aligned with what Sylvia Wynter calls "the new *eugenic/dysgenic* sociogenic code, as the code in whose terms the Western bourgeoisie, unable hitherto to legitimate its role as a ruling class on the basis of the noble blood and birth model of the landed aristocracy, was now to legitimate itself as a *naturally selected* ruling class, because the bearers and transmitters of an alleged eugenic line of descent" (quoted in Weheliye, *Habeas Viscus,* 148, emphasis in the original). At the same time, the "metaphorical" possession implied by aesthetic judgment does not repudiate the interest in real estate. Rather, in reflection, one explicates one's interests, untangling them from the pure operations of (the leisured, privileged) consciousness.

what threatens to entrammel it in conditions external to itself. In the explicative work of the *Critique of Pure Reason,* Kant displaces the problem of the subject's affectability, making subjectivity a "function" of interiority itself. According to Kant, the internal coherence of experience, immured within the laws of cognition, answers to "a hidden art in the depths of the human soul."[59] For although his analysis of the Categories of the Understanding aspires to exhaust the basic criteria according to which anything can be said to exist, the profoundly abstract Categories cannot, on pain of infinite regress, prescribe the rules for their own application. In the first *Critique,* judgment — as the power that marshals the particular and concrete under the understanding's facultative government — inscribes the limits of Kant's own critical explication, locating the depths from which an affectability threatens to overwhelm the *I* after all. The theory of aesthetic judgment posits a "free play" that buoys the *I,* playing on the surface of that opacity. I have argued that we should understand this play as a kind of laboratory for liberalism, a playground for taking pleasure in the latter's insistence, to quote Saba Mahmood, on "a detachment between the inner life of a self and its outward expressions wherein the experience of the former cannot be adequately captured in the latter, and where its true force can only be felt within the valorized space of personal self-reflection."[60] Evading "capture," the "true force" of this self is projected beyond the body, *not* in the form of "outward expressions," but as a feeling for its own universality. And I have suggested that the valorization, by modernity's dominant idioms, of this "space of self-reflection" comports with principles of hierarchy and exclusion that police that space. Indeed, it even requires them. If the "vulgar" — an appellation that might as easily be applied to bourgeois philistines as to proletarians — do not partake of the *sensus communis,* they can, at least, "[lay]

---

59 Kant, *Critique of Pure Reason,* 273; See also Ferreira da Silva, *Toward a Global Idea of Race,* 62.

60 Mahmood, *Politics of Piety,* 147.

claim to the name of a human being." This is not a privilege that Kant extends to non-Europeans, especially not to the peoples targeted by European colonialism. The latter represent, in Fred Moten's words, "the not but nothing other than human."[61]

Mirroring that "valorized self-reflection" theorized by Kant under the heading of aesthetic judgment, the composure of the white liberal subject is policed internally by what it projects, a de-humanizing and othering gaze that poses the non-white body, and in particular the Black body, as existing outside of that potential universal community of selves to which this subject, by virtue of a social positioning that can neither be relinquished nor avowed, enjoys access. Frantz Fanon calls this projection or projectile of white supremacy the "white gaze":

And then we were given the occasion to confront the white gaze. An unusual weight descended on us. The real world robbed us of our share. In the white world, the man of color encounters difficulties in elaborating his body schema. The image of one's body is solely negating. It's an image in the third person. All around the body reigns an atmosphere of uncertainty.[62]

---

61 Moten, "Preface to a Solo by Miles Davis," 222. For other works treating of Kant's views on race, see Robert Bernasconi, "Will the Real Kant Please Stand Up," *Radical Philosophy* 117 (February 2003), https://www.radicalphilosophy.com/article/will-the-real-kant-please-stand-up; Meg Armstrong, "'The Effects of Blackness': Gender, Race, and the Sublime in Aesthetic Theories of Burke and Kant," *The Journal of Aesthetics and Art Criticism* 54, no. 3 (1996): 213–36; and Zakiyyah Iman Jackson, "'Theorizing in a Void': Sublimity, Matter, and Physics in Black Feminist Poetics," *South Atlantic Quarterly* 117, no. 3 (July 2018): 617–48. Gayatri Spivak points out that Kant excludes non-Europeans from his vision of human teleology, i.e., of purposiveness (*A Critique of Postcolonial Reason: Toward a History of the Vanishing Present* [Cambridge: Harvard University Press, 2003], 26–30).

62 Frantz Fanon, *Black Skin, White Masks,* trans. Richard Philcox, rev. edn. (New York: Grove Press, 2008), 90.

In Fanon's narrative of his journey from the Antilles to France, the "burdened" composure offered to the colonial subject as the price of their admission to "the white world, the only decent one," is revealed to be a fraud. In the eyes of the European whites around them, the colonial subject can never hope to measure up, never transcend their Blackness.[63] Under the heat of the gaze, the Black subject — in Fanon's text, the Black *man* — stands caught in a catch-22. As Lewis Gordon puts it, "Try as I may, whenever I choose, no matter what I choose […] the fact of the matter is that it always turns out to be a black man who chooses."[64] The judgments of white subjects truncate the agency of people of color, consigning their character to caricature, their flesh to token, fetish, stigma, anathema: when the white child encountered by Fanon leaps into his mother's lap, terrified that "the Negro's going to eat me"; when the white woman riding the elevator with a Black academic philosopher involuntarily broadcasts, by a web of subtle gestures, her conviction of his "dark body's 'intention' to do her harm"; when the justices sitting on the nation's highest court tacitly endorse the "language of Indian savagery"; when the university's administration of "diversity" means that "people of color were classified, moved around, counted, recounted, and overcounted, [their] bodies extended across each of the School's seven divisions," according to "the nonconsensual agreement [they] had presumably made to remain within those proscriptions."[65] Like the antiracist and decolonial literature it has inspired, Fanon's account of racism and colonial violence begins from a phenomenologi-

63   Ibid., 94. "Burdened composure" is a riff on Saidiya Hartman's concept of "burdened individuality." See *Scenes of Subjection*, 115–24.

64   Lewis R. Gordon, *Bad Faith and Antiblack Racism* (Amherst: Humanity Books, 1999), 133.

65   Fanon, *Black Skin, White Masks*, 93; George Yancy, *Black Bodies, White Gazes: The Continuing Significance of Race in America*, 2nd edn. (Lanham: Rowman & Littlefield, 2016), 41; Robert A. Williams, Jr., *Like a Loaded Weapon: The Rehnquist Court, Indian Rights, and the Legal History of Racism in America* (Minneapolis: University of Minnesota Press, 2005), 34; Alexander, *Pedagogies of Crossing*, 130.

cal insistence on the flesh as the site of judgment. Exposure to the white gaze occurs against the background of that "implicit knowledge" to which a person ordinarily has recourse in navigating their surround, like what guides the hand in reaching for a pack of cigarettes.[66] But in Fanon's account, judgment is neither the determinate outcome of the laws of cognition, nor the valorized play of reflection. For judgment does not arise within an atomic consciousness, but it occurs within a deeply embodied tissue of social relations. Fanon confronts white people's suspicions, condescension, and revulsion, and these judgments divide him from his own body. As Fanon describes it, they cut his color out of his flesh.[67] For the presence of whiteness, hence white supremacy, in Fanon's social milieu violates his "bodily schema," intruding an "epidermal racial schema" that warps his ability to trust what his body knows. The body's implicit knowledge is undermined by, or entangled in, the countless ways in which Fanon is forced, as a matter of survival, to make *explicit to himself* the racist judgments of whites:

> I was responsible not only for my body but also for my race and my ancestors. I cast an objective gaze over myself, discovered my blackness, my ethnic features; deafened by cannibalism, backwardness, fetishism, racial stigmas, slave traders, and above all, yes, above all, the grinning *Y a bon Banania*.[68]

66 Fanon, *Black Skin, White Masks,* 93.
67 "Peeling, stripping my skin, causing a hemorrhage that left congealed black blood all over my body" (ibid., 92).
68 Ibid., 92. Along one dimension, this "epidermal racial schema" clings to the surface of the flesh, but along another it pierces the present, reopening a traumatic historical depth. Because unacknowledged by the white world, which nonetheless keeps the violence of this history alive, the latter becomes the sole burden of the Black body, which is conscripted into a double duty: representing both the racialized and undifferentiated historical present of oppression, and the individualized, atomized subject whom this oppression disables from fully assuming the rights and duties of the liberal social contract.

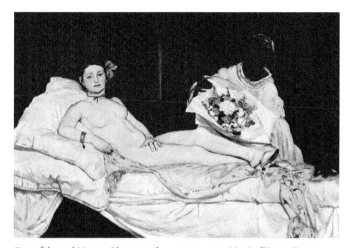

Fig. 1. Édouard Manet, *Olympia,* oil on canvas, 1863, Musée d'Orsay, France.
Source: Wikimedia Commons.

Fanon's account highlights instances of racist aggression, large and small, that awaken him to the positioning of the Black colonial subject in France. But white supremacy operates even without the presence of identifiable aggression (which is to say, aggression that white people might identify as such). Its judgments saturate the milieux where whiteness dominates, seeding the atmosphere with a question: "What stigmata do they see?"[69] These judgments discompose Fanon, weighing him down with the sediment of "racial-historical" relations for which he is, perversely, made to assume responsibility.

To be clear, I am not opposing Fanon's lived phenomenology of racism to Kant's aesthetic theory in order to show where the latter falls short. Doing so would have the perverse effect of treating Fanon's account as *the case,* thereby replicating the logic of liberalism that positions its colonial others as standing outside the trajectory of Western progress, stuck in a phase of pre-history. Thereby re-inscribing the colonizer's civilizing ped-

---

69 Inoue, *Antiracist Writing Assessment Ecologies,* 38.

agogy as the teleology proper to the colonial subject.[70] To borrow from Moten again, I am suggesting that we read Kant and Fanon in *apposition*. I am suggesting that Fanon's experience of racialization reveals another side of the aesthetic as delineated by Kant, a fold, as it were, inside the very structure of feeling that, for Kant, is at once universal and the special province of suitably "cultivated" subjects. Instead of distance, we are dealing with an intimacy that confounds autonomy and dependence; freedom and domination; taste, appetite, and disgust. Under the white gaze, Fanon "cast[s] an objective gaze" over himself, aestheticizing himself, splitting himself into both subject and object of reflection. But what fills the frame is not even the representation of a body reduced to an invitation to dominance (like the figure of Olympia in Manet's painting, see fig. 1). For Blackness here functions as the frame, the *parergon*.[71] As the overdetermined signifier of "cannibalism, backwardness, fetishism, racial stigmas, slave traders, and above all, yes, above all, the grinning *Y a bon Banania*," Fanon is forced, as Sylvia Wynter writes, "to make himself into a fact of negation, which alone enables the experience of being 'white.'"[72] What fills the frame, then, is only

70 Dipesh Chakrabarty, *Provincializing Europe: Postcolonial Thought and Historical Difference* (Princeton: Princeton University Press, 2012).

71 See Moten, "Preface to a Solo by Miles Davis": "But blackness, even though it is the sensuality that negatively bodies forth the supersensible, precisely insofar as it is 'merely' sensual, is not subject to the intersubjective validity of judgments of taste that it could be said to ground. Rather, as mere sensuality, it occupies and quickens a series: the stupid, the irrational, the deformed and/or deformative, the unfinished and/or disruptive, the driven and/or transportive, the irregular and/or anti- and ante-regulative, the blurred and/or blurring, the curved, the arabesque, the *parergon*, the outwork and/or mad absence of the work, the outlaw, the would-have-been-outside, the thing of nature that defies or defers, rather than presupposes, representation. That series will have always been inseparable from a natural history of inequality that it animates and by which it is animated" (221–22).

72 Sylvia Wynter, "Towards the Sociogenic Principle: Fanon, Identity, the Puzzle of Conscious Experience, and What It Is Like to Be 'Black,'" in *National Identities and Sociopolitical Changes in Latin America*, eds.

the empty itinerary of the other's gaze as it colonizes the racial-ized subject's self-reflection.[73] Agonized, parergonized, the flesh is cut off, not only from its milieu, but from the affective agency of its material being: "I hailed the world, and the world ampu-tated my enthusiasm."[74]

Mercedes F. Durán-Cogan and Antonio Gómez-Moriana (New York: Routledge, 2001), 42. Wynter continues: "And for this to be done, within the plotlines of the narratives which alone makes it possible, he must experience the corporeal reality of his body, as one that has always already been transformed by the negative stereotypes placed upon it, into a subhuman reality."

73 Of the role of the *parergon* in Kant's aesthetics, Derrida writes, "one cannot do without it. But in its purity, it ought to remain colorless, deprived of all empirical sensory materiality" (*The Truth in Painting*, 64).

74 Fanon, *Black Skin, White Masks,* 94. In these encounters, instead of a reflection on the object in which the subject pleasantly discovers an enlarged perspective and purposiveness, breathing in a generality that encompasses other autonomous agents like himself, *both* parties find themselves locked in a narrowing field of perception, bombarded by painful interests: fear, anger, contempt, and repressed desire. As a modality of judgment, the white gaze collapses the agency of both the judge and the judged. Their reflectiveness stands at the mercy of ingrained reflexes; their autonomy falls captive to an autonomic response. For the white person, this capture results from their own habits of judgment, which may present themselves symptomatically, as a pervasive but free-floating unease. For the racialized other, the situation is, of course, far more acute. It bears an edge that, even in mundane situations, can all to easily slide into verbal or physical assault, even murder. Thus, Fanon's use of visceral metaphors to render the emotional consequences of racism reminds us that the threat of *racist violence* is what makes racism such a powerful tool of oppression.

It is also true that the white gaze can become a source of pleasure to the person who wields it, especially when they pursue a conscious and intentional relation to their dominance. The power of the gaze, then, reflects and re-affirms that dominance. I am thinking here of the pleasure white people have taken in the spectacle of minstrel shows and other degrading depictions of Blackness (which persist, in different forms, to this day), as well as in the perpetration of heinous acts of anti-Black violence and terror. Such cases illustrate that the racializing gaze of white supremacy is not incompatible with the structure of aesthetic judgment. Indeed, the white gaze gives access to the *sensus communis* adduced by Kant, the *sensus communis* being defined, in this case, as a property appertaining exclusively to whiteness.

Fanon's encounter with the white world figures in his text as a profound emasculation. But as Hortense Spillers reminds us, the materiality of the flesh maintains an impossible intimacy with the question of its maternity. And in the case of the flesh marked as Black and female, this intimacy remains the zone of a double negation, or of a negation folded in on itself, in which the subject is not only objectified twice over (as Black and as female), but also barred from the femininity that serves as the white woman's patriarchal wage and racial alibi.[75] Both Fred Moten and Saidiya Hartman have written carefully and incisively about how the Black female body can, in the same moment of violent fixation, function as both object and frame, as Moten writes, "always crossing the borders between invisibility and hypervisibility, seriality and aesthetic criminality."[76] It is as though the detour of reflective judgment got caught in a recursive loop, vertiginously supplementing itself. But as Moten and Hartman in their separate ways insist, the closure of this figuration harbors fugitive possibilities. A fugitive agency that resists, and survives, the multiple fronts of violence marshaled against it, violence meant to deny Black women and girls any agency, any purpose. For as Spillers insists, "[t]he subject is certainly seen, but she also *sees*. It is this return of the gaze that negotiates at

---

75 Spillers, "Mama's Baby, Papa's Maybe." See also Jackson, "Theorizing in a Void"; Denise Ferreira da Silva, "Hacking the Subject: Black Feminism and Refusal beyond the Limits of Critique," *PhiloSOPHIA* 8, no. 1 (2018): 19–41; and Moten, *In the Break*, 14–24. With the exception of one chapter, "The Woman of Color and the White Man," Fanon's text is silent about the *other* colonial Other. On Michelle Wright's reading, this silence performs the disappearance of Black women, positioning the Black subject, in the first place, as implicitly male; and in the second, as standing in opposition or conflict with white women: "[W]hite women are deployed to symbolize the rejection of the Black male as a citizen/subject by the white nation" (*Becoming Black*, 128).

76 The occasion for these analyses is a late nineteenth-century photograph of an anonymous Black child, a girl, posed nude in the style of Manet's model, and probably taken by Thomas Eakins. See Moten, "Preface to a Solo by Miles Davis," 231; and Hartman, *Wayward Lives, Beautiful Experiments*, 24–30.

every point a space for living."[77] If the racializing cut disables
the subject, casting its *I* out of transparency, it does not exhaust
the subject's capacity for resistance, for looking back in defiance,
but also for seeing with a knowledge that eludes the position of
a weaponized autonomy, a treacherous transparency.[78] The sur-
vivors know too well that purpose is a sieve, a convenient mesh
for the flesh that the singular subject does not control. Denied
the wages of whiteness and masculinity, they know, too, when it
comes to the promise of freedoms bestowed from above, whose
money is where the mouth is:

> *not everybody knows my name,* but everyone knows what I
> taste like. salt after malt liquor. vault where the soul is kept.
> everyone knows my sweat under their tongue when they try
> to say free market. wet wild wick when they try to spark it on
> the fourth of july again. mildew of what i do for you. every-
> one knows the bloom of the brackish floor of the living room
> America. i taste like hysteria sedated with a case of the blues.
> i taste metallic like tap shoes Morse coding no. i taste like
> dirty city snow that can't stay white. i taste like your morning
> breath after waking up all night afraid your stuff is gone. i
> taste like sparrow song and hunger, taste like blackened coal
> mined lungs. i taste like military blunders limping up and

77 Spillers, "Interstices," 163.
78 Fanon's own text multiplies the dispositions available to the writer (and
the reader) into a series that undermines the impoverished binary between
"black skin" and "white masks." As Katherine McKittrick writes, "[e]ach
site Fanon encounters gives rise to a different sense of identity, a different
kind of self, and a different sense of place. His positionality and status
shift from moment to moment, comprising some, or all, of his identities
and identifications as a black man, an activist, a poet" (*Demonic Grounds,*
27). And as a white reader and auditor and citer of voices and texts that
speak from and to multiple and irreducible moments of Black lives, not
to mention the silences and gaps that haunt us with their muted ability,
I must learn how to open myself to being moved by more than just the
vicarious experience of the violence that situates the Black in a/opposition
to the white. For my capacity to be affected becomes, in such a case, a part
of that very violence, its reduplicative after-effect.

down the street. i taste like used rag fermentation that gets used again another week. can i speak?[79]

In a poetic work celebrating Black feminist praxis, Alexis Pauline Gumbs voices a fugitivity that "spills" over the containerized aesthetics of patriarchal white supremacy. At the root of those events we call the senses, which are the site of our history, the flesh exceeds the judgments of "taste" that preach a hierarchy of bodies and police their pleasures. Barred from that nominative membership in the *sensus communis* that full and unburdened citizenship requires, Gumbs's poetic speaker performs a labor of taste that is copulative, not transitive. Her speaker "tastes like," performing the position of the object of taste. And yet, in its figurative abundance, this performance disrupts the power of aesthetic or critical judgment to fix objects in the circuit of the subject's autotelic pleasure. For the creative powers of survival, Gumbs's prose suggests, are due to the mutability of the flesh where a thousand cuts do their work. The fugitive's flesh, in particular, disrupts the performative economies of capitalism and liberalism that their labor makes possible ("my sweat under their tongue when they try to say free market"). Just as the over-determination of their flesh by sexist and racist stereotypes ("wet wild wick") frustrates the coherence of the national project ("when they try to spark it on the fourth of july"). To the fugitive belongs a resistance encoded in performances that play to such stereotypes ("tap shoes Morse coding no"). And theirs, too, is a resilience throwing into relief what those *I*'s indentured to the ruses of whiteness and cishet masculinity would rather not know that they know. The fugitive's flesh, desired and disavowed, dispossesses them ("afraid your stuff is gone"), indexing the otherness that whiteness cannot do without. Indexing, too, that labor thanks to which even the white laborer's body "can't stay white," maimed by "military blunders," ailing with

79 Alexis Pauline Gumbs, *Spill: Scenes of Black Feminist Fugitivity* (Durham: Duke University Press, 2016), 30.

"blackened coal mined lungs." A sort of linking agency, the fugitive's "tastes like" entangles the transparent *I*'s with their own flesh, which they are afraid to bear, whose "song and hunger" accuse them.

global intimacies and guilt over ignorance

"Can I speak?" Subalternity's untimely question haunts the composure of the "typical good" liberal subject. It threatens to discompose the optimism that locates a kind of universal destiny in *what one has to say,* a phrase suggestive of a possession or property that doubles as a duty or imperative. "I feel very strongly about the way I write," writes Joseph Harris's Heather in her revised draft. "Whatever I write on that piece of paper you know it's me. […] My writing is my identity."[80] This sentiment complicates, I think, Harris's account of discursive agency as "a strong use of the work of others and a reflectiveness about one's own aims in writing."[81] Blurring the line between critical judgment and conventional self-expression, Heather's revision expresses a relation to writing that locates strength in feeling, not use, and which values intimacy and inspiration over distance and control. Indeed, the idea that her readers are "critics" both troubles Heather and stokes the enthusiasm that she attaches to her writing, leading her to project a sense of herself through writing onto a space occupied by the other ("you know it's me"), and to project her readers' reactions to her text onto herself. Hearing her "readers' opinions" is accompanied, for Heather, by "a flow of relief that rushes through [her] body." In a moment of relief (and release), Heather exhales the bated breath with which serious writers and idle talkers alike navigate their sense of audience. Hardly disinterested, her pleasure cashes in on her readers'

---

80 Harris, *A Teaching Subject,* 50.
81 Harris, "Revision as a Critical Practice," 577.

(imagined) assent: to her argument, yes, but also to her body and its presence.

In what follows, I explore the entanglement of the composing subject with the otherness that often figures, in the classrooms and elsewhere on the campuses of the neoliberal North American university, as a globality summoning this subject to her destiny in the world. I use the cis-gendered female pronoun here on purpose. For the posing/positioning of this subject by neoliberal pedagogies draws on liberalism's traditional construction, at the hands of elite white men, of bourgeois white femininity as the embodied site for the management of affective tensions unleashed by capitalism and empire. *Her* labor of "true feeling" makes space and time for the pleasure *he* takes in his exercise of distance and control.[82] Furthermore, this arrangement requires, if not the subaltern's silence, then the latter's halting (i.e., halted, forestalled, suppressed) efforts to be heard. In this triangular structure, performing whiteness involves performing one's disidentification from the position occupied by the racialized, globalized other. And performing white femininity requires a supplemental appeal to the position that refuses to identify with the gendered/feminized (white) other ("you know it's me"). At the same time, I am mindful of the fact that these subject positions, abstractly delineated, do not fix particular bodies, no matter how strenuously the biopolitical apparatus tries to tamp them down. The subject remains a palimpsest, its fleshy folds a trap for the particulars of history and fantasy, the traces of suffering and desire. I am also mindful that, as one who has been taught to identify with a dominant position in the structure, I cannot hope to disinterest myself in that identification or suspend its violence. I write, I persist in writing, this, therefore, from an attitude of general, critical optimism but quite particular pessimism, while striving not to let what I feel for my own case

82 Lauren Berlant, "The Subject of True Feeling: Pain, Privacy, and Politics," in *Left Legalism/Left Critique,* eds. Wendy Brown and Janet Halley (Durham: Duke University Press, 2002), 105–33.

collapse the space of resistance required if we are to imagine the future otherwise.

The cruel optimism of whiteness consists, for those identified as white, in an attachment to the white world's promise. This promise is that its transparent supremacy indefinitely extends in space and time. Certainly, the prevailing milieux of North American and Western European societies reinforce the sense that, as Shannon Sullivan puts it, "for a white person, *qua* white, the world presents no barriers to her engagement with the world."[83] Relative to people of color living under the white gaze, white people enjoy an untroubled relation to their agency *as whites,* whether in their occupation of public space, or in their identification with dominant narratives of national belonging. At the same time, the white world remains a fraught place, for the ambitions of capitalism and empire have never permitted this world to exclude its racialized others *tout court.* Indeed, as Lisa Lowe has shown, the world of empire is composed of trans-national, trans-generational intimacies created and sustained by human trafficking, resource extraction, migration, and trade, no less than by the diverse lineages and multiple trajectories of resistance to colonial violence and capitalist exploitation.[84] Denise Ferreira da Silva explores the "ontoepistemological" side of this intimacy, arguing that in "post-Enlightenment" Europe, the privileged attributes of autonomy and transparency, becoming less self-evident, more volatile, pressurized by the "sciences of man" and the needs of capital, could be preserved only by scientific "strategies." In particular, the disciplines of evolutionary biology, evolutionary psychology, and anthropology arrived on the scene to redefine these attributes. Or more precisely, to redefine their exclusivity, making them the properties of the dominant subjects of European empire. But these subjects were

---

83 Shannon Sullivan, *Revealing Whiteness: The Unconscious Habits of Racial Privilege* (Bloomington: Indiana University Press, 2006), 103.

84 Lowe, *The Intimacies of Four Continents,* 1–42.

themselves now racialized and historicized.[85] The white European or "Western" subject henceforth was to enjoy an autonomy produced, not by laws interior to consciousness, but by "exterior" laws governing organic and/or sociocultural development. Thus, autonomy's prize and transparency's treasure signify only in relation to a *global* context populated by those who have yet to earn or discover it, the peoples colonized and exploited by European imperial designs. And *these* others, of course, are marked by racial difference and divergent historical trajectories. The "white world," then, is the globalizing figure of that projective dis/identification, that "engulfment" (in Ferreira da Silva's words), as well as of its economic and material conditions and supports.

But the white world "can't stay white" for the simple yet profound reason that it's *not* the world. As sentimental subjects, "persons who shop and feel," what we consume promises to realize our participation in a phantom community of people like ourselves.[86] Thus, although nearly everything that we consume bears the traces of its transnational circulation, we who are identified as white still identify ourselves, through our possession of these objects, as subjects of a Western nation or civilization. Taste is the exercise of that claim to sovereignty. And yet, as the sense most intimate with acts of consumption, and host to the corporeal pleasures of engulfment, taste is also the sense that is most palimpsest. The intimacy of taste with otherness remains a problem inviting moral re-education, moral and aesthetic discipline. Such is the pedagogical import of much sentimental

---

85 Ferreira da Silva's argument is complex, and I strain to do justice to it here. See *Toward a Global Idea of Race,* esp. 115–51. This text extends a line of thought found in Sylvia Wynter's work, in particular in the essays "The Ceremony Must Be Found," "1492," and "Unsettling the Coloniality of Being/Power/Truth/Freedom." See also Alexander Weheliye's reading of Wynter's work in *Habeas Viscus.*

86 Lauren Berlant, *The Female Complaint: The Unfinished Business of Sentimentality in American Culture* (Durham: Duke University Press, 2008), 13.

literature: a training in what Lauren Berlant calls the "juxtapo-litical," signifying a nearness to the complexities of domination and power but also a desire for "relief from the political."[87] That desire is nowhere more conspicuous than in the literature of hu-manitarian philanthropy, which presents "global" crises, which have their roots in transnational capitalism and settler-colonial institutions, as amenable to resolution through the generosity of Western consumers. Such a text is Nicholas Kristof and Sheryl WuDunn's *Half the Sky: Turning Oppression into Opportunity for Women Worldwide,* which our imperial university one year laid a copy of on the pillow of every incoming undergraduate. Under the auspices of the university's "First Chapter" program, the dis-tribution of *Half the Sky* was meant to foster a classically liberal exercise in community among the incoming class by providing occasion for critical discussion and debate. But more than that, the choice of this particular text (and its placement in the inti-mate space of sleep and sex) seems to have been intended to in-vite performances of the kinds of feeling appropriate to subjects who are positioned not only to "make history," but also to culti-vate their moral agency through their desire for a better world.

Half the Sky is not a call to organized resistance to trans-national violence and inequality. Nor is it a work of policy or scholarship, nor a narrative of oppression told by the oppressed. It comprises a series of case studies, as written by an American journalist and a banker, and with the participation of women and girls in India, Cambodia, the Democratic Republic of the Congo, and elsewhere. These case studies concern the preva-lence of "sex trafficking and forced prostitutions; gender-based violence, including honor killings and mass rape; and maternal mortality."[88] Though they do not stint on harrowing details, the

---

87 Ibid., 10. Berlant describes feminized performances of the sentimental as arising from "a sense of [...] collective sociality routed in revelations of the personal, regardless of how what is personal has itself been threaded through mediating institutions and social hierarchy."

88 Nicholas D. Kristof and Sheryl WuDunn, *Half the Sky: Turning Oppression into Opportunity for Women Worldwide* (New York: Alfred A. Knopf,

authors position their book "not as a drama of victimization but empowerment," where the empowerment in question is primarily entrepreneurial: "transform[ing] bubbly teenage girls from brothel slaves into successful businesswomen." As critics have pointed out, Kristof and WuDunn's book has little to say about the institutions and policies that constrain the lives of neocolonial subjects, creating poverty and insecurity in the global South as the condition of privilege and comfort in the North.[89] Its focus on gender-based violence and sexual exploitation acknowledges neither the role of capitalism and empire in forging modern hierarchies of gender, nor the ways in which neoliberal economies are implicated in sustaining sex work.[90] Rather, *Half the Sky*'s narratives deploy the rhetoric of what Ferreira da Silva calls "engulfment." The women and girls whose suffering lies sensationalized and exposed in its pages appear as victims of "underdeveloped" societies, the implication being that these societies still require our tutelage.[91] For instance, while the authors ac-

2009), xxi–xxii.

89 For a thorough critique of the larger context for Kristof and WuDunn's interventions, see Jason Hickel, "The 'Girl Effect': Liberalism, Empowerment and the Contradictions of Development," *Third World Quarterly* 35, no. 8 (September 14, 2014): 1355–73. Hickel notes that "in a context of neoliberal globalisation, policies justified on the basis of women's empowerment — such as expanding access to the labour market and to credit — often end up placing women in new forms of subservience as workers, consumers and debtors" (1356). See also Rupal Oza, "The Entanglements of Transnational Feminism and Area Studies," *Environment and Planning D: Society and Space* 34, no. 5 (October 1, 2016): 836–42; Sunil Bhatia, "Op-Ed: Nicholas Kristof and the Politics of Writing About Women's Oppression in Darker Nations," *The Feminist Wire,* March 3, 2013, https://thefeministwire.com/2013/03/op-ed-nicholas-kristof-and-the-politics-of-writing-about-womens-oppression-in-darker-nations/.

90 On the neoliberal contexts of modern sex work, see Patty Kelly, *Lydia's Open Door: Inside Mexico's Most Modern Brothel* (Berkeley: University of California Press, 2008).

91 However unintentionally, this representation rehearses classically liberal apologetics for the exclusion of the "territories" of empire from the social contract. On the history of the latter, see Uday Singh Mehta, *Liberalism and Empire: A Study in Nineteenth-Century British Liberal*

knowledge "the complexity of gender roles in the Islamic world," they conclude that "the best clue to a nation's growth and development potential is the status and role of women. This is the greatest handicap of Muslim Middle Eastern societies today, the flaw that bars them from modernity."[92] When "a nation's growth and development potential" is legible only in capitalist terms, it is ironic that one of the primary engines of primitive accumulation — a gendered division of labor that devalues women's roles — here becomes the "bar" to that modernization.[93] But an exclusive focus on gender permits the more troubling element to fade from view: the devaluation of these women's lives by the *racializing* logics of coloniality. As their juxtaposition of brothels, businesswomen, and "bubbly teenage girls" suggests, the authors appeal to an image of femininity familiar to their intended audience, an image that signals the universality of white "Western" values (i.e., the innocent ebullience of childhood and adolescence). Contact with the (racialized) "global" tarnishes this femininity, provoking moral outrage, but it also provides occasion to relieve that outrage through the re-inscription of the heteropatriarchal logic of capitalism as the engine of innocence redeemed. (In this world, of course, the categories of businesswoman and sex worker are mutually exclusive.)

The university's selection of this book to promote the imagined community of its incoming class is a gesture both banal and ambivalent. Does it mark the entrance to adulthood of the "bubbly teenagers" who found it waiting on their pillows like a bible of liberal hopes and bad dreams? Does it signify the pain-

Thought (Chicago: The University of Chicago Press, 1999), 46–76. Rebecca Dingo argues that Kristof and WuDunn "often resort to old colonialist stereotypes of Third World women as passive and meek to justify neoliberal practices that promote personal responsibility, tenacity, and will" (*Networking Arguments: Rhetoric, Transnational Feminism, and Public Policy Writing* [Pittsburgh: University of Pittsburgh Press, 2012], 151).

92 Kristof and WuDunn, *Half the Sky*, 154–60.

93 On femicide, the gendered division of labor, and primitive accumulation, see Silvia Federici, *Caliban and the Witch* (New York: Autonomedia, 2014).

ful, if not necessarily traumatic, end of their innocence, as they prepare for a precarity for which, by comparison with the traumas on display in this book, they should, presumably, be grateful? Gratitude, with a dash of guilt: that, at least, seems to be the book's recipe for social change. For both the power of its exposés and the appeal of its solutions imply the reader's assent to a narrative about the superiority of the white world, i.e., a world (presumably) free from violence against women.[94] A world of citizen–subjects, morally autonomous agents whose responsibility for "global" suffering stems from their benevolence and magnanimity, rather than from their complicity in the political and economic structures that cause suffering to proliferate.[95] But having said that, I must also admit that, for somebody even modestly acquainted with the discourses of post-colonial and/ or transnational feminist critique, taking down *Half the Sky* is an easy task. Too easy, I would say, when that somebody is a white, well-educated cishet male worker in the academy. At issue is neither fairness to the authors' intentions, nor the critic's intellectual honesty. At issue is whether the performance of such critique actually deepens the critic's engagement with his own complicity, whether it furthers his "accountability to the person defined as nobody" or not.[96] In my case, complicity includes the fact that I was a member of the committee that selected *Half the Sky* for our "First Chapter" program (even if it was not my choice). I was also involved in a project to solicit and antholo-

---

94 This narrative is one according to which, in the words of M. Jacqui Alexander in *Pedagogies of Crossing,* "patriarchy was irrelevant to modernity and […] 'traditional patriarchy' had only a single archaic source, which Western modernity automatically dissolved" (188).

95 As Rebecca Dingo argues, while "the book should be commended for offering information about women's struggles in places that are often discounted in common, everyday reporting," the authors "do not offer any real solutions to the problems, nor do they offer a cogent analysis of how audiences might holistically understand problems that women face— they do not network each woman's story to wider contexts" (*Networking Arguments,* 151).

96 The phrase is from Gumbs, "Nobody Mean More," 254.

gize responses to this book written by incoming (first-year un-dergraduate) students, a project that framed its work in terms of the cultivation of discursive or critical agency. So whatever af-fects Kristof and WuDunn's text helped to circulate in this case, my labor is entangled with that circulation, too. The challenge is to expose my own entanglement with the whiteness of this work and its feminizing disciplinary force, in the hopes that, by dis-rupting its self-evident texture, we might weave this entangle-ment otherwise. I propose to recruit as my interlocutors in this work a couple of student writers whose responses to *Half the Sky* sustain a certain intimacy with my thinking here.

These pieces, albeit brief, position the writers in relation to the text and its narratives as subjects of complicity. In her essay, Julia contrasts her own privilege, as a "rich white girl" in the United States, to the harms that befall the women and girls in *Half the Sky*:

> After I read the story of Dina, the seventeen-year-old girl from eastern Congo who was brutally raped by a gang of Hutu militia members, I felt a little sick to my stomach, not only because of the sheer goriness and brutality of the rape, but because I had been ignorantly taking my safe walks home from school for granted.[97]

"Sick to my stomach." This writer's response performs what seems to exceed a disinterested feeling. The narrative of geno-cidal rape provokes a visceral interest. But if the details of the incident incite disgust, this disgust prompts the writer to pivot, to turn toward herself. Her essay relates an upsurge of dis/iden-tification with the figure of Dina, noting how their vulnerability to patriarchal violence is inflected differently (by the racializing forces of empire) with respect to its likelihood and severity.[98]

---

97 Excerpts are used with the author's permission.
98 That the stories in *Half the Sky* stimulate a species of lurid pleasure is no doubt crucial to the book's appeal. I am not claiming that this pleasure

Her "safe walks home" come to signify a fact about the writer's standpoint, and Julia endeavors to make explicit the role that race and class play in shaping that standpoint, thereby complicating *Half the Sky*'s approach to gendered violence. In response to another moment in the book, she writes: "And yet another wave of guilt over ignorance washed over me. If I went missing, one could be sure the police and probably FBI would work tirelessly to find the rich white girl." Here she centers the fact of her conscription to the ranks of white femininity, exposing, too, how membership in those ranks is, quite literally, policed.[99] A pedagogically optimistic reading of Julia's essay, à la Joseph Harris, would amplify the ways in which the writer signals her difference from the subjects of Kristof and WuDunn's narrative, thereby discovering that she "has something to say." And this discovery, as we have seen, orients the (occidental) subject toward the universal liberal public of "merely possible others" with whom one identifies, not in virtue of common conditions of embodiment, but because, like them, one possesses a singularly identifying discourse. But what interests me is how Julia's writing, like Heather's, attests to her embodiment of that something.

With regard to neoliberalism/neo-imperialism, the "global" functions as the other to the universal public imagined by the liberal text. As Ferreira da Silva writes, "the racial subaltern sub-

is incompatible with disgust. Rather, I want to suggest that the Kantian model of aesthetic/reflective judgment begins to fray under the pressure of this disgust, this sense of what Kant describes as "imposing the enjoyment which we are nevertheless forcibly resisting" and which is, for that reason, incompatible with "aesthetic satisfaction" (*Critique of the Power of Judgment*, 190). On Derrida's reading, disgust signals the threat of an "unrepresentable, unnameable, unintelligible, insensible, unassimilable, obscene other" to "the hierarchizing authority of logocentric analogy," because the "vicariousness" of disgust would "undo […] the power of identification" ("Economimesis," trans. R. Klein, *Diacritics* 11, no. 2 [1981]: 25).

99 For the idea of "conscription" to the racializing embodiment of whiteness, see Alexander, *Pedagogies of Crossing*, 140.

ject is placed before (in front of) the ethical space inhabited by the proper national subject."[100] This placement stages an awkward confrontation that "the proper national subject" struggles to find a vocabulary and a syntax for. In describing her parents' ability to provide for her college tuition as a "smart decision," and describing herself as "fortunate" and "blessed," Julia's essay situates its author in that context wherein, as Fanon notes of "Europe [...] and every so-called civilized or civilizing country," "the family represents a piece of the nation."[101] In this context, the "ethical space" of nuclear family and nation are continuous, while the intimate dependence of both on the spoils of empire remains veiled by its own aestheticization in the commodity-form. In Julia's essay, the predicates of empire appear obliquely, as a passive construction, when the writer describes herself as "truly spoiled." Many of the other student responses we anthologized — mirroring, it should be said, the book's reception in mainstream media — either celebrate reading *Half the Sky* as a consciousness-raising event, or take up the book's invitation to the techno-bureaucratic ploys of policy analysis and recommendation. Unlike those responses, Julia's essay seizes the occasion to perform a critical self-reflection. At the same time, the feelings that this reflection surfaces, rendered primarily as shame and guilt, exceed the composure proper to the critical, attaching themselves to a sentimental lexicon. Lacking the address to a specific prior fault, liberal shame or guilt appears as a melancholy in the face of structural imbalance. It arises in the gap between the shape of one's optimism — as a typical good liberal subject, wanting to believe that everyone is rewarded according to her merits — and a world order marked by injustice and inequality.[102] For young people with racial and class privi-

---

100 Ferreira da Silva, *Toward a Global Idea of Race*, xl.
101 Fanon, *Black Skin, White Masks*, 121. The white family is also that thing, per Spillers, "pledged to maintain the supremacy of race" ("Mama's Baby, Papa's Maybe," 219).
102 For a trenchant genealogy of liberal guilt that doesn't dismiss its critical potential, see Julie Ellison, *Cato's Tears and the Making of Anglo-American*

lege at the imperial university, being relatively insulated from the causes and consequences of the privileges they enjoy, and having been raised in an environment of highly structured permissiveness, the shock of confronting such failure can be acute. But note the ambiguity of Julia's phrase "guilt over ignorance." Is this guilt awakened by the failure to know a certain thing? Or by the failure to exhibit the capacity for certain kinds of thinking or awareness?[103] Does it suggest the moral value that critical judgment holds for somebody who has been taught to attend to the particularity of her own social position? If so, this guilt testifies to an intention to compose the self through reflection on the suffering of others.[104]

But liberal guilt frequently seeks relief for its pangs in philanthropic discourse, which no less than the scientific and na-

Emotion (Chicago: The University of Chicago Press, 1999). According to Colin Dayan, writing about liberal jurisprudence, "all definitions of personhood […] rest ultimately on the ability to blame oneself" (*The Law Is a White Dog: How Legal Rituals Make and Unmake Persons* [Princeton: Princeton University Press, 2013], 89).

103 Alain Ehrenberg argues that the drift of capitalism during the last several decades has replaced the neurotic dynamics of guilt with the depressive dynamics of an anxiety over one's abilities and capacities. We might extend this point to the kinds of moral capacities prized by liberalism: sympathy for the plight of the racialized and gendered other, and awareness of the political and economic determinants of one's own position (*The Weariness of the Self: Diagnosing the History of Depression in the Contemporary Age* [Montréal: McGill-Queen's University Press, 2010].

104 As Dipesh Chakrabarty argues in *Provincializing Europe,* the moral vocation of the modern liberal subject depends on "the capacity […] for a generalized picture of suffering," i.e., upon an intimacy with others' suffering *at a distance.* The distance between the sufferer and the observer — "even if," remarks Chakrabarty, "it be one's own suffering" that one observes — permits "a certain moment of self-recognition," in which the observer observes their capacity to "notice" the other's suffering, and in this observation, they (the observer, not the sufferer) discover their participation in the teleology of the "abstract, general human being." As an observer, one does not suffer, or not in the way that one does in sharing the burden of a loved one's illness or distress. Rather, one "documents […] suffering in the interest of eventual social intervention […]" (119). See also Berlant, *The Female Complaint,* 35.

tionalist discourses analyzed by Ferreira da Silva, constructs the global as the site of the non-white other's engulfment. As another student author, Chiara Corso, writes in her response to *Half the Sky*:

> A huge stumbling block for every breed of activism tends to come from an unacknowledged sense of privilege — a sort of well-meaning ethnocentrism that paralyzes altruism and keeps sympathy from evolving into empathy. We're not "saving" the women described in *Half the Sky*. We're cooperating with these women to better the world as a whole, and we need to do this in a way that respects different cultures instead of stripping them bare in favor of plasticized, "superior" Americanization.[105]

Corso's trenchant observation that "we're not 'saving' the women described in *Half the Sky*" reminds us, too, of the role that a racialized gender plays in this engulfment. For the figure whom Chandra Mohanty calls "the Third-World Woman," flitting through the pages of *Half the Sky,* appears to need saving because she functions rhetorically to assert the agency of the (presumptively) Western reader.[106] Such a reader is thereby invited to indulge in what Scott Richard Lyons calls the "persistent, uniquely American, and imperialist notion of recognition-from-above."[107] The subaltern's "need," in other words, indexes

---

105 Corso, in George Washington University, *Reflecting Half the Sky: Responses by the GW Class of 2014* (Washington: The George Washington University Libraries, 2011), 22. Cited by permission of the author.

106 Chandra Mohanty, "Under Western Eyes: Feminist Scholarship and Colonial Discourses," *Feminist Review* 30 (1988): 61–88

107 Scott Richard Lyons, "Rhetorical Sovereignty: What Do American Indians Want from Writing?" *College Composition and Communication* 51, no. 3 (2000): 452. As Glen Coulthard explains, "There is no mutual dependency in terms of a need or desire for recognition. In these contexts, the 'master' — that is, the colonial state and state society — does not require recognition from the previously self-determining communities upon which its territorial, economic, and social infrastructure is

her silence, and her silence is required, lest she have something to say about her situation. Something, perhaps, that might indict the ways in which, as María Lugones insists, colonial violence has "fractured" social relations by its inscription of gender as a normative category that is always already racially marked.[108] The "Third-World Woman" needs "saving" in order that she might become, in a future perpetually deferred by the needs of trans-national capital for her lands and labor, a Western, i.e., transpar-ently human, woman. A rehearsal of this claim in the interest of decolonial critique should not minimize or efface the very real threats everywhere (inflected by the structural positions of sexuality, race, class, and bodily ability) to cis and trans women's bodily, social, and political autonomy and security. At the same time, the representation of need in mainstream philanthropic discourses dovetails with a picture in which the structural po-sition of the philanthropic agent, as implicated or complicit in these threats, remains disguised. Corso's image of "stripping [other cultures] bare" aptly suggests how philanthropic reason recruits the subaltern as a foil for the white gaze, which denudes the former of her cultural situation in a gesture that joins aes-theticizing prurience to biopolitical control. And Corso's refer-ence to "plasticized […] Americanization" suggests something else, too. In the figuration of the subaltern as *culturally* affect-

constituted. What it needs is land, labor, and resources" ("Subjects of Empire: Indigenous Peoples and the 'Politics of Recognition' in Canada," *Contemporary Political Theory* 6, no. 4 [2007]: 451). Lyons and Coulthard are writing about the settler-colonial state in its relationship to Native and Indigenous peoples. Their analyses further expose just how fictive and fraught with internal contradiction this "Western" perspective is, which tucks a structure of political domination and violence behind a putative fact of geography.

108 Lugones, "Toward a Decolonial Feminism," 749. See also Lowe, *Intimacies of Four Continents,* on "the colonial division of humanity" (189). Andrea Smith, writing about this dynamic as it plays out in the settler-colonial context, points to the rhetorical construction of "the Native as the infantile 'citizen' that enables the future of the white, settler citizen" ("Queer Theory and Native Studies," 51).

able, laden with the remnants of what resists modernization, the white world encounters an indictment of its own cultural etiolation by white supremacy and the demands of capital.[109] (And wouldn't a department store mannequin, demonically animated, insist on its superiority to all those poor things of flesh and blood?)

To understand that we should be "cooperating with these women" whose struggles are limned in *Half the Sky* requires an acknowledgment that the "global" comprises sites of collective resistance to the violence of capitalism and empire.[110] That this book has nothing to say about women and girls laboring in the *maquiladoras* owned or hired by North American corporations, nor about the women working for much less than the minimum wage as farm workers or domestics *north* of the border, etc., is no accident. (The index to *Half the Sky* contains no entry on "labor" and only a handful of references to "sweatshops." One of these is the unqualified assertion that "sweatshops have given women a boost."[111]) The text traces a careful outline around its subject, such that the only violence that counts is intimate violence (rape, forced prostitution, honor killings), and the only intimacies that count are those that reaffirm the nuclear family as the seat of liberal selfhood and mirror of the nation-state. This focus would suggest that harm against (cishet) women and

109 "*Y a bon Banania*": A figure of endless, restless patience, the subaltern is also a figure of consumption whose bottomless appetites, like that of the grinning Senegalese on the cocoa ad cited by Fanon, provide fodder for Western laughter, pity, and disgust. Or the subaltern is the victim of barbaric cannibalism, like a bolus in the lily-white throat of civilization. Of course, this cannibalism is only that of imperial capitalism itself, with its vampiric appetite for natural resources, cheap labor, and consumer goods. See also David Marriott, "On Racial Fetishism," *Qui Parle: Critical Humanities and Social Sciences* 18, no. 2 (May 21, 2010): 215–48.

110 Alexander notes that the "local circuits that secure transnational profits […] are simultaneously the very places that collectivize women's labor and provide the contexts in which women come to understand the meaning of exploitation" (*Pedagogies of Crossing*, 102).

111 Kristof and WuDunn, *Half the Sky*, 210.

girls persists because of the underdevelopment of explicit norms and rights around gender. It also suggests that Western societies are superior because of their explicit commitments to such rights and norms, even if the philanthropic text cannot exactly afford to be explicit about this suggestion. What results is a sentimental narrative, full of the *fort-da* of a rhetorical imperialism struggling to keep its own promise up in the air.[112] No wonder, then, that a close reader like Julia, interpreting the text within the frame of its philanthropic logic, can conclude that although "world leaders and charities strive to give greater balance to the world in terms of social and economic equality," there may not "ever be a time when the world will be completely equal."

Whereas *Half the Sky* wields vicarious despair between the mitts of market rationality, Julia's response sits closer to that despair's serrated edge. The proposition that "world leaders" (e.g., the banker-backed governments of the EU and the US) and "charities" (many of them funded by these same banks) would collude in a "balance" other than that of their bottom lines is, in her words, "far-fetched." But that distance turns fetching insofar as philanthropy's appeal to a feminized influence depicts inequality itself as a natural order (an order inherently out of "balance," but natural nonetheless):

112 I mean in part what Dean Spade dubs the "empty promises of 'equal opportunity' and 'safety' underwritten by settler colonialism, racist, sexist, classist, ableist, and xenophobic imprisonment, and ever-growing wealth disparity" (*Normal Life: Administrative Violence, Critical Trans Politics, and the Limits of Law* [Brooklyn: South End Press, 2011], 41). As Spade's work shows, such promises target populations within the Western nation-state, too. For instance, queer and trans people in the US are invited to participate in "the liberal rights-focused framework" through narratives of opportunity and safety that center "incidents of intentional, individual negative action, discrimination, and violence," neglecting the structural causes of disproportionate harm endured by queer and trans people of color, especially those lacking economic means (102). "Rhetorical imperialism" is Scott Richard Lyon's phrase, which he defines as "the ability of dominant powers to assert control of others by setting the terms of the debate" ("Rhetorical Sovereignty," 452).

> I believe this inequality is necessary to connecting the world [*sic*] at a deeper level. Perhaps the reason some girls like me are born into well-off situations is so we can reach out and help others around the world who have less money and rights than we do. Giving always leaves a better feeling in your insides than receiving.

Like Kant's critic, seeking in nature a shape and purpose that prove elusive to the rigors of the rational understanding, the writer finds within the suffering described by philanthropic discourse a "form of purposiveness." In place of a causal nexus that implicates the possession of material and social privilege in the deprivation that others suffer, this operation makes "inequality […] necessary to connecting the world at a deeper level." An aesthetic logic discovers the "reason" for the privileged subject's privilege in that subject's capacity for an enlargement that "reach[es] out." As in the settler-colonial discourses analyzed by Aileen Moreton-Robinson, we might say that in *Half the Sky,* "virtue functions within the ontology of possession" to justify "racial and gendered maintenance and domination in the guise of good government." If the settler-colonial state's virtue "occurs through the imposition of sovereign will-to-be on Indigenous lands and peoples, which are perceived to lack will," the logic of transnational philanthropy construes virtue as closing the gap between the transparent and the affectable, the sovereign and the suffering.[113] But this virtue remains the property of that sovereignty. It appeals to the universalizing "will-to-be" of the power of judgment (the feeling that everyone should assent to the disinterested pleasure I take) as grounds for a promise that inequality does not foreclose the capacity for intimacy. If, for the socially engaged liberal, "giving […] leaves a better feeling in your insides than receiving," then social and economic privilege

---

113 Aileen Moreton-Robinson, *The White Possessive: Property, Power, and Indigenous Sovereignty* (Minneapolis: University of Minnesota Press, 2015), 178–79.

becomes a pure fund of "giving," a magic lamp that, though it cannot repair inequality (being inequality's source), can conjure something much more special. It can conjure, as an affection of the subject, the transparency of liberal humanity itself. Philanthropic reason promises to earn its keep, not by connecting to the world, but by "connecting the world," as though its purposiveness bore the power of the universal within itself.

critical negligence and the undercommon sense of us

One might read the expression of such sentiments as a case of the "ontological expansiveness" that Shannon Sullivan attributes to white privilege, referring to the belief that "all cultural and social spaces are potentially available for one to inhabit."[114] This is the belief projected by the white body in its transactions with the world. And as a belief inhabited by the student writer, this expansiveness might be said to violate the distance and control sought by critical thought. As Hannah Arendt cautions, "critical thinking does not consist in an enormously enlarged empathy through which one can know what actually goes on in the mind of all others."[115] But that would be an easy reading, and a negligent one. Negligent in its liaison or entanglement with a certain suspect pedagogy. This pedagogy makes suspects of those whose labor it needs in order to stage its own relevance to that labor's overcoming. As Stefano Harney and Fred Moten write in their manifesto with and against the university, with and against academic critique, this pedagogy performs its critical "opposition to the unregulated and the ignorant without acknowledging the unregulated, ignorant, unprofessional labor that goes

---

114 Sullivan, *Revealing Whiteness,* 25. This expansiveness accompanies the foreclosure, in the white imaginary, of the spaces of resistance inhabited by Black women and other women of color. On this point, see McKittrick, *Demonic Grounds.*

115 Arendt, *Lectures on Kant's Political Philosophy,* 43.

on not opposite […] but within" it.[116] The ignorant labor within me includes this neglect, which I perform in my belated critical address to somebody's composing at the university's behest. I perform it by making her labor the object of my charity or lack thereof. Perhaps the critical, in its academic practice, cannot escape this uncomfortable intimacy with the philanthropic, which is the love of humanity that presumes to make somebody out of nobody. For at stake in both instances is an unacknowledged debt. Somebody steals from all those nobodies (their lands, their labor, their love, their lives), so that this somebody might make themselves more like somebody. And then, giving back a sliver of what they stole, somebody steals from nobody even the fact of that theft, rewriting nobody's claim to justice as somebody's act of benevolence, somebody's name on a plaque. And so the illness begets itself all over again. In the echo chamber of imperialism, the subaltern contributes their silence — which is only the ongoing erasure of their voice and their name by the machinery that produces nobodies — giving the citizen–consumer occasion to speak on the other's behalf. And in composition's echo chamber at the imperial university, the student without something "distinctively her own" to say, contributes their vulnerability, their vulnerability to error, to the admission of a conventional particularity that has yet to learn how to stage its own overcoming in critical abstraction and judgments of taste. Their vulnerability produces the contrast between student and teacher, novice and expert, (feminized) reader and (masculine) critic.

116 Stefano Harney and Fred Moten, *The Undercommons: Fugitive Planning & Black Study* (Wivenhoe: Minor Compositions, 2013), 32. Harney and Moten write out of an allegiance and in debt to "the maroons [who] refuse to refuse professionalization, that is, to be against the university. The university will not recognize this indecision, and thus professionalization is shaped precisely by what it cannot acknowledge, its internal antagonism, its wayward labor, its surplus. Against this wayward labor it sends the critical, sends its claim that what is left beyond the critical is waste" (31–32).

These operations do not happen in parallel, by analogy, but in sequence. The one is the fractalization or folding-in-on-itself of the other.[117] Their conjoint production is the source of what Robert McRuer calls "a certain pathos" specific to critique, which vitiates the promise of a truly embodied, collective, critical agency. This pathos appears in the thought that composition's normative "straightness" (or whiteness, or cis masculinity, etc.) might be inevitable, which yields a melancholy pleasure, a "sweetness" that clings to the underside of that judgment.[118] It reveals a taste, in the critic, for "the remainder, the forgotten, the hidden," which we might call an indulgence in that quotient of experience that cannot be made explicit. A fool for this sweetness, the critic's voice quivers on the verge of expansive address to a sovereign public that "regards itself," in Julie Ellison's words, as "inescapably imperial."[119] In the classroom, in the boardroom of the trustees, the somebodies discharge their duty to the trust that they keep on behalf of all those bored, worn-out, affectable *I*'s, who are always losing their composure and cannot be trusted to think for themselves. They are, in fact, lightning rods for the charge that keeps trust flowing through the system. Overwhelmed by the white-out of their own promises, liberalism's institutions must harness this charge, which neither the trustees' composure nor that of the professional critics could handle, in order to satisfy the illocutionary conditions of liberalism itself.

117 As Spivak points out, "when the [European] Woman is put outside of Philosophy by the Master subject, she is argued into that dismissal, not foreclosed as a casual rhetorical gesture. The ruses against the racial other are different" (*Critique of Postcolonial Reason,* 30).

118 McRuer, *Crip Theory,* 155. Likewise, Linda Martín Alcoff argues that by positing the inevitability of the suture between whiteness and white supremacy, white anti-racist critics frequently participate in a kind of "white exceptionalism" (*The Future of Whiteness* [Cambridge: Polity Press, 2015], 91–135).

119 Ellison, *Cato's Tears,* 60. According to Ellison, the concept of sentimentality refers back to "ongoing crises of masculinity." In the scenes of neoclassical tragedy and latter-day liberal guilt she analyzes, (white) masculine sentimentality returns as the repressed.

However naive, the hope reposed in "connecting the world" testifies to the fraying of those networks (national, institutional, professional, familial) by which the liberal subject has been trained to sustain their sense of belonging, even as their implication in empire's engulfment of the globe, and in its dire consequences for human and non-human life, becomes denser. And if the "typical good" subject's composure entails the capacity to reflect on their own intents and purposes and those of others (for the sake of a typicality that feels universal and commands assent), this composure might be said to underwrite the attenuated promissory chains of transnationally networked capital itself. The vigilance of our negligence seeks to shield that promissory logic from the illusory, fictitious, impractical, and unreal.[120] These are some names for how sense exceeds reference, how sensation envelops more sides of a thing than reason can tabulate, how reality is how the world feels, coming together in the gap between us, in the folded cut that conjoins us while keeping us apart. In those folds, intentionality is at once dense and incomplete, inescapable and fugitive in the same breath. But the rubrics of explicitness, which our vigilance requires, express a fantasy of escaping from the folds of intentionality altogether.

Not all ways of learning and teaching presuppose this negligence. If doing the professional academic's work involves helping "students […] come to see themselves as the problem," Moten and Harney celebrate a place to which the problems run, "a nonplace called the undercommons."[121] In the undercommons, they are feeling and practicing forms of agency that are not sin-

---

120 For Ryle, sentimentalists are "people who indulge in induced feelings without acknowledging the fictitiousness of their agitations" (*The Concept of Mind,* 107). Ann Douglas describes sentimentality as having "no content but its own exposure" (*The Feminization of American Culture,* 254). As Adela Pinch observes, the sentimental subject "appear[s] really to be feeling emotions that themselves seem hackneyed, conventional […]" (*Strange Fits of Passion: Epistemologies of Emotion, Hume to Austen* [Stanford: Stanford University Press, 1996], 69).
121 Harney and Moten, *The Undercommons,* 29, 39.

gular but collective. They are decomposing and recomposing, sampling from and remixing, queering and cripping and translating traditions of practice rooted in the everyday emergency of embodiment as the ground of individual survival and collective power. They are "weav[ing] the fractured locus" of de/colonial agency. This agency is woven into the very texture of exploited labor, whereby the laborers weave into the social conditions of their work the conditions of its resistance.[122] They are studying and practicing and multiplying an "enmeshment" open to the generative possibilities of the encounter.[123] You could even call it sovereignty, if by that you meant "the ability to assert oneself renewed — in the presence of others." Such sovereignty "is a people's right to rebuild, its demand to exist and present its gifts to the world."[124] Perhaps this work "cannot be reconciled with the project of recuperating the lost voices of those who are written out" of the dominant narratives in order "to bring their humanism and strivings to light."[125] Perhaps it does not seek to re-inscribe the lost within the telos of their composition as full subjects of modernity. Rather than supposing that the object(ified) can be unlocked, like a jack-in-the-box, to reveal the subject trapped inside, these undercommon practices turn toward lived experience as generative of its own rigors, its own ruses for survival. These are plaited into the person, as densely a part of them as their sinews and their nerves. Surviving our socialization at the hands of parents, teachers, peers, employers, and agents of the state requires learning to sift others' words and gestures in search of their (not infrequently baleful) purposes: in order not to get bullied or hurt, in order to receive the

---

122 Lugones, "Toward a Decolonial Feminism," 749.
123 Mahmood, *Politics of Piety*, 38.
124 Lyons, "Rhetorical Sovereignty," 457.
125 Mahmood, *Politics of Piety*, 154–59. Apposite here is Alexander Weheliye's question, "Why are formations of the oppressed deemed liberatory only if they resist hegemony and/or exhibit the full agency of the oppressed? What deformations of freedom become possible in the absence of resistance and agency?" (*Habeas Viscus*, 2).

praise you're desperate for, in order to walk home safe, in order to clear the hurdle of another day. Many of our students arrive already having had to weave out of their own experience, and in solidarity with others, a fabric strong enough to withstand these abrasive structures. Like the rigidity of gender roles, the invidious nature of class distinctions, the toxic violence of heterosexual masculinity, the deadly boring work of internalizing white supremacy. And some arrive in spite of, in defiance of, the unrelenting force of the state's paramilitarized, carceral apparatus. Relish for the academy's critical lessons might depend, then, on a prior estrangement from the signifiers in your behavior, from the appearance of your body, from the baggage you have been taught to regard as your specific gravity in the world. And what of the university that receives them? As Moten and Harney write, "it cannot be denied that the university is a place of refuge, and it cannot be accepted that the university is a place of enlightenment. In the face of these conditions one can only sneak into the university and steal what one can."[126]

From the body, which "does not stay quite composed," or from the flesh in its intimacy with otherness, beginning with the (m)otherness from which we all emerge, I want to take my cue.[127] But it is not mine to take, nor is this my story to tell. I intrude upon a texture the trace of which I have been taught to rub out in myself, to expunge from my senses. A cruel optimism promises that explication's purgative thrust can leave me pure enough to merit whatever it is I desire. As Lauren Berlant writes,

> a poetics of attachment always involves some splitting off of the *story* I can tell about wanting to be near *x* (as though *x* has autonomous qualities) from the *activity* of the emotional habitus I have constructed, as a function of having *x* in my

126 Harney and Moten, *The Undercommons,* 26.
127 Gumbs, "Nobody Mean More," 257.

life, in order to be able to project out my endurance in proximity to the complex of what *x* seems to offer and proffer.[128]

Cruel optimism's "attachment to [...] a problematic object"
echoes Kant's reference to what lies beyond the limits of what
we can think. A horizon of explication, this concept lacks the
logical identity of a substance (where a thing is equal to itself).
Rather, in Kant's words, "the object = X."[129] Experience, like optimism, has a problematic object, an X that marks the spot that
cannot really be a spot for us, because all we can be sure of is
that our dispositions aim somewhere else. We have as fact only
these acts of loving, wanting, hoping, fearing, hating, etc., which
have a direction, a history, a structure, but we do not possess the
object as such. The pedagogies of patriarchal white supremacy
are indescribably cruel in their efforts to fix as objects the others
whose fixation might (though it never does) anchor white cishet
masculinity to itself. If, othered by that fixation, somebody can
still enjoy the thrills of expansiveness and manage to feel their
judgments thrum with the rhythms of a purposiveness satu-
rating their surround, that may be precisely *because,* as Moten
suggests, an intimacy with the lived ways of Blackness teaches
respect for "a physicality that is indexed to something more
than the 'merely' physical."[130] In its non-place, in the wonder
of the undercommonality of sensation, feeling, and breath, this
"breathed critique," this indexical encounter in, of, and with the
flesh, is not necessarily without reflection.[131] But as reflection, it
involves, involute to the movement of abstraction, a homing,
fugitive flight toward the embodied in its excess of the human

---

128 Berlant, *Cruel Optimism,* 25 (emphasis in the original).

129 Kant, *Critique of Pure Reason,* 232.

130 Moten, "Preface to a Solo by Miles Davis," 223.

131 Ashon T. Crawley writes: "Such life, such breathed critique, speaks
    back and against this totality, makes evident the incompleteness, the
    incompletion, of the project of white supremacy. And this because of the
    open-endedness to movement, to change" (*Blackpentecostal Breath: The
    Aesthetics of Possibility* [New York: Fordham University Press, 2017], 46).

body in its guise as singular thing, composed and strapped into place. This flight is expressive of the world's fragility, the cut of its presence under the tongue. This is an actuality prior to possibility, a materiality prior to form, not in the sense of what form informs, but what informs form in the repeated summons to form's constitution and its undoing. We might call this movement the ontologically deepening or implicating awareness that it is *this* world (not another) to which you assent, and which you discover in its deferral and refusal and prolongation of your assent. This world has futurity as its permanent, fugitive gift. As Fanon writes, "there had always been the unforeseeable."[132] In such a moment, somebody might even say with W.E.B. Du Bois, writing of his matriculation into Fisk University, "I leapt into this world with enthusiasm."[133]

As an invited ghost at the scene of composition, enthusiasm suspends purpose in favor of attention to the moment at hand, alive to the swerve, to the rhythm, always incomplete, of fervor and exhaustion, defiance and defeat, by which the hand writing or the mouth talking tries to fill the volutes of our lives. In thrall to that suspension, what occupies the page declares the writer's flesh at once familiar and foreign (*unheimlich* in Freud's words), home to a capacity unlooked for in the institutes of composure, the capacity for surprise. This capacity, and the way words can court it, puts us in mind of an etymology: ἐνθουσιάζειν, meaning "to be inspired or possessed by a god."[134] And if there is no god to take possession, are we clay pots filled only with dogma, ideology, bad images, the murmur of the masses or the lies of demagogues? To what does it leave us open? What lies on the other side? What beckons from that crack open to the uncanny that, misquoting Kant's stroke of enthusiasm, we could call the

132 Quoted in David Marriott, "Inventions of Existence: Sylvia Wynter, Frantz Fanon, Sociogeny, and 'the Damned,'" CR: *The New Centennial Review* 11, no. 3 (2012): 45–89, at 65.

133 Quoted in Paul Gilroy, T*he Black Atlantic: Modernity and Double Consciousness* (London: Verso, 2007), 116.

134 *Oxford English Dictionary*, s.v. "enthusiasm," https://www.oed.com.

"other = X"? Call it a dodge, if you like. But this X introduces a certain *frisson*. Call it *ex-thusiasm,* to register the sense of a god's going out, a god's exit from the world. There remains the space for something, a shuffling of the papers on the desk, a billowing of the drapes. As David Marriott writes about Fanon, "to leap is to escape and yet remain, to continue to relate to the 'historical' and yet never abandon the possibility of an open-ended traveling where reaching toward the universal is to reach for oneself as other."[135] And so the critic's optimism, perhaps, is of this Cheshire sort. For only in this all too brief felicity, which they will not name as such, can the writer find what they need to bring surprise into the world. They need the pressure of this enthusiasm against the sphincter of what our history bequeaths us, against the reflex of doubt, disbelief, even despair. How ill-prepared we are even for these breaches of felicity, and nothing preaches our finitude quite like falling in love with the first flush of inspiration. Whole lives traffic in the aftershock.

135 Marriott, "Inventions of Existence," 86.

2

Composition as White/Mansplanation: Bureaucratic Grammars and Fugitive Intimacies

I am quite straight-faced as I ask soberly: "But what on earth is whiteness that one should so desire it?" Then always, somehow, some way, silently but clearly, I am given to understand that whiteness is the ownership of the earth forever and ever, Amen!
— W.E.B. Du Bois, "The Souls of White Folk"

The proposition is a lure for feeling.
— Alfred North Whitehead, *Process and Reality*

A white hunter is nearly crazy.
— Gertrude Stein, *Tender Buttons*

On December 24, 2015, George Yancy's "Dear White America" appeared on the *New York Times*'s blog "The Stone." In his letter, Yancy exhorts white readers to wake up to their own racism as a step toward dismantling white supremacy. Yancy's focus in this text is on habits of racism that escape the subject's conscious awareness. Habits that very well might contradict what such subjects would declare, at that fraught border between consciousness and its occupied territories, as their intentions. For many whites, racism remains a matter of unreflective habits precisely because whiteness saturates the milieux of those identified as white, like a kind of background noise of embodiment. Against this background, Black lives and the lives of other people of color appear as signals bearing an impossible burden of information, encoding, as it were, a history wrapped in a fantasy wrapped in a fiction.[1] That this history is ongoing and unredeemed, in part because the fantasy persists, motivates the persistence of the fiction. The signals propagated by racism profit white people in part because they — both the signals and the race of those who receive them — need not be recognized as such.[2] Aware

1   For my thinking about whiteness and racism in relation to information theory, I am indebted, albeit belatedly, to Marisa Parham, "Sample | Signal | Strobe: Haunting, Social Media, and Black Digitality," in *Debates in the Digital Humanities 2019*, eds. Matthew K. Gold and Lauren F. Klein (Minneapolis: University of Minnesota Press, 2019), ch. 11. The history in question is, of course, that of the expropriation of Black labor and Black lives by acts of organized violence and calculated terror, in concert with the genocide and dispossession practiced against Native and Indigenous peoples, and the exploitation of successive waves of immigrant labor. Such violence and exploitation have secured the political and economic dominance of Europeans and their descendants in the Americas. The fantasy accompanying this history entangles the persecution of others as objects of domination with a relation to those others that construes them as both inviting this domination (through their passivity) and requiring it (through their untamed animality). The fantasy promises to allow the subject who dominates the racialized other to have his cake and eat it, too, by enjoying the pleasures of domination even as he disavows the violence that he practices, locating its source in the dominated other. Gorged on this double pleasure, such a subject, sleeping the sleep of the unjust, can afford not to recognize the acts of resistance to his power offered by those others, which, nonetheless, fracture his own sense of coherence, driving the fantasy deeper into the fissure of the self. Hence the persistence of the fiction, covering over that fractured place, that spells the irrelevance of the suffering and struggles of people of color to the everyday lives of whites.

2   As Yancy writes, "you are part of a system that allows you to walk into stores where you are not followed, where you get to go for a bank loan and your skin does not count against you, where you don't need to engage in 'the talk' that black people and people of color must tell their children when they are confronted by white police officers" ("Dear White America,"

that whites are taught to disavow their roles in white supremacy, Yancy encourages his readers "to listen with love, a sort of love that demands that you look at parts of yourself that might cause pain and terror." Referencing his own struggle to identify and undo his habits of sexism and misogyny, he models the vulnerability that he asks of his readers: "Please don't take this as a confession for which I'm seeking forgiveness." For "confessions can be easy," presupposing a moment of absolution, a clean break between the past and future. A practice of love, on the other hand, or of loving audition, requires an ongoing struggle. It requires that we first claim as our own, in order to combat, that which we disavow. It requires not only that we make explicit to ourselves the privileges "sutured" to our identity, but also that we learn how to feel their collateral human cost, the lives wasted and destroyed by a system that rewards and protects whiteness.[3] But the spirit of Yancy's letter is therapeutic. Its author exhorts us to "take a deep breath," writing, "I can see your anger." Rather than "wallow in guilt," which is a performance that centers the privileged subject's bad feelings, he would have us "make […]

The Stone [*The New York Times*], December 24, 2015, http://opinionator. blogs.nytimes.com/2015/12/24/dear-white-america/).

3   Yancy's approach is in tune with the embodied, "transactional" analysis of white privilege offered by Shannon Sullivan, *Revealing Whiteness: The Unconscious Habits of Racial Privilege* (Bloomington: Indiana University Press, 2006). See also George Yancy, *Black Bodies, White Gazes: The Continuing Significance of Race in America,* 2nd edn. (Lanham: Rowman & Littlefield, 2016); George Yancy, *Look, a White! Philosophical Essays on Whiteness* (Philadelphia: Temple University Press, 2012); Thandeka, *Learning to Be White: Money, Race, and God in America* (New York: Bloomsbury, 2013); Alexis Shotwell, *Knowing Otherwise: Race, Gender, and Implicit Understanding* (University Park: Pennsylvania State University Press, 2011); Lewis R. Gordon, *Bad Faith and Antiblack Racism* (Amherst: Humanity Books, 1999). On the political expedience of anti-Black racism and white supremacy in the formation of the United States, see Ibram X. Kendi, *Stamped from the Beginning: The Definitive History of Racist Ideas in America* (New York: Nation Books, 2017).

space" for the other's pain, the pain that white selfhood prolongs in its possessive drive to dominate.[4]

The hundreds of comments archived alongside Yancy's post run the gamut from grateful amplification to gratuitous and fragile outrage. As Yancy anticipates, many white readers make their anger visible. They do so with tautological, pathological insistence, each one registering the same point for themselves, such that the comments thread becomes a piston of grievance and verbal assault. Many seek to deflect the idea that they might be racist back onto Yancy himself:

> Just because someone has a skin color doesn't mean that skin color means anything. Just because you have staked your entire career on that color always mattering, it doesn't mean that you're not frequently making fallacious assumptions. Is my skin color white? Sure. I also have brown eyes…a height…and a lot of other things that really tell you very little about me. You presume to sum up the beliefs and attitudes of millions of people you've never met largely on the premise of projected stereotypes. […] "white america [*sic*]"? Racist.[5]

This commentator weaponizes the liberal pieties that construe racism in atomic terms, as a transaction between two individuals, shorn of the social and institutional contexts of power. As Yancy reminds us, Black folk endure disrespect, degradation, and physical violence at the hands of white people *collectively*.[6]

---

4   White guilt is part of the structure of feeling that sutures whiteness, violence, and power. As Fred Moten writes, "bad conscience is the self's familiar spirit, accompanying it, as its necessary and irreducible supplement, not merely as a reaction to the self's enveloping use of force but as, itself, the very force, the very power that animates relation in and as unbridled use" (*Black and Blur* [Durham: Duke University Press, 2017], 250).

5   Will End, Los Angeles, December 28, 2015, comment on Yancy, "Dear White America."

6   If I resort to the Du Boisian expression, it is not in order to flaunt my seduction by the monolithic fetish of the other endemic to dominant

The targets of anti-Black racism are intimate and definite (this man, this woman, these children), while white supremacy's ideological force derives from sedimented material arrangements and a cluster of mythic ideas that, even in the absence of explicit judgments, cloak Black (and Black-adjacent) bodies in an aura of fear, contempt, or disgust. But in calling Yancy a racist, the white commentator insists on a symmetry between anti-Black racism and Yancy's attribution of a single, definite property (i.e., being racist) to "white America" as a collective. Such responses demonstrate, of course, the feints and dodges of white fragility. At the same time, these responses show the tenacity of the white person's, and especially the white cishet man's, commitment to what James Baldwin calls "the tyranny of his mirror."[7]

Outside the nominal civility enforced by the moderators at the *New York Times,* these performances of aggrieved whiteness turned more violent, disclosing the white supremacist in his true colors.[8] Yancy was subject, in the days and weeks following his letter's publication, to a barrage of threats and harassment.

discourse. Rather, I mean to appeal to the dignity that Du Bois sought to grant his subjects (including, of course, himself). A dignity to be reclaimed, with each enunciation, from the violence by which the subjects of white supremacy (including, of course, myself) designate those whose designation as others shores up the former's putative humanity.

7   James Baldwin, "The Fire Next Time," in *Collected Essays,* ed. Toni Morrison (New York: Library of America, 1998), 341. In that mirror, Blackness appears as "the shadow projected by [the] white subject to produce himself as subject" (Michelle M. Wright, *Becoming Black: Creating Identity in the African Diaspora* [Durham: Duke University Press, 2004], 113). On "white fragility" as the state of susceptibility to "racial stress," which stems from white people's privileged lack of exposure to such stress, see Robin DiAngelo, "White Fragility," *The International Journal of Critical Pedagogy* 3, no. 3 (2011): 54–70. As DiAngelo notes, white fragility breeds "a range of defensive moves" in the white person who is unprepared and unwilling to engage with the topic of race or with situations in which white privilege is made explicit or called into question (54).

8   See Mike King, "Aggrieved Whiteness: White Identity Politics and Modern American Racial Formation," *Abolition,* May 4, 2017, https://abolitionjournal.org/aggrieved-whiteness-white-identity-politics-and-modern-american-racial-formation/.

I quote from Yancy's sampling of these responses because they shed a sulfurous light on what lurks below the surface of whiteness in its more composed guises. One piece of hate mail, signed "the white guy," reads,

> All your studies have forced me to examine my self image and my white racist mind. You clearly state that no matter what I think, I'm a racist. OK, cool…thank you for clearing that up. Now I am forced to say, because you tell me I can say nothing else […]![9]

The address then veers into overt hate speech — "designed," as Yancy observes, "to violate, to leave [him] psychologically broken and physically distraught" — which I don't reproduce here, not wanting to reiterate harm.[10] I quote the foregoing in order to consider the logic (if you can call it that) that the writer invokes as though to authorize their use of the expletive and its violence, a violence that their rhetoric suggests is otherwise barely kenneled by the norms of white masculinity, expressing a kind of salivating, frequently murderous impulse. In the grip of this impulse, the privilege to have the last word becomes, perversely, the conviction that one "can say nothing else." As Yancy's letter suggests, my white readers and I need to reckon with the idea that such speech-acts are intimate with, rather than anomalous to, performances of whiteness that inhabit the hegemonic space of modern subjectivity.[11]

---

9   Quoted in Justin Weinberg, "Internet Abuse of Philosophers (2 Updates),"
    Daily Nous, January 15, 2016, http://dailynous.com/2016/01/15/internet-abuse-of-philosophers/.
10 George Yancy and Brad Evans, "The Perils of Being a Black Philosopher,"
    The Stone (*The New York Times*), April 18, 2016, https://opinionator.blogs.nytimes.com/2016/04/18/the-perils-of-being-a-black-philosopher/.
11 I am entertaining the possibility that the passage in question is not the utterance of a particularly "abnormal" individual, nor even of an open and avowed racist, but rather that it belongs to someone who is in other respects an unremarkable specimen of twenty-first-century white American masculinity.

For doesn't the slur peek out from behind the word "racist" in the first comment quoted above? Calling a Black writer racist for their calling out whites' anti-Black racism is a bit like donning blackface. Albeit an angry blackface, a mode of minstrelsy that caricatures Black resistance to white supremacy as the work of charlatans out to defraud the (white) American public. As though *white* people haven't, in fact, "staked [their] entire career on that color always mattering." But as in the second comment, a catachrestic logic collapses Yancy's address to a generalized, plural *you* (white America) with a personal address. Indeed, these readers register Yancy's critique as a personal affront, an offense inviting a deeply visceral response. What aggrieves both readers is the specter of their own racialized particularity, the vulnerability of their white flesh to its inflection by the grammar of another person's speech-acts. One would like to point out to them, as Yancy has already pointed out, that the bodies of people of color remain vulnerable to particularization by race in ways that white bodies hardly ever are. "[A]ttacked as a *black man,*" Yancy is remanded, as it were, to the custody of his own body, which is a site marked by America's dominant institutions for shame, degradation, and trauma, if not incarceration and death.[12] A body coded by white people as an existential threat.

12 Ibid. (emphasis in the original). On the phenomenology of the Black body, see also Frantz Fanon, *Black Skin, White Masks,* trans. Richard Philcox, rev. edn. (New York: Grove Press, 2008); Gordon, *Bad Faith and Antiblack Racism*; Charles Johnson, "A Phenomenology of the Black Body," *Michigan Quarterly Review* 32, no. 4 (1993): 599–614; Sylvia Wynter, "Towards the Sociogenic Principle: Fanon, Identity, the Puzzle of Conscious Experience, and What It Is Like to Be 'Black,'" in *National Identities and Sociopolitical Changes in Latin America,* eds. Mercedes F. Durán-Cogan and Antonio Gómez-Moriana (New York: Routledge, 2001), 30–66; and Yancy, *Black Bodies, White Gazes.* For approaches that address embodiment from a Black feminist perspective, see Rizvana Bradley, "Living in the Absence of a Body: The (Sus)Stain of Black Female (W)holeness," *Rhizomes: Cultural Studies in Emerging Knowledge* 29 (2016); Denise Ferreira da Silva, "Hacking the Subject: Black Feminism and Refusal beyond the Limits of Critique," *PhiloSOPHIA* 8, no. 1 (2018): 19–41; Evelynn Hammonds, "Black (W)Holes and the Geometry of Black Female Sexuality," *differences: A*

As a white man reading Yancy's letter, I have a duty to acknowledge that the experience of this kind of embodiment lies beyond my ken, though not beyond my responsibility.

Some (white) people would decry the comments I have cited as evidence of the fraying of civility, or an atavistic eruption of hate that threatens the social contract. Others would rightly point out, as Yancy has done, how they extend and magnify a history of white supremacist violence. The social contract may be fraying, but the affects uttered by such voices do not occupy the fringes of the national imaginary. Nor is a logic of scarcity sufficient to explain the reproduction and circulation of white male rage in all its vicissitudes.[13] Such a logic underestimates the force and ferocity of this rage no less than its strategic goals. Whether behind a badge or on 4chan, on the playground or in the bully pulpit, white boys and men leverage public structures of racist and misogynist feeling in order to defend and consolidate their privilege. Accounts of white supremacy must attend to how these affects move and spread, how they accumulate within the most apparently rational edifices, how they take hold of old forms and structures and reanimate them. They seep under our skin. They distort the haptic bandwidth of human contact. They function as a viscous barrier that teaches us not to feel what we feel.[14] In this essay, I take up Yancy's invitation to "quiet that

Journal of Feminist Cultural Studies 6, nos. 2–3 (1994): 126–45; Hortense J. Spillers, "Mama's Baby, Papa's Maybe: An American Grammar Book," in *Black, White, and in Color: Essays on American Literature and Culture* (Chicago: University of Chicago Press, 2003), 203–29; and Alexander G. Weheliye, *Habeas Viscus: Racializing Assemblages, Biopolitics, and Black Feminist Theories of the Human* (Durham: Duke University Press, 2014).

13 According to the logic of scarcity, uncivil or violent outbursts by otherwise tame liberal subjects stem from lack: a lack of education, a lack of (respect for, exposure to) the facts, or in more materialist terms, a lack of economic opportunity. If we want to talk about lack, we need to account for a lack that functions as a principle of structure and also as that structure's displacement into the violence of its effects.

14 On the limitations of "cognitivist frameworks" for understanding white supremacy's "hegemonic emotional economies," see Paula Ioanide, *The Emotional Politics of Racism: How Feelings Trump Facts in an Era of*

voice that will speak to you of your white 'innocence,'" inflecting his invitation with Christina Sharpe's powerful question: "What happens when we proceed as if we *know* this, antiblackness, to

Colorblindness (Stanford: Stanford University Press, 2015), 12–16. I don't mean to suggest that white men are the only people who give vent to anger in defense of their privilege, nor do I mean to overlook what a properly intersectional analysis might teach us about the differential consequences of such a defense for people occupying different subject-positions relative to that privilege. White women as a group reap material benefits from the racist elements of institutional white supremacy, if not from its patriarchal and misogynistic features, even though some white women defend it on both fronts. Likewise, men of color can assert patriarchal privileges vis-à-vis women of color (though not, of course, unilaterally), even though in some situations, e.g., when confronted by the police, that masculinity becomes a liability, not an asset.

But the position of "the white guy" in the social hierarchy entails, by default, a resistance to seeing the world in intersectional terms. And if the violence, intimidation, and public terror wrought by white men, especially white cishet men, seems, in the present moment, to have gone off the charts, we would do well to recall the sanguinary history of patriarchal white supremacy in the United States. We would do well to remember the brutality of the slave-holders' state, the segregationists' state, and the carceral capitalists' state that recapitulates them both. And we would do well to remember the role that organized paramilitary groups of white men (e.g., the Ku Klux Klan) have played in extending the state's power to terrify, maim, incapacitate, and kill. On the violence of enslavement, my understanding is indebted to Saidiya V. Hartman, *Scenes of Subjection: Terror, Slavery, and Self-Making in Nineteenth-Century America* (New York: Oxford University Press, 2010); and Edward E. Baptist, *The Half Has Never Been Told: Slavery and the Making of American Capitalism* (New York: Basic Books, 2016). A keystone for analyses of slavery in terms of its production of the racialized and gendered body is Spillers's essay "Mama's Baby, Papa's Maybe." On white supremacy and the history of extra-judicial racist terror, I would refer the reader to Ida B. Wells, *The Light of Truth: Writings of an Anti-Lynching Crusader,* eds. Mia Bay and Henry Louis Gates, Jr. (New York: Penguin Books, 2014); Philip Dray, *At the Hands of Persons Unknown: The Lynching of Black America,* rpt. edn. (New York: Modern Library, 2003); and Robyn Wiegman, *American Anatomies: Theorizing Race and Gender* (Durham: Duke University Press, 2002). On the latter-day iterations of this history in the white power movement, see Kathleen Belew, *Bring the War Home: The White Power Movement and Paramilitary America* (Cambridge: Harvard University Press, 2018).

be the ground on which we stand, the ground from which we attempt to speak, for instance, an 'I' or a 'we' who know, an 'I' or a 'we' who care?"[15] But the *I* and *we* of Sharpe's invocation are not automatically, unproblematically available to me if I am to quiet the voice of innocence that plots in me, Iago-like, against the other. White innocence articulates part of white supremacy's schemes. Its feeling comports with a certain calculating reason.

In what follows, I propose to understand the "ground from which we attempt to speak" as white supremacy in its entanglement with bureaucratic-capitalist rationality.[16] The latter I approach, à la Wittgenstein, as a kind of grammar, productive of ways of picturing the world. This grammar privileges what can be made explicit, in the form of rules, norms, standards, formulae, and procedures. But what disappears from, or remains illegible in, the pictures so produced? At the beginning of the twentieth century, Max Weber defined bureaucracy as the organization of knowledge in the service of domination. By separating the possession of legal and institutional authority from qualities inherent in, or attached to, a person (such as nobility or charisma) — by teasing apart, at least on paper, power's exercise from its embodiment — bureaucracy makes domination

15   Yancy, "Dear White America"; Christina Sharpe, *In the Wake: On Blackness and Being* (Durham: Duke University Press, 2016), 7.

16   For the lineaments of this argument, I am indebted to the work of Ronald Takaki, George Lipsitz, and David Graeber, as well as Theodor Adorno and Max Horkheimer's critiques of enlightened reason. Ronald T. Takaki, *Iron Cages: Race and Culture in 19th-Century America,* rev. edn. (New York: Oxford University Press, 2000); George Lipsitz, *The Possessive Investment in Whiteness: How White People Profit from Identity Politics,* rev. and exp. edn. (Philadelphia: Temple University Press, 2006); David Graeber, *The Utopia of Rules: On Technology, Stupidity, and the Secret Joys of Bureaucracy* (New York: Melville House, 2015); Max Horkheimer and Theodor W. Adorno, *Dialectic of Enlightenment: Philosophical Fragments,* ed. Gunzelin Schmid Noerr, trans. Edmund Jephcott (Stanford: Stanford University Press, 2002). See also Kathy E. Ferguson, *The Feminist Case against Bureaucracy* (Philadelphia: Temple University Press, 1984).

particularly effective.[17] But in Weber's picture, we can discern an impulse to disembody domination. The theory of bureaucratic rationality makes domination seem both transparent and devoid of meaning. As a property of reason itself, or a condition of reason's efficient operation, domination becomes, like one of Kant's Categories, something the causes for which we cannot seek, the consequences of which we must accept. But relations of domination and subordination are never *not* embodied. And in the twenty-first-century United States, bureaucratic reason — in the design of economic policy, in the running of schools, in the management of infrastructure and public services, in the administration of prisons and the police — remains intimate with the everyday violence of patriarchal white supremacy.[18] Like the rabbit in Wittgenstein's account of aspect, such violence functions as the overlooked aspect in the pictures traced by bureaucratic grammars. Trained *not* to notice it, we who profit from the domination of others ignore the labor they do that sustains domination's transparency to itself. Just as we ignore the resistance that they mount to their own domination. The latter is a repertoire of fugitive creativity, the gifts of which are so central to modern culture that they can rightly be said to represent modernity's measure of itself.[19] Meanwhile, this unmeasured ignorance, this innocence born of domination, has an edge: a kind of anger stipples the back of the head; an appetite for others' suffering bristles at the base of the spine.[20] If the President of the

17 Max Weber, *Economy and Society: An Outline of Interpretive Sociology,* eds. Guenther Roth and Claus Wittich (Berkeley: University of California Press, 1978), 2:956–58.

18 See Dean Spade, *Normal Life: Administrative Violence, Critical Trans Politics, and the Limits of Law* (Brooklyn: South End Press, 2011).

19 Nahum Dimitri Chandler, "Originary Displacement," *boundary 2* 27, no. 3 (2000): 249–86; Fred Moten, *In the Break: The Aesthetics of the Black Radical Tradition* (Minneapolis: University of Minnesota Press, 2003); Clyde Woods, *Development Arrested: The Blues and Plantation Power in the Mississippi Delta* (New York: Verso, 2017).

20 In Eve Kosofsky Sedgwick's memorable words, "obtuseness arms the powerful against their enemies" ("Privilege of Unknowing," *Genders* 1

United States sounds like a schoolyard bully, perhaps it should not surprise us. Perhaps the troll is the technocrat in a different guise.

The link that Sharpe makes between knowledge and care requires, for me, disrupting my sense of innocence. But that shouldn't mean replacing innocence with a conviction of my own irretrievable fallenness. I mustn't confuse cynicism for knowledge, or melancholy for care.[21] In order to make space for that link and for the voices of those who know and care, I have sought in what follows to leave argument and critical analysis open to what occurs in the interstices of the explicit, via a series of encounters with the work of some poets—Claudia Rankine, Dionne Brand, and Tracie Morris—and the composer Julius Eastman.[22] Their work, as I read it, is addressed to fugitive practices of reading and listening. It realizes a labor of critical resistance but also recuperation, drawing strength from multiple aesthetic registers and layered traditions of Black women's and Black queer survival and flourishing. Borrowing from Morris, I cite these works in the spirit of *handholding*.[23] I take her word to refer to a non-possessive way of holding, an intimacy of entanglement that centers tactility and care. As a gesture between people, handholding suggests a picture of the social that belies the priority given to the metaphysically and anatomically carved out, atomized, and epidermalized modern self.[24] As aesthetic practice, these works offer a shifted aspect of the ground from which we speak, a picture that both confounds innocence with

[Spring 1988]: 103).

21 As Linda Martín Alcoff remarks, "whiteness is not *nothing but* racism" (*The Future of Whiteness* [Cambridge: Polity Press, 2015], 98).

22 Hortense Spillers describes the interstice, in relation to Black women's experience, as "that which allows us to speak about and that which will allows us to speak at all" ("Interstices: A Small Drama of Words," in *Black, White, and in Color,* 156).

23 Tracie Morris, *handholding: 5 kinds* (Tucson: Kore Press, 2016). On fugitive reading and listening, my thinking holds hands with Fred Moten's work in particular. See Moten, *Black and Blur*; and Moten, *In the Break.*

24 On epidermalization, see Frantz Fanon, *Black Skin, White Masks,* xv.

the inevitability of its implication in processes of violence and subjugation, and summons us to the uncertainty of a knowledge that, among the plights of bondage, there exist threads of escape, lines of flight.[25]

In *Citizen,* her lyric meditation on the perils and travails of Black being in this white grimace of a nation, Claudia Rankine writes,

> The rain this morning pours from the gutters and everywhere else it is lost in the trees. You need your glasses to single out what you know is there because doubt is inexorable; you put on your glasses. The trees, their bark, their leaves, even the dead ones, are more vibrant wet. Yes, and it's raining. Each moment is like this — before it can be known, categorized as similar to another thing and dismissed, it has to be experienced, it has to be seen. What did he just say? Did she really just say that? Did I hear what I think I heard? Did that just come out of my mouth, his mouth, your mouth? The moment stinks. Still you want to stop looking at the trees. You want to walk out and stand among them. And as light as the rain seems, it still rains down on you.[26]

The grammar of bureaucratic reason privileges the flat, self-evident locution: "Yes, and it's raining." This grammar authorizes statements such as "Not all white people are racist" or even "Yes, racism still exists." These are statements that presuppose an em-

25 I am wary of calling these works, and the practices that they exemplify, a "counterdiscourse." For one, that term grants a kind of priority to the discursive that I think these works themselves defy. Moreover, as Alexander Weheliye argues, that label belies "the centrality of [...] blackness [...] to Western modernity" (*Phonographies: Grooves in Sonic Afro-Modernity* [Durham: Duke University Press, 2005], 5). Perhaps they are better considered as participating in an aesthetics and ethics of revision, re-working, re-mixing, a labor of making the modern world a more livable place.

26 Claudia Rankine, *Citizen: An American Lyric* (Minneapolis: Graywolf Press, 2014), 9.

pirical warrant or justification, where what is empirical can be presented, laid out for inspection, made explicit. The empirical participates in the hegemony of the visible, the scopic, and the specular in post-Enlightenment, Eurocentric versions of reason: "[Y]ou need your glasses to single out what you know is there."[27] But Rankine's prose focuses on the labor that produces the empirical as such: "[Y]ou put on your glasses." This labor is physical, intellectual, and affective ("you want to stop looking") all at once. The vignettes in *Citizen* render palpable how unevenly this labor is distributed. How the epistemic structures of white supremacy involve an ignorance/innocence that strands people of color in the plight of constantly having to make explicit to themselves and others what white subjects refuse to see. Inexorably recurring, this plight unravels the trust held between the flesh and its world ("Did that just come out of my mouth, his mouth, your mouth?"). But the necessity of experience, figured here as the subject's inexorable burden, also suggests, or summons, a kind of sensate grammar, a tactile bridge to the world in its fugitive becoming ("as light as the rain seems, it still rains down on you"). In this still-ness of the light rain, fugitivity persists as the freedom of the flesh to be elsewhere than here and otherwise than itself.

white wages and a speaking rage

As W.E.B. Du Bois pointed out long ago, white supremacy amounts to a kind of civil religion for modernity, and the republican norms of rational deliberation and informed consent have never sounded in this country without the background hum of racist (and racializing misogynist) violence. What Du Bois calls the "public and psychological wage" of whiteness encourages

---

27 On the ocularity of racializing reason, see Wiegman, *American Anatomies*; and Harryette Mullen, "Optic White: Blackness and the Production of Whiteness," *Diacritics* 24, nos. 2–3 (1994): 71–89.

white people to cultivate a sense of superiority to, and dominion over, those who would otherwise be their social equals.[28] As a *wage,* whiteness — and more particularly, able-bodied, middle-class, white, cishet masculinity — is experienced as a personal possession. The wage shores up a sense of possessive, transparent interiority. Such a sense of transparent interiority, as Denise Ferriera da Silva argues, remains fundamental to Eurocentric notions of the self, and the possession of whiteness (and its allied norms) is construed as integral to that self-authorizing transparency.[29] Moreover, the wage teaches us who benefit from it that the meaning of our privilege entails the privacy of its meaning. Whiteness functions as the mirror's tain, the mirror in whose tyrannical clear glass we are taught to perceive ourselves. That very clarity blocks the development of habits of empathy with those whose image whiteness seems not to reflect. But the function of the wage is not to clear a space, by force of exclusion, for the realization, by those remaining, of freedom and equality.

28 W.E.B. Du Bois, *Black Reconstruction in America: An Essay toward a History of the Part Which Black Folk Played in the Attempt to Reconstruct Democracy in America, 1860–1880* (New York: Atheneum, 1977), 700–701. The wage, in the form of white supremacy, grants all whites, irrespective of social class, a degree of license that is withheld from Black folk and others marked as non-white. In addition to access to goods and spaces more or less reserved for white use, and a degree of leniency from the law with respect to infractions for which Black (and Black-adjacent) people are more severely and routinely punished, the wage includes the license to abuse, demean, or actively discriminate against non-whites. In tandem with the privileges afforded cishet masculinity, the white wage serves the white male ruling elite by dividing the working class against itself, while justifying the exploitation of labor on which elite rule depends. For a thorough historical treatment of white supremacy as a lure used by elites to secure the cooperation of the white working class, see David R. Roediger, *The Wages of Whiteness: Race and the Making of the American Working Class* (London: Verso, 2007).

29 Denise Ferreira da Silva, *Toward a Global Idea of Race* (Minneapolis: University of Minnesota Press, 2007). On the "possessive logics" of whiteness, see also Aileen Moreton-Robinson, *The White Possessive: Property, Power, and Indigenous Sovereignty* (Minneapolis: University of Minnesota Press, 2015), xi–xii.

(The lie of the wage is that freedom and equality obey a logic of scarcity. Believing this lie is the price of its enjoyment.) The wage functions, rather, to justify the saturation of a putatively democratic space by the capillary forces of domination and hierarchy. Polished by racism and its force-multipliers, misogyny, homophobia, transphobia, xenophobia, classism, and ableism, the mirror of whiteness instills emulation, envy, and competition as the body's destiny. It summons us to a stunted achievement, a *mise en abyme.*

"The dominant know plenty" about their roles in domination, a knowledge that is lodged in the body's carriage, that flecks the senses, that thrills the nerves.[30] But the wage binds them to a refusal to be held accountable for the consequences of their roles. This is true even when the facts of this consequence are themselves ready to hand, collected and made explicit by the same bureaucratic practices that keep whites' wages secure.[31] This tactical ignorance amounts to another kind of tacit knowl-

---

30 Moon-Kie Jung, *Beneath the Surface of White Supremacy: Denaturalizing U.S. Racisms Past and Present* (Stanford: Stanford University Press, 2015), 23. The enjoyment of embodied social privilege and power is perhaps most often, though certainly not always, present to the subject as a kind of negative liberty, as a freedom from constraints imposed on others. This negative liberty also carries, in virtue of its structural conditions, a negating force. That is to say, its enjoyment is inextricably tied to the deprivation of others' liberties. Others are followed and discounted and policed because I, qua white person, am not.

31 For instance, Moon-Kie Jung points to the white American public's general indifference to the systematic underemployment in Black communities — a measure of well-being that is readily recorded in a number of official statistical sources — and compares this indifference to the recurrent panics about unemployment that are triggered whenever the latter afflicts white communities in particular (*Beneath the Surface of White Supremacy,* 141–68). Even when represented as fact, the suffering of the oppressed cannot transcend its facticity in the dominant imagination, cannot become tragedy. Consider by contrast what qualified 9/11 for its role as national trauma. It was an attack on the very heart of elite (white) economic power, and its victims included members of those working-class professions whose iconic masculinity remains closely allied with the powers of the state (firefighters and police). The attack got the nation hot under its

edge, a knowing how not to know. It grants those who inhabit it, especially white cishet men, a wide latitude for interpretive license: the freedom to believe in all manner of good stories about the self and the world. Yet this license belies a fragility, a proneness to the fanaticism that chants, in defense of whiteness, "Amen!" When challenged to justify their privileges, white men's wage becomes their *rage,* experienced as justified anger over a violation of their property rights. Aristotle defines anger as a "man's" desire for revenge against those who have "slighted" the "man himself or one of his friends."[32] The slight in question must be, according to Aristotle, "undeserved," suggesting that what's at stake are the goods (the wages) that one expects to receive in respect of one's social position. And what matters is not only the nature of the slight but the status of the person delivering it, insofar as "men think that they have a right to be highly esteemed by those who are inferior to them."[33] When someone calls the phrase "white America" racist, or when someone identifies with the beleaguered voice of patriarchal white supremacy ("As always, the white guy"), their responses reflect the grievances of the dominant when the oppressed dare address them as equals. The assertion that "[j]ust because someone has a skin color that doesn't mean that skin color means anything" does not deny the meaning of skin color. It denies the right of another (Yancy) to interpret (to slight) that (white) color's meaning. In other words, the vehemence of this denial has everything to do with the meaning of *Yancy's* skin color, and with what *that* implies about the latter's right to pass judgment on white men. For the fragility of the wage is at stake. As if by being made explicit, it is made vulnerable, like a magic charm that works only

white collar, so to speak, as well as the version of its blue collar that white American men still pop with pride.

32 Aristotle, *The "Art" of Rhetoric,* trans. John Henry Freese (Cambridge: Harvard University Press, 1926), 173.

33 Ibid., 177.

if no one thinks of it as such.[34] Likewise, a verbal challenge from someone without the wage seems to have mythic power, as if Yancy's words could conjure racism *into* his white readers: "I am forced to say [a racist epithet], because you tell me I can say nothing else."

Social and political domination, as Aristotle's analysis suggests, entails not only a monopoly on physical violence, but also a monopoly on interpretation. The legitimacy of anger is secured by social hierarchy. One is angered (justly) by the judgments of another who is not positioned to pass judgment on one, or whose express judgments do not convey the respect that one is due.[35] As a corollary, "those who do not get angry at things at which it is right to be angry are thought to be foolish, and so are those who do not get angry in the right manner, at the right time, or with the right people."[36] For Aristotle, there is a propriety to anger that attaches to social position. And yet, if anger regularly afflicts the subjects of social privilege and power, so much so that it seems to be the signature affect of such subjectivity, given anger's suture to ideas about honor and respect, then anger's centrality to the practices of domination suggests that the monopoly at their heart teeters on the verge of a violence that undoes its claim to reason. Your typical white guy should be *less* prone to anger than other people, given his access to the lion's share of social privilege. But the anger of white guys is not only over the top; it also displays a demonic infelicity, re-

34 On the property interest in whiteness as social status, see Cheryl I. Harris, "Whiteness as Property," *Harvard Law Review* 106, no. 8 (1993): 1707–91. On the "magic talisman" of white supremacy, see Ta-Nehisi Coates, "The First White President," *The Atlantic,* October 2017, https://www.theatlantic. com/magazine/archive/2017/10/the-first-white-president-ta-nehisi-coates/537909/.

35 Aristotle doesn't say whether a slave in Athens can, or should, be angry for the perpetual insult that is enslavement, or whether an Athenian woman can harbor rage over her exclusion from the full rights of citizenship.

36 Aristotle, *The Nicomachean Ethics,* trans. H. Rackham (Cambridge: Harvard University Press, 1926), 231.

vealing what the writers claim to deny.[37] Asserting their monopoly on interpretations of whiteness, they reveal the dependence of whiteness on its racialized others. This dependence, with its violently unequal conditions of intimacy, breeds an asymmetry of knowledge and judgment, as James Baldwin, with his usual trenchant poignancy, explains:

> [T]here is, thereafter, forever, a witness somewhere: which is an irreducible inconvenience for the makers and shakers and accomplices of this world. These run together, in packs, and corroborate each other. They cannot bear the judgments in the eyes of the people whom they intend to hold in bondage forever, and who know more about them than their lovers. This remote, public, and as it were, principled, bondage is the indispensable justification of their own: when the prisoner is free, the jailer faces the void of himself.[38]

In calling out racism, the witness demands a reckoning from those who make and shake whiteness into a world. A reckoning with the thing that whites must keep mum about. For control over what can be said aloud, written down, or otherwise dragged or coerced into explicitness is one of the enabling conditions of the power to hold others in bondage. As M. Jacqui Alexander writes, the option always stands open to the powerful "to pretend that there was never any locution and to behave as if what was said carried no weight."[39] But their dominance depends on those who must, at dawn and day's end and during

---

37 On the "demonic" as the "unfreely disclosed," see Søren Kierkegaard, *The Concept of Anxiety: A Simple Psychologically Orienting Deliberation on the Dogmatic Issue of Hereditary Sin,* eds. and trans. Reidar Thomte and Albert B. Anderson (Princeton: Princeton University Press, 1980), 123.

38 James Baldwin, "The Devil Finds Work," in *Collected Essays,* ed. Toni Morrison (New York: Library of America, 1998), 563.

39 M. Jacqui Alexander, *Pedagogies of Crossing: Meditations on Feminism, Sexual Politics, Memory, and the Sacred* (Durham: Duke University Press, 2005), 159.

all the hours in between, cope with this behavior. Who bear the weight of bondage, not only as a curtailment of their freedom, but also as a form of terrible knowledge, needing to be spoken of in order to be avoided, a thing to which the idea of explicitness is hardly adequate, the "Danger" sign that identifies the sheer drop beyond the cliff's edge.[40] This demand for reckoning, when presented to the white subject as a means of loosening the thing's hold on them, prompts the latter to make their commitments to that thing explicit in the act of disavowing it. Even as they insist that this thing, whiteness or white supremacy, *cannot* be made explicit because it does not exist.

There is violence there, unacknowledged by those who carry it in themselves, where it waits, one slip of the tongue or finger's twitch away from ruining someone's day or destroying someone's life. And if those in bondage know their captors better than their captors are known by their lovers, this fact tells us something about the kinds of love that comport with the captor's place. And it reminds us that bondage, even when "remote, public, and as it were, principled," remains a deeply embodied relation. In the words of Saidiya Hartman, "the bounded bodily integrity of whiteness [is] secured by the abjection of others."[41] Hate speech is illustrative in this respect. The speech-act produces (by reiterating) the incommensurability of social positions that might otherwise be thought to speak from a shared ground.[42] Hate speech, like other racist acts, shatters the chance for reciprocity. Back-and-forth, even of a confrontational sort, becomes untenable. In hurling an epithet or making a threat,

---

40 As David Graeber observes, "[t]hose on the bottom [...] have to spend a great deal of imaginative energy trying to understand the social dynamics that surround them — including having to imagine the perspectives of those on top — while the latter can wander about largely oblivious to much of what is going on around them" (*The Utopia of Rules,* 81).

41 Hartman, *Scenes of Subjection,* 123.

42 As Sianne Ngai notes, questions about the range of proper affective responses to acts of racism expose "a symbolic violence in the principle of commensurability itself" (*Ugly Feelings* [Cambridge: Harvard University Press, 2007], 188).

the speaker ventriloquizes the power of the law and the state in their capacity to declare the state of exception, to carve out the boundaries of bodily integrity that protect some and exclude others from these protections.[43] Even if the target doesn't feel physically endangered, there is, structurally speaking, no adequate comeback. As Patricia Williams writes, recounting her experience of being turned away from a Benetton in New York by a white clerk, "There was almost nothing I could do […] that would humiliate him the way he humiliated me. No words, no gestures, no prejudices of my own would make a bit of difference to him."[44] The propriety of anger is open (like the Benetton store) only to members of the dominant group, and the targets of hate speech and other racist acts might be said to suffer from an impropriety that inflects, and infects, every possible response. At least, that is the intended effect of such acts. They seek to render another maximally affectable, i.e., prey to an onslaught of affects (Williams describes feeling "a blizzard of rage") that forecloses them from a subject position defined by reason's transparent articulation onto social hierarchy.[45] Thus, Yancy's attackers in the comments thread and elsewhere seek to disable, rather than refute, his argument, insisting that as a Black person, reason is not his to claim.[46]

And yet, in their bid to claim sovereignty by way of others' abjection, these movers and shakers and minions and alibis are "forced" to disclose a vulnerability that the other's abjection is meant to remove. Security by abjection is, we might say, inher-

---

43 On the "ventriloquism" of power by its accomplices, see Alexander, *Pedagogies of Crossing,* 167–68. On Giorgio Agamben's concept of the "state of exception" and its function in modernity's "racializing assemblages," see Weheliye, *Habeas Viscus,* 53–75.

44 Patricia J. Williams, *The Alchemy of Race and Rights* (Cambridge: Harvard University Press, 1991), 45.

45 Ibid. On the affectable and the transparent as mutually exclusive positions occupied by racialized subjects, see Ferreira da Silva, *Toward a Global Idea of Race.*

46 Alexander theorizes this process of "illocutionary disablement," drawing on the work of Rae Langton, in *Pedagogies of Crossing,* 123–24.

ently unstable, since it requires violence or the threat of violence to sustain it. Between the power of judgment and judgments of power, the chiasmus discloses a chasm. Speaking into/out of this chasm, echoing the redundant and tautological force that speaks him, the subject of white supremacy can "say nothing else," nothing other than whiteness, which, per Baldwin, is only another name for the "void in himself," or the raw place that chafes so easily beneath the call for justice because that call exposes the self's habitual forms of justification as a farce. Admittedly, the temptation of this kind of analysis runs us into the danger of evacuating the other's agency, too, with the result that the whole scene appears overdetermined, devoid of escape. But for what it's worth, that's not my intention. Rather, I am thinking about the other's agency in these scenarios (Yancy's agency, or Williams's) as a kind of (un)originary problem for modernity and for modernity's most privileged subjects.[47] We might posit that resistance to the seduction of another's agency or judgment constitutes, in general, the hard kernel of a privileged and dominant subjectivity, precisely because without the other's judgment, the structure (of privilege, of dominance) as such would not exist.[48] But where the other's judgment concerns the justice of privilege itself (and not just the validity of one's claim to it), we might imagine that this subject, sometimes at least, receives this judgment as a shock. In such moments, even someone packed tightly into his white cishet masculine flesh, corroborated from crown to toe, might feel the stink of the moment as their stink,

47 See Chandler, "Originary Displacement." I am thinking also here of Fred Moten's thinking about Blackness and the Black avant-garde as "the ongoing event of an antiorigin and an anteorigin, replay and reverb of an impossible natal occasion" (*In the Break,* 14).

48 Resistance to the other's judgment is different from indifference to it. One might suppose that someone self-assured in either his feelings of superiority to people of color or in his freedom from such feelings would not be bothered by the charge of racism, much less by "white America's" being so accused. By his resistance, however, the subject shows what he *needs* — i.e., the deference, if not the approval, of the other — even as he strives to appear above needing it.

and the motions they go through, as the ragged jerk of a marionette: standing their ground, secretly wanting comfort, yet face to face with the desperate, forsworn knowledge that, here and now, there is no *there* there.

a cage of speech

Imagine two anonymous people, A and B. Anonymous, but not unmarked, not without position. For the first is the one in charge (a teacher, a trainer, or a manager) and the second a subordinate (a student or a worker or an apprentice). Their working relationship at this moment answers to an apparently simple division of labor. B "has to write down a series of signs according to a certain formation rule" as furnished by A.[49] The rule doesn't matter, except that it must be explicit. Suppose it is the arithmetic function: $x_n = x_{n-1} + 2$. (The scene is a sort of test, perhaps a qualifying exam, preparatory to B's being allowed to do a certain kind of task.) After writing down a long sequence, B makes a mistake. They write down the wrong sign: "1004," instead of "1002." In exasperation, pointing to the mistake, A declares that B "doesn't understand" the rule. A insists that they "meant" for B to do otherwise.[50] At this stage in Wittgenstein's *Philosophical Investigations,* the inquiry concerns the grammar of the words *meaning* and *understanding*. But like many of Wittgenstein's examples, this one is also about labor and power. It touches on, however obliquely to Wittgenstein's own intentions (and what, he might ask, do we *mean* by that?), a certain grammar of domination. And this grammar, in its serial, self-evident redundancy, iterates over the asymmetry that sutures understanding to socio-political standing and that binds meaning to acts of possession and the defense of property.

49 Ludwig Wittgenstein, *Philosophical Investigations,* trans. G.E.M. Anscombe, 3rd edn. (Malden: Wiley-Blackwell, 1991), 48.
50 Ibid., 63.

"What you are saying, then, comes to this: a new insight — intuition — is needed at every step to carry out the order '+n' correctly." — To carry it out correctly! How is it decided what is the right step to take at any particular stage? — "The right step is the one that accords with the order — as it was *meant.*" — So when you gave the order +2 you also meant that he was to write 1002 after 1000 — and did you also mean that he should write 1868 after 1866, and 100036 after 100034, and so on — an infinite number of such propositions? — "No: what I meant was, that he should write the next but one number after every number that he wrote; and from this all those propositions follow in turn." — But that is just what is in question: what, at any stage, does follow from that sentence.[51]

The grammar of domination requires that one be prepared to give certain kinds of answers to the question of what follows from a sentence. It requires that one entertain a certain picture of what it means to make, to be authorized to make, a decision. Partaking of that "white managerial masculinity [that] travels everywhere," *A* feels that their instructions explicate a rule, and that this explication is both necessary and sufficient to understand *B*'s role in the process.[52] *A* would endorse Weber's claim that in bureaucracy, "the management of the office follows *general rules,* which are more or less stable, more or less exhaustive, and which can be learned."[53] That the rules can be learned does not vitiate the necessity of hierarchy. Following the rules requires mastery, but in relation to the work that they direct and oversee, Weber's managers must have mastered more *general* rules, or mastered them more thoroughly, than the people they manage. The rules remain management's intellectual property.[54]

---

51 Ibid., 64.
52 Alexander, *Pedagogies of Crossing,* 139.
53 Weber, *Economy and Society,* 2:958 (emphasis in the original).
54 As Pete Richardson concludes, "[m]anagement insists that it is properly in control of the conception, of what work should be done" ("Doing Things with Wood: Builders, Managers and Wittgenstein in an Idaho Sawmill,"

With managerial foresight, *A* asserts, "I already knew, at the time when I gave the order, that [*B*] ought to write 1002 after 1000."[55] *B*'s work becomes evident *as work* — as a thing performed by another person — only in its deviation from *A*'s rules. In order to lay claim to their authority, the manager must be able to have meant his rule in a different way (a "*unique* way", Wittgenstein says) from how their subordinate would be capable of meaning it. And yet, the manager's meaning must be available to both parties if the work is to get done, i.e., if managerial authority is to succeed. This fugitive parity both underwrites and undercuts the manager's place.

Jacques Rancière insists that this parity reveals a revolutionary potential latent within the grammar of domination. From the fact that "the inferior has understood the superior's order," we can deduce that "the inferior takes part in the same community of speaking beings and so is, in this sense, their equal."[56] But following Wittgenstein, we might say that this proposition

Critique of Anthropology 29, no. 2 [June 1, 2009]: 173). Bureaucracy, then, exhibits in a fashion internal to itself the features of the modern liberal social contract governing the relationship between state, citizens, and the people. Vine Deloria, Jr. argues that "in the form in which the men who framed the Constitution received it, the philosophy of social contract was oriented wholly toward a certain restricted class of individuals and could neither include any divergent groups nor provide any significant guidance or protection for the mass of people. Its primary virtue was to encourage a clever, established elite to benefit at the expense of others and perpetuate itself" ("Minorities and the Social Contract," *Georgia Law Review* 20 [1986]: 919).

55 Wittgenstein, *Philosophical Investigations,* 64.

56 Jacques Rancière, *Disagreement: Politics and Philosophy,* trans. Julie Rose (Minneapolis: University of Minnesota Press, 2008), 49. In a distinct but related vein, Nahum Dimitri Chandler argues that "'[c]ontrol,' especially 'absolute' control, over someone else's intention requires recognition of that intention: There is no need to control that intention which has no force" ("Originary Displacement," 281). Chandler's attention to force troubles Rancière's appeal to equality as what characterizes the "community of speaking beings." Chandler might insist that there is no appeal to equality that is not already (borrowing a figure from Fred Moten) cut by the operation of this force.

is precisely what is in question. How are we to understand this sense of equality, and what might follow from laying claim to, or being cut by, such a sense? And turning the question on Wittgenstein himself, we might ask, what kind of therapeutic engagement does the philosopher pursue in this section of his text, and why does it focus only on *A*?[57] Why does *A* need the therapy? Or if their need appears self-evident, why does it trump *B*'s need, whom the text denies a voice? If *A* represents the standpoint of the reader to whom the *Investigations* is addressed, or if *A* represents a version of the philosophical inner voice we are to imagine as in dialogue with the more properly Wittgensteinian one, what does *B*'s silencing say about the presuppositions of voice and standpoint in Eurocentric modern thought?[58] Fred Moten remarks on the "fundamental disqualification" besetting the one

57 My reading of Wittgenstein is closely informed by Stanley Cavell, who explores the notion of Wittgenstein's therapeutic aims in great depth in *The Claim of Reason: Wittgenstein, Skepticism, Morality, and Tragedy* (New York: Oxford University Press, 2009).

58 Bureaucratic grammar preaches the centrality of the managerial standpoint, which, like white culture at large, masks the privileges of domination in the homogeneity and boredom of the impersonal. From this standpoint, it requires will and imagination to see what transpires elsewhere, after the order has been given, or in the rifts opened by the official rules. Imagine *B,* this time hunched over "an unlimited supply of paper," meticulously performing calculations in accordance with "fixed rules [...] supplied in a book" (444). She is a low-wage employee and "has no authority to deviate from [the rules] in any details." Although the rules vary with the task, they also take up residence in her head and in her fingers. They follow her home at the end of the day. They scramble her dreams. Imagine *B* fighting the temptation to walk away, to look up, to think about a hundred other, more pressing things (she is trying, after all, to make ends meet on a clerical salary). Imagine the courage it takes to stifle her anger at her boss's roaming eyes and paws (she has rent to pay and food to buy). Imagine the pride and stamina that lets her master the pain climbing the trellis of her spine (she has been sitting for hours without a break), careful not to make a mistake, since one of the few rewards she manages to eke from her work is the knowledge that she does it better than most of her white colleagues. Imagine *A*, shirt-sleeves rolled up, supervising her work, keeping a close eye on it, closer, perhaps, than on the other clerks in his office. He is quicker to pounce on her mistakes

who "speak[s] from the position of the not supposed to speak," who persists in speaking from the standpoint of having been denied standing.[59] This speaker, this *B*-ing, "relinquishes the possibility of thought or of being thought insofar as [they] (merely) provid[e] the material conditions […] for another's thought and for another's being thought."[60] *A*'s condition of "being thought" involves the a priori postulate of their thinking (for) themselves.

because *B* is a woman of color. She is more than qualified, in fact, to do *A*'s job, but only white men in this department get promoted.

I have extrapolated this example from one of Alan Turing's seminal papers, in which Turing models the digital computer on something more familiar to his contemporary readers: "the human computer" ("Computing Machinery and Intelligence," in *The Essential Turing: Seminal Writings in Computing, Logic, Philosophy, Artificial Intelligence, and Artificial Life: Plus the Secrets of Enigma*, ed. B. Jack Copeland [New York: Oxford University Press, 2004], 441–64). In the popular imagination, Turing himself belongs to that pantheon of canny white men who leveraged their tinkers' pleasure to remake the world. But "the human computer" is the digital computer's originary displacement: the workers who did the heavy lifting of manual calculation and record-keeping, in fields as diverse as accounting and cryptography, before the advent of their digital surrogates. Performing feats of "intellective skill" by crimp of the hand and crick of the neck, these workers were typically well-educated, highly intelligent women taking advantage of the highest station not barred to them in the ranks of intellectual and academic life.

Today's "human computers" reappear in new guises: the Uber drivers bound to the "fixed rules" dictated by an automated dispatcher, the food-service or call-center employees whose every move is monitored for optimal efficiency. Their labor prepares the next generation of digital surrogacy in the form of artificial intelligence. On "intellective skill," see Shoshana Zuboff, *In the Age of the Smart Machine: The Future of Work and Power* (New York: Basic Books, 1996), 185–95. On the gendered history of human computers, see Wendy Hui Kyong Chun, *Programmed Visions: Software and Memory* (Cambridge: MIT Press, 2013); and David Alan Grier, *When Computers Were Human* (Princeton: Princeton University Press, 2013).

59 Fred Moten, "Preface for a Solo by Miles Davis," *Women & Performance: A Journal of Feminist Theory* 17, no. 2 (July 2007): 217. For a critical reflection on the idea of the standpoint and the question of standing, see Alexander, *Pedagogies of Crossing*, 122.

60 Moten, "Preface to a Solo by Miles Davis," 217.

But this postulate is, as Wittgenstein would say, only a picture. And like any picture, it requires "material conditions" for its production. The picture commits *A* to the "idea […] that that act of meaning the order had in its own way already traversed all those steps: that when you meant it your mind as it were flew ahead and took all the steps before you physically arrived at this one or that one."[61] Wittgenstein is concerned to show *A* their mistake, which is to have imagined that the act of delivering a rule, or more precisely, of explicating how they intend the rule, could somehow determine the totality of that particular act's serial effects. Such a determination or overdetermination is what *A* means or pretends to understand by the word "meaning." But this picture is coherent only if meaning resides entirely inside the head. Or more precisely, inside the head of the subject positioned to deliver, rather than (merely) to obey, the rule. But even Wittgenstein, who takes great pains to trace the emergence of meaning in the context of language use, neglects that, strictly speaking, it is *B,* not *A,* who "physically arrive[s]" at each step in the sequence. *A*'s commitment to a possessive model of meaning maps the hierarchical relation between manager and subordinate onto the relation between an invisible mental act and a visibly physical series, thereby rendering *B*'s labor not only secondary but meaningless, superfluous; not invisible, but opaque. *B*'s labor exists, for *A,* only in the lag-time of a supplement to what *A* always will have meant. And Wittgenstein's slip or omission confirms this dis/placement, this opacity of a labor and a body that exists only to be absorbed by the finished product or else extruded by the error that halts production. Likewise, the iterable, embodied labor that *A* performs, in the act of uttering commands and corrections, vanishes into the think-hole of their authority and expertise.

61 Wittgenstein, *Philosophical Investigations,* 64. *A*'s picture recapitulates what Stefano Harney and Fred Moten refer to as the "fantasy that capital could exist without labor" (*The Undercommons: Fugitive Planning & Black Study* [Wivenhoe: Minor Compositions, 2013], 80–81).

If *B*'s labor disappears from this picture, even more pro-found is its refusal of their knowledge. I mean, the knowledge that those who labor have of the conditions of their labor, in-cluding, of course, the violence that produces those conditions. This knowledge becomes more acute the closer one stands to the condition of having the kind of body that the prevailing re-gime remands to the place of the "zero degree" of social being, a being construed to exist only as a source of labor (physical, sexual, emotional, intellectual).[62] Thus, the "sense" of equality among speaking beings cannot lay claim to the transparency of a meaning that becomes available to the subject through a shift in standpoint. For if it rests on the mutual understanding of "inferior" and "superior" (even as it points toward the horizon of hierarchy's overcoming), we must acknowledge that mutual understanding is, in itself, the continuous outcome of a deeply unequal division of labor, knowledge, and responsibility.

When a woman you work with calls you by the name of an-other woman you work with, it is too much of a cliché not to laugh out loud with the friend beside you who says, oh no she didn't. Still, in the end, so what, who cares? She had a fifty-fifty chance of getting it right.

Yes, and in your mail the apology note appears referring to "our mistake." Apparently your own invisibility is the real problem causing her confusion. This is how the apparatus she propels you into begins to multiply its meaning.

What did you say?[63]

---

62 Spillers, "Mama's Baby, Papa's Maybe," 206. In "Interstices," Spillers glosses the kind of knowledge Black working-class women have had to wrest from the rules that governed their movements inside and outside of the workplace: "At the level of analysis and experience, we witness no arbitrary bonding between a signifier and signified so that […] the word, the gesture that fulfills it, and the actual consequences of both converge on a literal moment of time. To lose control of the body is to be hostage to insufferable circumstances; the lack of control is also in the historical outline of black American women often enough the loss of life" (172).

63 Rankine, *Citizen,* 43.

Not unlike Wittgenstein's, Rankine's sense for the "ordinary" attunes us to the infra-political, dispositional forces that rupture and fortify it. Here whiteness plays the alpha role, as the manager of the situation. The second-person narrator's (presumably) white colleague demands shared responsibility (i.e., mutual understanding) for her own error.[64] Although "you" don't necessarily work *for* the other woman, "you" already work on her behalf, bearing emotional burdens, to the imposition of which no adequate response is possible. That "you" do this work as a matter of course testifies to the efficiency of the "apparatus," which answers to the needs and desires of the dominant, saving them from accountability for their mistakes. Rendering "you" invisible, incredible, and available for exploiting, the apparatus does the dominant this further service: it signals to "you" that it is "your" interpretive labor, "your" knowing-better, and "your" caring that taints "you," that marks "you" as unsuitable for an equal share.[65]

The violence of the apparatus that "she propels you into" consists, in this case, of the racialized subject's consignment to a work of enunciation, producing meanings over which the speaker is denied control. The meanings "multiply" along axes of past and present harms, magnetizing memory in the flesh of other aggressions endured, micro- and macro-, and reanimating history as an ever-present threat to the subject's well-being, if not, indeed, her existence.[66] The apparatus constrains the de-

---

64 The (white) woman in this scenario might be said to exemplify the dominant standpoint of white liberal feminism, performing a commitment to mutuality that effaces white women's roles in the oppression of women of color. See Spillers, "Interstices."

65 On the concept of "interpretive labor," see Graeber, *The Utopia of Rules.*

66 On Alexander Weheliye's reading of Spillers's work, "flesh, while representing both a temporal and a conceptual antecedent to the body, is not a biological occurrence seeing that its creation requires an elaborate apparatus" (*Habeas Viscus,* 39). The apparatus Weheliye and Spillers refer to is, in the first instance, that of circum-Atlantic slavery, which has its afterlife in the racializing violence of the prison-industrial complex. Rankine's work reveals how so-called ordinary language, in

grees of freedom that she has to tell her own story, to record her version of the events. And it seems pertinent that this "mistake" happens in a workplace, where the norms of bureaucratic reason insist on a transparency behind which racism and other forms of prejudice and discrimination find it easy to hide. Bureaucratic language is supposed to be free of implication, but the freedom belongs to those with power, who take credit for the work they direct yet are somehow never around when it turns out that mistakes were made. If the one harmed by this mistake refuses, for instance, to accept her colleague's specious apology, or if she otherwise presses the issue, she risks her further eclipse by racist stereotypes. If, on the other hand, she acquiesces, she lends her tacit, normalized, but nonetheless painful support to her invisibility as a social subject. Her white colleague's "fifty-fifty chance of getting it right" mirrors her own double-bind. In either case, the house wins. That Rankine does not spell out this logic amplifies the power of her prose: the piece ends with the weight of a decision hanging in white space: "What did you say?"

We are meant, I think, to feel the embodied grammar of that question, to let its gravity sink in. I'm trying to understand, from the respectful but nonetheless inappropriate (because expropriating) distance of the white space that I occupy, what it means to confront the capture of one's speech by the apparatus of white supremacy. That this capture is necessarily incomplete does not diminish the regular awfulness of it. For make no mistake: the apparatus yields profit for the "movers and shakers" and their "accomplices," a surplus-value produced by the work of being and breathing and feeling and thinking in this world:

For so long you thought the ambition of racist language was to denigrate and erase you as a person. [...] [Y]ou begin to understand yourself as rendered hypervisible in the face of

the bureaucratic contexts of modern life, prolongs the apparatus in a multitude of more subtle forms.

such language acts. Language that feels hurtful is intended to exploit all the ways that you are present. Your alertness, your openness, and your desire to engage actually demand your presence, your looking up, your talking back, and, as insane as it is, saying please.[67]

Rankine's challenge to the picture of "racist language" as a negating, nullifying force draws attention to the productivity of its violence.[68] In the same breath, *Citizen* enriches readings of the speech-act that focus on the latter's illocutionary aspects as vectors for power.[69] I want to say that it is not only the case that, in

---

67 Rankine, *Citizen,* 49.

68 Racism's productivity, in very "real" economic terms, remains key to the global success of US capitalism. Ronald Takaki puts it succinctly: "The removal of Indians and the expansion of black slavery made possible the Market Revolution" (*Iron Cages,* 78). Today's carceral regime extends slavery's legacy into the private-prison boom. See Michelle Alexander, *The New Jim Crow: Mass Incarceration in the Age of Colorblindness* (New York: The New Press, 2012); Ruth Wilson Gilmore, *Golden Gulag: Prisons, Surplus, Crisis, and Opposition in Globalizing California* (Berkeley: University of California Press, 2007).

69 In his theory of speech-acts, J.L. Austin restricts "meaning" to the classical idea of semantic reference (or reference and sense, in Fregean terms), i.e., that which seems to attach to the proposition qua logical entity, floating free from any particular context. In addition to this dimension of the speech-act as *locution,* Austin famously posits an *illocutionary* dimension, wherein the speech-act gathers force by virtue of its engagement with social convention. Thus, the "meaning" of my promise to come tomorrow would be the idea of my coming tomorrow (perhaps a mental image of my arrival on your doorstep), but the "force" of my promise would arise from the product of my ability and my intention to show up. It is in virtue of force, not referential meaning, that as Austin says, "our word is our bond." The force of the illocutionary is, for Austin, governed by convention. What makes a proposition a promise is our mutual (and generally tacit) expectation that certain kinds of abilities and intentions will accompany its utterance. A promise that fails to satisfy those conditions is, for Austin, not meaningless, but it is "infelicitous." Finally, Austin posits a third dimension of the speech-act, the *perlocutionary,* to account for the fact that our use of language is not strictly conventional, but that it achieves practical effects in virtue of its power to recruit feelings and motives. For my promise may or may not persuade you, excite you,

its indefinite repetition, the speech-act must both institute and displace the conditions of its legitimacy, opening the space for resistance inside the capture of the performative by governing conventions.[70] For within this schema, it is also the case that the presence of the other ("[their] looking up, [their] talking back, and as insane as it is, saying please") furnishes the speech-act with what it needs to accomplish its rhizomatic work. Or perhaps that's not quite right. Perhaps the emphasis ought to fall not on the other (which may also, of course, be the self), but on their *presence,* which could mean their dis/placement before the being instituted by language in its use. This presence is movement, enacted (as Rankine describes) in gestures of *being* present. (And I'm thinking also of what Wittgenstein says: "meaning something is like going up to someone".)[71] In its presence to the speech-act, the flesh becomes part of the "material conditions […] of another's being," the conduit or channel by which meaning takes effect.[72] And hate speech, like other forms of violence,

frighten you, etc., or all of those at once. Nonetheless, Austin's focus on the illocutionary — which has been fruitfully taken up by philosophers in the Continental tradition like Judith Butler — privileges the conventional over the affective components of language use. See J.L. Austin, *How to Do Things with Words,* eds. J.O. Urmson and Marina Sbisà (Cambridge: Harvard University Press, 1975); Judith Butler, *Excitable Speech: A Politics of the Performative* (New York: Routledge, 1997). My thinking about the perlocutionary is indebted to Stanley Cavell, *Philosophy the Day after Tomorrow* (Cambridge: Harvard University Press, 2006).

70 Butler writes, "[t]he speaking subject makes his or her decision only in the context of an already circumscribed field of linguistic possibilities. One decides on the condition of an already decided field of language, but this repetition does not constitute the decision of the speaking subject as a redundancy" (*Excitable Speech,* 129).

71 Wittgenstein, *Philosophical Investigations,* 112.

72 This approach to the performative has been developed within traditions of Black feminist theory. For instance, Zakiyyah Iman Jackson writes, "[b]y suggesting that representation performs, I mean to imply a doing and an implementation that forestalls the vertical bifurcation of representation and matter into respective planes of transcendence and immanence and, instead, places both on the same plane in the (un)making of being"

propels the flesh into an address designed to sever it from the possibility of redress.[73]

Make no mistake: as an accomplice to patriarchal white supremacy (and its interlocking structures of oppression), I, too, contribute my presence to "the violence of being required to behave as if democracy and reasonableness truly existed, when in truth they do not."[74] The possession of whiteness and cishet masculinity (and other normative attributes) does not exempt me from *this* violence, though the wages I receive do allow me to buy something back in the form of bodily integrity, security, and a modicum of autonomy. And yes, in the form, too, of the pleasures of domination, of propelling others into the apparatus of their subjugation. These wages, I want to say, are most days enough to subdue the sense of what else I might have lost (to begin with: of openness, of alertness, of desire). You might say that the apparatus operates without your consent to produce your consent. And yet, how do I, in my complicity, inhabit the space of the "you" addressed by Rankine's prose? I want to say that the device of *this* address works to unsettle the transparency of the standpoint that I imagine is mine to occupy. Ordinarily, in virtue of that standpoint, my identification with another's experience, when the latter is marked by an absence of those possessive attributes that condition my subjectivity, remains deeply qualified. Having a sufficiently well-trained literary imagination, I can perform my understanding of narrative or critical figurations, for example, of Black women's experience *because,* as a subject of racial and gendered privilege and power, my identity as a white man remains subordinate to my status as a subject. But I am entertaining the thought (about which I

("'Theorizing in a Void': Sublimity, Matter, and Physics in Black Feminist Poetics," *South Atlantic Quarterly* 117, no. 3 [July 2018]: 631).

73 On redress, see Hartman, *Scenes of Subjection,* 49–58. As David Graeber observes, violence as a mode of communication functions to "[stifle] the possibility of sending any further messages of any kind" (*The Utopia of Rules*, 102).

74 Alexander, *Pedagogies of Crossing,* 141.

may be mistaken) that Rankine's use of the second-person pronoun does something else, outside of the circuits of sympathetic
identification. That for the white reader, at least, it repeatedly
poses *the problem* of identification. Which is also the problem
of knowing what follows from the other's words, from my presence to their sentience and their sentences. *What did you say?* I
am neither the subject of this question, nor am I exempt from its
address, which is a summons to accountability. Accountability
for my words and for my silence, for my acts and my inaction.
As Wittgenstein says, "a new decision [is] needed at every stage."
There is no flying ahead of my meaning, no flight from my mistakes. As a part of the apparatus, an apparatchik, I am moved, I
am shaken.

composing the withheld page

White America has always catered to "nervous white men." As
Ronald Takaki recounts, Thomas Jefferson fathered a foundational anxiety in his insistence that "men could not live 'at random' and [that] all behavior had to be a 'matter of calculation'
or else the strongest passions would overwhelm the moral sense
and rationality."[75] These passions were and are unleashed by the
violence of imperialist accumulation, wage exploitation, and
capitalism's more direct forms of bonded labor, no less than by
bourgeois rationality in its suture of competitive acquisitiveness
to self-surveillance and a deep distrust of the flesh. But even as
the spread of urban, industrial capitalism ramped up the energies of randomness, the transformation of both profit-making
and politics into bureaucratic enterprises promised to reduce
the dilemma of republican self-governance to an "engineering
problem." This phrase comes from Claude Shannon's 1948 article
inaugurating information theory, a text with nothing explicitly
to say about capitalism or bureaucracy. But in its bracketing of

75 Takaki, *Iron Cages,* 142, 64.

the social aspects of "communication" in favor of a purely formal, mathematical approach, Shannon's seminal text might tell us a lot about the grammars that dominate modernity.[76] Shannon's text also hides a kind of Easter egg for the humanist, a glimpse or glitch, amid this technical prose, of the avant-garde:

THE HEAD AND IN FRONTAL ATTACK ON AN ENGLISH WRITER THAT THE CHARACTER OF THIS POINT IS THEREFORE ANOTHER METHOD FOR THE LETTERS THAT THE TIME OF WHO EVER TOLD THE PROBLEM FOR AN UNEXPECTED[77]

Generated, Shannon claims, by algorithmic means, this passage is meant to demonstrate the statistical regularities of the English language. Knowledge of these regularities permits someone with tabulations enough and time to construct, by roll of the dice, an almost not nonsensical approximation of written English.[78] But as I read it, the passage smuggles in, under the cover of scientific

76 C.E. Shannon, "A Mathematical Theory of Communication," *The Bell System Technical Journal* 27, nos. 3–4 (1948): 379–423, 623–56. The "engineering problem" of communication has played a central role in the development of capitalist bureaucracy. On this topic, see JoAnne Yates, *Control through Communication: The Rise of System in American Management* (Baltimore: Johns Hopkins University Press, 1989).

77 Shannon, "A Mathematical Theory of Communication," 388.

78 For the curious, Shannon's procedure can be approximated as follows. Select a large, fairly representative textual corpus — e.g., the works of a prolific author of unexceptionable style. Split the corpus into short sequences of either words or letters, each sequence being exactly n elements long. (Letting n equal 3 or 4 tends to achieve the best results.) Next compile a table showing, for each sequence of elements $1 \ldots n{-}1$ found in the corpus, the probability of transition to any given element in the nth position. This method, which treats written language as a Markov process, can be used to generate new text by starting with one n-gram and rolling a weighted die to select the next element (based on the transition probabilities in the table), and so on. Though laborious to do manually, a Markov-chain algorithm can be implemented with a few lines of code in any number of modern programming languages. For a recipe, see Brian W. Kernighan and Rob Pike, *The Practice of Programming* (Reading: Addison-Wesley, 1999), 62–63.

illustration, a sly joke. A "frontal attack on an English writer" evokes the very algorithm that Shannon used to compose this passage, purporting to show that potentially meaningful phrases need not arise in a writer's head. The algorithm is "another method for the letters," as is Shannon's "mathematical theory of communication" itself, which extends a venerable tradition ("the time of who ever told") of thinking about the phenomenon of communication as "the problem" of "an unexpected," that is, of mapping the overlap of convention and invention, regulation and intuition, expectation and surprise.[79]

Shannon grounds his theory on the premise that the "semantic aspects of communication are irrelevant" to the design of communication systems, since the messages that these systems relay can be decomposed into their formal, quantitative properties.[80] To oversimplify matters: understanding the probability with which certain *signals* occur in a set of messages displaces, as the proper object of scientific interest and knowledge, consideration of their role as *signs* that refer to things in the world. This displacement, with its promise that mastery of the signals can render the messiness of messages irrelevant, answers to a powerful modernist fantasy. As Wendy Hui Kyong Chun argues, writing about the history of software and the hubris of the Information Age, "the dream is: the more that an individual knows, the better decisions he or she can make."[81] And yet, in excess of

---

79 For a thorough and provocative reading of Shannon's work in the context of twentieth-century Modernist literary experiments (James Joyce's *Finnegans Wake*), cybernetics, and psychoanalysis, see Lydia H. Liu, *The Freudian Robot: Digital Media and the Future of the Unconscious* (Chicago: University of Chicago Press, 2010).

80 Shannon, "A Mathematical Theory of Communication," 379.

81 Chun, *Programmed Visions,* 8. In a sense, Shannon's information theory operationalizes Max Weber's definition of bureaucratic rationality as optimizing "the probability that a command with a given specific content will be obeyed by a given group of persons" (*Economy and Society,* 1:53). The probabilities in Shannon's theory describe the content of messages transmitted over a channel, while the probability to which Weber alludes concern the consequences of those messages' transmission. Both, however,

Shannon's scientific aims or dreams, the passage above performs a displacement of that displacement, suggesting that the tension or slippage between the meaningful and the mechanical is undecidable. It opens the door to what Aristotle calls *to automaton,* performing the eruption of randomness as meaning inside the apparatus designed to reduce language to a set of a-signifying facts.[82] The undecidability of the significance of this passage for the theory that it illustrates (does it bolster or subvert Shannon's project?) mirrors the undecidability of the status of the phrases that constitute it (are they nonsense or not?).

Shannon's pseudo-poetic apparatus is also about violence. Typography highlights an aggression signaled by the phrase "frontal attack." If, in reading this passage, one feels the onset of melancholy, too (identifying, perhaps, with the "English writer" whose relevance is under attack), it's not a stretch to say that this text has, in addition to its train-wrecked semantic content, a certain tone. Indeed, that it can have such a tone might be the more "unexpected" result of this experiment. For if *tone* names the torque that speech-acts produce in us, then meaning is, from one perspective, *mostly* about tone.[83] Shannon's text

concern the crux of modern capitalism: the reproduction of authority and trust within structures that remain hierarchical, but in which the imperatives of domination and control, spread over space and time, cannot rely on the embodied and implicit repertoires of power between people working face to face. In the modern firm, as in the offices of the modern state, authority may be miles away, emanating from a disembodied source known only through its written protocols.

82 Aristotle, *Physics, Volume I: Books 1–4,* trans. P.H. Wicksteed and F.M. Cornford (Cambridge: Harvard University Press, 1957), 161. Though more loosely translated as "accident" or "chance," the Greek term carries the suggestion, surviving in the English loan-word, of that elusive quality Kant called "purposiveness without purpose," a phenomenon to which it feels irresistible to ascribe agency and intention, though we know (or suspect) that it can have none. See Alison James, *Constraining Chance: Georges Perec and the Oulipo* (Chicago: Northwestern University Press, 2009).

83 "What do you *mean* by that?" is a question that typically has little to do with the denotative signification of what was uttered, and a great deal to do with how the utterance was *meant,* i.e., with the consequences that it

might be read alongside any number of twentieth-century literary experiments that recruit the procedural and the aleatory as a means of disrupting the privileged place of authorial intention. Yet more emphatically than these experiments (cordoned off as they are from so-called ordinary language by the conventions governing the reception of the literary text), Shannon's text provokes a serious question. For if meaning remains "irrelevant" to the bureaucratic grammars of modernity, then where does meaning reside? For these grammars have hardly jettisoned the possessive personal, nor have they dislodged from its privileged spot the picture of reason as what transpires in a transparent, autonomous consciousness. Though language may be reduced to a table of probabilities, the Cartesian ego reappears in the guise of the engineer, i.e., he who has mastered the probabilities in advance. This is the fantasy of "a sovereign subject, for whom there is no difference between command given and command completed."[84] Like Wittgenstein's *A,* imagining that the com-

---

may or may not have been intended to produce. That is to say, meaning in language use concerns, above all, the affective information that utterances carry, which is information about the relation between the speaker and the addressee and/or the world. As Silvan Tomkins's work suggests, linguistic reference would have no traction on us were it not for the affects that motivate our response. Yelling "Fire!" in a crowded theater is not an act of descriptive magnanimity; most uses of language do not (at least, not in any straightforward sense) describe the world. For Tomkins's information-theoretic approach to the affects, see Silvan S. Tomkins, *Shame and Its Sisters: A Silvan Tomkins Reader,* eds. Eve Kosofsky Sedgwick and Adam Frank (Durham: Duke University Press, 1996); Silvan S. Tomkins, *Affect Imagery Consciousness: The Complete Edition,* 2 vols. (New York: Springer, 2008), vol. 2. For an extended meditation on the elusiveness of tone in the literary text, see Ngai, *Ugly Feelings,* 38–88.

It is also worth pointing out that the figurative and tonal aspects of communication accrue particular urgency in situations where speakers and/or listeners do not enjoy the liberty to communicate in the open. Such has been the formative context of many communities of color in the United States. As Marisa Parham writes, the "signals" of Black folk's discourse "might be understood as protection, as a way of transmitting important information under surveillance" ("Sample | Signal | Strobe").

84 Chun, *Programmed Visions,* 49.

mand he had given "had in its own way already traversed" the labor required to fulfill it, but being brought back, again and again, to the gap between intention and action, desire and possession.

The tone of Shannon's found poem is angry, but to whom is this anger addressed, and where does it come from?[85] A fugitive feeling, it partakes of an impersonality that is nonetheless passionate, or more precisely, *impassioned*.[86] Within the apparatus, a proposition functions less as form or content than as a lure. It entrains, entrammels, entices, implicates. As another student of meaning's (ir)relevance once wrote, "A sentence of a vagueness that is violence is authority and a mission and stumbling and also certainly a prison."[87] It is from the fugitive nature of meaning that speech derives its power to harm. This power makes language the primary vector for human authority. As speakers (or writers), we are missionary and errant and cagey and fenced in by words (by our own and by others'). The apparatus propels now with pain, now seduces with promises of pleasure or redress. But even, or perhaps especially, when one wields words to do harm, the speaker, as Denise Riley imagines, "is dispossessed of his own words in advance. The rhetoric of rage speaks him mechanically and remorselessly."[88] My intention is not to exculpate the one who causes injury. Nor is my intention to replace the abuser's magical thinking, which locates agency in the targets of their abuse, with the magical thinking that locates agency in language itself. Rather, my point is that agency occurs

---

85 Sianne Ngai argues that "[i]f a literary work's organizing semblance of feeling cannot be identified entirely with a reader's response to it, or said to be a feeling represented or signified by the text, it evokes [Brian] Massumi's description of affect as that which perpetually 'escapes' the particular forms or perceptions in which it is 'captured,' while also remaining 'alongside' them" (*Ugly Feelings*, 56).

86 See Denise Riley, *Impersonal Passion: Language as Affect* (Durham: Duke University Press, 2005), esp. 9–27.

87 Gertrude Stein, *Tender Buttons* (San Francisco: City Lights Books, 2014), 40.

88 Riley, *Impersonal Passion,* 17.

in the act (of saying, hitting, spitting, penning the poison letter, pulling the trigger, etc.) and in all the acts that are preparatory and subsequent to it. There is no "inward, spiritual act" that
we might hope to isolate prior to all those whose consequences
snowball, whose consequences others suffer and endure.[89] If our

89 Austin, *How to Do Things with Words,* 10. When a Black or brown person
    is accused of a crime, the search for motive does not usually preoccupy the
    white American public. We whites assume that we know what the causes
    are, and whether attributed in a spirit of liberal concern (with eyes averted
    and a sanctimonious shaking of the head) or conservative hysteria (with a
    righteous wag of the forefinger or drumming of the fist), these attributes
    depersonalize and dehumanize the accused: it was poverty that made
    'em do it, or Black crimin/animality. But when a white person commits
    a crime sufficiently horrific or salacious that the white public is forced
    to take notice — and especially when a white cishet *man* commits such a
    crime — one can observe a contrary hurry to *humanize* the perpetrator,
    to plumb the depths of his past for a deeply personal motive. On the one
    hand, this search for motive shields the rest of us whites from a reckoning.
    For then it's not "whiteness" that ambushed worshippers in the Emanuel
    African Methodist Episcopal Church, or that lay surrounded by emptied
    magazines on the thirty-second floor of the Mandalay Bay Hotel, or that
    sits behind the camera on *Dateline,* fighting back tears of self-pity. On
    the other hand, this search confirms the perpetrator in possession of his
    agency, securing his status as the transparent and autonomous subject.
        The specter of this subjectivity haunts scenes of "random" mass
    violence in a particularly perverse way. We might note, with Sally
    Robinson, that "the fall of white masculinity from the heights of
    disembodied 'universality' into the depths of embodied particularity"
    can be accompanied by a kind of existential crisis, as well as a kind of
    sadomasochistic pleasure (*Marked Men: White Masculinity in Crisis*
    [New York: Columbia University Press, 2000], 56). (One of Robinson's
    examples is the Hollywood film *Falling Down.*) Perhaps, like the hate-
    mailer who "can say nothing else" but racializing hate, the perpetrators
    of such violence desire to exchange rational agency for total compulsion,
    autonomy for *to automaton.* That so many white cishet men should feel as
    though only these two extremes stand open to them attests to their vexed
    position within a system that demands the reduction of the working body
    to the conditions of a machine, a system that also affords some workers
    the privileges of dominating others. It attests, in other words, to the false
    promise of the wages of domination, which spectacularly fail to recuperate
    the humanity of the dominator. Likewise, the spectacular pleasure that
    such men take in the possession and use of firearms (especially automatic

agency is not ours to possess, it is something for which we are responsible, something for which we must take care.

"*'Sine ira et studio'*: without hatred or passion, hence without affection or enthusiasm."[90] Thus runs the motto, according to Weber, of bureaucratic reason. Like Weber's motto, the framing of communication as an "engineering problem" seeks to solve a prior problem by fiat. By muting our words' affective reverb, bureaucratic or engineering reason prescribes a tonic for subjects caught up in the barrage of contradictory signals that strafe modern life. As Nahum Dimitri Chandler writes, "The system in which […] subordination occurs, because it exists, is analytically presupposed." Patriarchal white supremacy, alongside other forms of domination, appears as a "preestablished matrix" limiting the subject's degrees of freedom, just as the tabulated probabilities describing the signals available are supposed to delimit what can be communicated.[91] Of course, no one ever said that meaning was in the table, just as no one seriously believes that freedom can be found in the matrix or the ledger or the marketplace. And that is the point. Once banished from the operations of reason, meaning or freedom as shared endeavors can be treated as irrelevant. Such is the lure offered to those who can afford to subscribe: none of that matters outside your head. Your triumphs are your own, as are your failures. The individual, working hard, not just following but intending the rules as his own, is shielded from the downstream consequences of his actions and inaction, just as he is discouraged or forbidden from knowing the structural causes of his pain.[92] The ruse is meant

and semi-automatic weapons) owes something to the way that the gun promises to reconcile these contradictions in the subject whose agency it amplifies into deadly force: the shooter becomes, for a brief moment, a *dominating machine.*

90 Weber, *Economy and Society,* 1:225.

91 Chandler, "Originary Displacement," 281.

92 The acute dysfunction of bureaucratic reason is only deepened by the increased demand for explicit and intentional performances of emotional labor in the workplace. We are increasingly expected to invest not only our skills, our knowledge, and our time, but also *ourselves* — or more precisely,

to work, to the degree that it does, for the subject identified as white, cishet male, and middle class. Relevance hinges, for him, on this knowing what not to know.[93] For others, the ruse was only ever a cruel joke, and the hinge, whose friction they feel in their bones, swings another way. In the words of Marisa Parham, "it is knowing *to know* that pivots comprehension toward the unsaid, toward the meaningfulness compressed in a signal."[94] This unsaid meaningfulness is not *in* the head, though its compression's force is felt there. But that force also unleashes emancipatory energies.

Dionne Brand's *The Blue Clerk* imagines this force as splitting the subject of enunciation into two. These halves, speaking by turn in her poetic text, Brand calls "the author" and "the clerk." As the counterpart to the author's public persona, the clerk leads, we might be tempted to say, an interior, private, cryptic existence, working behind the scenes. And yet, Brand depicts the clerk's purview as an exterior and profoundly bureaucratic space:

The bales have been piling up for years yet they look brightly scored, crisp and cunning. They have abilities the clerk is forever curtailing and marshaling. They are stacked deep and high and the clerk, in her inky garment, weaves in and out of them checking and rechecking that they do not find their way onto the right-hand page. She scrutinizes the manifest hourly, the contents and sequence of loading. She keeps account of the cubic metres of senses, perceptions, and resis-

our will to believe, feeding the system with a credulity that it desperately needs to stave off the certain knowledge of prolonged crises, repeated catastrophe, and impending collapse. On the intensification of emotionally performative labor, see Eva Illouz, *Cold Intimacies: The Making of Emotional Capitalism* (Malden: Polity Press, 2016).

93 Wendy Chun describes the abstractions of software engineering as what "both empowers the programmer and insists on his/her ignorance," since the programmer almost never knows how, exactly, the computer fulfills their commands (*Programmed Visions,* 37).

94 Parham, "Sample | Signal | Strobe" (emphasis mine).

tant facts. No one need be aware of these; no one is likely to understand. Some of these are quite dangerous.

And, some of them are too delicate and beautiful for the present world.[95]

The clerk works on a wharf or dock, sorting and cataloging "bales" of "left-hand pages," which represent "what is withheld" from the rectos (the right-hand, the correct) pages produced by the author. The author is, nominally, "in charge" of the clerk, overseeing the latter's work, which means overlooking, as much as possible, her labor: "I forget the bales of paper fastened to the dock and the weather doesn't bother me. I choose the presentable things, the beautiful things. And I enjoy them sometimes, if not for the clerk."[96] We might be tempted to regard the clerk as representing the author's unconscious. But if her labor seems altogether too clerical for Freud, that is because it hearkens to a very different economy of language and representation than what the theory of repression comprehends. The clerk's tireless scrutiny, her "checking and re-checking," her "keep[ing] account," speak to the discursive reality, as adduced by Hortense Spillers, of "the racialized subject":

> his history has dictated that [the] linguistic *right to use* is never easily granted with his human and social legacy but must be earned, over and over again, on the level of a personal and collective struggle that requires in some way a confrontation with the principle of language *as prohibition,* as the withheld.[97]

95 Dionne Brand, *The Blue Clerk: Ars Poetica in 59 Versos* (Durham: Duke University Press, 2018), 5.

96 Ibid., 3–6.

97 Hortense J. Spillers, "'All the Things You Could Be by Now, If Sigmund Freud's Wife Was Your Mother': Psychoanalysis and Race," in *Black, White, and in Color,* 400–401 (emphasis in the original).

As I read this passage, Spillers suggests that for the racialized subject, confronting and surviving the ledgerization of life, language does more than encode or encrypt a prohibition.[98] Rather, as an engine of that racializing and gendering apparatus by which access to discursive privilege, legal recognition, and rhetorical sovereignty can be foreclosed, language is, in some way, the very thing prohibited or withheld.[99] The clerk's vigilance in Brand's text speaks to her "confrontation" with the "principle" that loads speaking with danger, that makes it a matter of life and death. Over and over again, the clerk's voice returns the text to a figuration of a being-in-the-flesh that, in its inescapable, suffering seriality, exceeds the ruses of abstraction and condensation. And this voice interrupts the Viennese waltz of interiority and exteriority that the aspirational bourgeois subject imagines as her milieu: "If the poet doesn't do more, the clerk will be inundated by bundles of sheets tightly fastened with gnats and

98 On the ledgerization of Black lives as an ongoing process, beginning with circum-Atlantic slavery, see Simone Browne, *Dark Matters: On the Surveillance of Blackness* (Durham: Duke University Press, 2015).

99 Scott Richard Lyons defines "rhetorical sovereignty," in the context of Native and Indigenous struggles, as "the inherent right and ability of peoples to determine their own communicative needs and desires in the pursuit of self-determination," which involves "setting at least some of the terms of the debate" ("Rhetorical Sovereignty, What Do American Indians Want from Writing?" *College Composition and Communication* 51, no. 3 [2000]: 462). As Spillers maintains, the "right to use" begins with literacy, the "achievement" of which, for oppressed populations, represents "an emancipatory aim" ("Psychoanalysis and Race," 400). An emphasis on the right to use language, and especially (though by no means exclusively) to use it to assert one's legal, political, and social relevance in contexts where that relevance has been systematically denied, stands in contrast to those strains of liberal thought and activism that focus on the explicit *representation* of certain groups or classes in law and policy. To be represented as equal before the law provides no guarantee that one will receive a fair hearing or be granted access to the tools necessary for adequately representing one's own interests, much less for "setting at least some of the terms of the debate." On the limits of liberal activism, see Spade, *Normal Life.*

wire."[100] The clerk's task, you might say, lies in accounting for the evidently irrelevant, for the affective and sensuous weight of both action and inaction (e.g., the poet's *not* doing more), for all that the withheld pages hold: "The cynical clerk notes, in her cynical English, all the author has elided, the diagonal animosities and tiers of citizenship. The author wants a cosmopolitan city. Nothing wrong with that. But the clerk who orbits her skull has to deal with all the animus."[101]

In her querulous dialogue with the author, the clerk sustains a certain resonance with Adam Smith's "spectator in the breast," the figure by which Smith sought to address the social engineering problem of capitalist modernity.[102] But while Smith's spectator is an exercise in abstraction, producing the subject in transparency through a synthesis of the hypothetical perspectives of his fellow citizens, Brand's clerk indexes a kind of surplus or remainder of the flesh. The clerk, in other words, accumulates those aspects of her particular embodiment that the author might prefer to forget: "I am not really in life, the author says. I am really a voyeur. But the part of me that is in life is in pain all the time. That's me, says the clerk."[103] For the work of surviving embodiment, which is the labor that conditions the author's oeuvre, includes the political, social, and economic violence, past and present, that inscribes her flesh within — or more precisely, as the foundation for — "the diagonal animosities and tiers of citizenship." Hence the dock where the clerk waits and sorts, watching the weather, "expecting a ship." It is a space haunted by the arrival of the ships bearing stolen life across the Atlantic. This haunting not only marks the author's identity, but also serially institutes modernity itself, fixing the modern subject — and with particular force, the Black female

---

100 Brand, *The Blue Clerk,* 67.
101 Ibid., 23.
102 Adam Smith, *The Theory of Moral Sentiments* (Indianapolis: Liberty Classics, 1982).
103 Brand, *The Blue Clerk,* 205.

subject — within "a triangular trade of censorship."[104] Such censorship is not an exercise in abstraction, not the triangulation (as in Adam Smith) of perspectives under the equalizing light of republican reason. Rather, as the author explains to the clerk, it begins, again and again, in "the sirens that are turned on, that come alive whenever we step outside, you and I."[105] To step outside is to step into the apparatus, to plunge again into a propulsion that powers the economy by a traffic in commodities from which the self, as the flesh's truncated, anagrammatical fiction, is hardly exempt.

Brand's clerk might remind us, too, of another famous thought-experiment: James Clerk Maxwell's demon, the hypothetical being whose clerical labor keeps a closed system away from the entropy toward which it tends.[106] Maxwell's demon defies the second law of thermodynamics by sorting faster and slower (i.e., hotter and colder) gas molecules into two sides of a partition within a box. Absent the demon, the gas in the box remains at equilibrium, a uniform average temperature that corresponds to a maximally random distribution of the molecules. In Claude Shannon's theory, *information* becomes another name for entropy, making relevance a function, you might say, of maximal bombardment, of the ballistic conditions of exchange.[107] On the standard physical interpretation, the demon's

104 Ibid., 5, 125.
105 Ibid., 208.
106 My reading is motivated here by Katherine McKittrick's invocation of the "demonic" in relation to the work of Sylvia Wynter. For McKittrick, the demonic signifies "a non-deterministic schema; it is a process that is hinged on uncertainty and nonlinearity because the organizing principle cannot predict the future" (*Demonic Grounds: Black Women and the Cartographies of Struggle* [Minneapolis: University of Minnesota Press, 2006], xxiv).
107 The theory represents the signal content of a message as a function of the volume of state-space (probabilistically defined) that its signals can be said to occupy. Thus, a more informative signal (one with higher entropy) is one belonging to a larger space of possible signals. (The least informative signal is the one that occurs with a probability of one; no other signals are

feat remains impossible, because did such a being exist, its own
entropy would increase as a function of its need to keep track
of which molecules belong here or there: "[E]very […] *bringing
together* of distinct conditions […] can only be accomplished
at the cost of a corresponding bringing *apart* in the demon
himself."[108] Which laws does Brand's clerk defy by bringing together the left-hand pages, thereby making possible, even as she
interrupts, the composure of the authorial voice? What does her
impossible labor accomplish at the cost of a "bringing apart" in
the clerk herself? As modernity's more critical students have ob-
served, the disorder of "men […] liv[ing] at random" increases
(*pace* Jefferson) the more that experience becomes "a matter of
calculation." For the requirement of calculability, which is also
the imperative of commensurability or equivalence, leads to the
transformation of life itself into a field saturated by the logics of
surplus value and commodity exchange. In the United States,
where capitalism's imperial ambitions are realized through the
vectors of corporate media and information technology, we live
in a society dominated by what Silvan Tomkins calls "informational greed." Ours is a society whose subjects "must have too
much information too quickly."[109] Or as Brand's author opines:
"All information is available, all history is available, all thought
is available. Consuming is the obvious answer to life."[110] In Tomkins's affect theory, "informational greed" is symptomatic of a
set of maladaptive personality traits in which anger predomi-
nates, anger being (for Tomkins) the affect produced by the un-
remitting bombardment of any stimulus.[111] Tomkins's articula-

possible.) Or as Wendy Chun writes, "information increases with vapor,
with entropy" (*Programmed Visions*, 21).

108 David Z. Albert, *Time and Chance* (Cambridge: Harvard University Press,
2000), 101 (emphasis in the original). Albert's valuable book actually
contests the philosophical validity of the standard interpretation of
Maxwell's demon for statistical mechanics.

109 Tomkins, *Affect Imagery Consciousness*, 2:705.

110 Brand, *The Blue Clerk*, 110.

111 For Tomkins, each distinct affect has its own stimulus profile, answering
to a certain evolutionary need of the organism for processing a particular

tion of information theory onto the study of affect invites us to think about economies of signals that circulate neither within nor without, but via the channel of, the flesh. With respect to these signals, the subject is that "affectable thing" (in Denise Ferreira da Silva's words), the embodied medium through which a labor of being affected produces meaning.[112] In addition to commodities (and information as a commodity), the exchanges that capitalism demands include information about each individual's value as a commodity in the marketplace of exploitable labor, which is also the market of power and prestige.[113] An impassioned calculation, driven by the impetus to establish one's worth in a system that denies the stability of value in the

kind of information. He describes eight (sometimes nine) distinct affects: startle, anger, fear, shame, distress, disgust, interest/excitement, joy, and a ninth that he calls, on analogy with disgust, "dissmell." The siren that erupts when you step outside startles you, forcibly re-directing your attention from whatever authorial thoughts to your immediate environment. For someone who knows to know what sirens can mean for people like her, the siren will probably also cause fear, which is the affect profile of rapidly escalating stimuli: e.g., a quickened pulse, an associative rush of images, a frantic search for more information or a plan of escape. The siren's persistence or recurrence turns fear to anger, as the flesh is wracked by signals that it remains powerless to modulate. Of critical importance to Tomkins's theory is the idea that each affect "imprints" its physiological response with the same profile as its stimulus, creating a feedback loop that persists until the problem posed by the original stimulus has been resolved. Anger, for Tomkins, is the most dangerous and destructive of the affects, since its painful profile tends to be self-perpetuating. For an insightful analysis of how anger fuels the racializing animus of agents of the white supremacist carceral state, see Ioanide, *The Emotional Politics of Racism,* 55–80.

112 Ferreira da Silva, *Toward a Global Idea of Race.*

113 As Luc Boltanski and Eve Chiapello argue, the self represents the horizon of surplus value, beyond even labor-power (which can be replaced by machines). This self, as they note, is construed as immanently capitalist, in virtue of the fact that the person exploits himself or exploits the contributions of others that go into maintaining the self. The privileged, entrepreneurial self is the commodity into which disappear others' labor and creativity and care (*The New Spirit of Capitalism,* trans. Gregory Elliott [New York: Verso, 2007]).

reiteration of every value's reification, produces the subject as a perpetually angry one.

The subject desperate to fix the signals of whiteness and masculinity into the signs of personal success knows how *not* to know that on the ground floor, capitalism rests on the power to make human life into a thing that can be bought, sold, and disposed of at will. In other words, his desperation and anger reiterate the forgetting of that violence, and the violence of his forgetting exploits the labor of those who know to know because they cannot do otherwise. With their knowledge, wrought on the edge of a living disposability, they forge the tools to make a different future, another world. Despite the fact that "every aspect of life is an emergency," in the face of that, on the docks where ships come with their freight in the (choke)hold of modernity, these voices "work to make the world intelligible": to stave off unreason where unreason insists on its identity as the world's *raison d'être*.[114] And yet, alongside what profits us in that work, something escapes its capture as profit, something that becomes intelligible only as inheritance or as gift. The clerk's left-hand pages accumulate the emergency but also "a small present happiness and an eternal hope, even also, joy," which offer themselves as part of what emerges, radiant strands of what plights one generation to the next.[115] They accumulate, those pages, the author's memories (beginning with her grandfather's life and work beside the sea). They propagate transformative moments: the music of Mingus, a silence in the desert, the breath of ancestors, and something like an ongoing inventory of the improbable possibilities of language itself:

114 Brand, *The Blue Clerk,* 208; Alexander, *Pedagogies of Crossing,* 118. As Hortense Spillers remarks: "It is striking that precisely because black cultures arose in the world of normative violence, coercive labor, and the virtually absolute crush of the everyday struggle for existence, its subjects could imagine, could dare to imagine, a world beyond the coercive technologies of their daily bread [...]" ("The Idea of Black Culture," CR: *The New Centennial Review* 6, no. 3 [2007]: 25, emphasis in the original).
115 Brand, *The Blue Clerk,* 242.

This is what the clerk thinks: lemon documents, lemon fac-
tors, then lemon, watch lemon, lemon nails, wasp lemon,
lemon summary, slap lemon, lemon dangers, lemon cre-
vasses, there are a few documents that came, lemon defec-
tions, why allow a certain kind of speech, lemon vines, lemon
ankles, distance lemon, knotting lemon, bay lemon, lemon
reaches. This is what we have.[116]

If information theory measures the value of a message as a function of the probabilities that its signals represent, then information is a property available only to the one who, in lieu of the
labor of interpretation, decides the assignment of probabilities
that govern the field. The *relevant* decision cannot, by fiat of the
theory, occur either in the production or reception of the message itself. "What the clerk thinks" defies the grammar of this
theory for another kind of enumeration of possibility. A catalog
of the unrelieved decisions that living requires, born of an insistence that "a word is not an easy thing, it is not a light thing."[117]
Not a thing, in other words, to be trifled with. At the same, the
gamble (or gambol) of it "is what we have." Because the emergency must be lived over and over again, endured anew each
instant, its "inventory," as Brand writes — using a homonym I
read in both of its senses — "is agape."[118]

Brand's practice of inventory evokes that custodial love described by James Baldwin: "The custodian of an inheritance,
which is what blacks have had to be, in Western culture, must
hand the inheritance down the line. So, you, the custodian, recognize, finally, that your life does not belong to you: nothing
belongs to you."[119] That "nothing belongs to you": if whiteness, as
George Yancy claims, is a "sutured" identity, this thought pulls

---

116 Ibid., 225. For a powerful reading of Brand's text in relation to "the hold"
and "the wake" as figures for Black life in its inflection by circum-Atlantic
slavery, see Sharpe, *In the Wake*, 17–19.
117 Brand, *The Blue Clerk,* 208.
118 Ibid., 61.
119 Baldwin, "The Devil Finds Work," 566.

against the suture.[120] This nothing is the "cut" that each new performance, every fresh decision, makes in the series that it prolongs and extends. The suture presupposes the cut of which it is a mode, a mask, of forgetting, while the cut makes memory possible. Thinking "in the break" with Fred Moten, we might say that the cut creates rhythm, granting us access to "an experience of meaning," rhythm being what the flesh endures, the oscillation of pain and pleasure, want and sustenance, dread and desire that quickens us and is how songs live and die in the gut.[121] Or as Harney and Moten write, "the black aesthetic turns on a dialectic of luxuriant withholding," ensuring that "the trouble with beauty […] is always and everywhere troubled again and again."[122] The cut is in-formation, ingress — the world pressing upon the flesh — the world realizing itself in the here and now. And if the organism experiences this pressure as the image of a durable past and an imminent future, it does so because in the present, the shock of becoming overwhelms the being that is, that brims over with "the indefinite complexity of what is felt."[123] That no decision exhausts the decidable, that there is always a residue: this is how the lure of the proposition comes into play, like a wriggle inside knowledge, a fluke in the laminate, a ludic squirm beneath the grammar in which I have learned to say "I am."

"This information can never be lost, only irrevocably given in transit": Harney and Moten invite us to the scene of a performance equally tactile and auditory, where messages are passed, not exchanged, in an intimacy that joins us hand to hand.[124] Lis-

---

120 Yancy, *Black Bodies, White Gazes,* 12–13.

121 Moten, *In the Break,* 92.

122 Harney and Moten, *The Undercommons,* 48.

123 Alfred North Whitehead, *Process and Reality: An Essay in Cosmology,* corr. edn. (New York: Free Press, 1978), 153. Riley, *Impersonal Passion,* writes from a Whiteheadian or Baldwinesque perspective that "a vivid part of an instant is its drawing into itself the reverberating past as the impacted persistence of earlier ravages" (142).

124 Harney and Moten, *The Undercommons,* 51.

tening to Julius Eastman's serial compositions for multiple pianos, I am called to such a scene. Just as Brand's writing disrupts
the grammar that would either lock meaning up in the subject's
head or banish it to irrelevance, Eastman's music, with its col-
laborative, improvised sound, renders information as something other than the process by which inert matter receives the
imprint of an intentional and transparent form. Eastman's music
gives us a slice of "phonic materiality" in transit.[125] Privileging
neither melody nor its negation in dissonance, each piece creates
a texture of repetition and improvisation, echo and emphasis, in
which a musical surface of repeated phrases is roiled by changes
in timing and dynamics that occur across multiple instruments
in antiphonal arrangement. On the recording I have, four pianos play the score, overdubbing it onto itself in real time. The
music pools into momentary equilibrium, only to be dislodged
by the eruption of previously heard strains that sweep the piece
toward another basin of attraction. The music swarms. On one
piece, Eastman's own voice joins the pianos at regular intervals,
clerically counting aloud — "One, two, three, four" — before the
pianos redouble their attack.[126] Eastman's voice performs "the
break," gathering the rhythm, as it were, to unroll it into the next
segment, summoning time.

A liminal and long-neglected figure in the history of the
twentieth-century avant-garde, Eastman described his compositions as "organic music," a term that elicits both their use of
additive structure, and their dependence on improvisation to
realize structure in the act of transformation:

> [T]he third part of any part (of the third measure or the third
> section, the third part) has to contain all of the information
> of the first two parts and then go on from there. So therefore,

125 The phrase is from Moten, *Black and Blur,* 30.
126 Julius Eastman, *Unjust Malaise* (New York: New World Records, 2005).
    The pieces, which have titles consisting of the words "evil" and "crazy"
    prepended to the n-word, defy even my citation of them here.

unlike Romantic music or Classical music where you have actually different sections and you have these sections which for instance are in great contrast to the first section or to some other section in the piece...these pieces they're not... they're not exactly perfect yet. They're not perfect. But there's an attempt to make every section contain all of the information of the previous sections, or else taking out information at a gradual and logical rate.[127]

Eastman's aesthetic approach, like James Baldwin's ethical vision, might be described as custodial. At any rate, it deploys a concept of information that gets itself reformed by the idea of tradition, a carrying forward, handing down, or passing along in which innovation and loss are inevitable but "gradual," suggesting that the artist as custodian does not rush to seize the material as his own to make anew. Unlike the Markov chains of Shannon's information theory, Eastman's version of information is not memory-less. Rather, it describes a practice of memory as an embedding of the past in the present, which involves the placement or disposition of the body itself in space and time.[128] The freedom of the composer lies in making space for improvisation, and the freedom of the improviser lies in inhabiting that space, embellishing it without violating it, and making possible its transfer to the next phase of performance. Improvisation, as Moten writes, realizes itself as "sound become dispersive sensuality," which offers an apt figure for Baldwin's idea of inheritance, too.[129] Aesthetically, this orientation centers the embodied, engaged performer, including the listener or reader,

---

127 Eastman, from oral remarks before a performance at Northwestern University, quoted in Ellie M. Hisama, "'Diving into the Earth': The Musical Worlds of Julius Eastman," in *Rethinking Difference in Music Scholarship*, eds. Jeffrey Kallberg, Melanie Lowe, and Olivia Bloechl (Cambridge: Cambridge University Press, 2015), 276–77.

128 On the knowledge that the body bears in its spatial orientation, see McKittrick, *Demonic Grounds*.

129 Moten, *In the Break*, 47.

who performs the music by absorbing the rhythm in a resonant *habitus* (nodding along, tapping his foot, etc.), or who performs the text by elaborating on its imagery and narrative and following (silently or aloud) the contours of its phonic, sonic, somatic, graphic drift. Rather than the disinterested pleasure in form that entitles one to speak universally, this aesthetics has its (an) originally displaced and therefore fugitive home in a dis-possessive experience of layering and loss. Like affect itself, tradition is — e.g., in the "black radical tradition" described by Moten — a figure for the flesh burdened into time.

Moten's phrase echoes Eastman's explanation on being pressed about the scandalous titles of his compositions. Describing slavery as "the basis of the American economic system," Eastman refigures the primary and persistent signifier of that violence as a name for "that thing which is fundamental [...] that person or thing that obtains to a basic-ness, a fundamental-ness, and eschews that thing which is superficial or, can we say, elegant."[130] The being of Blackness is a radical thing partly because, as Moten argues, its resilient, resistant being (its insistence on being, you might say) unsettles the borders of humanity as policed by that class of beings who exempt themselves from the violence that makes commodities out of everything else in the world. Blackness as the basis of modernity, including its economic systems, but also its aesthetic achievements. The tradition communicates itself, per Moten, via a "soma-sonority

---

130 Eastman, "Julius Eastman's Spoken Introduction to the Northwestern University Concert," *Unjust Malaise*. This anthology features two pieces out of what Eastman refers to, in the pre-concert remarks included on the same album, as a series of fifty-two. This anthology also includes the piece "Gay Guerilla," the title of which Eastman explains as follows: "There aren't many gay guerillas, I don't feel that gaydom has that strength. So therefore I use that word in the hopes that they will. [...] A guerilla is someone who is in any case sacrificing his life for a point of view. [...] If there is a cause, and if it is a great cause, those who belong to that cause will sacrifice their blood, because without blood, there is no cause. So therefore, that is the reason that I use 'gay guerilla,' in hopes that I might be one, if called upon to be one."

that refuses to disavow itself." It can be heard and felt, not only at the summits of literary, musical, and artistic achievement, but also "beneath speech," insofar as speech remains the privilege of those who allocate the illocutionary conditions of the human on the basis of skin color and other abusively arbitrary categories.[131] If the white guy, voiced by this apparatus, "can say nothing else" but this violence, which is the "Amen" of whiteness, then Eastman's claiming of the hateful epithet, like his counting aloud during performance, enacts "a series of strategies and/or techniques of corporeality" that disturb that field.[132] They demand to count, they demand to matter, they demand accountability from those who hide behind their "Amen," and at the same time, they refuse to be counted, tallied up, held down, or held in place. Such strategies do not work in isolation, only in concert, like the calls by which guerrillas and outlaws improvise survival, always on the move, imps of probability who outflank your frontal attack.

I hear Eastman's remark that "they're not perfect" as more than an admission about his own compositions or about their "finished" state. Because the improvisational work is, by definition, unfinished, i.e., open to (re-)interpretation, it remains a stranger to perfection. Or at least, a stranger to the senses of perfection that connote closure, completeness, comprehensiveness. (An improvised performance might yet be "perfect" in an-

---

131 Moten, "Preface for a Solo by Miles Davis," 217. Or as Alexander Weheliye puts it, writing about the radical energy that the flesh communicates in its resistance to capture and control, "[h]ardly anterior to language and therefore the human, these rumblings vocalize the humming relay of the world that makes linguistic structures possible, directly corresponding to how the not-quite- and nonhuman give rise to the universe of Man. [...] [T]he flesh engulfs not only Man's visually marked others via instruments of torture and the intergenerational transmission of hieroglyphics but emanates rays of potential enfleshment through the far-flung corners of Being in the world of Man" (*Habeas Viscus*, 172).

132 Weheliye, *Phonographies*, 38. In Weheliye's words, "the white subject's vocal apparatus merely serves to repeat and solidify racial difference as it is inscribed in the field of vision" (42).

other sense: singular, not admitting of replication, indelible, one of a kind.) This estrangement of perfection applies as much to the moral work (the work of love and care) as the aesthetic one (the work of sense). Love cannot afford to wait on perfect information. Bureaucratic grammars can pretend to such perfection only because the processes that model communication as information are memory-less. They institute the erasure of every particular trajectory in the postulate of a probabilistic, abstract, but still deterministic space. But this erasure has its own particular trajectory. As a frame for political violence and economic exploitation, it underwrites the systematic ruination of lives and the destruction of communities and even entire peoples. While we decry a few spectacular examples of crimes against humanity as bureaucracy run amok, the equally bureaucratic processes that help to produce humanity as a field partitioned against itself touch nearly every aspect of modern life.[133] No wonder, then, that this drive toward erasure should be embodied. It is felt, I would argue, as the demand for mastery over all channels of communication, for complete control of the present as a means

133 On the divisions within the category of the human as a tool of domination, see Sylvia Wynter, "Unsettling the Coloniality of Being/Power/Truth/ Freedom: Towards the Human, After Man, Its Overrepresentation—An Argument," CR: The New Centennial Review 3, no. 3 (2003): 257–337; Weheliye, Habeas Viscus; and Ferreira da Silva, Toward a Global Idea of Race. As Dean Spade argues, the "administrative norms" central to bureaucratic rationality (for instance, being allowed or denied the right to register a change of gender on your driver's license) are frequently "less visible," in terms of the harms they cause, than "those moments when people are fired or killed or excluded explicitly because of their race or body type or gender […]." Yet administrative norms, whose very explicitness as impartial and impersonal rules seems to shield them from scrutiny, retain the power to "structure the entire context of life" (Normal Life, 24). Especially at the level of populations (rather than individuals), advantages and disadvantages, "security and vulnerability," opportunity and exploitation, etc., can be distributed in ways that, by appearing not explicitly to exclude anyone, not only perpetuate harm but also function to erase the contexts in which the individual might be said (i.e., by those enjoying said advantages, security, opportunity) to have a legitimate claim to the redress of wrongs done them by the system (117).

of rendering irrelevant the meaning of the past. It is akin, in a way, to the "nuclear scripts" described by Silvan Tomkins, which structure experience as the endless repetition of "good scenes" becoming "bad scenes," reproducing the chance for perfection as the rehearsal of its failure.[134] The nuclear demand is fundamentally reactionary, not radical or revolutionary. It is insensible to the history wrought by its own repetitions. Thus, it remains committed to an inversion of good and bad as these are experienced by a self for which autonomy remains the gauge. The nuclear script numbs one to the reality of others, to their necessary contribution to the work of changing the conditions of the polarity itself. I don't want to suggest that whites, or white men, or white cishet men, have a monopoly on maladaptive affect, any more than I wish to center or privilege their feelings as a precondition for understanding patriarchal white supremacy. Rather, it is the very process of centering and polarizing that remains integral to the wages of whiteness and white masculinity, which is a mode of identity premised on the promise of dominance insofar as this dominance can never be durably achieved.[135] Thus, the answer to Du Bois's question, "What on earth is whiteness that one should so desire it?" is tautological. The answer, indefinitely deferred, is whiteness itself. A love animated by a desire for dominance, by a desire to know the self as dominant in that relation, requires avoidance. Collectively, we white cishet men should stand astonished by the spectacle

134 Locked into a maladaptive spiral, in which some kernel of scenes (e.g., a mother's affection, a father's anger) have been "magnified" into mythic images of perfection and its opposite, the personality in the grip of a nuclear script finds, at every turn, that the bad implacably succeeds the good, and such a personality insists on the unconditional reversal of this dynamic. But it is their very commitment to that reversal that drives them, again and again, back to scenes of humiliation, betrayal, etc. In thrall to a nuclear script, "the self victimizes itself into a tragic scene in which it longs most desperately for what it is too intimidated to pursue effectively" (Tomkins, *Affect Imagery Consciousness,* 806–9).

135 Thomas Dipiero, *White Men Aren't* (Durham: Duke University Press, 2009).

of what our own desires have wrought. But we turn away, or we redouble the terror we know too well how to produce. (If the white male shooter is only nearly a terrorist, that is because he does not use terror for a political end; he uses terror as an end in itself. His spectacular violence aims to cement a meaning whose vulnerability to change he cannot abide.)

As Baldwin suggests, Black lives not only matter, but they serve as custodians of honesty and compassion in a society premised on self-deception, prejudice, and plunder, wherein the wages of another's exploitation become the invidious signs of success. A society still organized around forgetting the labor without wages that Black folk and other people of color have done to make the modern world intelligible in spite of itself. Considering the case for reparations, Ta-Nehisi Coates writes, "perhaps no number can fully capture the multi-century plunder of black people in America. Perhaps the number is so large that it can't be imagined, let alone calculated and dispensed."[136] Coates's point is that the possible failure of the calculable does not absolve us of the work of imagination. Demanding reparations becomes the necessary condition for imagining them, for imagining their necessity. By which I mean, for reckoning with the plunder and the terror and the underhanded dealing by which white success has always consolidated itself in America. Coates, like Baldwin, helps us understand the American nation itself as a kind of epic nuclear script. But one in which the bad scenes keep playing out on the backs of those whose suffering would appear to be what white people's idea of the good requires, the nation having staked its career on one color mattering more than any other thing. To break the spiral, whites must shake off the lulling sense that the past and its burden of "delinquent debt […] can be made to disappear if only we don't look."[137] We must

136 Ta-Nehisi Coates, "The Case for Reparations," *The Atlantic,* June 2014, https://www.theatlantic.com/magazine/archive/2014/06/the-case-for-reparations/361631/.
137 Ibid. Coates proposes that, with respect to questions about reparations (e.g., to whom, how much, when, how to pay for it, etc.), "wrestling

demand reparations for slavery, Jim Crow, redlining, disparate policing and sentencing, etc. However hard the accounting, it won't be anything compared to the burdens so many have borne and continue to bear for our collective failure on this account. And we must demand, too, a true acknowledgment and recognition of Native American sovereignty. Only through such forms of reckoning can we hope to find our way to the practices of responsibility that we humans desperately need.[138] Our collective survival rests on the cultivation of tactics for keeping the future alive in the abundance of being together, tactics that amount to an ethos of love, creativity, and care.

Suppose the past can be reckoned with, suppose it can be dealt with in a reparative way, but only through scripts that disperse affect into processes of compassion and solidarity. Suppose that such processes need not exclude modes of organized, even militant, resistance. But suppose that their very militancy might be grounded in an ethos and an aesthetics that teach one to "act so that there is no use in center."[139] Suppose, furthermore, that we supplement Stein's injunction to dispersively sensuous performance with an invitation to perform a sensuous acknowledgment of, and with, others. The written texts collected in Tracie Morris's *handholding* are accompanied by audio tracks that consist, for the most part, of recordings of Morris reading aloud. Both textual and vocal performances are meant to accompany pieces by other artists (films, poems, and musical/sonic compositions) to which they respond and on which they riff. Morris's introduction encourages the reader/listener to "read along/ listen along with me and Kubrick, Akomfrah, Stein and Schwit-

publicly with these questions matters as much as—if not more than—the specific answers that might be produced."

138 Andrea Smith proposes that we redefine "sovereignty" as a way of "being responsible for the land," such that "nationhood can engage all those who fulfill responsibilities for land" ("Queer Theory and Native Studies: The Heteronormativity of Settler Colonialism," *GLQ: A Journal of Lesbian and Gay Studies* 16, nos. 1–2 [2010]: 62).

139 Stein, *Tender Buttons,* 63.

ters and Cage."[140] But these modes of explicit accompaniment also bring to mind the tacit accompaniment of those others, the traces of whose voices, gestures, touch, and flesh cut against our flesh (like waves against the shore) as we think, speak, write, listen, and think. Morris's engagement with modernist and post-modernist texts enacts a composing-with as "a poetics of survival, a queer relationality," an improvisatory relation to cultural materials that serves at once as homage, critique, archaeology, formal experiment, and personal testament.[141] These pieces perform a re-membering of what their source texts partially suppress, the real and figurative dismemberment of Black life and Black female life. Like Eastman's, Morris's compositions come together like fractals, in which a fragment of experience, a momentary and intimate facet of attention, discloses an array of other facets. Any word may participate in multiple networks of association and affinity (by alliteration, rhyme, metaphor, paronomasia, etc.). And like Stein's *Tender Buttons*, which it annotates and accompanies, Morris's work illuminates ordinary objects, spaces, and occasions as they participate in orders of cultural and economic value.[142] With a "basic-ness" these things

140 Morris, *handholding, 7*.
141 The quoted phrase is from Alexis Pauline Gumbs, "Nobody Mean More: Black Feminist Pedagogy and Solidarity," in *The Imperial University: Academic Repression and Scholarly Dissent,* eds. Piya Chatterjee and Sunaina Maira (Minneapolis: University of Minnesota Press, 2014), 254.
142 On "annotation" as a method of Black aesthetic/critical practice, see Sharpe, *In the Wake,* 102–34.
    Writing about Stein's purported "unreadability," Natalia Cecire argues that this critical stalking-horse responds to the ways in which Stein's texts insist on foregrounding the gendered taint of the body writing them, a body supposedly fit (in virtue of its assigned gender) only for "unwaged labor, especially repetitive labor including housework and information work" ("Ways of Not Reading Gertrude Stein," ELH 82, no. 1 [2015]: 303). For Cecire, Stein's repetitive, paratactic prose, together with its subversion of the reader's expectations for narrative or grammatical coherence, does more than defy the conventions of both masculinist literature and "women's writing"; it appears to indulge in a kind of excess that defeats interpretation. And it does so, Cecire suggests, by seeming (at least,

shine in their mattering as the interface between thought and feeling, sensation and abstraction, speech and act, where the texture of language opens us to a dispersal beyond what we can hope to possess: "To add, to adorn is not superfluous, it's the essence to get at something. To take it in, to complete."[143] Morris's work, in this sense, provides an essential supplement to Stein's method, an extended riff on Stein's claim that "the difference is spreading."[144]

The radically beveled vision of domestic space in *Tender Buttons* remains circumscribed by the fact that Stein's dispersive attention lacks a history. The objects that populate her text are just *there,* even if they restlessly gesture elsewhere, toward a horizon now whimsical and humorous, now ominous, now ecstatic. Morris's "re-viewing" of Stein's text annotates the latter with a fugitive montage of narrative gestures that themselves "spread" outward into other histories via the lateral logic of image, apposition, rhyme, and pun. In the first section, "If I Re-viewed Her / Objectively" (annotating the "Objects" section of *Tender Buttons*), Morris imagines a woman moving among the things. She is a bride and then a widow, and her domestic toil ensures that the domestic objects that shine for Stein do not lose their luster:

to many male readers) somehow too embodied. Which is to say, not necessarily undisciplined, but disciplined in "the wrong kind of work," not the kind of work that produces value in the literary marketplace. "Stein's unreadability, then, is always ready to risk (and receive) the charges of 'fraud' or 'hoax'; it insists on the value of repetitive labors without presupposing that that value must come on capital's gendered terms (as wage-eligible 'hard work')" (304).

If Morris's approach to Stein as "handholding" suggests an embrace of the embodied nature of reading as the accompaniment of writing, perhaps it advocates, too, for a different relation to the question of readability. Reading becomes not a matter of interpretation (or its absence), of assigning and registering (or denying) the value of a commodity on the basis of assumptions about the labor behind it, but a labor in its own right, a cooperative mode of engagement that can also function, not as an accounting for value, but as a holding to account.

143 Morris, *handholding,* 104.

144 Stein, *Tender Buttons,* 11.

"After all this, heartache, this bruise, she has to do the washing too. After she sits."[145] And the capillary action of Morris's lyric voice links up such moments with collective histories of struggle and oppression, with life and death on a larger scale. The Triangle Shirtwaist Factory fire, for instance, haunts the tenderness of Stein's buttons: "She's a prism. A triangle of a waist. The scythe, the window. The fire."[146] Morris's work is cut by the knowledge of whose labor produced these objects, and whose flesh, in its vulnerability to violence and exploitation no less than its creative power, sustains the difference celebrated by the poet's gaze.[147] Prompted by Stein's ruminations on "an ordinary color" in the "Food" section of *Tender Buttons,* Morris writes/recites,

A regular color is translucent. It's "unaffiliated." It's neutral. It's "natural." Everything else isn't essential. So they say…and most of us mean "we" when we say "they." It doesn't make juice, it's the absence of juice. It's water. Cocoanut water. Bathwater. Rosewater. Porcelain ablution.[148]

145 Morris, *handholding,* 75. Morris's "re-viewing" of Stein through the figure of a domestic worker resonates with Patricia Hill Collins's remark that "[d]omestic work allowed African-American women to see White elites, both actual and aspiring, from perspectives largely obscured from Black men and from these groups themselves" (*Black Feminist Thought: Knowledge, Consciousness, and the Politics of Empowerment,* 2nd edn. [New York: Routledge, 2009], 13).

146 Morris, *handholding,* 76.

147 In a passage that shuttles between the distinct but interlocking forms of violence that are domestic waged labor, settler-colonial occupation, circum-Atlantic slavery, and lynching — and between the strategies of communal survival and resistance by which Black folk and Native and Indigenous peoples have created livable worlds in defiance of white supremacy — Morris makes this point emphatically: "If I had to review her, if I had to rewind, if I had to redo, reuse, renew…I'd think about where those foods come from. She know? I'd wonder how they'd get full. I'd wonder if what we did with pig parts of necessity, they did to us out of luxury. The abundance of us growing in the fields" (ibid., 85).

148 Ibid., 94. As Morris notes in her preface to this work, "[w]hen I went to the 'food' however, the text seemed to feel more and more distanced from the source, from Stein. […] My muse is off on her own, talking to other muses

The ordinariness of Stein's (unspecified) color reflects a posture in which the subject views their own experience as a universal standard, as the neutral transparency against which all others will be judged biased and opaque. Or worse yet, condemned as inessential, i.e., lacking in essence, as an imperfect mixture that violates the rule. But even if "most of us" succumb to the egoism of perspective, the dominant perspective belongs to the color that has no color, to the whiteness that attends my lady's bath, to the whiteness that promises to absolve how many crimes, to wash away what volumes of blood.

Stein's next paragraph in *Tender Buttons* deepens the domestic intimacy of this ordinary color, riffing on "a work" that is "dainty and really dainty, very dainty, ordinarily dainty" — although, as is often the case in this text, menace rears its head: "all of that in most violent likely."[149] Tracing a more narrative passage through "bath" and "breakfast," Morris asks us to acknowledge the intimate violence of the labor that Stein wants only to glance at (can't keep from glancing at):

There's this weak-day kind of water that this is. The bath that one takes before getting out there, in the work world, whirling down the drain. You need breakfast before heading out to work. [...]

Being late is no excuse. Eating is no excuse. The traffic is no excuse. The transportation is no excuse. Waiting is no excuse. There's no excuse not to be here. To not exude enthusiasm. To not talk about anything that isn't work-related. To not re-

like Etheridge Knight's, my ancestors' kitchen aesthetics. The way they manifested art in kitchens at home and homes away from home [...]. They had a whole other conversation about food that Stein could not enter" (ibid., 71).

Stein's text reads as follows: "An ordinary color, a color is that strange mixture which makes, which does make which does not make a ripe juice, which does not make a mat" (*Tender Buttons,* 44).

149 Stein, *Tender Buttons,* 44–45.

lated anything to not work is not related. There's no excuse.
There's no cue. There's no ex. There's only cause. The cause
is to work one's way towards it. And by "it" he means "me,"
meaning him. Singular.[150]

In this passage, the one who tolerates no excuses, like *A* in Wittgenstein's vignette, asserts his monopoly on the meaning of the
other's work. He, the one in charge, is the "singular" meaning,
the sole final "cause," on account of which one works. Or one
works "towards it […] meaning him" because in the grammar of
domination, the decisions imposed by those in power represent
the alpha and omega of every labor, every process, like a closed-
circuit video in which the other appears as a grainy ghost on the
screen. Every decision, every meaning, presupposes the radical
mattering of the flesh, but this grammar demands the erasure
of the relative, the relational, and the real acts of bearing, sup-
porting, and suffering that lie packed against the cut of whatever
we decide, calling for their belated (*B*-laden) acknowledgment.
As a result, the logic that best serves domination is an incoher-
ent one: "To not related anything to not work is not related."
He who "means 'me'" clings to a grammar that groans under
the weight of its disavowals. But to be clear, it is the other who
groans, grimaces, forcing a grin to satisfy the requirement that
they "exude enthusiasm"; that they "remain sweet. That's what
everyone said you should do" (see "your saying please").[151] The
etiolated perspective privileged by patriarchal white supremacy,
like the dead labor congealed in the commodities of capitalism,
requires infusions of affect and desire by those who shoulder
the yoke. (But as Morris reminds us, "When they put the bit in
we were not smiling. When they put the yoke on, we were not
pastoral.")[152] The meaning that the system pays out, a meaning

---

150 Morris, *handholding,* 94.
151 Ibid., 95.
152 Ibid., 84. If Stein's "white hunter is nearly crazy," his whiteness signifies
     the nearness to a madness that projects its own unreason onto the other's
     resistance. This resistance is nothing but the eminently reasonable

that is, to each one of us, though by violently unequal degrees, a belief in their own singular endowment, derives from the very meaning, or meaningfulness, that it stole from us, collectively, taken together in our misery and our strength.

Like the texts of Gertrude Stein (and of many other writers who hark back to her example), Morris's work expresses a practice of dwelling where meaning and sense emerge in the world's manifestation as a process of being-affected-by. But here what cuts is also the question, as Dionne Brand puts it, re-encountering the racism evident in Stein, "How many micro-abrasions, as they say, do you think I could take?"[153] There is an accounting to be had, but not in any sense of what might totalize things, letting any of us off the hook, endorsing my *ergo sum*. Morris holds hands with Stein's text in order to hold Stein, and us, to account. The vocal accompaniment (intended to support "listening and/ or reading both texts simultaneously as legal proofreaders do") heightens our sense of the phrase, its fraught boundaries, its silent, boundless, bonded freight.[154] Where Morris slips up or stutters in her recitation, she lets it stand or else re-doubles it, making the "mistake" part of the take, refusing to withhold what can be held-with, but giving the voice over to, spacing it out into,

response to a violence that drives reason out of the one who wields it. As with the jailer who keeps prisoners in order to fill the prison he has made out of the void in himself, this violence and this madness mutually suture themselves into the "enlightened" human being, an apparatus that destroys the evidence. As Morris muses in one her text's most explicit sections,

"I wonder if they ate us. I wonder, if there was another reason we were roasted. I wonder what Leopold hosted? Why'd he burn the evidence? What I'd like to see Conrad write about: the heart, the heartlessness. What did they do with it? How'd it taste? I mean, if we were chattel. If they were cackling. If they were as crackled as the prepackaged snacks in store. Like the scalping, like a head scratched clean off, they said the Reds did, they did against Red. Against red. A contrast. A ghast. I wonder what they ate? I wonder why they talk about Aztecs like that? I wonder if they are saying something again? Something in ink again? Something about Incans? About the spilling" (84–85).

153 Brand, *The Blue Clerk,* 116.
154 Morris, *handholding,* 7.

what Christina Sharpe calls "wake work."[155] One doesn't read for proof, but with a clerical precision not at odds with a certain abundance, though the *A*-men would hardly think to look for it there: "Concepts and intangibles are what. What it means is what it is. We decide and that decision is not a noun it's a feeling."[156] Morris's work, like that of the other artists, writers, and scholars whose handholding this essay depends on, reminds me of the urgency of deepening a phenomenology of feeling into an ethics of love and care. Without making a spectacle of violence and suffering, that work strives to keep alive for the reader the density of the circum-Atlantic history that, for Black folk, Native and Indigenous peoples, and many other communities of color, remains virtually inescapable in the present-day United States. And that remains, for whites, all too virtuously escapable. The reader encounters this density in the layered resonance of image and idiom, foregrounded by the hesitations and slippages performed by Morris's recorded voice. These kinks in the chain of association feel less like moments of searching for the "right"

155 Sharpe explains, "I want to distinguish what I am calling Black being in the wake and wake work from the work of melancholia and mourning. And though wake work is, at least in part, attentive to mourning and the mourning work that takes place on local and trans*local and global levels, and even as we know that mourning an event might be interminable, how does one mourn the interminable event?" (*In the Wake,* 19). Sharpe's "wake work" shares, as I take it, an ethos and an aesthetics with Baldwin's idea of tradition as inheritance, and with Moten's concept of improvisation, which also aptly describes (part of) what Morris is up to in these "sonic, textual engagements." As Moten claims, "improvisation is the unacknowledged grapho-spatiality of material writing" ("Preface for a Solo by Miles Davis," 240). In the way of describing Morris's work, I'm also drawn to what Marisa Parham calls "Black glitch aesthetics." Morris's tongue-tripping recitation underscores a phenomenology in which "meaningfulness is continually re-encoded as anticipation is re-experienced itself as a kind of knowledge, surfing between dreadful and delicious, break dancing is a non-binary state" (".break .dance," *sx archipelagos* 3 [July 2019], http://smallaxe.net/sxarchipelagos/issue03/parham/parham.html).
156 Morris, *handholding,* 113.

word, than an artful handling of strands of meaning that threaten to tie up speech itself:

> There's a crescent moon, a sliver of light from the clouds making a cross on the tree where He's hanging. There is a sexta-star and it's all at the same fixed spot. I see it all and still don't believe it. I believe what I see but nouns are subjunctive, um, subject, er, suspect.[157]

The hanging figure in this passage evokes, of course, the specter of white supremacist terror that haunts Morris's text. The tree is also, in context, what a widow sees outside her window, as she stands rooted in a claustrophobic world of domestic waged labor, in a place fixed by both her race and gender, a "lady who was on her way someplace and got something said to." (In counterpoint to the "Rooms" section of *Tender Buttons,* this section of Morris's text is titled "Enclosure.") The threading of the past, which is always multiple, through the dispositional grammar of action and speech yields the present moment as the lure of our futurity (as the shimmer skipping across the water at which we leap). Stein's *Tender Buttons* teaches us how "the sensible decision" loses its luster when we are properly attuned to the actual luster of experience, its variety, its spreading difference, in the light of which the sensible decision is "not even more likely to be pleasing."[158] Stein's text, at its enigmatic conclusion, even suggests that the errancy haunting each decision — in the cut, you might say, between the sensible and the sensuous — makes possible our wonder at the phenomena that confront us, and that this wonder discloses the only true grounds of justice and care:

> The care with which the rain is wrong and the green is wrong and the white is wrong, the care with which there is a chair and plenty of breathing. The care with which there is incred-

157 Ibid., 117.
158 Stein, *Tender Buttons,* 76.

ible justice and likeness, all this makes a magnificent aspara-
gus and also a fountain.[159]

Wonder is, for Stein, rooted in the body and its situation ("a
chair and plenty of breathing"). In its attention to the texture of
wonder and embodiment in Stein's text, Morris's work teaches
us to deepen this reading by acknowledging how our access to
wonder, like our bodies, inherits a history and, as such, summons us to a reckoning. I suppose this is to say that Morris's
work thinks more carefully about the illocutionary and perlocutionary dimensions of poetic language: "The luxury of saying
why is there a difference is to be able to ask."[160] Or that it takes
more care to insist that the alternative to the bureaucratic lure
of the "sensible decision" is not poetic license (for they are, after
all, two sides of the same coin). The alternative, rather, might
feel like dwelling in the decision (not in *in*decision, but in the
cut that accompanies decision), feeling the accumulated weight
that each occasion ushers into the present:

> Why's the world's knowing attached to that one little area of
> the planet. To the victors go the victims' gaze, I guess. It's not
> exactly translucent, not exactly opaque. More like a veil one
> could be born with.
>   The ocean is encircling all things, whatever they mean.
> The ocean is lapping the tree…
>   Take care. Take care.[161]

159 Ibid.
160 Morris, *handholding,* 112,
161 Ibid., 117. Such a reckoning is the gift with which George Yancy's "Dear
     White America" concludes: "Take one more deep breath. I have another
     gift. If you have young children, before you fall off to sleep tonight, I
     want you to hold your child. Touch your child's face. Smell your child's
     hair. Count the fingers on your child's hand. See the miracle that is your
     child. And then, with as much vision as you can muster, I want you to
     imagine that your child is black." The gift of care for another, of a care
     that exceeds the nuclear confines of family and the political and economic
     conspiracies of race, gender, class, etc., is not reciprocal in the restricted

The weight of our history, like the encircling ocean, does not only burden things. It sustains them. Just as what sustains us is not being loved and cared for, but the imperative to love, to take care.

sense of what closes the loop of an exchange. Rather, as Rauna Kuokkanen writes, inviting us to make space for the forms of knowledge and praxis that Native and Indigenous worldviews communicate, "gifts are not given primarily to ensure a countergift later on, but to actively acknowledge kinship and coexistence with the world; without this sort of reciprocity, survival — not just of human beings, but of other living things — would be impossible" *(Reshaping the University: Responsibility, Indigenous Epistemes, and the Logic of the Gift* [Vancouver: UBC Press, 2007], 43–44). A gift that deepens the breath and the breadth of the world. A gift of, in, and with the flesh, which is "the loophole of retreat, the liminal space, and the archipelago for those revolutions that will have occurred but remain largely imperceptible within Man's political and critical idioms [...]" (Weheliye, *Habeas Viscus,* 135).

3

Confusions of a White Man/qué:
An Apocryphal Case History

So we must be careful — lest we lose our faith — and become possessed.
— James Baldwin, *The Devil Finds Work*

The worst words revivify themselves within us, vampirically.
— Denise Riley, *Impersonal Passion*

My father was a great lover of imprecation, and a fan of the explicit and the illicit and the tabooed. From him, the *Verboten* received its due. He cussed like one trying to command, by sympathetic magic, the flesh that bothered and tempted him and crossed his will. *Bitch. Cocksucker. Sonofabitch. Motherfucker.* Occasionally, the n-word. He would say the last with a grimace, in a sort of sideways whisper, as if to say, though you don't want to hear it, it has to be said. As if a nod to the impropriety of the word boosted its force. But even as they amplify the feelings they give voice to, slurs tighten the strictures of a basic infelicity. In the act of casting another into the dirt, such speech can expose the speaker as being at the mercy of his own body and its affects, struggling against the difference that he cannot master in himself (the flushed face, the spittled lip). At the end of his life, shrunken inside his frame, my father had lost none of his flair for cursing. A piece on the news or a reminiscence might provoke it. But the words shook the will that had become too frail for them (or so I imagined) as he bowed beneath illness and old age, tired of that burden that the flesh bears as its gift. And so, I thought, the self closes, in the end, over the riddles and secrets and primal scenes that have sustained it, becoming wholly crypt.

My father died the year white supremacy lost the popular vote but won the election, sounding again that furious nothingness within the white male American soul. My father had retired to Lucerne Valley, California, a sparsely populated stretch of desert, with dilapidated settlements, Joshua trees, and tumbleweeds, a place of bluster and desuetude, like a long, harsh note from the archangel's trumpet. To drive the four hours from LAX through the San Gabriel mountains to see him was to endure a monotony made for the end of days. Made on a Hollywood sound stage, but all the same. On the porch of the cabin where he lived, a marble bust of Jesus stood, looking in. From inside the cabin, framed by pink drapes, mountains rose behind the Savior's locks and held the last rays, along brown slopes dotted with brush and boulders, of the evening sun. My father was not a religious man, unless camp counts as a religion. Sentimentality strove in him against an equally strong current of cynicism, producing a sacrilegious bent. But sacrilege is basically nostalgic. As an old man, he slept between zebra-striped sheets on his mother's antique four-poster bed. When not shuttling between specialists to manage an obscure disease, he spent his last years swearing at the news, watching reruns of *Gunsmoke,* and coddling and baby-talking to his two small dogs. *Aw, there's a baby, Daddy. Say, who loves you, Daddy? Aw, who loves you?*

I wrote this book as a way of talking back to my father. Of addressing the insistent narcissism of that question: Who loves you? Any number of books have been written in the straits of that address. The question doesn't admit of an answer. Or the only answer is its repetition. Not a rhetorical question so much as a question that installs a rhetoric, it hollows out an interiority as the space of its resound. My father's demand that I desire his love remains one of the conditions under which, and against which, I write, since writing, or the ostentatious performance of "being a writer," was, from quite early on, one of the ways in which I learned to court and weather his approval. All of that would be banal to rehearse here, yet another rerun of the day-time Oedipal drama of the white male bourgeois subject, with its smoking guns around every corner and its sponsorship by psychopharmaceuticals. But I wrote this chapter out of a resolve to tackle the neglected aspects of the question (neglected by the subject in question, I mean). That I am white, cishet, male, and middle-class: as the song says, *What's love got to do with it?* But love *does* have to do with it. From these social and political as-pects of being, which are styles of having a body, of occupy-ing one's parcel of space and stretch of time, one derives ways of being lovable, along with a formidable sense of where love comes from. And where, or to whom, it returns. James Bald-win's observation that Black folk know white people "better than their lovers" reminds us that love, under certain conditions, can become an obstacle to self-knowledge. It reminds us that being loved, or seeking to be loved, might, in fact, enact what Stanley Cavell calls the "avoidance of love," insofar as the conditions un-der which one seeks love require that one refuse to acknowledge the totality of that love's conditions.[1] This requirement is love's pact with power. Perhaps it comes into play wherever loving and being loved get mixed up with enjoying and jockeying for one's place in the social hierarchy. But the requirement cuts especially close where the romantic and the familial provide cover for that hierarchy and its ravages. And for white Americans, whose place in the hierarchy collectively can be said to rest on what Ta-Nehi-si Coates calls "the vending of the black body and the sundering of the black family," a sundering that continues to this day, to

---

1   James Baldwin, "The Devil Finds Work," in *Collected Essays,* ed. Toni Morrison (New York: Library of America, 1998), 563; Stanley Cavell, *Must We Mean What We Say? A Book of Essays* (Cambridge: Cambridge University Press, 2008).

see oneself as worthy of love in virtue of one's social position requires a special effort to avoid the truth.[2] This avoidance is a kind of concealment. Baldwin calls it "white privacy." It entails the idea that one's "situation must always transcend the inexorability of the social setting."[3] But it's a curious kind of concealment, at once spectacular and intimate. A performance in front of others that is designed to persuade the self, to come between the self and the uncomfortable truth. One doesn't just draw the heavy velvet drapes against the light, one makes a dress out of them. Indicting the Hollywood fictions that sponsor so much of white Americans' understanding of love, Baldwin writes, "the white chick is always, somehow, saved or strengthened or destroyed by love — society is out of it, beneath her: it matters not at all that the man she marries, or deserts, or murders, happens to own Rhodesia, or that *she* does: love is all."[4]

Love here, i.e., the love of the white male subject, ciphers for whiteness, in the sense that whiteness is both *all* (the social setting for everything that one should aspire to) and *nothing* ("out of it," irrelevant to one's achievement). Of course, whiteness, particularly in its cishet masculine and moneyed isotopes, grants power. But as Kiese Laymon argues, this power is most visible, at the level of the individual, as a kind of absence or negation. The rich white man enjoys "the power to never be poor

---

2   Ta-Nehisi Coates, "The Case for Reparations," *The Atlantic*, June 2014, https://www.theatlantic.com/magazine/archive/2014/06/the-case-for-reparations/361631/.

3   Baldwin, "The Devil Finds Work," 564. By the phrase "in virtue of one's social position," I mean insofar as one measures self-worth primarily in comparison with other members of one's race and class, which remains the typical yardstick for white Americans' sense of self. It is the opposite of the thought that one might be lovable in spite of some aspect of "the social setting," such as poverty or another source of stigma. In the latter case, one is painfully aware of love's conditions. Baldwin's use of "transcend" points to the particular contradiction of white American subjectivity, which must insist on the meaning of social position while denying the relevance of its wider context, a feat only possible through a kind of willed and aggressively defended ignorance, a tactical forgetting.

4   Ibid., emphasis in the original.

and never be a felon, the power to always have his failures treated as success no matter how mediocre he [is]."[5] His power is evident in all the things that do not touch his life, like lead in the water, like searchlights through the windows at midnight, like whispers and cries you can't get out of your head. But this power not to fail, or more precisely, to escape liability for one's mistakes and misdeeds, even when the misdeeds are criminal, remains the outcome of social and political conspiracy. And conspiracy is obviously not the rare metal that is supposed to make whiteness worthy of love. For it shows the heart of whiteness, of what whiteness and white cishet masculinity are, to be the refuge of mediocrity, defended by the redoubt of a collective denial.[6] *Love is all.* In thrall to its institutional, social, and familial sanction, a white person, this white person, feels that denial itself as the desire for some always elusive sovereignty, the power to decide my own fate. What I have instead is access to power over the fate of others, insofar as I succeed at their expense. But the root of such desire taps into the fear of that which whiteness, as the wages of white fathers, gotten through enough plunder and spilled blood to fill all hell, both ushers in and promises to save me from.

Who loves you? That your white Daddy does, and that his love is all, encodes the power not to fail, the power to decide, as the promise of success. But such success remains a volatile, violent, jealously guarded thing, unevenly distributed even among the white male population. The true meaning of this promise is an open secret, as Baldwin suggests, well known to people of color, and which whites expend boundless energy to conceal from themselves. *"Wo Ich war soll Es werden"*: the *I* appears, irradiated, in its place.[7] *It* is what Hortense Spillers

---

5   Kiese Laymon, *Heavy: An American Memoir* (New York: Scribner, 2018), 190.

6   I borrow the phrase "the heart of whiteness" from Julian B. Carter, *The Heart of Whiteness: Normal Sexuality and Race in America, 1880–1940* (Durham: Duke University Press, 2009).

7   Nicolas Abraham and Maria Torok, *The Wolf Man's Magic Word: A Cryptonymy,* trans. Nicholas Rand (Minneapolis: University of Minnesota

calls "the blankness of 'race,'" an emptiness "where something else ought to be," signifying nothing.[8] But the blankness must be covered over; that is the condition of its power. The privacy that covers it, this white privacy, outs itself perpetually. As a fondness for moralizing, as hypocrisy, as brutal pettiness, as self-indulgence, it commits one to "moral mediocrity."[9] I wrote this book, struggling with my own costive, compulsive privacy. I wrote this book and this chapter in and out of the shadow of my father's hatred of mediocrity. And as I re-wrote and revised, I have had to reckon with how that hatred, passed on to me, harbors mediocrity within itself. My father was a highly intelligent and charming man, a brilliant architect, a charismatic and hardworking teacher. He loved a lot of Black music, and I think he truly cared about the Black students whom he taught for decades at Southern University in Baton Rouge. At least, I remember his being an advocate for the excellence of their work. But my father could not, or would not, do the work of discernment that his own case required. I mean the work of learning to feel the radical difference between an excellence demanded as the price of survival, and one assumed as the empty sign of membership in the posse. My father devalued Black lives and Black works lest their excellence impugn the deferred promise of his own.[10]

Press, 2008), 81. The phrase is a reversal of Freud's famous epigram about the emergence of the ego from the unconscious, "Wo Es war, soll Ich warden," which can be translated as "where it was, there I shall be."

8 Hortense J. Spillers, "'All the Things You Could Be by Now, If Sigmund Freud's Wife Was Your Mother': Psychoanalysis and Race," in *Black, White, and in Color: Essays on American Literature and Culture* (Chicago: University of Chicago Press, 2003), 385.

9 Laymon, *Heavy*, 190–91.

10 I don't mean to suggest that whiteness can be understood dialectically in relation to Blackness. For one, the insights of Black feminist theory remind us that "patterns of subordination intersect," including race, gender, sexuality, class, and physical ability, such that any person's experience of having or lacking power is a complex, multifaceted, highly contextual, and embodied process, which explicit categories of racialization alone cannot render intelligible (Kimberlé Crenshaw, "Demarginalizing the Intersection of Race and Sex: A Black Feminist Critique of Antidiscrimination

He believed that by talent, one (meaning, primarily, he and his sons) could "transcend [...] the social setting [...]." Including what Coates calls "the long tradition of this country actively punishing black success."[11] Such punishment is part of the landscape of whiteness across the US. But in the milieux of southern Louisiana where I grew up (as in many other places), a certain proximity to, and intimacy with, the scenes of that success and its punishment (beginning with the communities whose ability to sustain themselves in the teeth of white supremacist terror includes forms of self-expression deeply woven into the fabric of the local culture) necessitate, in defense of white privacy, intimate practices of misrecognition and neglect. My father's sense of excellence was founded, in part, on a lie, the lie of whiteness and its negating, neglectful power, and he passed that sense on to me. Likewise, his defensive, spectacular privacy, bound up with a kind of bereaved masculinity, took a serious toll on everyone in his life, especially the women he loved or sought to be loved by, and on his children. He was a loving father. But it's the nature of that love that I want to understand, and how it failed

Doctrine, Feminist Theory and Antiracist Politics," *The University of Chicago Legal Forum* 140, no. 1 [1989]: 139–67.). Or to put it another way, white patriarchal power depends on what Alexander Weheliye calls "assemblages" that deploy race and gender, along with other classifications, to delimit who has access to the full panoply of rights and privileges that are supposed to belong to human beings (*Habeas Viscus: Racializing Assemblages, Biopolitics, and Black Feminist Theories of the Human* [Durham: Duke University Press, 2014]). These assemblages include various interlocking and hierarchically structured modes of racialization, reflective of the entwined processes of settler-colonial occupation, circum-Atlantic slavery, imperialism, immigration, globalization, etc. Whiteness, per Barbara Tomlinson, "is not an embodied identity but a privileged standpoint and structural advantage" ("Wicked Problems and Intersectionality Telephone," in *Antiracism, Inc.: Why the Way We Talk about Racial Justice Matters*, eds. Felice Blake, Paula Ioanide, and Alison Reed [Earth: punctum books, 2019], 163). But the identification with whiteness serves those who can afford it as a means not only of enjoying structural advantages, but also of forgetting their foundation in stolen land, labor, and life.

11   Coates, "The Case for Reparations."

us. And how that failure functions as part of my sense of being (as) a white man.

The sense of having privilege, of having the power not to fail, warps the senses. I am thinking about what the senses have been trained to exclude. Or to enclose. I'm thinking of a term that Kierkegaard uses, "inclosing reserve," to describe a self constituted by acts of reservation, withholding, and enclosure. A self folded in on itself, as it were. Kierkegaard contrasts inclosing reserve with what he calls "inwardness."[12] We might appeal as well to what certain Black spiritual and aesthetic traditions call "soul," the latter signifying the presence of resources that, while housed in the self or the body, realize themselves in performances of shared feeling and desire.[13] In the grip of inclosing reserve, by contrast, one refuses the openness to change that is the occasion for (a) soul. Shunning what is collective, one seeks to protect the sovereign privacy of the self. Although such a person may flout social convention, he (and I use the pronoun advisedly) founds his projects for living and loving on a fundamental failure of nerve.[14] The conviction of one's own fallenness — of one's failure to be lovable — can even become the fantastic preserve of a negative freedom from how the flesh changes us, through the wager of loving, into others we don't yet know how to recognize. Kierkegaard calls the personality prone to inclosing reserve a "demonic" personality. White privacy — some would spell it "piracy" — might be said to make one demonic because it

---

12 Kierkegaard's discussions of inclosing reserve and inwardness can be found in *The Concept of Anxiety: A Simple Psychologically Orienting Deliberation on the Dogmatic Issue of Hereditary Sin,* trans. and eds. Reidar Thomte and Albert B. Anderson (Princeton: Princeton University Press, 1980), 123–38.

13 See, for example, Ashon T. Crawley, *Blackpentecostal Breath: The Aesthetics of Possibility* (New York: Fordham University Press, 2017).

14 According to Kierkegaard, such a person is nervous or in despair about possibility, but what terrifies him is possibility as embodied, lived, and endured. Kierkegaard writes, "[h]e desires in one way or another to be more than the empirical, historically qualified, finite individuality that he is" (*The Concept of Anxiety,* 143).

grounds a sense of self-possession in the violence of possession itself. As Fred Moten argues, "[w]hile subjectivity is defined by the subject's possession of itself and its objects, it is troubled by a dispossessive force objects exert such that the subject seems to be possessed — infused, deformed — by the object it possesses."[15] The predatory dream of self-possession passes from one generation to the next. What enables its passage is the scope and encouragement given to habits of possessing, and of wanting to possess, others and the fruits of their labors. Such habits translate flesh and world into the relations between a subject and its objects, relations that become explicit as judgments of value.[16] How does a child of white cishet male privilege come to abide in, and by, his possession? How does the white nuclear family, that supposed crucible of "American wealth and democracy," stage its sense of love as an intimate drama funded by "the for-profit destruction of the most important asset available to any people, the family"?[17]

I might be asking whether white privacy has a primal scene.[18] But Freud's talking cure affirms explication (as the unraveling of

---

15 Fred Moten, *In the Break: The Aesthetics of the Black Radical Tradition* (Minneapolis: University of Minnesota Press, 2003), 1.

16 My thinking on this score is indebted to Shannon Sullivan's account of the "unconscious habits of white privilege" as a matter of sensory and somatic traces. See *Revealing Whiteness: The Unconscious Habits of Racial Privilege* (Bloomington: Indiana University Press, 2006).

17 Coates, "The Case for Reparations."

18 In his case history of the patient he calls the Wolf Man, Freud posits that his patient's neuroses stem from a singular event in the patient's life: witnessing, as an infant, his parents' having sex ("From the History of an Infantile Neurosis," in *The Standard Edition of the Complete Psychological Works of Sigmund Freud,* trans. James Strachey, new edn. [London: Vintage, 2001], 17:3–124). Lodged in the Wolf Man's unconscious, the scene becomes formative of the maturing subject's relation to his own sexuality. But the scene sows confusion by scrambling domination, gender, and pleasure. Having seen his father mounting his mother from behind, the child identifies as pleasurable both the dominant (masculine) position and the subordinate (feminine) one. If the Wolf Man's case complicates Freud's earlier theories of infantile seduction, it nonetheless remains a story about the ontogeny of the European bourgeois male subject. The subject,

the logic of the symptom) as the destiny of the subject. This destiny, as Hortense Spillers argues in her profound meditation on race and psychoanalysis, by definition excludes "the stigmatized subject […] whose access to discourse must be established as a human right and cannot be assumed."[19] The subject barred from full humanity by the logics and ledgers of empire bears, in their flesh, the traces or hieroglyphics of a very different set of pri-

that is, whose accession to heteronormative sexuality and patriarchal gender roles plays out, on an intimate scale, the management of primitive urges by Western civilization writ large. And since the primal scene produces neurosis, involving the Wolf Man's psyche in the elaboration of a complicated language of symptoms and dreams whose meanings the analyst alone can unpack, Freud's story of the primal scene is also a story about the subject's entrance to discourse.

What happens, then, if we complicate Freud's explication with the question of sociogeny? If we keep in mind that the Eurocentric category of the human, or of civilization, is overdetermined by its violent emergence on the scene of empire? And that the subject of this discourse inherits practices that have, in the course of prolonging and promoting empire, discursively banished Europe's racialized others to the realm of the primitive, the primal, and the non-human?

The "sociogenic principle," taken up by Frantz Fanon in his analysis of colonial oppression, serves as a corrective to what Sylvia Wynter calls "our present culture's purely ontogenetic and/or biocentric conception of the human identity," which is at the same time an "ethno-class (i.e., Western bourgeois) conception" ("Towards the Sociogenic Principle: Fanon, Identity, the Puzzle of Conscious Experience, and What It Is Like to Be 'Black,'" in *National Identities and Sociopolitical Changes in Latin America,* eds. Mercedes F. Durán-Cogan and Antonio Gómez-Moriana [New York: Routledge, 2001], 49). In other words, the ontogenic/phylogenic perspective on human psychology remains inseparable from the processes that inscribe race (and a racially inflected gender) as the boundary-line, never stable however violently imposed, between those whose claims to humanity are taken for granted, and those who must fight for this (always revocable) recognition. (Who, as Fanon's work makes clear, may have to fight for such recognition even from themselves.) The "sociogenic principle" insists that "we can *experience ourselves as human* only through the mediation of the processes of socialization effected by the invented *tekhnē* or cultural technology to which we have given the name *culture,*" including the technologies of race and gender (Wynter, "Towards the Sociogenic Principle," 53, emphasis in the original).

19   Spillers, "Psychoanalysis and Race," 425.

mal scenes.[20] Such scenes, whose description pushes against the fascia of the imagination, and in which the brutality of plunder becomes, in its recurrence, an engine of both the psychic and the market economy, are a far cry from Freud's lupine peepshow. But with Moten, we might interest ourselves in the farness of that cry, which is also its closeness under (the) cover(s), in order to trace these scenes' "ongoing disruption" of the privacy of the white masculine subject. They skid beneath the railings of the Freudian interpretation, which would safeguard the totality and privacy of Daddy's love. In Freud's rendition of the Wolf Man's primal scene, the presence of the parents' flesh, becoming something else in an act of passion, something other than what their anatomically distinct bodies represent, disrupts the Oedipal trajectory. And yet, the structure remains airtight, a cryptic moment in the individualized, pathologized psyche, as long as we neglect the role of the flesh as vulnerable to a possession that is not only figurative and legible (as in the father's possession of the mother's body during sex), but also scandalously literal, legal, and lethal. As the site, that is, of a repeated capture countered by an ongoing resistance. Following Spillers, we could say that "'individual,' 'family,' and 'society' are […] particles in constant bombardment," scattered in complex trajectories by the social and material forces that produce the distinctions of race, gender, and class as morally and legally salient in the distribution of wealth and power.[21] The field of that scattering is the flesh. "Before the 'body,'" the flesh carries forward, across generations, the common energy that animates us in its folds.[22] But empire's trash talk renders the human cover for the cryptonym of the flesh-as-a-thing.[23] When Baldwin refers to the

---

20 On the flesh and its hieroglyphics, see Hortense J. Spillers, "Mama's Baby, Papa's Maybe: An American Grammar Book," in *Black, White, and in Color,* 207; as well as Weheliye, *Habeas Viscus.*

21 Spillers, "Psychoanalysis and Race," 388.

22 Spillers, "Mama's Baby, Papa's Maybe," 206.

23 The cryptonym, in Abraham and Torok's re-working of Freud's case study, refers to a word buried in the unconscious part of the ego, where it

white American public's refusal "to make black privacy a black and private matter," he alludes to the fact that white privacy, and by extension, an American public that recognizes itself as white, depends on the regime that once treated Black lives as private property, and which has never stopped devising new ways to keep private property out of Black hands. And Daddy's love, as the love that has law and power on its side (the law of the father and the power of whiteness), has for its inexorable social setting the scene of untold, unaccounted-for, as yet unreckoned-with crimes. Crimes, as Spillers reminds us, practiced with special force against Black motherhood, with enduring consequences for the situation of the Black family.[24] To "mak[e] white privacy

performs an "active vital and dynamic function" (*The Wolf Man's Magic Word*, 81). Neither literal nor figurative, the cryptonym exceeds the referential model in which the opposition between those terms makes sense. For the cryptonym occupies a site that can be expressed only by a series of detours through a lexicon. The word, rather than the thing to which it refers, eludes consciousness. Like a slip of the tongue in reverse, operative at a more radical level than the metaphorical and metonymic logic of repression, the cryptonym recruits orthographic and phonetic echo-effects, as well as chains of semantic association (synonymy). It belongs to the realm of the "false friend," the anagram, paronomasia, onomatopoeia, and other ruses that involve a slippage between the matter of language and its formal or semantic dimension. For Abraham and Torok, the cryptonym's career describes the fate of pleasure *inside* repression: "This particular area within the Ego, the place that shuns symbolization and is the site of the death of pleasure, knows the word that says pleasure." The languages of patriarchal white supremacy are cryptonymic, perhaps, insofar as the ingredients of fantasy no less than the armature of common sense remain, for those who take up those languages, linked to the buried pleasure of the word as a vehicle of unrestrained power over others (the power to terrorize, the power to possess). Then again, this pleasure is hardly buried in much of the discourse, historical and contemporary, through which the white American public identifies itself and its common interests. Rather, spectacular and mundane forms of degradation practiced against its racialized and gendered others sustain the white patriarchy in the non liquet of its own laws about rightful possession and the just exercise of power.

24 Spillers, "Mama's Baby, Papa's Maybe," 228. Her analysis focuses on the situation of the enslaved, arguing that "the female" was systematically

real," then, might mean learning to hear, to stand exposed to, "the broken and irreducible maternity [...] of the commodity's scream."[25]

In that scream's haunting of the discourses of political economy, Fred Moten wants us to hear "a literary, performative, phonographic disruption of the protocols of exchange."[26] Not like cryptic words in a "garbled, private language," the scream amplifies the voice, in excess of language, as a material, maternal trace.[27] A voice not hidden, but there to be heard. A voice that is here, and if you don't hear it, then it means that you have been taught to tune it out. Or maybe it makes you a hieroglyph to yourself. Maybe it deposits, among the names you give yourself,

---

"ungendered" — denied even the limited rights of womanhood and motherhood — in the service of her captor's sexual prurience and his economic interest in her fertility. As a result, writes Spillers, "(1) motherhood as female bloodrite is outraged, is denied, at the very same time that it becomes the founding term of a human and social enactment; (2) a dual fatherhood is set in motion, comprised of the African father's *banished* name and body and the captor's mocking presence" (ibid., emphasis in the original). The white stereotype of the "matriarchal" Black family thus misrecognizes what is actually, according to Spillers, the legacy of this violation of motherhood and the concomitant erasure of the patronymic by the institution of slavery.

25 Baldwin, "The Devil Finds Work," 564; Moten, *In The Break,* 12. Moten refers to the scene of a child's literal awakening to the terrors of slavery in Frederick Douglass's *Narrative,* a scene which is as much seen as heard: "I have often been awakened," Douglass writes, "at the dawn of day by the most heart rending shrieks of an own aunt of mine" (quoted in ibid., 19). On this scene and "the ease with which such scenes are usually reiterated, the casualness with which they are circulated, and the consequences of this routine display of the slave's ravaged body," I refer the reader to Saidiya V. Hartman, *Scenes of Subjection: Terror, Slavery, and Self-Making in Nineteenth-Century America* (New York: Oxford University Press, 2010), 3. See also Christina Sharpe, *Monstrous Intimacies: Making Post-Slavery Subjects* (Durham: Duke University Press, 2010); Claudia Tate, *Domestic Allegories of Political Desire: The Black Heroine's Text at the Turn of the Century* (New York: Oxford University Press, 1992); and Weheliye, *Habeas Viscus.*

26 Moten, *In the Break,* 10.

27 Spillers, "Psychoanalysis and Race," 396.

a cryptonym in your inclosing reserve. Maybe the voice tunes *you,* with a resonance in the gut. This resonance is the "dispossessive force objects exert," an interference you might mistake for white noise when it disrupts the sales pitch, love story, lecture, diagnosis, game show — when it breaks in on Daddy talking out of his hat. But Freud was right about one thing: talking back to Daddy is how Daddy learns to talk. In other words, the appeal to that dispossessive force in the service of an Oedipal narrative repeats, in however muted a register, the desire for domination that blinds kings and makes mothers scream. The narrative links a possessive investment in the self to patrilineal descent.[28] On this logic, I am my own man because I am my (white) father's (legitimate) son. Hilton Als writes of feeling "a horror of my I, since that meant being a him — my father."[29] If I, as a white man, feel moved to attest to something like Als's horror, I must also acknowledge how much of it, in my case, stems from my father's embodiment of whiteness as well as masculinity. Which is to say, his ways of possessing them, of making them *his.* And this horror, if that word even fits the case, requires a different frame of reckoning with the sociogeny of primal scenes. To assume his position is to learn how to be, at various times, a perpetrator, an alibi, and a bystander. For one is always the potential witness to trauma who has been taught not to see, taught to speak a language that entombs the open secret of his complicity.[30] The subject as witness, as whiteness,

28 According to Spillers ("Mama's Baby, Papa's Maybe"), slavery and its aftermath have barred Black families from the patronymic, patrilineal logic that renders personhood legible and verifiable, and which signifies the white person's exemption from the plight of the commodity.

29 Hilton Als, *White Girls* (San Francisco: McSweeney's, 2014), 30.

30 In *The Wolf Man's Magic Word,* Torok and Abraham revisit the Wolf Man's case, imagining that the patient suffered, not from the repressed memory of a spectacle, but from the persistence of a word (the Russian *tieret,* meaning "to rub"). As a child, the Wolf Man had thought or spoken or heard this word spoken in connection with a traumatic scene, about which he was subsequently admonished by his mother never to speak again. Rather than catching his parents have sex, Abraham and Torok

living for that sense of reckless freedom afforded by the slippage of the tongue, fails to make sense. In what follows, I return to some scenes that fashioned my sense of self as something both more and less than the subject/object of a father's love, trying to feel the force with which it rubbed me into being, and the loss of what got rubbed out along the way, in pursuit of the question that proves most elusive: "How did it feel?"[31]

posit that the child must have witnessed something yet more taboo: an act of incest between his father and his sister. The patient's subsequent fixations and dream narratives, which Freud interprets according to a logic of symbolism and condensation, Torok and Abraham read as ways in which the patient talks around the nub of a story he dares not retrieve. The cryptonym is thus the marker of the primal scene, an entry in an index that has been whited out. It is also the mark borne by the witness to violence, whose silence has been bought by threat or bribe. The cryptonym signifies the witness's implication in that violence. His possession of the word seals the pact of his complicity, even as he talks around it endlessly, his very acts of confession performing his fidelity to the secret that they conceal.

31 Brian Blanchfield, *Proxies: Essays Near Knowing* (Lebanon: Nightboat Books, 2016), 134. I have also taken a cue from Brian Casemore's call for critical texts that perform "the process of working through a cultural symptom," and which use the reconstruction of a life narrative as a form of pedagogy (*The Autobiographical Demand of Place: Curriculum Inquiry in the American South* [New York: Peter Lang, 2008], 5). And perhaps there is a more elusive question still. For someone whose claims to humanity can remain unspoken in every case, because guaranteed by his occupation of the subject-position enclosed by whiteness and cishet masculinity (those rooms of ownership crowding out the world), doesn't the project of exposure, for someone like that, fail to amount to more than an exercise in self-justification? Another telling of the story of which there are already too many, endless tales of exemption, lullabies for the infantile citizen, Daddy's baby boy? And doesn't this impulse to register the question, i.e., to register it explicitly, represent the writer's gambit to signal his story's exemption from the ilk of those padded out with the stuff of plunder and oppression, taking up too much space and time? Isn't it time to give it a rest? In the silence of my failure to answer that question, this book is the blush of an erasure that cannot accomplish itself. (On the "infantile citizen," see Lauren Berlant, *The Queen of America Goes to Washington City: Essays on Sex and Citizenship* [Durham: Duke University Press, 1997], 25–54).

I was my mother's first child and my father's fourth. She wanted to name me Fred, after her father, killed in an industrial accident only a year or two before. This was the man whose death she carried as she grew pregnant with me, whose life she saw in the brown hair and dark brown eyes that announced me a Deshotels. But my father wouldn't hear of it. *Freddy? They'll tease the shit out of him.* He countered with Wolfgang, being okay with Wolfie but conjuring me a Mozart. *Dolsy* represents a compromise of sorts: the name belonged to my paternal great-grandfather, a Louisiana state senator (a portly man in white linen or seersucker when he was photographed in a friendly handshake with Huey Long). Had I been a girl, I was told — having been delivered one day after the Fourth of July — I might have been named America. I don't think the idea was an access of patriotism on my father's part. Rather, a child's name, like the title of a movie or a show, should be full of marquee potential. During those first years, my mother was my primary caregiver, but my father insisted on feeding me my infant formula every night, pacing the floor of our small New York apartment twelve floors above Times Square, my head resting on his shoulder until I drifted off. Bing Crosby or Al Jolson crooned on the Weltron. Though not a large man, my father possessed a stature magnified by charisma and a hot, jealous temper. His hands, in particular, always struck me as huge, like a physical manifestation of his personality, although I imagine they were also comforting to a small child's body, cradling my haunches and gently beating time. That tempo would have told me I was his Yankee doodle boy, and with Broadway below and Fifth Avenue nearby, we had white Christmases galore to dream of.

From the beginning, I was my father's child. In his telling, I popped out of the womb wide-eyed and alert, smiling, and with a head full of hair. In a photo he took of me at age three or four, my eyes are wide for the camera, in a face covered in white grease paint, with a red dot on my nose, and a bright feather headdress. A true paleface, decked out for trick-or-treat like

Hollywood in the spoils of genocide. To my father, I was a cash advance on the possible — *my son, the genius* — and his invest-ment in that service was such that he could ignore whatever evidence to the contrary I might have offered, had I dared. As a toddler in New York, I was his sidekick, and he trotted me off to movies, museums, concerts in Central Park. By his side, on his shoulders, or strapped to his chest, I discovered the privilege of travel, of purpose in the wide, white, masculine world. The ho-rizon pivoted about his shoulders, crowded by skyscrapers, our course interrupted here and there as he hoisted me up to peer through the porthole at a construction site. My father's stories would fill those years with a mythology of precociousness: How as a toddler, I stood through a long program of Brahms or Mo-zart, miming the conductor. How I stood, straight as a bolt and giggling, while my father lifted me up in his palm. Though dis-couraged from playing with children my age, I was flaunted be-fore adults, and it tickled him when, tugging at my leash on the sidewalks near Time Square, I stopped to banter with strangers: a busker, a homeless man selling secondhand paperbacks, the Korean-American woman who ran the produce stand down the street. Our apartment building housed members of New York's artistic and theatrical unions, and there I was my father's ticket to an audience with the kinds of people whose friendship he wooed: the burlesque dancer who let me play with the rings on her toes, or the wizened Russian émigré Petroschanko, an au-teur of adult movies whose advice my father sought on a film project of his own. *But why do you want to make pictures, when you can make more children like this?* For my father the racon-teur, fresh out of Louisiana's Cajun country, I was his torch song, his lovelorn address to the faint and tawdry starlight of Manhat-tan in the late 1970s.

My own memories of those years splutter with wonder, fleck-ed by the city's soot and grit. A pair of hairy legs skids into view as their owner, a tall and bearded roller skater, stoops to indulge my curiosity at the Chelsea Piers. The sweet, fluffy warmth of a corn muffin rises in my mind, something I think we would have bought at Penn or Grand Central Station, but shorn of context, it arrives like a missive from some transatlantic fantasy, a fleecy golden secret that abridges time. Ditto the taste of kosher hot dogs and orange soda, awash somewhere in the noise of an artificial waterfall. From those years, images of my mother flicker with work and care: trailing after her on our way home from the grocery store, my legs burning with exhaustion, or chasing behind her as she cleaned house, pushing a toy whose wheels tumbled a clear globe full of plastic balls. Of the nearness of her body, I remember less, no doubt because the stories that I heard growing up were those my father told, the photographs those that he took. As she tells it, she was young and alone and inexperienced, with her family far away, struggling to satisfy a domineering older man who demanded her allegiance to the promise, never fulfilled, of Bohemian lives. Lives devoted to flouting social convention and to the pursuit of beauty and adventure. My mother's plight, as I came to imagine it later, was the disappointment and regret described by Adrienne Rich as "the daylight coming / like a relentless milkman up the stairs."[32] And as in a naive reading of that poem, I used to lay the blame squarely on my father, imagining my mother and myself as allies against his overbearing need and the threat of his rage. But in a poem in her own hand that I found among my father's papers when he died, dated from the year that I turned two, my mother writes:

He knows no consideration
Dolsy doesn't
Never knows when to be quiet
When to be loud
When to absent himself
Or when to be near.
He will talk when you want silence,
Jump and stomp when you want peace.
[…]

---

32 Adrienne Rich, "Living in Sin," *The New Yorker,* January 23, 1954.

The child's wantonness offsets the wife and mother's

[…] responsibility
Of seeing to it that
You are silent when silence is asked for,
That you are there when your help is needed,
That you give when a hand is opened to you.

As a toddler, standing up tall, pushing around my noisemakers, I was both my father's favorite and his factor, embodying a willfulness that was our exclusive privilege. My mother's poem rehearses what Rich's "relentless milkman" suggests: the demands imposed by patriarchal logic on women for the care of the law's vessels. At the same time, my mother herself was compelled to become a kind of vessel, bottling up anger and resentment in her silent, yielding presence. According to Freud's account of Oedipal dynamics, the impossible demand falls on the son. *You must be like your father; you may not do as your father does.* The father's presence casts a shadow that lengthens on a long afternoon into that pointer of bourgeois rectitude, the super-ego, which keeps the self in check until its gin and tonic at five o'clock.[33] But what becomes of the super-ego if the son inherits the father's privilege, including his fantasies of sovereign speech

33 Sigmund Freud, "The Ego and the Id," in *The Standard Edition of the Complete Psychological Works of Sigmund Freud,* trans. James Strachey (London: Hogarth Press, 1961), 19:34. The Oedipal super-ego, as theorized by Freud, depicts the psychic economy of privilege as a demand for emulation (you must aspire to be like your social superiors) intertwined with a prohibition (you must respect your superiors and never usurp their place). But the place of the mother/daughter in the Freudian canon, as many of Freud's feminist interlocutors have argued, remains one defined by a lack. This lack speaks to the patriarchal frame of the theory itself. On Freud's neglect of mothers, see Madelon Sprengnether, *The Spectral Mother: Freud, Feminism, and Psychoanalysis* (Ithaca: Cornell University Press, 1990). Hortense Spillers goes further, linking Freud's avoidance of the "dark continent" of female sexuality to the racialization of the non-European man or woman. See Spillers, "Psychoanalysis and Race," 393.

and action and his sense of entitlement to a woman's care, while the mother occupies the place from which emulation is forbidden? The self might coalesce around the nub of a different sort of prohibition: *you must not be like your mother.*

How did my mother's poem fall into my father's hands? "The hand […] opened" demands gratification, nutrition, love. It might also be the hand my father raised against my mother at least once. For me, his hands bore gifts, like the new Matchbox car he brought home every Friday evening, a token of masculine power. It was his voice, raised to a pitch indicative of just how much he cared whether the neighbors or anybody else could hear him, that was the instrument of his displeasure. A handsome man, handy with tools and all sorts of manly accoutrements, and like Yankee Doodle, handy with the girls, my father carried himself (or tried to) in that way of white American cishet men that projects confidence in their right to own the world. In his stories, he carried himself undaunted every morning, on his way to work at 4 AM, through a Times Square rife with prostitution and drugs, down to the subway, where once a teenage girl tried to mug him. *You'll have to kill me, sweetheart, because I don't have any money.* He never said whether, in that moment, he had bothered to put up his hands. In trying to understand how those hands dispensed whiteness and manhood, how they invested me with it, I am thinking of what Spillers writes: that on account of the fraught place that the Black family occupies within the logic of the patronymic and the patrilineal, "[t]he African-American male has been touched […] by the mother, handed by her in ways that he cannot escape, and in ways that the white American male is allowed to temporize by a fatherly reprieve."[34] And I am thinking of this temporality or tempo of the white paternal in terms of another half-memory, a long ride into the Bronx, where the subway line emerges into daylight and the empty lots and broken infrastructure that mark America's steady war of attrition on Black and Latinx communities. The

34 Spillers, "Mama's Baby, Papa's Maybe," 228.

train trundled us through that landscape to the zoo, where I slid down a slide carved out of a tree and poked my head up with the prairie dogs. With our two heads in that scuffed and scratched Plexiglass bubble, we stood looking out, my father and I, a man-to-be of his ilk — a pair of milkmen, looking for all the world. In that bubble blown of privilege and power, we enjoyed a spectatorship perpetually erupting into the midst of what white America would call blight, decay, "the crack epidemic," without having to notice the suffering that was the opportunity for our opportunity. And oblivious, too, to the resistance and play and labor and care that sustain lives never offered a reprieve.

As a product of that bubble, learning the arts of self-enclosure, my fantasies gave vent to a desire to shrink the world down to a more manageable scale. On a long road trip with my parents and baby brother back up to New York (I was five or six, and we had moved down south a year before), I repopulated the landscape, as it scrolled by the pickup's window, with people my size. Effacing family, I made the voyage alone, anticipating the white masculine promise of autonomy as my imagined self traveled north among other child-adults, riding in style in the pink plastic big-wheeled trike I coveted but that my parents couldn't afford or wouldn't buy. In addition to the other drivers, and the construction crews on the side of the road, and the denizens of towns beyond the interstate, my mind's eye miniaturized their concerns and their machines, replacing the real thing with the bright plastic or die-cast replicas that, as FAO Schwarz had taught me, were in endless, invidious supply. It was on this trip, too, that my parents impressed on me, the sometime babbler on the streets of the Big Apple, the danger of strangers. At a KOA campground, where we had parked our Airstream trailer for the night, I struck up a conversation with a shirtless man, the proprietor of a massive motor home. *Do you want to take a look inside?* The magic of such machines was irresistible, like paternal power crystallized, pure, self-contained purpose. But my mother or father intervened, taking the opportunity to equip me with a paranoia that is patriarchal white supremacy's underside: *There are people who will steal children and chop them into little bits.* This was, in a sense, the mantra of the 1980s and 1990s, as the Reaganite consensus replaced the welfare state with a renewed program of assault on poor communities of color. But in the white American imaginary, it was a war for the body of the white, middle-class child. In their fantasized dismemberment, the milk-carton kids testified to more, I think, than a reckoning with the tabooed reality of child abuse. Just as elite white men attacked Reconstruction with the myth of the white woman at the mercy of the emancipated Black man, so white men at the end of the twentieth century, facing social and political challenges to their power, mustered a moral panic over the white man's progeny.[35] And like the earlier retrenchment around white womanhood, the nightmare of the missing child spoke of threats to the hegemony of the white middle class, threats intensified by the neoliberal program of privatizing public goods. As Frantz Fanon reminds us, a strong, cruel state caters to the father's fantasies.[36] A meaty threat, a temporizing terror, when the white father's hands give, their gift becomes the vehicle of a compulsive pleasure. *Fort-Da,* says Freud. The tiny blue Honda Prelude (it had real, working doors!) skids out of sight beneath a chair. The white child vanishes at the end of a street. A vessel we freight with our longing for innocence, the child's flesh bears, in its imagined voyage toward sacrifice, the proof that our privilege is innocent, or else the expiation of our guilt.[37] To be chopped

35 In *American Anatomies: Theorizing Race and Gender* (Durham: Duke University Press, 2002), Robyn Wiegman provides an astute reading of the dynamics of patriarchal white supremacy and white supremacist terror in terms of the anxieties of white American men.

36 Frantz Fanon, *Black Skin, White Masks,* trans. Richard Philcox, rev. edn. (New York: Grove Press, 2008), 121.

37 Richard Dyer writes, "whiteness aspires to *dis*embodiement as the condition of its enjoyment of the privileges of the public sphere (self-determination, negative liberty, etc.)" (*White: Essays on Race and Culture* [New York: Routledge, 2017], 39, emphasis in the original). And Julian Carter, writing about the close association between whiteness and neurasthenia in the nineteenth century, postulates that white people's "belief in their own weakness helped to excuse them from accountability

into bits: that's the fate of Bluebeard's wives. They are captives to a privilege the fee for which is enclosure, a cryptic prohibition, and ignorance of the fate that precedes them and awaits (their coming to) their senses.

They met during a production of *Romeo and Juliet.* This was in Mamou, a small town on the prairie in southern Louisiana. A son of one of the prominent white families in town, my father in his early thirties cut a vulpine figure in the pages of a local newspaper, looking aloof and androgynous beside an article about the leisure suit. Mamou back then was a town like many other towns in the South, a place whose fortunes had sprung up on the shoulders and backs of unfree labor. A town founded by men wearing white linen suits in the photographs we were shown by our parents, never bothering to inquire about what went on outside the frame. My father belonged to a caste of white men with a towering sense of their own self-importance. Men whose achievements must have seemed larger than life, in a context where, for them, upward mobility promised to magnify a multigenerational sense of ownership over the place, a promise buttressed, of course, by the privileges they derived from Jim Crow. By the time my parents met, my father had established himself as an architect of stylish homes in the region, mid-century modern designs that commanded their surroundings like Wallace Stevens's anecdotal jar. My mother, meanwhile, was only 17, a child of the prairie and the pine woods, where Cajun and Creole families worked as tenant or small independent farmers on land that the French and Spanish had stolen from Choctaw tribes. Tales floated in our family about a Cherokee (or Choctaw) ancestor somewhere down the line, though that stopped none of us from claiming the advantages of whiteness. Like my mother's

for the suffering that made their privileged positions possible" (*The Heart of Whiteness,* 155).

father, the white men of my grandparents' generation had begun to leave the fields for more lucrative work in industry, a path barred to their Creole of Color neighbors.[38] Among the photographs my father took of that production, a number capture my mother alone, posing on a bare stage, her jet black hair curled and bobbed, her lithe figure clad in a short white dress of muslin or some other fabric, tempting and sheer, with a ruffle along the hem. Her knees, of which she has always been ashamed, are bare, and bare her feet, as she clutches with one hand a wooden beam above her head. *He was the first person,* my mother often said, *who talked to me like an adult.* My father had Mercutio's gift for gab. *He could make you believe it,* she said, meaning his wild schemes, full of moonlight and held together by spiderwebs. Though his idol was Frank Lloyd Wright, I think my father fancied himself a Howard Roark, or Gregory Peck playing Howard Roark in the Hollywood version of that noxious book that I doubt he ever read. And for all his accomplishments as an architect, it was theater and film that called to him, those vehicles for investment in apocryphal selves, telling you that love can be all if only you believe it.

But you had to help him believe it. Or else a plague on both your houses. In his work on irony, Kierkegaard describes a person who pins their sense of self to their power of negation.[39] Their subjectivity depends, as it were, on the availability of the factory reset, the blank slate, the next feature in the matinee. Of course, this power is really a delusion. But delusions have power, and the white man as ironist may need failure, repeated failure,

---

38 Sylvie Dubois and Barbara M. Horvath, "Creoles and Cajuns: A Portrait in Black and White," *American Speech* 78, no. 2 (2003): 192–207.

39 The ironist "craves the subjective freedom that at all times has in its power the possibility of a beginning and is not handicapped by earlier situations" (Søren Kierkegaard, *The Concept of Irony, with Continual Reference to Socrates,* trans. and eds. Howard V. Hong and Edna H. Hong [Princeton: Princeton University Press, 1989], 253). "In irony," Kierkegaard writes, "the subject is continually retreating, talking every phenomenon out of its reality in order to save itself — that is, in order to preserve itself in negative independence of everything" (257).

as a reminder of his freedom from the circumstances that, for others, might determine or ruin a career or a life. My father's life and career comprised a string of such failures: two marriages abandoned; a successful architectural partnership dissolved; a movie left unfinished; the union job in New York (painting sets on soap operas) that he quit for the vaporous promise of a commission down South; the rural homestead that he carefully restored, only to abandon it to foreclosure; the fanciful real-estate ventures in Florida and Mexico that came to naught. When he should have been at the height of his architectural career, he built little. True, teaching duties, along with the task of raising a family, got in the way of more creative pursuits. But he hurt his prospects by a sworn commitment to the idea that *clients don't know shit,* and he wasn't afraid to let them know it. (He reserved special vitriol for his clients' wives. *It's always the bitch,* he would say, misogyny providing failure's perfect alibi.) On top of that, he was something of a sucker. But whenever a project crashed and burned, Queen Mab's sails whisked him off to another. Such is the stuff of white masculinity. My mother, as long as she believed or wanted to believe that his love was all, must have suffered on account of my father's fondness for the apocryphal in himself. My mother, who could read people much better than he could, taught me how to read (I am five years old, puzzling out words in the newspaper on her lap), and she tried to teach me the hazards of such self-delusion. We are walking around our tiny subdivision in Lafayette, with its drab townhouses and its streets that force the pedestrian to thread a narrow selvage of grass between asphalt and ditch. I am amusing myself by pulling my shirt up over my face, plunging ahead with a child's newfound conviction that he knows better than his mother. *Don't do that, or you'll hurt yourself.* Then in that slow-motion agony with which love, as time's instrument, rakes the flesh, she watches in silence as I walk smack into the side of a neighbor's mailbox.

Can I expose the apocryphal in myself as the texture of the patronymic, the damage and slippage of its law? What did it sound like, with its hedges and pronouncements, its promises and smack talk and cryptic proscriptions? A frequency haunts the dial, like a station hard to catch: my father's voice on the road, driving. I sit beside him, miming him, hands on the wheel of my Fisher-Price dashboard. The road is dark, with the beacon ahead of a Gulf or Phillips 66 sign, its orange globe high and warm in the night. My father's voice, in this moment, has that warmth and that glow. It radiates security but also the promise of success. Its authority about the world feels like a luxury, like the Cadillac Brougham he owned a bit later, with its Italian leather and its tail fins, and the low growl of its dual-quad engine as we drove into town from the country for orange sherbet on Sunday afternoons. But the voice mystifies, too. It spits commands, demanding that you learn its tempo, like my father in one of his fits of rage. Or like the auctioneers at the rural estate sales my parents dragged us to, looking for antiques. We would follow the dirt roads around Eunice and Mamou to an old house in the woods, after a death had spilled its contents onto the dusty, unkempt yard: a battered and wobbly armoire; frayed folding chairs; a heavy cast iron and enamel juicer whose handle I pumped until I was told to stop; a meat grinder; two enormous and (as we discovered upon bringing them home) afflicted television sets, on which the picture jumped and sizzled; and an assortment of medical equipment (bed pans, a walker, a blood-pressure gauge). Where my parents hunted for treasures, I saw only objects cursed by obsolescence, either their own or that of the bodies they were meant to serve. But under a canopy of oaks, the auctioneer — an elderly white man with a hanky over his microphone and another for his brow — kept the bids coming by an incantatory stammer, in a frenzy of vowels and consonants that turned these objects into cash. As though in the summer heat, something was being lulled to rest there, or conjured to rise from the dust.

A blunted bullet, the Airstream trailer stood in the middle of six acres. Pine woods, threaded by a small bayou, flanked the property on three sides. These were the woods of my mother's childhood, where the pine needles made a pungent floor beneath the tall, resinous trunks and the prickly undergrowth, full of burrs, mosquitoes, and the mites we called red bugs. Trumpet flowers hung at the wood's edge, mingled with the invasive Chinese tallow or "chicken" trees. A dirt road led you to the property from the two-lane blacktop running between Eunice and Mamou. Behind the fishpond, which never lived up to its promise, lay the "tennis court," a rectangle of grass that, like my father's ambition, jarred with its milieu. Behind that stood the trailer, where we lived for a year while restoring our "Cajun house," which my parents had transplanted from some place less auspicious, and which now straddled a hardly green hill that sloped down to the bayou in back. A gravel drive girdled the property, and to the west stood "the barn," a white half-dome of corrugated metal, full of masculine pleasures, where my father kept his tools and the rusty, disassembled bodies of two antique cars. Originally home, perhaps, to Choctaw peoples, the land had passed to my mother on my grandfather's death. Here my parents bonded over their commitment to a story about the past, one of those stories that centers settler-colonial experience as authentic in virtue of its connection to the land. My mother had a connection to the land, but for my father, it was something else. I can see the two of them now: Her with a bandanna around her forehead, hardly stopping to wipe her brow as she lays bricks or scrapes the varnish off an old rocking chair. Him in his work boots and painter's pants, a chunky grease pencil in the pocket of his carpenter's apron, striding about with a level in his hand. For my mother, the place held a link to long hours of childhood spent hiding in the woods with a book or her favorite cousin, away from the tumult of too many younger siblings. My father had a vision for the place, to be sure, a romantic vision, springing from the chasm of his own archaic temperament. But *the place scared him,* my mother told me much later. *I think he was afraid of the neighbors.* Our only neighbors were my mother's second cousin who lived down the road, and a family of Creoles of Color who had farmed the land across the way for generations. I don't know, but I can imagine that their holdings might have shrunk throughout the years under the pressure of white terrorism and subtler forms of white encroachment.[40] So what terrified my father about this place? I don't imagine that he thought about that history when he glanced across the dusty road at the little house where, as I recall, an elderly woman lived, and where her grandson or great-grandson went every day after school. There was no place for them in my father's Xanadu. No place for history, either, only for its dress rehearsal (the "Cajun" house, the antique cars). Perhaps it was the woods themselves, with their ancestral voices, that scared him. He could not comprehend their claim upon him, the command of that high, hot silence, and the solace of the shade below.

Neither could I. Shooed out of doors on muggy Sunday mornings, playing on the hard dirt, which, when scratched, revealed red clay, or at the margins of the woods, always on the lookout for fire ants and paper wasps, I found our rural life rife with a savagery that only compounded the anger seething in our home. Fat black ants threaded their way through the bark of the live oak that held our tire swing. After a rain, the crawfish mounds appeared, tidy mud towers in the grass, but always vacant to the reach of prying fingers. Among the heads of the tall grass, dragonflies hovered in pursuit of prey. Dirt-dauber wasps packed any crevice neglected too long with their nests, wombs of baked clay that disclosed, when dislodged, desiccated bodies. These mundane graves filled me with disgust, perhaps

40 As James Dormon explains, the term "Creoles of Color" generally refers to the mixed-race descendants of those who had won their freedom from slavery before the Civil War and "occupied a special, intermediate place in the racial and social order of antebellum Louisiana and the Gulf port cities […]" ("Preface," in *Creoles of Color of the Gulf South,* ed. James H. Dormon [Knoxville: University of Tennessee Press, 1996], 1–27). The social and economic standing of Creole of Color families, many of whom had been self-sufficient or even prosperous farmers and landowners in the antebellum period, came under fierce attack in the wake of Reconstruction and throughout the period of Jim Crow, as whites sought to consolidate their power in part by erasing all gradations of racial and ethnic distinction beyond white and Black.

because they suggested that the only thing harder than fending off all this life (the ants beading their chemical trails across the kitchen counters, the cobwebs in the corners, the mosquitoes at the screen) was to keep death at bay. More than once my brother and I watched a wasp and a daddy-long-legs dance a fatal waltz on a windowsill, as the sun beat through the glass, the one fighting to defend itself, the other to feed her brood.

And then there were the visits and sleepovers at Gram's. This was not the old house in the woods where my mother had grown up, but a prefab, vinyl-sided affair squatting in mud-logged fields. It was an epicenter of grandchildren (and great-grandchildren) needing a babysitter or a place to crash, large and lonesome-eyed dogs, discarded farm equipment, stray cats, chickens and guinea fowl, and one or two horses, all wandering in haphazard commerce with one another, all of whom could expect from their Gram a minimal standard of attention and care. Hers was a compassionate fatalism that I associate, rightly or wrongly, with the survival of a kind of European peasant culture, simmering with mischief. To provoke in her and our mother a fit of giggling was a child's delight — next to the eagerness with which my brother and I awaited the Little Debbie snacks, tastelessly sweet, that were Gram's bribe for good behavior. The house and its grounds seemed untouched by the years, suspended in the boredom of a Sunday afternoon beneath a wide and scoured sky, the domestic quiet inside punctuated by the tick of a grandfather clock. (That tick-tock tortured my nights there, spent tossing between polyester sheets that made me itch and sweat.) We played long hours with our cousin, a plucky, rambunctious, troubled kid between our ages, with something in him, an alloy of anger and grief and untaught curiosity, wound tight as the coiled copper in the motors he loved taking apart. From a discarded dryer, a new toy, it didn't matter. A kind of Cartesian hunger drove him, who was practically an orphan and lived with Gram full time. Playing with him plunged me into a world of physicality to which I was a stranger. To act out our fantasies there (fending off aliens or enemy soldiers) was to embody them, not in a sanitized way, with plastic limbs and sialagogic sound effects, but by dint of sticks and clumps of dirt, chasing each other across the wide yard or crouching in ambush in a ditch by the road. It was to struggle sometimes to save narrative from the swerve into physical violence, and sometimes to encourage the swerve. And it was a poor moment of triumph when I realized that I was bigger by enough to hurt this cousin whenever he hurt my baby brother, to repay tears with tears, pushing pain down the line. For he (our cousin) was, as a boy, already a casualty of a certain type of white manhood — rural, Southern, working-class — in which boredom and dwindling opportunities conspire to produce a steady pulse of resentment that courts risk and ruin. Perhaps the sense of white masculine entitlement in such places, embattled and desperate, needs the sting of punishment to feel its power.[41]

Where my cousin and my brother had, as kids, a kind of generous energy written on their faces and in their builds, I was skinny, quiet, and sedentary, physically and socially self-contained, and covetous of my toys. Those I loved best were foundlings or castaways. First there was Benjamin, a thumb-sized Fisher-Price boy with an orange tunic and a cowlick, sole survivor of a plastic ferry that had vanished during our move from New York. He was supplanted by Mr. Peabody, a rotund character I liberated from one of my brother's toddler sets, and later there was an anonymous G.I. Joe with gun and backpack, the lone hero of my furtive forays into normative masculinity. Mine, after all, was the generation reared in the shadow of *Home Alone* and Doogie Howser, the generation of the child prodigy and the lost boy. Or did these fetishes stage, in miniature, my father's desire that I be special, like a Christ, *sui generis* and at the same time every inch his father's child? Perhaps I invested them with a child's intimation of precarity: that my parents struggled

41 Although many white people do get caught up in the carceral system, it is also true that to be poor and white and cishet male and to engage in risky or illicit behavior — at least in the American South — is to conform to the rubric of the "good ol' boy," i.e., to warrant tolerance from the authorities and often a second (or third, or fourth) chance.

to make ends meet, that their marriage was doomed. We were not poor in those years, or like many white families on the bottom rungs of the middle class, we would not have called ourselves that. My father always lived for the big win waiting just around the bend. In that horizon of entitlement, material straits are less something to reckon with — or even to defy, through the outbursts of recklessness to which, as I watched them grow up, some of my cousins grew prone (hard drugs, drunk driving, petty and sometimes serious crimes) — than the chronic occasion for a melancholy whose lost object is abundance itself. Or to be precise, the promise of an abundance that wasn't necessarily real to begin with, but a story handed down from one generation to the next, a trove of images on the threshold between memory and desire. To this day, the vacant tree lots after Christmas do the trick. Suddenly, I am remembering things we never, or rarely, had: fancy candies, like creamy swirled peppermints (not Brach's) and marzipan animals; fresh fruit singly wrapped in colored foil; a large wheel of dried apricots, glossy prunes, and fat dates. And there I am, all through November and December poring over the endless newsprint pages of the Sears Wish Book. Its pictures of boys and girls enjoying their bunk beds, Huffy bicycles, and monumental Lego sets engrossed me more than any narrative of knights and dragons and damsels in distress. Serving not as tokens of what we enjoyed, but as nubs or stubs of what I thought we were supposed to have, these images make concrete a sense of privilege, expressing a child's feeling of loss in the face of what he does not possess (enough of). Almost as though his parents' failure to provide it amounted to abandonment. And unlike my father, I could not muster the will to pretend that what we had, we had entirely by choice, and that this spurious choice rendered our lot best. After years of being played with and carried about in my pocket, Benjamin lost the two dots he had for eyes. Lovingly, tenderly, my father gave him a new pair, using his best India ink. No doubt a magic marker would have done the trick, but when the ink promptly rubbed off, he promised to restore my pilgrim's sight with his smallest drill bit. Which was, alas, not small enough: Benjamin's eyes were not only missing, now they were gouged out, and I cast him off for good.

We were all regular casualties of my father's love (including the man himself), which, in its pursuit of something that wasn't there, bored past the envelope of tenderness to the pain and fear where he sought to anchor it. He seldom laid hands on us, although a light rap of his knuckles on my brother's or my scalp was his preferred method of keeping us in check. But when anything set him off, his voice and posture projected a fury not to be trifled with. Some of my memories of his threats are so outrageous that I almost doubt their veracity. *Open that goddamn door, or your eyeballs will be rolling across the tennis court!* Bombarded by white-hot anger, we were objects in collision. Because my mother (so he said) had left the radio on in the Volkswagen and killed the battery, he flipped over the dining room table where we all sat at lunch. Tomato soup seeped across the floor. My mother stood in a corner of the room, clutching my brother to her side, and I stood in another corner, too afraid to run to her, or too used to the structure into which any other alliance was destined to collapse. My father stood at the apex, dispensing love and discipline, and my mother and I occupied the other vertices, by turns targets of his rage and rivals for his love. Another time, in the tight quarters of the trailer, my slowness or sloppiness at my chores sparked a row, my father and mother shouting at one another until he hauled off and hit her. She crumpled to the floor, her thighs pale and wide and soft where they stuck out from her shorts. A change came over him, and turning on me, he hoisted me into the air and shook me, the trailer's plastic molding creaking at my back. Neither of my parents is a stranger to anger, but my mother's has always been slow to develop, proceeding by reasons and cautions, her voice edged with a hardness that lends the image of your fault the finality of proof. In the heat of it with my father, she could, for the most part, hold her own, though I don't remember that she ever resorted to screaming, or tried to match the insults that he unleashed. *Go to grass!* Maybe she conserved her idioms out of concern for our ears (in earshot of my father's vulgate, a piece of parenting decidedly moot). Or perhaps *to grass,* conjuring an old horse out to pasture, was meant to sting worse than telling him to go to hell. As for my father, he fumed, his anger a prodigious and rapidly rising column of foul matter and wasted energy; the feeling spent, he just as quickly regained his cool. But for the moment, he was a man possessed, and his anger's "enigmatic messages" shook me longer after the episode had passed.[42] But I was fazed in a way that my younger brother, his impishness abetted by a hearing deficit, was not. Well into adolescence, I would wake in a start on a Saturday or Sunday morning to the sound of our father's tantrums somewhere in the house. I was the rabbit to my brother's duck, hiding in my burrow while he shook it off, plunging ahead in the knowledge that the noise would pass. More flexible than I in body and temperament, able to bend where I buckled, my brother inherited our father's artistic ferocity, the severity of the standards to which he was prepared to hold others and himself. To me, our father passed on the liability to anger that roils in the wake of that severity, a surge that renders me a different person, a stranger to myself.

The land around Eunice and Mamou straggles past its heyday into the present, its fields littered with oil wells that eke out a profit or have stopped for good; its highways lined with homesteads, some new and ambitious, some modestly hanging on, and some consigned to a limbo of mystery and neglect (their windows papered over with foil, their fences fallen, their yards littered with rusted farm equipment); its pine trees and wildflowers and circling hawks and strutting egrets like ghosts of the prairie to which, one day, this farmland will return. In Eu-

---

42 I borrow the term from Shannon Sullivan, who draws on Jean Laplanche's theory of infantile seduction to argue that habits of racism and white privilege communicate themselves from parents to child via "enigmatic messages that operate in and through the child's body" (*Revealing Whiteness,* 66).

nice, white middle-class promise and respectability persist in the wide boulevards, manicured lawns, cement statuettes of the Virgin, and Victorian mansions ensconced in dogwood and azaleas. When I was nine or ten, my parents bought a shuttered building on Eunice's traditional commercial street — in an effort, perhaps, to give my mother the creative and social outlet she craved, or to distract my father from the disappointment that had settled in, now that work on our Cajun house was done. The building had high, vaulted ceilings and black-and-white tile floors. My mother made special-occasion gowns to order in the back, and in the front, she and my aunt sold handmade crafts on consignment. There were Mardi Gras masks in every medium from porcelain to *papier mâché,* alongside articles of mass manufacture that someone had taken the trouble to turn "Cajun": aprons and oven mitts embroidered with crawfish, a barometer mounted by an alligator, a percussive pair of steel spoons. The word had been something of a slur during my parents' childhoods, an epithet for the uncouth white people who lived off the land, a population whose hard work never rose to the level of respectable living. But by the 1980s, "Cajun" culture had become something to celebrate and commodify.[43] In school, we studied the history of the Cajuns in their exile from Acadia to the Louisiana coast, absorbing a narrative of white diaspora that stood in for — effacing white people's accountability for — the history

43 Although Cajun and Creole of Color communities have historically worked the same lands and occupied, at times, similar positions in the social and economic hierarchies of southern Louisiana, Cajuns can claim the structural advantages of an identification with whiteness, including better access to jobs, education, healthcare, etc. And these advantages extend to the commodification of local cultures themselves. As Sylvie Dubois and Barbara M. Horvath note, "Cajuns have clearly benefited more than Creoles from […] ethnic revival; almost all of the highly prized aspects of the French Louisiana culture are designated as 'Cajun' […]" ("Creoles and Cajuns," 202). See also James H. Dormon, "Ethnicity and Identity: Creoles of Color in Twentieth-Century South Louisiana," in *Creoles of Color of the Gulf South,* ed. James H. Dormon (Knoxville: University of Tennessee Press, 1996), 166–79.

of settler-colonial expropriation and genocide and the circum-Atlantic slave trade.[44] We celebrated jambalaya and gumbo, ignorant that the latter was a Choctaw invention.[45] In fifth grade, I donned overalls and a straw hat for a class rendition of Cajun life, in a rehearsal of my own ersatz performance of a few years before, when my parents had outfitted me in overalls and brogans for my very first day of school. (Although a Yankee transplant, I had, back then, evidently fooled the principal, who shamed me for my Cajun manners: *We say* Yes, sir *around here, country boy.*)

My mother's shop in Eunice, with its trickle of visitors, mostly elderly white women who stopped by to finger a few knick-knacks and gossip with my aunt, was a welcome change from our life in the country. Out there we hardly saw our neighbors (*country people,* my father sneered), apart from the occasional Catahoula hound that strayed onto our property, which my father chased off with a slingshot. But in Eunice, our mother introduced us kids to a more sociable world. We visited my father's old friend at Wrights' men's clothier down the street, with its dark racks of gabardine and its air heady with cedar and leather. On weekends we danced to Cajun bands at the Liberty Theater or took in a movie at the Queen. While our mother worked, we sometimes played in the corners of the florist's shop next door, among roses and gardenias, the shelves full of baubles I knew better than to touch, where the staff gave us a faintly sweet lemonade. It had the texture, this town, and this shop in particular, of what whiteness seemed to promise me. The cold marble, the icy lemonade, the chilled whiteness of the gardenias, it was like a frozen tableau, not exactly a safe space, but a space outside of time. For there was so much time. We rode our bikes dur-

---

44 On the recruitment of Cajun cultural identity to shore up whiteness (and justify the exclusion of people of color), see Sara Le Menestrel, "The Color of Music: Social Boundaries and Stereotypes in Southwest Louisiana French Music," *Southern Cultures* 13, no. 3 (September 17, 2007): 96.

45 Tony Marks, "A Cultural Gumbo," *Evangeline Today,* July 9, 2018, https://www.villeplattetoday.com/news/cultural-gumbo.

ing interminable summer afternoons up and down and around
Park Avenue, from the white concrete municipal building at one
end, to the playground at the other in its nimbus of shade, our
tires thumping over the seams of the sidewalks where the oak
roots had split them, our faces scrunched against the glare from
parked cars and mowed lawns. In our roaming, we tethered
ourselves, by some force of tacit knowledge, to the white and
middle-class parts of town. Our parents would not have been
able to afford these homes, but we could afford to play along the
streets in front of them, unmolested, without anyone's bothering to call the cops or ask us where our parents were. There were
other parts of town, I knew, neighborhoods where Black and
brown folk lived, where mothers also sewed and worked and
where children rode their bikes and played. (Just as there was
another seamstress on the same block as my mother's shop, a
woman of color, whom I never met.) But that knowledge itself,
like the fact of my father's rage, was a thing not to be scratched
at, a blank spot that offered no traction to curiosity, wonder, or
critical inquiry in my otherwise fertile imagination. A few years
later, I would learn to wonder at and inquire into the sources
of my father's rage, even to devote my energies to escaping its
power. By then, I would have formed the habit of treating my life
as a story, and my father as one of its main characters. But this
other knowledge, more grammar than narrative, or a story in
which the character of whiteness blotted out the others, has remained opaque for much longer. It was, and is, a kind of primer
of the white self, picked up less through explicit instruction than
by what rubs off on the flesh, in the shade under the oaks, on a
slow summer day.

It was on top of this priming that I began to fashion an intentional self, motivated, in cryptic ways at first, by a desire not
to be like my father. Just as my mother adored the artist in him,
and just as he admired and encouraged, if he did not necessarily
respect, the artistic streak in her, they encouraged my younger
brother and me in our creative pursuits. Indeed, my father expected it of us, and at eight or nine, trotting after him with my
kid's toolbox, I still longed to master those manly arts. But for

Christmas one year, Gram gave me a sewing kit. And it filled me with enthusiasm for the work that I now saw my mother do, in the back of her shop, for hours on end. With my own shears, thimble, and laboriously threaded needle, I made my first creation: a pillow that looked less like the strawberry it was supposed to be than an inflamed kidney. My interest in sewing did not survive the divorce. But I like to think that my mother's practice offered me a different model of labor and art. For my father, each new project demanded a fresh surplus of passion, and once that was spent, or thwarted, the project fizzled out. The house in the country and the store in Eunice in time grew rank to his tastes and were abandoned to the weeds and the bank. But my mother worked differently, steadily, at a pace marked by the hum, halt, click, reverse, and hum again of the Singer, as the fabric bunched and stretched beneath her fingers, pooled in her lap and at her feet. While my father, hunched over his drafting table or walking around a building site, aspired to an aesthetic characterized by its fascination with the rectilinear control of space, my mother poured herself into a discipline of the sinuous and its interruption. A dance of dart and pleat and hem, creating those accents to the body's natural beauty that, by covering and constraining, give it new ways to express itself. Just as poetry or prose can recruit the rhythms of speech, rhythms that reveal an allure we had almost forgotten, buttoning to undress the mother tongue, allowing us to revel in her dishabille.

It was around then that I began to follow my own line, and books welcomed me into their dark and private corners. I especially loved *The Wind in the Willows* and *Eight Cousins*. The travails of Rat and Mole, and Toad's reckless adventures with his motorcar, transpire amid the comforts of a scaled-down world. Though already a world beset, in subtle ways, by what lies beyond its borders. As Christopher Bollas writes, describing an early scene in the book, "the reader […] discovers that in fact Rat and Mole are experiencing the sunrise, but they cannot see the sun, they only experience its effect on their environment.

The object casts its shadow on the subject."[46] The shadow of the object could describe how the white cishet masculine subject, having been taught to make objects out of others — or out of the otherness of others' flesh, and of his own — is informed and deformed by what escapes a structure of possessiveness. What escapes includes the matter of solidarity and care. As a male child, I was learning that my father's love, present as "the projection of a surface" of emulation, obedience, and desire, was not all. But as a white child, bred up to feel middle-class, I had only an inkling of how love spreads wider than its entanglement with the nuclear family.[47] And like any number of white men or women who grow to adulthood without being able to recall, for instance, the first thing about the women of color who minded them as toddlers — beyond the aura of a smile, warming some Manhattan apartment — I had less than an inkling about whose labor sustained our tidy white version of the world. Perhaps that's why I took to the stories of orphans, following the hardships of Alcott's Rose, as a bit later I gobbled up Oliver Twist. The literary orphan-story spiritualizes the privileges of the European bourgeoisie. The white orphan girl, in particular, embodies what the disciplines of capitalist exploitation otherwise repress, her femininity a vessel where passion and vulnerability are transformed, under the pressure of a singular sense of virtue, into nurture and

46 Christopher Bollas, *The Shadow of the Object: Psychoanalysis of the Unthought Known* (New York: Columbia University Press, 1987), 38. Bollas's work expands on Freud's idea of "the shadow of the object as it falls on the ego," the object, in its loss, becoming "the hand of the fate" (34). For Bollas, the first such "transformational object" is the mother, who is "'known' as a complex process of care […] as the infant develops, the ego assumes the transformational function" (51). In other words, the ego assumes the role of care vis-à-vis the self, "inheriting" from the mother the structure of those early relations. Bollas re-writes Freud's theory of the ego in explicitly relational terms, focusing on the bond between mother and infant. But this focus can also obscure intimacy's porousness, how intimacy always carries, as it were, shadows of the wider social world.

47 The quoted phrase is Freud's description of the ego, as cited in Sullivan, *Revealing Whiteness*, 67.

care. Dickens's novels expose the rifts between moral sentiments and the marketplace, but it is Alcott's book that I treasured. I can still see myself seeing myself as Rose, waiting all day by the skating pond for her cousin, falling ill with a fever from which her uncle nurses her back to health. With chronic headaches at eight or nine years old, was I waiting for my guardian to arrive and bring me up to a proper, healthy whiteness? As a child, I felt precious and fragile, my privilege an eggshell, awaiting a future of cracked ambition and broken love. (Had my mother, herself the eldest of eight, with a mother who had little time for her older children and a father who worked to exhaustion in the fields, been waiting for that guardian, too, when his flesh-and-blood shadow rode into town?)

In fifth grade, I wrote poems for Ms. L—, and I joined the informal sorority that followed her around the playground at recess. *Girls, Dolsy's a catch.* And oh, how I wanted to be. I desired domesticity's latch on the self, and I saw, or thought I saw, the way whiteness, economic security, and provincial middle-class values could lock it down. After all, what else secured my classmates' limbs in that confidence they showed on the soccer field, or when passing notes in class, or when running for class president? When I ran for class president, I lost, and I cried, ashamed to have lost and more ashamed to be crying. But I couldn't help it. My orphan inside "wept." There were only two Black kids in my class that year, identical twins who (it was rumored) used to swap places without the teacher's noticing. I think it was Darren with whom I swapped words at recess, new polysyllabic acquisitions like "persistent" and "perpendicular." He and his brother were friendly and funny and put words together in creative ways that I didn't understand, like "jack it up." I used phrases like "public address system" (borrowed from an elderly substitute teacher). Travis, the one white kid who came from a working-class household or a broken home (to us, they were the same), and who had hung around my mother's shop in an effort to befriend me before the florist chased him off, got expelled for bringing a scalpel to school. Before that, Travis told the class that he believed in evolution. *Some people think that mankind was descended from the apes,* Ms. L—had said during a biology lesson. When I said or implied that I believed in evolution—quietly, to two popular girls over lunch, repeating something I only dimly understood about Carl Sagan and the Big Bang—I was told I might be a Satanist. (There was some shouting, then, and tears, I think, all around.) But I craved the discipline that kept lawns trim, that promised to hold at bay the looks and the questions that my own upbringing seemed to provoke. *Who's your Daddy?* That's what almost anyone in a small south-Louisiana town wants to know upon meeting a child. By the time I learned that the answer to this question was not tautological, I had reason to feel that the patronymic could be an ill-fitting thing. Or an omission that one had to atone for by conspicuous good behavior. I felt sure I would gladly trade the latitude I had to enjoy things deemed by my peers' parents too "adult" (R-rated movies, staying up late on weekends), for freedom from my father's eccentric regime: the foods we were not permitted to eat (pizza, hot dogs, chewing gum); the tastes and activities we were dissuaded from by sarcasm and disdain (the Boy Scouts, church, team sports, anything on TV with a laugh track). My white classmates had pizza parties and sleepovers, played sports, and prayed with their families every Sunday. They drove ATVs through the rutted fields and roamed their housing tracts in small groups. *What are those?* they would ask, pointing at my lunch of dried fruit and nuts (never having encountered, perhaps, a pecan outside of a pie or a walnut apart from a sundae). I didn't mind how it tasted, but I couldn't stand my lunch for looking so rustic and austere beside the cafeteria's spread of roast meat, brown gravy, white rice, and glossy buttered rolls.

My parents were early adopters of what we now call a healthy diet, but as in everything, my father hungered for the fanatic's monopoly on the truth. To the end of his life, he would cite Arnold Ehret, a turn-of-the-century nutritionist who advocated regular fasts, a diet of fruits and leafy vegetables, and strict avoidance of all "mucus-causing" foods. Ehret's work, as far as I can tell, occupies a transitional zone between Victorian mores about the body and modern clinical approaches to fitness and health. In one sense, his prescriptions seem ahead of their time, but they also express the moralism of a deep disgust for the body's functioning. In the dog-eared, brittle little paperback that my father kept among his books, the following passage is underlined:

> Perhaps in an entirely healthy condition the so-called mucus membrane should not at all be white, slimy, but clean and red like on animals. Perhaps this "corpse-mucus" is even the cause of the paleness of the white race! Paleface! Corpsecolor![48]

Curiously, Ehret's prescriptions suggest a desire to purge the white body of what, by homology, makes the body white. In this passage, mucus functions as a metonymy, not for whiteness as a racial category, but for the corporeality of that category, which Ehret figures as a form of corruption and decay. And like any number of white men before and after him, he appeals to an image of the primal, the "healthy condition" of "animals," as a cure for what ails whiteness itself. But Ehret's book promotes a return to this primal condition as an ascetic practice. My father's fasts lasted at most a few days at a time. It was my mother who, not long before they split up, once fasted for nearly two weeks straight, subsisting on water and lemon juice. By the end, she lay in the soft well of their feather bed, unable to get up without assistance, her wan face looking scared and severe. I guess she did it, in part, in order to show up my father, forcing him to reckon with the presence of a kind of stamina, a strength of will, that he never could muster. Such was the resistance she offered to his demand that she occupy or be his shadow. Or maybe she merely wanted (as I, too, have wanted, when drawn toward self-harm) to make the pain visible, to surface it (as the ego is "the projection of a surface"). In her case, that might have meant act-

---

48 Arnold Ehret, *Rational Fasting for Physical, Mental and Spiritual Rejuvenation* (Dobbs Ferry: Ehret Literature Pub. Co., 1987), 37.

ing out the anguish of years wasted in the composure of a body and a face never allowed to say no. The composure of someone whom her culture has trained to assent to an effort to transcend the inexorable, an effort that becomes her inexorable condition. Just then, that face, whiter than usual, might have said: *To escape this, you have to learn how to disappear.* To turn into an object, or take refuge among its shadows. Like those that, after days without food, would have begun to cling to her face, its usual softness sharpened into something I didn't quite recognize.

When I was ten, their marriage broke up, and a car ride delivered my younger brother and me into a new world. Our father was at the wheel of his cherished cloth-top MG, and my brother, five years old, lay curled up on the coupe's back seat. We drove through a winter thunderstorm to New Orleans, leaving our mother behind. Our father had decided to move the family again. But she refused. She told him that she wanted a divorce. He left, taking *his* children, the way one might seize, in a huff, household items (the radio, the electric mixer, the flatware). In the MG, the heater, a noisy red box below the passenger seat, incubated our passage. With his hands looming in that tight space, filling me with the raw material for any number of bad adolescent verses to come, he railed against her betrayal. He swore that he could have killed her. I knew he had at least one gun that he kept out of sight, part of some secret phallic armature. *If it wasn't for you two angels,* he said, his voice steely in the effort to persuade himself, *I would give them what they've got coming.* Her and her lover, *that goddamn cocksucking bastard.* The affair, I knew even then, was an expedient fiction, cooked up in order to dignify, before us and himself and the rain-swept night and no one in particular, the fact of his desertion by a woman. The night before (or was it another night thereafter?) the four of us had spent in a motel, my brother and me tucked into a cot at the foot of the room's double bed. Our parents were discreet, but I woke in the morning to their bare legs under the covers as they fumbled for their underwear. At first, they presented the break-up in amicable terms. But as the car spirited us away from, yet deeper into, the threat of our father's rage, I understood how the stage was set. Understood that I could not, for the foreseeable future, take our mother's side or cry or call for her. My father was the child needing comfort, the sovereign robbed of his plea-sure dome, the man possessed. As for my baby brother (born at home, breast-fed until he was a toddler), even before the divorce he had clung to our mother's body with a child's foreknowledge that this blessed intimacy, the best he could know, would not last. After their separation, grief dragged him through a series of ailments, from pinworms to pneumonia. I, on the other hand, would do what I have done ever since: I would pretend to be an adult. I would start wearing suspenders, apply myself even more precociously at school, and for that first year, address every adult woman I met with a plaintive *Yes, ma'am* and *No, ma'am.* (Good orphans mind their manners.) But on that night, with the wind-shield streaming, and the road ahead grayed out by sheets of rain, in which taillights shimmered like the trace of something elusive and deferred, our mother — our mother's flesh, that zone of wonder and shame — became the object shadowed by loss. But what did any of us know of her flesh, to which we owed the comfort and integrity of our own?

What if Daddy's love was all you had? He had saved us, so he insisted, from the stultification of small-town life, in the grip of which we were bound to become something awful: Baptists, or Republicans. Our mother's love became an indulgence, along with fast food and watching sitcoms, reserved for two weekends a month. I said I wasn't allowed to grieve, but in truth, I don't remember grieving, so readily did I fall back into a groove pre-pared during those first years of my life, when my father doted on me and touted me and paced me to sleep across the par-quet floor. Being a single parent of two young boys must have been difficult and trying. But it was also a domestic idyll, this household of men, with one son responsible and sensitive and compliant, a wife-and-mother surrogate, and the other a boy after his own heart, mischievous and robust. And our father's fondness for adventures, braced by a conviction that brooked no reluctance on our part, was catching. We were Rat and Mole and Badger, arming ourselves with pistols and cudgels. We kept a clean house. We rode in a fine motorcar. He took us with him on trips to Mexico for weeks at a time. And whatever we did, his knowledge of the world, while almost never as sound as he believed, commanded a child's sense of wonder. *Look at this old camera — I used to have one just like it. The Acura is the most reliable modern engine in the world. There's a great book — you should read it — about a man who turns into a cockroach; there's another one about a man who eats an entire car. Is your toy broken? Let Daddy fix it. Did you hurt yourself? Let Daddy see.* We were latch-key kids, but that suited us just fine. It only whetted our sense of self-reliance in the face of a world whose love could not be trusted. *Don't, under any circumstances, open the door to strangers. Especially if they're from the sheriff's department.*

Now it was our father's turn to show us the town. I was generally afraid of or embarrassed by my father's friends, who came to the fore in his new bachelorhood. Like J.D., a lawyer who kept a fancy Lakeshore house in perpetual squalor, mirroring the man himself, an imposing pale heap with a drunk's glabrous legs. J.D. always had a new conspiracy theory on tap, or a piece of dubious advice — *You should get yourself a second social security number, just in case* — or worse, a tale of sadism and braggadocio. *That fucking cat scratched me, so, you know, I threw it against the wall three or four times.* He was the sort of man who, had he been anything other than white, would have wound up in prison long ago. J.D. drew up the divorce papers for my father, putting down the cause as spousal abandonment. Then there was the washed-up movie producer who beat his wife and called our house collect from a Mexican jail; and my father's favorite client, a real-estate mogul who treated him to steaks and strip clubs but skimped on his fees. White men with an insatiable appetite for possession, which possessed them in turn, like the flabby leather sofa at J.D.'s house that threatened to swallow me as I sat on it, waiting for J.D. and my father to return. But for them, life could be an abacus of conquests and off-color jokes, an endless supply of moonlit schemes, a raconteur's paradise.

One of my father's favorite spots in New Orleans was the Hummingbird Grill and Hotel, a dive on St. Charles Avenue with an ensemble cast of precarious men (and occasionally, their female consorts) in leather and denim and camo, their beards and hair unkempt, their skin chapped by cigarette smoke and the open road and a wind blowing only neglect from the stars. My father kept a cool distance from these characters, but he loved to brag about being there, with the hairs in the hamburgers and the roaches skittering across the floor. An amateur playwright, his feelers alert, I can see him "stand[ing] proudly inclosed within himself," "a spectator, even when he himself is the one acting."[49] My father slummed it, masquerading as him-

---

49 Kierkegaard, *The Concept of Irony,* 283. For Kierkegaard, the ironist smuggles egoism into the midst of his vaunted negativity. Hence the ironist's negativity is but a ruse, its critical incisiveness but a cheap trick: "It cannot really be said that the ironist places himself outside and above morality and ethics, but he lives far too abstractly, far too metaphysically and esthetically to reach the concretion of the moral and the ethical." For the ironist, the very activity of judging becomes the badge of his superiority, its rabbit's foot. But the irony that haunts the ironist is that the peerage to which he aspires remains elusive. It cannot, by definition, include those whom the ironist judges as being incapable of irony, the run-of-the-mill, mediocre, Philistine crowd, Hegel's "honest souls." Nor can it include those marginalized by the dominant morality. The latter serve merely as objects for his possessive gaze. The ironist may convince himself that he has cashed out of the rat race, but he has not cleared his debt to domination. It's just that he wants to dominate in virtue of himself. In other words, not on account of his embodiment of the common marks of privilege and power (his whiteness and masculinity). He's astute enough to feel, in some measure, the emptiness of those. But for him, his own astuteness knows no limits, so he deceives himself still. His identification qua white man hinges on the possession of some cryptic potential. But as Kierkegaard writes, the ironist "continually collides with the actuality to which he belongs."

Kierkegaard's critique of irony, and of the concept into which he develops it, the demonic, provides some phenomenological language for thinking about the abstract character of white cishet masculine identities, abstract in their metonymic relation to a nation of universal subjects

self in pursuit of the real. *Your mother always hated it here.* At ten or eleven, I felt shame in proximity to these tough, ragged customers. I felt my body's vulnerability, its fragility, as if their looks of having seen the other side of something, the undercarriage of their own desires, might prove contagious. But the budding ironist in me could already trace something similar in my father, with his icy gray eyes and high forehead and prematurely white hair. I squirmed at how those eyes hovered too long over the young women who waited on us at restaurants and department stores. How he called them *sweetheart,* or cracked a joke at their expense, the words spoken with a coyness that masked the care taken to secure his dentures while he spoke. And with a note of desperation, as his cool, aquiline handsomeness yielded, with age, to a hunger more basilisk-like. And like him, I fantasized about the lives of those men who tenanted the Hummingbird Hotel, tramping up and down a dark stairway beside the alcove where I fed quarters to the console that chimed with cheap thrills, playing Spyhunter or Pac-Man. Itinerant and, I presumed, lonely lives, they held out, in my ignorance of whatever hardship or trauma might have hounded them, a different kind of promise. A further edge of disintegration, in the flesh, having the courage to mortify the latter (my mother, fasting) and to sever its ties (my mother, leaving us). They promised,

conceived as equal in rights and opportunities, and equally abstract in their differentiation from others on the basis of a series of metaphoric binaries (white/Black, male/female, etc.) in which one term is imagined as superior to the other. Both of these modes of abstraction collide with the reality down on the ground, where most us have to work for a buck, trying not to get screwed over, fighting back the tears we forgot long ago how to shed, and mistaking our anger for dignity and courage. Or perhaps we should say that these abstractions collide with each other on the terrain of that reality, which far from diminishing their salience, requires it. As Dana Nelson argues, "what men are symbolically promised by national/ white manhood is almost never what they get: a space where men can step out of competitive, hierarchically ordered relations and experience the rich emotional mutuality of fraternal sameness" (*National Manhood: Capitalist Citizenship and the Imagined Fraternity the White Men* [Durham: Duke University Press, 1998], 19). See also Wiegman, *American Anatomies,* 170.

perhaps, a primal courtship of the object's "dispossessive force." Outside, it was Mardi Gras, the loaded crowd jockeying for a good spot to see the parades, shouting, cursing, elbowing their way to the curb, struggling to keep their costumes together, baring their flesh. Above the other revelers bobbed three giant phalluses of peach-colored foam. The three of us had staked out a booth at the Hummingbird after craning for a glimpse of Zulu along a packed meridian, and now we waited for Rex. At some point that day, a beer can struck my brother in the head. But we toughed it out until the Krewe of Comus, the last parade of the season, wound its way through the emptying and fetid streets, flanked by a troupe of white-clad torchbearers. It was a spectacle of white pride and terror, insisting that "plantation power" prevail even amid carnival misrule.[50] And our perseverance paid off, for the thinning crowds meant that we reaped handfuls of loot as Comus rolled through the swill and trash, torch-lit argosies of patrician largesse and jealously guarded power.

50 Clyde Woods, *Development Arrested: The Blues and Plantation Power in the Mississippi Delta* (New York: Verso, 2017). This would have been one of the last public appearances of the "Mystic Krewe of Comus." After the passage, in 1991 and at long last, of a New Orleans City ordinance mandating the desegregation of the Mardi Gras krewes, this oldest of the officially recognized organizations forewent parading altogether rather than integrate. On the history of Mardi Gras as a legally enshrined institution by which the white elite of New Orleans sought to discipline and displace the carnivalesque traditions of the working classes and communities of color, see Joseph Roach, *Cities of the Dead: Circum-Atlantic Performance* (New York: Columbia University Press, 1996), 1–25. Writing on the history of Mardi Gras parades and balls, Roach notes that these "upper class performances by a closely knit aristocracy" have served as sites to reinforce homosocial bonds among white men of property, even as they "express a kind of two-faced panic — queasy resignation punctuated by eruptions of outrage — that local government and its laws are passing from the control of white people" (265). Such performances provide a platform "where images of violent ridicule may stand in for violent action." Incidentally, the torchbearers or *flambeaux* of Comus were originally enslaved men and later free men of color, although membership in the Krewe itself has always been restricted to whites.

In those years, the movies were our babysitter. Our father would drop us off at Joy's Dollar Theater for a few hours while he met with a client or went out on a date. Sometimes we missed the first half of the feature and had to watch it out of sequence, or else we killed time in the Taco Tico next door. These were nights of grease and patience, in palaces of sovereign misrecognition. We became adept at waiting. We waited, with the feel of old upholstery pilling under our legs, eating stale popcorn and sucking on the last of the Coke we shared, for an audience with the selves that we longed to be, or that we felt compelled to desire. In the movies we loved, there was no need for patience and no hesitation. The Terminator terminates. With his cape and his scowl, Michael Keaton cleans up Gotham, and Robin Williams as Mr. Keating commands all the white boys' love, including, one might imagine, Christian Slater's gleaming skater and those irreverent imbeciles Bill and Ted. Icons of a misfit but saccharine masculinity, these white guys asserted the power granted by their social identity, either by gratuitous violence in a world skewed from the norm, or by irony and humor in world too straight-laced for its own good.[51] They promised us that the or-

51 I owe my frame for reading these films to Sally Robinson's trenchant look at works of literature and film from the late twentieth century that center the angst of white cishet men. Robinson reads these texts as expressive of the ways in which feminism, the Civil Rights movement, and identity politics have rendered the white cishet male body visible as a particular kind of body, thereby marking it as potentially "other" (as opposed to the "unmarked" status of the subject whose race, gender, and sexuality are taken as the universal, hegemonic norm). Robinson argues that these texts take masochistic pleasure in depicting this embodiment as traumatic — a claim compatible with my suggestion that some ways of embodying privilege can be understood according to Kierkegaard's model of the demonic. See Sally Robinson, *Marked Men: White Masculinity in Crisis* (New York: Columbia University Press, 2000). On the uses that such narratives of white male angst make of the representation of Blackness, see Hazel Carby, "Encoding White Resentment: Grand Canyon — A Narrative for Our Times," in *Race, Identity, and Representation in Education,* eds. Cameron McCarthy and Warren Crichlow (New York: Routledge, 1993), 236–48. Hollywood's sentimental revision of patriarchal white

der that most benefits elite white men might coexist with compassion and justice, spontaneity and love. And when it was over, we waited in the lobby, sometimes with a couple of quarters for the arcade games, which were quickly spent, as though in an airlock where we prepared for re-entry into the hot and motherless night. I didn't have trouble keeping my brother occupied, for he would sit rapt in concentration, drawing or playing with a toy. Already he showed signs of the physical and mental stamina that, as he grew up, would allow him to take comfort in working himself to exhaustion, a mother's gift to her stubborn baby boy. His hero in those years was Robocop, the cyborg struggling to retain his humanity in service to corporate greed and the police state. But if my brother would substitute those parts of himself touched by our mother with the hardness and polish of a machine, my most heroic wish was for a different body, larger, older, more capable, more graceful, more lovable. Which was also a wish for disembodiment, or self-effacement, as the prerequisite to self-possession. In sight of the teens and pre-teens who gathered at the movies together, I suffered, not from loneliness, but from the shame of being there alone. I had only the company of this child who, once my partner in mischief and make-believe, was increasingly my responsibility: his feet dangling from the seat, his toes in his Buster Brown sandals a scandal of immaturity. I fidgeted on the bench where we waited, shredding a napkin or empty paper cup, gradually awakening to the fact that Daddy's love was not, and had never been, all. That it left a large and growing gap that demanded, somehow, to be filled. Around us in the lobby, most of the other kids were Black. In relation to them, I took up, as a foregone conclusion, the white Southern man's sense that we — the nameless they and the blameless I — could not be friends, that we had nothing in common, ex-

supremacy, coming at the tail end of the cokehead decade, as bankers and financiers danced on the grave of the welfare state, dovetails with what neoliberal politicians during this period dubbed "family values," a renewed investment in Oedipal spectacles that transfigure political and economic violence into narratives of personal loss and private failure.

cept for our common awareness of the history and the current conditions that rendered us socially unequal. And I tasted, and buried in myself, the white Southerner's embarrassment at this riven commonality, which is the unease with which one makes an object of judgment out of someone whose judgment one is afraid to reckon with. Even as I failed to individuate them, *the Black kids,* so I felt, could surely see right through me. In their presence, my white flesh felt like some clumsily held secret, a purloined thing. And even as I failed to grasp the extent of the disparity between us — and the forms of violence and plunder that produced it out of white people's greed and fear — I missed, too, whatever we might have had in common. Like the fact that some of those Black boys and girls had younger siblings in their care, because their parents, not unlike mine, could not afford a babysitter. But solidarity melts into the whiteness whose heir you are, and I stayed put.

A supplement to the "absence of culture" characteristic of middle-class whiteness, Hollywood fantasy, as James Baldwin argues, projects a counterfeit privacy in place of public life.[52] With the lights down, the senses are bombarded to create a kind of cult space, a collective form of inclosing reserve. There violence becomes redemptive, romantic love triumphs, and history hardly exists, in an apocryphal, apocalyptic time devoted to the restoration of the secret of whiteness as self-enclosure. Walking out of the movies on a Sunday, with the hammered light

---

52 In "The Devil Finds Work," James Baldwin tells the story of American racism and patriarchal white supremacy through the lens of Hollywood cinema, for Hollywood has always taught white Americans how they should understand race. This teaching typically happens by erasing the relevance of race, as white heroes and heroines do their thing in a world devoid of people of color, or where non-white characters are either villains, props, or oracles of a sentimental minstrelsy. They are objects, in short, for the white characters' and the presumptively white audience's wish fulfillment. On whiteness and "the absence of culture," see David Roediger, *Towards the Abolition of Whiteness: Essays on Race, Politics, and Working Class History* (London: Verso, 2000), 13. On classic Hollywood cinema and the construction of whiteness, see also Dyer, *White.*

of late afternoon above the heat-soaked cement and asphalt of the suburbs, my body ushered me toward a melancholy that I couldn't understand, although I dreaded it, whatever *it* was: another night of homework, another week of school, another week without seeing our mother, puberty, adulthood, the final loneliness of waiting for that thing you always wanted to justify the strength with which you wanted it. There may have been, gathering in the lobby, an abundance beyond these returns, but it was lost on me. When I got home, I devoured the rest of a V.C. Andrews novel. Its embossed paperback cover promised a B-movie luridness, and its blue-eyed, blond-haired orphans, at the mercy of sadistic relatives, pursued an incestuous romance that would have made my rosy Victorian alter ego blush. A book-ish Black girl in my class had turned me onto those novels as I watched them engross her during recess. I wanted reason to blush. Especially in my father's presence, I was a put thing, a kind of human putty, my energies bent on anticipating where he wanted me to be, what he wanted me to say. *As soon as you're around your Dad,* my mother told me back then, *you just shut up like a telescope.* Under my father's *I,* I longed for the stars. But gazing at the stars, we read as destiny a light projected out of the past. A past that was itself the shadow of something prior. Or the fold of terror and trauma, the ravages of an insatiable appetite for domination, and the love and hope that sustain the resistance to it. A fold compressed, by the persistence of that appetite, into a failure to reckon with any of it.

In this telescoping of the nuclear and the national, in this tunnel hollowed out by Hollywood in the wreckage of our times, our mother's rejection of our father gave him license him to re-enact a primal fantasy of his own. He was in high school when he found out that his mother was having an affair with a young serviceman, hardly three years his senior. His parents were es-tranged but not yet divorced. My grandfather, an itinerant elec-trician during the Depression and the War, cut a distant but po-tent figure in my father's life. *Daddy never laid a finger on us, but he wouldn't take shit from any man. He laid flat more than one boss who spoke to him in a way he didn't like.* As for my grandmother, whom the town knew her whole life as Baby, she spoke to everyone in the way she liked, whether they liked it or not. In her teens, Baby had played piano at the picture show whenever it came to town. And well into her eighth decade, decked out in costume jewelry under Shirley Temple curls, Baby was still a flirt and a card, modeling Hollywood's "white chick" with aplomb. She was also the family's matriarch, coddled and defended by her doting sons. On this occasion, however, having caught Baby and her new beaux sneaking into the house late one night, my father felt hailed to protect the patronymic. Lacking Daddy's physique, he fetched the latter's revolver and aimed it at the beaux's head. I imagine that the scene — lit by an outdoor light outside their big house on the corner, under the magnolias, which would have lent the hot night, full of sweat and feral cat and perfume, a shade of cream — was stolen by Baby herself. For instead of shooting, my father went off to sulk, and he was still sulking many years later when our mother's *No* startled him like a cat jumping out of the magnolias. And again, reaching for his gun, he reached for a prop that didn't fit, in a lovers' tangle that left him crying out against his dispossession by the objects that he had been taught possessively to desire, and by the self that, as the reserve of those desires, had become objectified in turn. Crying out with no language for what ailed him, except for this confusion of tongues, these apocrypha flanking him — flanking us — on all sides.[53]

<hr>

53 "Confusion of tongues": the phrase comes from Sándor Ferenczi, who reminded Freud that the development of neurosis is not a matter only of the child's desire. Ferenczi's work suggests that the self-regulative subject is formed by passionate identification with a desire or need she is not ready for, a desire or need imposed on her by adults, and which comes laden with guilt and habits of self-reproach. What is contagious, on Ferenczi's model, is desire and judgment (criticism). See Ferenczi, "Confusion of Tongues between Adults and the Child," *Contemporary Psychoanalysis* 24, no. 2 (July 1, 1988): 196–206.

Driving from Baton Rouge toward Eunice on I-10, the Appian Way of south Louisiana's petrochemical empire, you pass above neighborhoods where working-class Black communities live in the shadow of a prosperity that their labor has secured, cut off by the interstate from the wealthy neighborhoods around the university, and sitting downwind from the toxic clouds spewed night and day by Exxon and Dow. Then you traverse a long stretch of swampland submerged by man-made overflow from the Mississippi and Atchafalaya Rivers, the causeway hemmed by a deep silence on either side. We made that trip countless times, barreling or crawling down that corridor of commerce and leisure and contraband. Those weekend visits were over almost before they began, our parents meeting stiffly to hand off the children in the parking lot of a truck stop or at the curb outside a granite-faced courthouse under live oaks. And yet, those weekends with our mother, even more than an afternoon at the movies, offered the reprieve of another kind of privilege, another kind of time. A time not structured by anxiety, but open to other senses dormant in the flesh: silliness and laughter, sadness and grief, excitement, and a serious and honest mutual confidence, in which secrets could be shared. Hers was not our father's privacy, which was neither private enough for me, nor something we were allowed to share with anyone, having been sworn to uphold a paranoid fraternity. Scraping by on Pell grants (she had gone back to college) and a meager income from dressmaking, our mother worked night shifts at Taco Bell, squirting sour cream and guacamole out of industrial-size tubes, before returning to her shop to finish a batch of bridesmaids' gowns, sitting up till dawn under a lamp that, as I imagined it, defied the snug darkness of the town and the wider darkness of the fields beyond. When we stayed with her, for the first year or so, we stayed in that shop, bathing in the bathroom's industrial sink and eating microwave dinners. But we defied the night together, cruising in her used Impala, which was green and barge-like, over the town's quiet streets and along its one commercial strip, and up and down the back roads that held, in the dappled afternoon shade of their curves, the promise of a fresh start and a new life: the ramshackle Victorian-era mansions in Iota and New Iberia that she loved; the aunts and uncles and cousins whose homes were full of family and food and gossip and lore. *Someday soon I'll buy a house, and my babies can come live with me.* In the meantime, as far as she could stretch her funds, our mother attended to our clothes, teeth, haircuts, and other aspects of child-rearing that our father was prone to miss. Of course, my mother's pluck expressed her privilege, too, particularly in the jobs and loans that she, a newly single woman, was allowed to get, her whiteness ensuring (at least, often enough) that the door wouldn't be shut in her face. She was encouraged to face forward, to look toward the love up ahead. But in the meantime, we traded stories about our silly crushes, she and I, with Bonnie Raitt's velvet voice on the tape deck and my baby brother pestering us from the back seat. Always a little heady inside with exhaust fumes, her Impala reminded me of the vintage Cadillac that my father had owned, but it was unencumbered by the latter's status as a privileged object, something one might be judged against and might not deserve. The car embarrassed my mother but not me, who was by then embarrassment's boon companion. Riding in that car, I felt somehow free. I'm not sure I ever allowed myself to believe that we would live with our mother again. But those weekends with her taught me how to indulge in fantasies untouched by the desperate edge of my father's desires. Or rather, in the cut across our lives made by that desire and its despair, my mother and I could find a reprieve in fantasy together. From her I learned what it means to have, and to be, a confidante.

That confidence had to sustain me on the long drive back to Baton Rouge, with the water spreading to the horizon in both directions, a brown-green mirror broken by cypress knees and now and then a solitary fisherman's shack. With dusk closing in, the gas flares began to burn at the refineries, towers of flame in the night sky. On those drives, the sunset dilated the world into a kind of golden ache, and time bled away from us more rapidly than usual, pooling in our wake as a homesickness we were always running from. A homesickness we were learning to repress or to channel into other desires. It was around then, at age twelve or thirteen, that I awoke to the outward shape of my flesh: its willowy frame; its musculature weak and clumsy; and above all, the deformity that pressed my ribs into a peak at the sternum, like a bird's beak, or a life-form about to burst from my chest. *Bruh, check out this shit! Somebody better call Ripley!* That deformity became, for me, the most acute point on a hyper-sensitive exoskeleton, grafting onto my senses a vigilance about how I looked. I stood with my arms folded across my chest. Walking down a crowded street, I checked my reflection in the store windows, hoping to throw this other character off my track. And now I encountered my father, too, as an explicit object of judgment. Daddy's love had become a liability, with his penchant for coddling and cursing, and his wiry aging body, and his hot temper, with his silk shirts and zebra-striped sheets, and the leather "purse" he wore slung across his torso, which mortified me less by its presence than on account of his propensity to call it that in public. *Boys, why didn't you say something? Daddy almost forgot his purse!* Why, indeed. And why can't Daddy be more like other adults? Like those who I imagined my peers' parents to be, solid in their whiteness, faithful in their allegiance to middle-class Southern values? Above all, I feared the shades of the demonic in him, suspecting that his strained protest against the world's good graces would alienate those whose approval I sought. And I disapproved of his disapproval of them, these *fat stupid Americans,* these *goddamn Baptists,* these *bloody Republicans.*

We had moved to Baton Rouge, a bastion of white Southern Baptist Republicans, where we lived in a sprawling apartment complex called Eden Point. Beside its sign's huge apple, at the edge of a highway without sidewalks and flanked by culverts, I caught the bus to Sherwood Forest Middle School. Such is the mythopoeia of white supremacy with which Baton Rouge abounds: a town of gated subdivisions, flagrant political corruption, and flagrant prejudice; a trading post in the swamp that fancies itself a city on the hill. In New Orleans, I had been learning how to make friends. But now the task was not to make friends but to fit in. The signs of election began with being white and middle-class, a sorting abetted by the curricular tracking that assigned us "gifted and talented" students to our own classes, segregated from the working-class Black students, whom the school system never bothered to test for talents nor grant an audition for their gifts. Beyond that, election rested on the distinctions by which the white American middle class tries to transcend itself. Who wore Girbaud jeans, with their designer label sewn right onto the fly, and who made do with Lees or Levi's. Or worse, with Wranglers and hand-me-downs, like polyester pants shrunken in the dryer. *Doesn't your mom know how to do laundry?* Who had the latest Nikes or Reeboks, and who shopped at Payless. Or worse, whose name-brand sneakers, brought back from a trip to Mexico, proudly acquired by haggling with a street vendor in seventh-grade Spanish, were, in fact, knockoffs. Who didn't know enough to remove the "fag tag" from his shirts. Who lived in which subdivisions. *White Oaks, Pleasant Pines, White Pines*: their names were homonyms, sharpening the effect. Mastery of the distinctions was itself a mark of distinction. I was never invited to play in those preserves of wealth and spiritual health. To be off-brand, that was my lot.

To be off-brand was to run scared within the ranks of white privilege, praying to pass muster. With limbs flailing to catch the football, to dodge the dodgeball, somehow to stand under but also to avoid the softball in its excruciating, tumescent descent toward the outfield, where I had hoped to escape notice, but now all eyes followed the ball to my failure's foregone conclusion. Or in the locker room, where my passive disposition provoked a fascinated cruelty; where I could be hoisted by the throat; where I smelled like onion rings; where there was no dodging other bodies, and the flesh was a thing I could get no purchase on, the theme of coded, salacious talk and the object of taunts and terror. To wrest self-possession from there was to train your feelings and fantasies and desires in a direction toxic to them, and to misrecognize this fact, as though toxicity were sweet.[54] With envy whetted against shame, to listen rapt to cherub-faced white boys wearing leather bomber jackets as they told tales of sexual conquest, and to laugh loudly as they taunted their exes to the tune of Guns N' Roses: *Back off, bitch!* And the girls, too, had to laugh it off, learning that white femininity required of them this tolerance for obnoxious behavior that could veer, without warning, into something far more severe. And for me, to be thrilled at being in on the joke — as if cruelty were something that could carry us, our voices giddy and aloft, across the sky, leaving our bodies back on earth — was only to stand, waiting, beside a swagger that did not suit me, longing for an intimacy with these girls on terms that I could not express. Not in my father's language, not in the language of these boys. With the soft voice on the phone saying, *My friend Sarah likes you, do you like Sarah?* I felt something like time itself leaking out of my chest, and it left a mother of a hole. And in that hole, I heard myself yelling, *I don't know! Leave me alone!* There was an overnight field trip, we were in a hotel. The other boys found a soft-core channel, which cast a blue hush on the room. As when my father, years before, had taken me to horror movies or whatever other R-rated fare he desired, I watched through thatched fingers, seeing nothing but myself on the edge of myself. A boy's leather bomber jacket lay draped over the back of a chair, its lining silkscreened with a map of the world.

Renunciation became my secret study: to be ready, at all times, to renounce love, for only this readiness can equip you for the

---

54 Quoting Silvan Tomkins, this desire might also be described as an attachment to "the good scenes that we can never permanently achieve or possess," but the pursuit of which embroils us in an endless rehearsal: we keep staging what should represent the site of boundless satisfaction, but which inevitably bottoms out in disappointment and/or punishment (*Shame and Its Sisters: A Silvan Tomkins Reader*, ed. Irwing E Alexander [Durham: Duke University Press, 1996], 183). Tomkins refers to these compulsive performances as "nuclear scripts." Nuclear scripts trap the self in a "mini-maximizing," all-or-nothing logic. They urge us on to melodrama, which is, of course, how white Americans shield themselves from tragedy, though they don't manage to escape farce.

failure that plagues the power not to fail. This thought arms Kierkegaard's demonic individual. It weaponizes the blankness of whiteness itself. "There was to be no more giving of myself — all giving was to be outlawed henceforth under a new name, and that name was waste."[55] What did I know about waste? But it was my body's study. Ashamed of being so skinny, and in defiance of our father's policed portions at lunch and dinner, I turned defiance inward and curbed my appetite. The brown bag lunch he carefully prepared — the sandwich in wax paper, with its single, slippery slice of turkey or ham; the apple, bruised on one side, squishing the sandwich on the other, and filling the bag with a noisome sweetness — got chucked every morning into the dumpster by the bus stop. Daddy's love came from a place of deep hunger. I knew that much, and I vowed to stamp out the same in myself. *You got to step into it, bring it to you, between your right arm and your chest. Put it in the breadbasket. Dolsy, put it in the goddamn breadbasket!* Try as he might to teach me, I could never catch a football. My chest, I felt, could hold no bread, nor could it stop a projectile hurled with that love's force. I taught myself to dodge Daddy's love, and I shrank into myself. With my backpack heavy with homework, I cultivated Victorian passions. Awake in my lower bunk, my clam-shell headphones throbbing, I thought about certain white girls in my class who seemed, through some rumored experience or secret trauma, to have been stranded ahead of their years, and in my mind, they led me by the hand back to some botanical attic where, in each other's arms, we could be children again. What did I know about sex, beyond a few verbal fetishes shared with my little brother, like "crotch-piece," a nonce word borrowed from the partible bodies of our G.I. Joes? But the flesh knew itself as partible, and soggy as bread, and full of a noisome sweetness. I broke my arm and wrote a poem. I held my cast gingerly against the small of a classmate's back at the eighth-grade prom, our bodies themselves like plaster casts protecting what we didn't know about

55   F. Scott Fitzgerald, *The Crack-Up* (New York: New Directions, 2009), 83.

278

ourselves. I held Sarah's hand, limply, for the space of a few tight breaths, in the bleachers at the homecoming game. We didn't know that we already knew what it was to be bruised by love and time. Under the glare of the halide lights, the bodies of the players, mostly Black, collided on the field below.

The radio and MTV sponsored our senses, rallying us with anthems by C+C Music Factory. Crushing, we drank from the gospel swoon of Boyz II Men and Whitney Houston. Bobbing our heads to Bell Biv DeVoe, we tasted something that raised the hair on the backs of our necks, as the beat sent shudders past the edge of what we understood. Our flesh was the hem of a garment that we touched, longing to be cured. But the poison that ailed us wasn't a girl. It was the distillate of a structure that granted our bodies the power to fail at others' expense, and to profit by their pain. We consumed Black pain, repackaged and commodified. We white boys sagged our jeans and salted our speech with "bruh." With the white girls in our grade, we made an enclosure of our bodies on the cement porch of McKinley Magnet High, inside a driveway separated by razor wire from the wooden-frame houses of a neighborhood that stood blocks away from the heart of planter affluence, rife with private security, manicured azaleas, and white colonnades. The vice-principal, a military-cut white man in a Sears-green polyester suit, strode up and down the halls with a wooden paddle at his side. We white boys cultivated cruelty in our voices and our postures — the cruelty that watched behind my father's eyes, that strikes at the gut, that sounds too much like love. We regaled each other and rolled our eyes, we shoved and joshed and egged each other on. We embodied the logic of "plantation power" that Clyde Woods has written about, keeping to our tight, cruel circle, policing our pyramid, while the meaty paramilitary arm of the state put the screws to all those who, against the white screen of our self-love, passed by in silhouette.[56] Collectively,

---

56 Woods, *Development Arrested,* chronicles the struggles of Black
    communities in the Mississippi delta against the power of white elites in

we ignored, avoided, and neglected our Black classmates, like the Black neighbors we avoided and the Black workers we ignored or talked down to. I have no doubt that there were more overt forms of racism at work around me, too, the overtness of which I was being trained to miss. But from the Blackness in our milieu, we white kids leached a language and a kind of hunger for being, which lit up our insides with feelings that we had no name for. Feelings borne of the radiance of a history of resilience that held no meaning for us as anything *but* feeling. And what was that feeling, for us, but the nimbus of moments promising a taste of our potential as it evaporated into the present? In the foyer of the state capitol, the waxed tiles rang with the coming and going of a grand old power, a power undaunted by the scandal of its brutality and proud, even, of its corrupt, predatory drive. This was the power of "a regime that elevated armed robbery to a governing principle."[57] There a young white man in a suit approached our Youth in Legislature group and singled me out for an officious pump of his hand. *Welcome to the capitol, son. I'm your state representative, David Duke.* He had a voice smooth and dangerous as oil. Did my home-school haircut and hand-me-down cardigan (the dressiest article I could muster) declare me ripe for radicalization? Or was it something else? Except when in the classroom, where the allure of being a white-lady teacher's pet proved irresistible, I studied how to be innocuous, inconspicuous, incognito. I gave assent when it was required, but hardly ever with fervor. I occupied the shadow of a participatory distance — part envy, part desire to please — that

the South and in Washington, who collude to keep the poor in this fertile region as vulnerable as possible. Their strategy proves effective in part by its ability to lure working-class whites away from the solidarity they should pursue with their Black counterparts. But Woods's book is also a paean to the knowledge and spiritual power of those Black communities, which cultivate ways of knowing that whites appropriate and commodify precisely because they cannot learn from them, ways of knowing that threaten white comfort and white profits.

57 Coates, "The Case for Reparations."

was calculated not to offend, posing no threat to those who felt entitled to be in charge. At the same time, my posture spelled, inside every offer of submissiveness, a refusal to disclose, my shoulders slouched, my eyes trained on the distance or the floor. *Hunched over like a professor,* my father said. And that refusal itself, like a thing soldered to the body, bore the stamp of Daddy's love.

One need not endorse the likes of a David Duke to profit by the latter's work on behalf of white privilege and power. The social distance between the devil and a good conscience is often great, but the moral distance is often not. My classmates and I back then knew that we weren't like Duke or the people who supposedly supported him.[58] (*Gross,* they giggled when he was out of earshot. *You'd better wash your hand!*) But some or many of us might have grown up to resemble a different young white man. He is the anonymous bystander, one of the faces in the leering, callous carousel of the mob or the crowd. But he has persuaded himself that he stands out because, although very much a party to the crowd's violence or neglect, he can play it cool. With his hands clean, he thinks he knows where he stands. James Baldwin describes him well:

> The bar was very crowded, and our altercation had been extremely noisy; not one customer in the bar had done anything to help us. When it was over, and the three of us stood at the bar trembling with rage and frustration [...] a young

58 Even this supposition was a lie secreted by the good conscience of middle- and upper-class whites. In fact, what catapulted Duke to legitimacy in Louisiana politics was the support of suburban voters outside New Orleans, upstanding citizens determined to improve their property values. Which determination has ever been the engine of white supremacy in the United States. Such people might cast their vote and keep their conscience intact in part because the mainstream media persisted in depicting Duke as the standard-bearer for poor whites in north Louisiana, ne'er-do-wells flying Confederate flags from their pickups (rather than business owners and high school principals who kept their Confederate memorabilia at home).

white man standing near us asked if we were students. I suppose he thought that this was the only possible explanation for our putting up a fight. I told him that he hadn't wanted to talk to us earlier and we didn't want to talk to him now. The reply visibly hurt his feelings, and this, in turn, caused me to despise him. But when one of us, a Korean War veteran, told this young man that the fight we had been having in the bar had been his fight, too, the young man said, "I lost my conscience a long time ago," and turned and walked out.[59]

By making small talk with Baldwin's group, perhaps this young man wished to affirm his superiority to the racism on display in the bar. But when confronted with his own failure in this instance (a failure of nerve, perhaps, or a failure to be conscientious, but a refusal, at any rate, of the solidarity that the moment offered and demanded), he abdicated responsibility. The conviction of having lost your conscience, answering here to the visibility of hurt feelings, reminds me of what Kierkegaard calls "demonic anxiety" or "anxiety about the good."[60] (Such a conviction, depending on the depth of its hold on you, might also be what, in another work, Kierkegaard describes as the most dangerous form of despair.)[61] Preferring a kind of hardened, sclerotic sense of actuality ("I lost my conscience a long time ago") to the possibility of being otherwise that failure discloses, demonic anxiety, which is the wellspring of inclosing reserve, chooses unfreedom in order to preserve its freedom of choice. In other words, by abdicating your responsibility, you

59 James Baldwin, "The Fire Next Time," in *Collected Essays,* 318–19. Baldwin and two Black companions had been refused service in the Chicago airport by a white bartender because, according to the latter, they "looked too young."

60 Kierkegaard, *The Concept of Anxiety,* 118–54.

61 Søren Kierkegaard, *The Sickness unto Death: A Christian Psychological Exposition for Upbuilding and Awakening,* trans. and eds. Edna H. Hong and Howard V. Hong (Princeton: Princeton University Press, 2006), 109–10.

seek to protect your sovereignty, denying others any claim on the meaning, or the meaninglessness, of your acts.[62] For the visibility of your feelings, the visibility of your hurt, threatens that cryptic sense of possession, threatens the apocrypha by which you recognize yourself. (Sometimes, staying with our mother for the weekend, we visited other people's homes. Not the bachelor pads of my father's bosom friends — J.D.'s Toad Hall, or the Episcopal priest's hushed house, with its leather-bound classics and operas on laser disc — but the homes of what I took to be typical families. White, ostentatiously middle-class families in suburban enclaves, where the kids played outside until the food was on the table, with plenty for seconds, too. Families, as it seemed, without stories, where happiness was punctual as it is in dreams sometimes, the distillate of moments without precedent or consequence. Playing hide-and-seek by flashlight with kids from the neighborhood. Racing and splashing in the pool. Shooting basketball on a driveway — no gym-class hierarchy, no taunts and jeers. Watching cable TV from a sprawling sofa set while gorging ourselves on pizza. Here, perhaps, was a privacy that didn't require you to disappear.)

The young man who had conveniently lost his conscience was, Baldwin tells us, "typical." Typical of a nation founded on the loss or setting aside of conscience in the interest of profit and plunder. A nation committed to its apocryphal stories. If the word "conscience" implies a knowing-with, a sharing or entanglement of knowledge that lays the foundation for responsibility, then I will have lost my conscience whenever I disavow my responsibility for others. Including those whom white America excludes from the stories that it tells about itself. In these stories, privacy is always emerging into the fullness of forgetting what it hides from itself as well as what it excludes. (Such privacy remains a liminal zone. It may welcome you across the threshold,

---

62 "[T]he self in despair," writes Kierkegaard, "wants to be master of itself or to create itself, to make his self into the self he wants to be, to determine what he will or will not have in his concrete self" (ibid., 69).

but not to stay. Because you are a poor relative or because your mother is earning extra money as the caretaker for the family's adult cousin, and you happen to be white. But you do the dishes without being told, and the white ladies in the house, drinking daiquiris on a Sunday morning, shower you with praise. *You'll make some woman very happy someday.*) The demonic promise of having lost my conscience entails a repudiation of my role in history, for the word "history" refers to how I am entangled with all the others, living and dead. My flesh — this flesh, exceeding or escaping the possessive — is the skein of that entanglement. Entanglement is rife with fear and trembling. Such anxiety, for Kierkegaard, is the precondition of freedom. (My brother, meanwhile, would embarrass me by hanging onto our mother, clamoring for her attention, lapsing into the baby talk that made her cross. But he needed her crossness as much as her comfort, needed all of it, squeezed into the space of a weekend twice a month.) But in the demonic subject, this anxiety, this necessarily "entangled freedom," strives to remain "entangled […] in itself," turning inward and away from that riskier engagement that m/others us to ourselves as beings in the world.[63] As Kierkegaard suggests, anxiety arises because "the individual," in sinning, replays the history of "the race."[64] Having a conscience does not mean being free from sin; it means confronting it. As a white man, whenever I choose not to confront and contravene the history of patriarchal white supremacy, I prolong and perpetuate it. Choosing not to be tested, having persuaded myself that I am not brave enough.

The story bunches under my fingers, and I risk knotting the thread, breaking the seam. But I am trying to find my way, in words, toward what passes by touch, by the avoided presence and promise of touch. Trying to find my way along the seam traced by James Baldwin when he writes about the white American "terror of any human touch, since any human touch

63 Ibid., 49.
64 Ibid., 28–29.

can change you."[65] My mother's touch tried to teach me how to handle my anxiety. (Reaching across the table to squeeze my hand, in a booth at Pizza Hut, tall glasses of root beer between us and greasy pieces of crust.) If a touch changes you, does it do so like "the leap" on which Kierkegaard dwells, whereby sin enters the world, and also faith? Even if you don't know at the time, or ever, that you have been changed? My mother, who had always wanted a daughter, tried to teach me how to listen to the women who would come into my life. (*I wasn't trying to turn you into girl. I wanted to raise you differently, that's all.* Beyond the windows, beyond the parking lot, spread the darkness of a night whose solitude she knew too well.) Does touch jump the frame in which Western philosophy depicts time as an inner sense, a self-awareness recording the passage of sensation and abstracting from this passage to the idea of an objective chronology valid for everyone everywhere? Does inclosing reserve express the folding in on itself of that sense of time, its buckling inadequacy to how we live and feel? As my mother knew, as her touch testified, typical white men become themselves through performances that defer the anxiety that they cannot escape. Boasting to test your credulity. Ready, always, to make someone else the butt of a joke. Busily explaining the world and themselves so as not to hear what others have to say. Policing themselves and others. It's like living on the edge of your own body, racing against some secret, on the lam from scenes of unfinished pain. And in hot pursuit, of course, of what Baldwin calls "the guilty, furtive, European notion of sex," which he relates to the "European dream of America [...] a dream which began as an adventure in real estate."[66] Under such conditions, love remains bound up with the ideology of whiteness as the right to property, and with white femininity as white patriarchy's possession

65 Baldwin, "The Devil Finds Work," 529.
66 Ibid., 509.

and alibi.[67] (*Silly boy.* For all that, sometimes we stumbled out of ourselves, in the silliness of our flesh, which knows what doesn't fit. In fits of laughter, with flailing limbs, we danced, my brother and I, our mother and Monica — whom my mother sometimes looked after on weekends, so that Monica's mother could take time to herself — romping around the living room to the radio. All smiles, Monica and I danced. Serious for a moment, you took me aside: *You're a child, but she is a grown woman, and she knows what she wants.*) What does the flesh want? In this story about Daddy's love, why does a mother's love wait in the parentheses? Perhaps, like a Hollywood heroine, I have wanted to leave her out of it, vesting her figure in my life with the apocryphal power to transcend love's conditions. For the knowing of the flesh, which lifts laughter and affection to the surface, warm with excitement and shame, are lessons still ciphered for me. Like the eloquence of a mother's care, and whose love selvages us, holding us from harm and from the damage we would do, not knowing ourselves.

When my father told me the story of a mother's betrayal and a son's near-revenge under the magnolias, the two of us — father and son, engaged in that awkward, desultory bonding in which parents and their adult children sometimes encounter one another as the shadows of what they never knew about themselves — sat perched on shiny vinyl stools in Slim's Y-Ki-Ki, a zydeco joint in Opelousas. My father pointed out the care with which Keith Frank tuned up his band, standing on the dance floor and listening to each musician in turn. Old age had slowed and mellowed him, my father, though he would still dance with the women who asked him to. He was a good dancer, and a lifelong fan of zydeco and the blues. Like white men everywhere, and especially in the American South, my father took more

---

67   Cheryl I. Harris, "Whiteness as Property," *Harvard Law Review* 106, no. 8 (1993): 1707–91.

from Black cultures than he would dare to admit. If his own manhood had begun in the shadow of those sinecures of whiteness, Hollywood musicals, he believed, like the early stars of that cinema, that his appreciation for this music made him special. When I was still a teenager, he had brought me to Tabby's Blues Box, in Baton Rouge (*Tabby and me go way back. I used to come here long before the LSU crowd discovered it*), where we had sat among other white faces as Henry Gray unspooled the way back to truths we would tap our feet to but that our heads were ill-disposed to hear. The blues is, as Clyde Woods puts it, a practice of "epistemology" that has always "held the feet of the community to the fire of African American realism."[68] My father might have thought he understood that realism, with its profound lessons about the erotic life as a dimension of political economy. But in his ironic determination to transcend his social setting, I suspect that the blues became a soundtrack to the apocryphal parts of himself. How did this art touch or haunt my father's ambition, I mean, his desire to create bold work that made a statement? The signature of that work may have been the catastrophe of those lessons neglected and misunderstood. Like his entry for a 1984 Times Square design competition: a skyscraper in the shape of Marilyn Monroe, with a central suspension structure evoking her flared skirt. The structure was meant, as his application explained, *to remind the gawking masses below of the plume of a mushroom cloud.* Marilyn's sexuality blowing up America's Great White Way, that symbolic epicenter of empire's weaponized entertainment system, with its guilty, furtive notions of sex on endless, feverish, mercenary display: he must have known it would never fly. He had to settle for the half-naked Art Deco caryatids, made of painted plywood, that flanked the interior of a truck-stop casino he built in Alexandria, Louisiana. These figures consign femininity to its role as a structural principle, but a disruptive one, frozen in a moment of exposure. They enshrine

---

68 Woods, *Development Arrested,* 72.

scopic sexuality in architecture, as if the rectilinear could put right some primal swerve.

Hortense Spillers argues that, because of the systematic violation of Black female sexuality and motherhood at the foundation of American economic power,

> the female, in this order of things, breaks in upon the imagination with a forcefulness that marks both a denial and an "illegitimacy." Because of this peculiar American denial, the black American male embodies the *only* American community of males handed the specific occasion to learn *who* the female is within itself […].[69]

Which suggests that the patronymic, as the sign of white privacy and legitimacy, bars the white masculine subject from contact with the female in himself. "The female" in Spillers's text is not the feminine, but the one who "stands *in the flesh,* both mother and mother-dispossessed."[70] The function of white femininity, on the other hand, is to encrypt the possessive impulse, keeping it at a distance.[71] White femininity locates the impulse out there, in space, where the skyscraper or caryatid, like the fashion model beaming from the billboard and the star strutting on the silver screen, monumentalizes sensuality. Otherwise, sensuality appears as a strain on time itself; as the tempo of a touch muffled or lost beneath layers of fear, anger, and shame; as the rap from behind Bluebeard's door. I'm imagining my father as Marilyn astride Manhattan, standing in for the unfaithful mother,

---

69 Spillers, "Mama's Baby, Papa's Maybe," 228, emphasis in the original.
70 Ibid., emphasis in the original.
71 Richard Dyer argues that "the geographic structure of imperial narrative confirms the binarism […]: the white woman as the locus of true whiteness, white men in struggle, yearning for home and whiteness, facing the dangers and allures of darkness" (*White,* 36). This narrative is related to "the idea of landscape, framed and perspectively organized" that "suggests a position from which to view the world, one that is distant and separate."

standing over the neighborhood, now Disneyfied, where years before he and my mother had created me (*Why do you want to make pictures, when you can make more children like this?*).[72] And then, of course, there was my father's actual foray into film-making, a project that, unfinished, occupied the position of a singular fetish in his life. *My movie.* He mentioned it often, saying the words with a jealous love. Made during the decade before I was born, it came with him whenever he moved, coiled inside dozens of metal canisters, each one weighing at least fifty pounds. Unable to be viewed (the one good print had virtually disintegrated, leaving only the negatives), it was, and is, the perfect apocryphal text. A musical black comedy of sorts with soft-core elements, *Dong!* takes place (as it's been described to me) on the night that King Kong climbs the Empire State Building, with song and dance and shenanigans afoot in an Art Deco bathroom or boudoir, and a pair of giant mechanical googly eyes peering through windows at the back of the set, mirroring the viewer's own. Husbanding his power not to fail, the movie marqueed in my father's stories about himself. There was the movie mogul in New York who had offered to fund its completion, and the producer from HBO who had promised a distribution deal. *I'm gonna turn it into a live-action animated feature, and I'll get George Lucas's company to do the special effects.* The film was his loot, carried away from the ruins of several professional relationships: the co-producer he had bought out; the cinematographer, just getting started in his career, whose requests for clips my father had refused; the composer whose friendship had

72 Lionel Trilling argues that the modern artist "seeks his personal authenticity in his entire autonomousness — his goal is to be as self-defining as the art-object he creates" (*Sincerity and Authenticity* [Cambridge: Harvard University Press, 1997], 100). While not wishing to endorse the putative universality of this claim, it strikes me as apt to the aesthetic that my father embraced and bequeathed to me. But this desperate pursuit of autonomy remains, in spite of itself, in contact with those traditions of modernity that don't disavow, because they can't afford to, the dependence of the artist on her audience, history, body, milieu — what Fred Moten calls "the black avant-garde" (*In the Break,* 32).

soured; my mother, who had helped edit the all-but-final cut. Growing up, it mortified me, this "porno" that my father loved like another, secret, prodigal son. *I don't want to hear about that queer movie,* I can hear my pre-teen self telling my mother, not really knowing what the word meant. But it amplified my shame that he promised to leave it to us, my younger brother and me. *When I'm gone, you boys will have to finish it. I can't trust anybody else.* White privacy, trusting no one, reproduces itself as patrimonial debt.

The brilliance of the "black avant-garde," for Fred Moten, stems in part from the matrical insurgence of the figure that breaks in on its denial by the American nation, which is also a denial of the rights of figuration. Moten wants us to hear the sounds of that insurgence, which, quoting Spillers, "stands *in the flesh,* both mother and mother-dispossessed."[73] Did the defense against that insurgence frame my father's body of work, his body in life, and the confusion at its center? Or was the work itself the frame, a set of relations that isolated, or sought to isolate, in the midst of its own confusion, a "bereaved relation to […] beauty"?[74] This sense of bereavement expresses, by "brushing against" it, "the exteriority of what is internal" to the work, or to the life, which Moten calls "the primordial actuality of its sensory materiality."[75] At pains to escape this actuality, yet drawn back to it, time and again, we sidle up to the tall stools or pull up chairs in the long hall where the music keeps going, where they're tuning up, keeping time. Without keeping it to themselves or under lock and key. Because this bereavement at the center, this bereavement that de-centers, this "dis-

---

73 For Moten's dialogue with Spillers's work, see *In the Break,* 15–16. Moten writes, "enslavement — and the resistance to enslavement that is the performative essence of blackness (or, perhaps less controversially, the essence of black performance) is a *being maternal* that is indistinguishable from a *being material*" (16, emphasis in the original).

74 Jacques Derrida, *The Truth in Painting,* trans. Geoff Bennington and Ian McLeod (Chicago: University of Chicago Press, 2001), 44.

75 Moten, *In the Break,* 248.

ruptive exteriority" that partakes of the "dispossessive force" of the object, remains *exemplary* (in the sense of the outwork, the out-take, the fugitive outward movement whereby what is cut off comes back to haunt the inside) in the blues and other art forms forged in the crucible of collective, improvisational revolt against intolerable, impossible conditions.[76] When you hear Lightnin' Hopkins confide that "the blues is a feeling," you brush up against an aesthetics that expressive theories of art fall short of.[77] It's not about something primal in the sense of being prior to, or situated before, reflective consciousness. But something that enacts what the idea of such a consciousness, in its Eurocentric bourgeois guise, would forestall: being as the condition of what *feels itself becoming* (time and again) a feeling thing.[78] In this becoming, crossed by history, bereaved and on the run, anguish awaits alongside hope. Depriving themselves of that hope without knowing it, "the multitudes who think of themselves as white […] hold this anguish far outside themselves," as James Baldwin says.[79] In doing so, they estrange themselves from the

76 Moten adverts to a "transference, a carrying or crossing over, that takes place on the bridge of lost matter, lost maternity, lost mechanics that joins bondage and freedom, that interanimates the body and its ephemeral if productive force, that interarticulates the performance and the reproductive reproduction it always already contains and which contains it. The interest [of such an analysis] is, in turn, not in the interest of a nostalgic and impossible suturing of wounded kinship but is rather directed toward what this irrepressibly inscriptive, reproductive, and resistant material objecthood does for and might still do to the exclusionary brotherhoods of criticism and black radicalism as experimental black performance" (ibid., 18).

77 Lightnin' Hopkins, "Blues Is a Feeling," recorded May 17, 1962, track 1, disc 1 on *Mojo Hand: The Lightnin' Hopkins Anthology,* Rhino Records, 1993, compact disc.

78 This is the human being in its disruptive guise as what Denise Ferreira da Silva calls an "affectable thing" (*Toward a Global Idea of Race* [Minneapolis: University of Minnesota Press, 2007], 44). Franklin Rosemont refers to jazz and the blues as aesthetic practices "in passionate revolt against the unlivable," practices that "demand nothing less than a new life" (quoted in Woods, *Development Arrested,* 39).

79 Baldwin, "The Devil Finds Work," 555.

truth, holding on for dear life to the promise of its substitute, wondering whom they can trust.

Truth, beginning with our finitude, which is our affection by and as the flesh, does not conceal itself, hoard itself, or require your acceptance and safekeeping. But trust obeys a logic of scarcity. There just isn't enough to go around. You have to earn another's trust by keeping their secrets. Did I write this book to refuse my father's trust? Or to earn it? I would like to imagine that his movie might have earned, somehow, the queerness that in my callous ignorance I once maligned it with. I'd like to imagine something transgressive in it, a campy antidote to the ponderousness of Dino De Laurentiis, locking arms with the cinema of John Waters and *The Rocky Horror Picture Show.* But I suspect that, as a sexually explicit musical that borrows its premise from *King Kong* and *Planet of the Apes,* the film traffics — how could it not? — in what Spillers has dubbed "pornotroping," by which "the putative surplus carnality and sexuality of black flesh ungendered" becomes, in the white imaginary, the vehicle of a kind of endlessly repeated primal scene.[80] In this repetition, the white masculine subject inscribes a figuration that projects the subject's own impulses, impulses weaponized by the political violence sustaining the settler-colonial regime, onto the flesh of those whose dispossession proves indispensable to the blank check of whiteness. Secure in his possession, Daddy walks out of the matinee into the late afternoon light. In the same movement, my own critical or ironic distance from the film invites or indulges in a pornotroping, too. I have never seen his movie, but it remains for me a site of fascination, encrypting what I refuse to see, keeping a lid on the bereaved shame I have mistaken for my inner sense, or for the interiority of sense, as if every moment froze in the effort to capture what won't stay put. I

---

80 Weheliye, *Habeas Viscus,* 106. See also Spillers, "Mama's Baby, Papa's Maybe," 206. Alexander Weheliye argues that "cinema enables the production of bare life as a politico-sexual form of life, wherein the remainder that is effected but cannot be contained by the legal order is disseminated in the visual realm" (98).

shouldn't want to keep its secrets, nor are they mine to keep. No more than they are my father's. By treating the film as *his* work, I disfigure the labor of all those who made its half-life possible. Like the aspiring young actors, drawn from New Orleans's theater scene, whom my father required to work in the nude and sing live on set. Like my mother, in her twenties at the time and devoted to my father in his outré pursuits. Like the librettist, a French Quarter poet whose name my father couldn't recall, and the well-known Black composer who wrote the score during one hot month spent in my parents' rickety renovated house on Esplanade. *He didn't want his name on the credits,* my mother says. After my father's death, I hunted for the soundtrack among his things, to no avail. According to her, the showstopper belonged to the role of "Queenie," sung by a classically trained singer with credits on Broadway. *His falsetto could shake the chandeliers.* He was, according to my mother, a queer Black man. How would he have inhabited or disrupted his role in this film, its humor rife with racism and homophobia?

He sang, I am told, a piece of his own choosing, one of Salome's arias from Massenet's *Hérodiade.* Would he have chosen the one where Salome intones, "I search ceaselessly for my mother"? Backed by swelling strings, Salome sings of her lost mother's voice, "melodious" and "tender," with a tenderness that she transfers to the "serene" words of the prophet.[81] As Salome, would he have sung as the motherless sing to comfort themselves? (Do I sing to comfort myself with more apocrypha? To put to sleep part of what I think I might know but have estranged from myself? And what do I know, really, of how Black lives touched my father's life, as students, as colleagues, as partners, as friends? Or what intermittent solidarity with them he might have achieved, and how they must have been hurt by and how

---

81 Jules Massenet, *Hérodiade,* with Choeur et Orchestre du Capitole de Toulouse, conducted by Michel Plasson, recorded November 19–27 and December 2 and 9–10, 1994, EMI Classics, 1995, compact disc.

they resisted his racism and misogynoir?[82] Not to mention how those forces of estrangement radiate outward from the individual and his circles of intimacy and acquaintance, being magnified by other ripples of predation and neglect, and becoming, in the aggregate, a power that divides the world. This power goes to work within the confines of the smallest spaces, sifting and dividing. Like the uneven elevations in a city that determine where the flood waters settle, and the policies and assessments that are invoked to decide who in a neighborhood is allowed to return and rebuild. Like the vastly unequal life chances of people sitting in the same classroom or eating at the same restaurant. *I'm going out tonight with a friend of mine.* My father looked sharp in linen trousers and a salmon-colored silk shirt. I never asked any questions, and he never brought those friends home. From

---

82　Elaborating on Moya Bailey's coinage of the term, the artist Trudy writes, "While anti-Black sentiments impact all Black people, because of how Black women experience gender — as 'non-women' via forceful masculinization as violence […] not via self-identification as empowerment […] and as sexual chattel via hypersexualization that reduces Black womanhood to a sexual object with non-person status because of gender in addition to race — misogynoir is conceptualized as a way to explain how it's more than racist misogyny or even objectification but complete dehumanization as a 'contradiction' to White womanhood" ("Explanation of Misogynoir," *Gradient Lair,* April 28, 2014, https://www.gradientlair.com/post/84107309247/define-misogynoir-anti-black-misogyny-moya-bailey-coined. See also Moya Bailey and Trudy, "On Misogynoir: Citation, Erasure, and Plagiarism," *Feminist Media Studies* 18, no. 4 (2018): 762–68.

　　Misogynoir, as I understand it, encompasses fetishizing forms of appropriation as well as more overt methods for the dehumanization that Trudy describes. An appeal to Black feminist theory, then, in pursuit of critically understanding my own relation to white masculinity, does not remain innocent of the motives from which my whiteness moves and shakes and for which it consoles itself. As Valerie Smith notes, "[w]hen black women operate in oppositional discourse as a sign for the author's awareness of materialist concerns, then they seem to be fetishized in much the same way they are in mass culture" ("Black Feminist Theory and the Representation of the 'Other,'" in *Changing Our Own Words: Essays on Criticism, Theory, and Writing by Black Women,* ed. Cheryl A. Wall [New Brunswick: Rutgers University Press, 1989], 46).

him I learned, perhaps, how to keep even your friends as strangers, a trick that comes easily when you are a stranger to yourself.) Like the prophet, the stranger is a figure of bereavement, of bereaved touch. The presence of the stranger disfigures what it frames, which is the identity that its invocation was meant to protect. "The stranger's presence," Baldwin writes,

> mak[es] *you* the stranger, less to the stranger than to yourself. Identity would seem to be the garment with which one covers the nakedness of the self: in which case, it is best that the garment be loose, a little like the robes of the desert, through which robes one's nakedness can always be felt, and, sometimes, discerned. This trust in one's nakedness is all that gives one the power to change one's robes.[83]

Figuration dresses and dissembles. In the possessive figuration of white cishet masculinity, the subject clutches his garment close. Of his nakedness, he is afraid. He remains covered even when seeming to bare it all, terrified that it, whatever *it* is, might turn out to be the tailor's dummy (the one my mother had acquired second hand, whose ventral and dorsal halves, gray felt stretched over a rusty metal frame, never made a perfect fit). And yet, this fear comes to feel like insurance. So long as his nakedness might be something inanimate, something mechanical, it can belong to him without his becoming it. Above all, his art and his life must be authentic, which means that they must not be exposed, not subject to change in contact with the world. We found, in a strongbox that our father kept on a shelf above his bed, a letter to be opened after his death. There he stipulated, again, that my younger brother and I should finish his movie, this rare gem that, aside from his children, was his only legacy. Though if not, *perhaps that, too, is for the best — let it return to dust.* Along with his passport, some old traveler's checks, and an unsigned will, the box held certificates of divorce from my

---

83 Baldwin, "The Devil Finds Work," 537, emphasis in the original.

mother and his previous wives, and documents attesting to the dissolution of some very old business partnerships. Perhaps having them close by helped him sleep at night. The white man would not be who he thinks he is without the power of division, which he holds outside of himself. And indeed, as if my father's film had sought its resting place, we found fragments of the only extant print, gone bad in storage and tossed out, scattered across the property, wrapped by the wind around rocks like the shed skins of rattlesnakes.

On its lost soundtrack, perhaps that song is the one that Baldwin describes as the "song which Europe let out of its heart so long ago, to be sung on ships, and to cross all that water," a song "now coming back to Europe, perhaps to drive Europe mad: the return of the song will certainly render Europe obsolete, and return the North American wilderness — yet to be conquered! — to a truth which has nothing to do with Europe."[84] That song makes strangers of us, my father and me. And in the years before his death, we kept one another as strangers, my father preferring that distance in which I would always be his wide-eyed baby boy, *my son, the genius.* (I first felt myself among strangers in the first grade, at Mamou Elementary, with its old, neglected buildings and its dusty yard littered in the fall with acorns and the brown bedroom slippers of the magnolia leaves. Feeling lost, I cried a lot back then, at the slightest provocation: a misplaced jacket, a broken crayon, a shortage of the promised candy.) For my part, I used that distance to hold at arm's length parts of myself that reminded and remind me too much of my father. Like the sexual jealousy that has roiled my relationships with women, driving me, on occasion, to the verge of self-harm. Like the rage rising in me when I am called on to acknowledge how I might have failed someone I love. Like the ambition, per-

---

84 Ibid., 510. The point is not, it must be emphasized, to conquer the wilderness. The point is to undo the idea of humanity as the exclusive purview of those who can impose the violence of their will to make profit out of prophecy, those who project, onto peoples and lands around the globe, a fantasy of wilderness that backs a claim to real estate.

petually ashamed of itself, that has touched my creative pursuits, provoking a tortuous dialectic of exhibitionism and self-effacement. (That was when tears still stood available to me — that labor that keeps the bereaved flesh moving — before the flesh itself became a source of panic, a thing to be avoided, neglected, whipped into shape, and shunted into channels of possessive desire. They told me, *You can't cry so much, son. You need to get a hold of yourself.* After a while, whatever the cause, my tears themselves became the problem.) These are parts of myself that mark my desire for excellence as *his* desire. My father and I failed and fail to hear what we cover in covering the sounds of Black cultures, of the matrix of white masculinity's others, of our mothers, living on stolen real estate.[85] (The only voice I remember coming to my defense when I cried at school belonged to a Black girl in Miss Judy's first-grade class. After solving my dilemma, she had to defend herself against those who knew I needed to get a hold of myself. *He's my friend, and he can have my crayon if he wants it.*) Harryette Mullen writes, "the white hand writes for the black voice, turning speech into text."[86] The white man's hand turns acts of honesty and loving and protest, written or spoken or sung, into the erasure of truth in what the white man thinks he knows, misspelling knowledge as possession. It's *his* story to tell, because he knows *from experience.* That's what my father always said, whenever I challenged him about his overt expressions of racism, which I did hardly often enough. That's what he said in our last fight about it, which was our last fight. My younger brother was driving us to the one decent restaurant within twenty miles of my father's desert cabin, in the battered Volkswagen Golf that, after his death, smelled

---

85 This idea is indebted to George Yancy's observation that "white America 'covers' the cultural productions of Black people. To acknowledge Blackness, after all, might lead to the uncovering of whiteness" (*Black Bodies, White Gazes: The Continuing Significance of Race in America,* 2nd edn. [Lanham: Rowman & Littlefield, 2016], 72).

86 Harryette Mullen, "Optic White: Blackness and the Production of Whiteness," *Diacritics* 24, nos. 2–3 (1994): 84.

of death, some critter having crept into its innards to expire. (I remember talking with this girl, my friend, on the swings, our feet kicking up dust, just as I remember holding hands with Tabitha or playing astronauts with Richard or being tattled on by red-haired Louis, whose daddy worked at the dump. But this girl who came to my aid, who named me as her friend, I don't remember her name.) During that drive, the conversation had turned, taking one of those abrupt detours that I dreaded, to the topic of young Black men *who can't stop shooting each other.* No doubt it was some talk-radio line item in my father's litany of complaints about southern California, which had replaced his litany of complaints about southern Louisiana. He had traded one hot and neglected part of the country for its dusty mirror image. *Well,* I said, *maybe we could talk instead about the young white men shooting everybody. Too bad, like most Americans, you're more comfortable with your prejudice than with the truth.*

Dolsy, I'm just trying to tell you what I know from experience. This was no longer the man whose anger, flaring white hot, the skin pulled tight against his jaw, could make me shrink back into myself, his whole body announcing, *You will not survive this.* With his hands on his bony knees, his fingernails yellow and brittle, his ankles swollen and crippling him with pain, my father's voice ran ragged in the back seat. Now I was the man I did not find that day in the rearview mirror. His voice had become my voice. His experience, which I was hot to repudiate, was wrapped up, in ways I didn't want to know about, inside mine. (Another story. I caught the school bus that year every day before dawn, groggy and morose, immuring myself among the high vinyl seats for the ride that jostled us over dirt roads and blacktop highways, trailing dust, taking me from a world where love could be terrible and confounding to a world that felt terrible and confounding and mostly devoid of love.) My brother kept his mouth shut and his eyes on the road. If experience had taught my father to defend, through explicit performances of racism and misogyny, the lie of his sense of superiority, then what of my own sense of superiority (to him, to his type of man)? That is founded on another kind of lie. This lie would make a virtue of my good white liberal's studied avoidance of such explicitness, an avoidance shading into an avoidance of experience itself. (But after school the bus buzzed with laughter and riot, as bodies rushed to spend their pent-up energy, and voices, buckled all day into the classroom's hush and rote recitations, clamored for the vocabulary that felt like freedom and desire. It was a voyage of excitement, made more exciting by the threat of shame and harm. A voyage toward forbidden knowledge. Lurching over a pothole, the bus might plant your lips on the hand of a classmate where she gripped the top of the seat in front of you, as you both scrambled, giggling, to get a better view. It would have smelled, her hand, like chewing gum and a big sister's lotion and the freight of secrets you already carried without knowing what they meant. If you and she found the nerve, you might even sit in the back with the kids from junior high or high school. Kids who might poke fun at your shaggy bangs and the duck tail tucked into the collar of your shirt. *Are you sure you're not a girl?*) Mine is a failure *of* experience, having failed, for the most part, to entangle my life with Black lives, much less to put my body on the line in acts of organized resistance to white supremacy. What could I say? How could I deliver myself from Daddy's love? *I'm speaking from experience, too. I'm speaking from the experience of a white boy who grew up full of anger and resentment, who grew up hating himself.* We had arrived at the restaurant, a stuccoed Italian joint with wrought-iron accents and Chianti in baskets, out of place here on a service road in the desert. *Why would you say that?* my father asked. *What reason did you have to hate yourself?* I could tell it hurt him, to be reminded of what he had known without knowing it. Just as it might have pained him, in a different way, to feel dwarfed now by my larger frame, which after three decades had finally filled out. (Slapping me on the back, *Look at my boy!* Then with that old edge in his voice, halfway teasing, halfway a threat, *Now don't you go getting fat.*) Holding open the door to the restaurant, I said, wanting it to hurt, *You could answer that better than I.*

That neither of us could answer his question shows how this hurt was and is the language we shared, or a thing coiled around the heart of our language, passed from father to son, a mutual confusion by which you shall know your name. (*I may look like a girl, but I can sure burn your ass with a balloon.* The words came out of nowhere, or nowhere I understood, and made the back of the bus erupt in laughter, as I wagged a red tongue of latex and a big boy's tongue. But it was less a feat of nerve than an accident of vocabulary. Thanks to my father, my six-year-old self already had a store of threats and curses I had not known the use for until the bus ride knocked them loose. Now they came tumbling out.) Did I write this book to expose how deeply the confusion is mine? (I must have kept up the act for a while, a bawdy Howdy Doody, ventriloquized by a desire on the edge of my senses, suddenly keen to steal the show. But it didn't last long. Later that afternoon, or another, after the bus had emptied out — we lived near the end of the driver's route — a much older boy, sitting in the last seat, leaned toward me. *Now you had better quit cussing,* he said, easing a knife out of the hip pocket of his jeans, *or I'm gonna have to cut off your pee-pee.*) I wrote this book seduced by the apocryphal in my life, which are the stories we tell to cover ourselves, to protect against our uncovering by those whose touch knows the places where we are cut, where we were cut out for this world. I wrote this book sleeved in shame. (I remember that young man on the bus as handsome, popular, with a mustache that made him look adult and an easy laugh. A cousin, as I think I thought back then or had been told, of the kid who lived across the road from us. A party, in other words, to that ethnic and cultural familiarity, deeply cut by the ravages of white supremacy, in which we would have smiled and nodded and regarded one another, neighbors who never or hardly ever talked, from opposite sides of the road. I do seem to remember his voice, full of a wry warmth, touching something that need not be said aloud. Something whose hard edge could be sheathed in wit. He had laughed at my act, now it was his turn to joke. There was almost a tenderness to this joke, or the promise of one. Perhaps he meant to spare me the indignity of the principal's finding out, who made the rounds with his paddle every Friday afternoon, or some worse punishment that might have awaited me at home.)[87] I wrote this book to travel again those roads, in an approach to the wisdom in them, winding and unwinding the bobbin of the world. The wisdom of those who live through the needle's eye, having reason to know that what reason we have is never our own. (I don't remember his name. *You had better tell your momma, so that she can sew it back on,* someone said. No need. My speech-bubble had already burst, drenching me with shame. Superfluous, too, was the driver's admonition as, red-faced, I climbed down from the bus. *If you keep cussing, son, I'm gonna have to talk to your folks.* More than anything, I remember the shame, its hot silence settling in. Wrapping this moment in that sense of private failure that white manhood excels at. Who did or said what? Did it unfold that way at all? It matters to no one, except my needful I. But it strikes me now that I can't remember what else I might have said that day on the bus. What names I might I have called him, whose name I have forgotten.) I wrote this book without hope of writing a conclusion. It may be that this confusion has no end. But as the blues teaches, love is a nonce word. It's never all there is, not in any transcendent sense, but you can reach for it in a pinch, if you know how. If you have the feeling. And to leap beyond the decision to hide behind failure's foregone conclusion, which dodges the chance for change, and to confront the history of that failure and its forgetting, beyond explication,

---

87 I am aware that my memory and my rendition of it here perform a kind of pornotroping, too. This memory-fragment crystallizes, in miniature, the white patriarchal fear of emasculation by the Black male. It's certainly not the only time someone told me that I looked like a girl. Nor was this young man's threat, judging by his tone, and even assuming I'm remembering it the way it happened, severe. (Not compared with what my father threatened me with many times.) But the salience of the memory seems to disclose something about how, as a white man, I learned about the power of words, a lesson intertwined with the desire to assert dominance in situations where selfhood seems to require cutting oneself off from the racialized and gendered flesh of others by cutting them down.

beyond expiation: what would *that* feel like? To dwell with the realization that "black history does not flatter American democracy; it chastens it"?[88] A sense of time beyond Daddy's temporizing, it might have to *begin* with shame. I don't mean in the way of some distant, primal signal, but in the way of a cut or a seam that breaches our separateness, in that darkness toward which our flesh gives us passage. And which dispossesses us — including those of us who have been taught to possess ourselves via our power to harm.

88 Coates, "The Case for Reparations."

Bibliography

Abraham, Nicolas, and Maria Torok. *The Wolf Man's Magic Word: A Cryptonymy.* Translated by Nicholas Rand. Minneapolis: University of Minnesota Press, 2008.

Ahmed, Sara. *Queer Phenomenology: Orientations, Objects, Others.* Durham: Duke University Press, 2006.

Albert, David Z. *Time and Chance.* Cambridge: Harvard University Press, 2000.

Alcoff, Linda Martín. *The Future of Whiteness.* Cambridge: Polity Press, 2015.

Alexander, M. Jacqui. *Pedagogies of Crossing: Meditations on Feminism, Sexual Politics, Memory, and the Sacred.* Durham: Duke University Press, 2005.

Alexander, Michelle. *The New Jim Crow: Mass Incarceration in the Age of Colorblindness.* New York: The New Press, 2012.

Als, Hilton. *White Girls.* San Francisco: McSweeney's, 2014.

Amadae, S.M. *Rationalizing Capitalist Democracy: The Cold War Origins of Rational Choice Liberalism.* Chicago: University of Chicago Press, 2003.

Anker, Elisabeth R. *Orgies of Feeling: Melodrama and the Politics of Freedom.* Durham: Duke University Press, 2014.

Arendt, Hannah. *Lectures on Kant's Political Philosophy.* Translated by Ronald Beiner. Chicago: University of Chicago Press, 1989.

Aristotle. *Physics, Volume I: Books 1–4.* Translated by P.H. Wicksteed and F.M. Cornford. Cambridge: Harvard University Press, 1957.

———. *The "Art" of Rhetoric.* Translated by John Henry Freese. Cambridge: Harvard University Press, 1926.

———. *The Nicomachean Ethics.* Translated by H. Rackham. Cambridge: Harvard University Press, 1926.

Armstrong, Meg. "'The Effects of Blackness': Gender, Race, and the Sublime in Aesthetic Theories of Burke and Kant." *The Journal of Aesthetics and Art Criticism* 54, no. 3 (1996): 213–36. DOI: 10.2307/431624.

Austin, J.L. *How to Do Things with Words.* Edited by J.O. Urmson and Marina Sbisà. Cambridge: Harvard University Press, 1975.

Bailey, Moya, and Trudy. "On Misogynoir: Citation, Erasure, and Plagiarism." *Feminist Media Studies* 18, no. 4 (2018): 762–68. DOI: 10.1080/14680777.2018.1447395.

Baldwin, James. "The Devil Finds Work." In *Collected Essays,* edited by Toni Morrison, 477–576. New York: Library of America, 1998.

———. "The Fire Next Time." In *Collected Essays,* edited by Toni Morrison, 291–348. New York: Library of America, 1998.

Baptist, Edward E. *The Half Has Never Been Told: Slavery and the Making of American Capitalism.* New York: Basic Books, 2016.

Barker-Benfield, G.J. *The Culture of Sensibility: Sex and Society in Eighteenth-Century Britain.* Chicago: University of Chicago Press, 1996.

Belew, Kathleen. *Bring the War Home: The White Power Movement and Paramilitary America.* Cambridge: Harvard University Press, 2018.

Berlant, Lauren. *Cruel Optimism.* Durham: Duke University Press, 2011.

———. *The Female Complaint: The Unfinished Business of Sentimentality in American Culture.* Durham: Duke University Press, 2008.

———. *The Queen of America Goes to Washington City: Essays on Sex and Citizenship.* Durham: Duke University Press, 1997.

———. "The Subject of True Feeling: Pain, Privacy, and Politics." In *Left Legalism/Left Critique,* edited by Wendy Brown and Janet Halley, 105–33. Durham: Duke University Press, 2002.

Bernasconi, Robert. "Will the Real Kant Please Stand Up." *Radical Philosophy* 117 (February 2003). https://www. radicalphilosophy.com/article/will-the-real-kant-please-stand-up.

Bhatia, Sunil. "Op-Ed: Nicholas Kristof and the Politics of Writing About Women's Oppression in Darker Nations." *The Feminist Wire,* March 3, 2013. https://thefeministwire. com/2013/03/op-ed-nicholas-kristof-and-the-politics-of-writing-about-womens-oppression-in-darker-nations/.

Blanchfield, Brian. *Proxies: Essays Near Knowing.* Lebanon: Nightboat Books, 2016.

Bollas, Christopher. *The Shadow of the Object: Psychoanalysis of the Unthought Known.* New York: Columbia University Press, 1987.

Boltanski, Luc, and Eve Chiapello. *The New Spirit of Capitalism.* Translated by Gregory Elliott. New York: Verso, 2007.

Bradley, Rizvana. "Living in the Absence of a Body: The (Sus) Stain of Black Female (W)Holeness." *Rhizomes: Cultural Studies in Emerging Knowledge* 29 (2016). DOI: 10.20415/rhiz/029.e13.

Brand, Dionne. *The Blue Clerk: Ars Poetica in 59 Versos.* Durham: Duke University Press, 2018.

Brown, Kimberly Juanita. *The Repeating Body: Slavery's Visual Resonance in the Contemporary.* Durham: Duke University Press, 2015.

Browne, Simone. *Dark Matters: On the Surveillance of Blackness.* Durham: Duke University Press, 2015.

Butler, Judith. *Excitable Speech: A Politics of the Performative.* New York: Routledge, 1997.

Carby, Hazel. "Encoding White Resentment: Grand Canyon — A Narrative for Our Times." In *Race, Identity, and Representation in Education,* edited by Cameron McCarthy and Warren Crichlow, 236–48. New York: Routledge, 1993.

———. *Reconstructing Womanhood: The Emergence of the Afro-American Woman Novelist.* New York: Oxford University Press, 1987.

Carter, Julian B. *The Heart of Whiteness: Normal Sexuality and Race in America, 1880–1940.* Durham: Duke University Press, 2009.

Casemore, Brian. *The Autobiographical Demand of Place: Curriculum Inquiry in the American South.* New York: Peter Lang, 2008.

Cavell, Stanley. *Must We Mean What We Say? A Book of Essays.* Cambridge: Cambridge University Press, 2008.

———. *Philosophy the Day after Tomorrow.* Cambridge: Harvard University Press, 2008.

———. *The Claim of Reason: Wittgenstein, Skepticism, Morality, and Tragedy.* New York: Oxford University Press, 2009.

Cecire, Natalia. "Ways of Not Reading Gertrude Stein." ELH 82, no. 1 (2015): 281–312. DOI: 10.1353/elh.2015.0005.

Chakrabarty, Dipesh. *Provincializing Europe: Postcolonial Thought and Historical Difference.* Princeton: Princeton University Press, 2012.

Chandler, Nahum Dimitri. "Originary Displacement." *boundary 2* 27, no. 3 (2000): 249–86. DOI: 10.1215/01903659-27-3-249.

Chatterjee, Piya, and Sunaina Maira. "The Imperial University: Race, War, and the Nation-State." In *The Imperial University: Academic Repression and Scholarly Dissent,* edited by Piya Chatterjee and Sunaina Maira, 1–50. Minneapolis: University of Minnesota Press, 2014.

Christian, Barbara. "The Race for Theory." *Cultural Critique* 6 (1987): 51–63. DOI: 10.2307/1354255.

Chun, Wendy Hui Kyong. *Programmed Visions: Software and Memory.* Cambridge: MIT Press, 2013.

Cintron, Ralph. "'Gates Locked' and the Violence of Fixation." In *Towards a Rhetoric of Everyday Life: New Directions in Research on Writing, Text, and Discourse,* edited by Martin Nystrand and John Duffy, 5–37. Madison: University of Wisconsin Press, 2003.

Coates, Ta-Nehisi. "The Case for Reparations." *The Atlantic,* June 2014. https://www.theatlantic.com/magazine/archive/2014/06/the-case-for-reparations/361631/.

———. "The First White President." *The Atlantic,* October 2017. https://www.theatlantic.com/magazine/archive/2017/10/the-first-white-president-ta-nehisi-coates/537909/.

Collins, Patricia Hill. *Black Feminist Thought: Knowledge, Consciousness, and the Politics of Empowerment.* 2nd edition. New York: Routledge, 2009.

Coppe, Abiezer. *Selected Writings.* London: Aporia Press, 1987.

Coulthard, Glen S. "Subjects of Empire: Indigenous Peoples and the 'Politics of Recognition' in Canada." *Contemporary Political Theory* 6, no. 4 (2007): 437–60. DOI: 10.1057/palgrave.cpt.9300307.

Crawley, Ashon T. *Blackpentecostal Breath: The Aesthetics of Possibility.* New York: Fordham University Press, 2017.

Crenshaw, Kimberlé. "Demarginalizing the Intersection of Race and Sex: A Black Feminist Critique of Antidiscrimination Doctrine, Feminist Theory and Antiracist Politics." *The University of Chicago Legal Forum* 140, no. 1 (1989): 139–67. https://chicagounbound.uchicago.edu/uclf/vol1989/iss1/8.

———. *On Intersectionality: Essential Writings.* New York: New Press, 2019.

Cvetkovich, Ann. *Depression: A Public Feeling.* Durham: Duke University Press, 2012.

Davis, Angela Y. *The Angela Y. Davis Reader.* Edited by Joy James. Malden: Blackwell Publishing, 1998.

Dayan, Colin. *The Law Is a White Dog: How Legal Rituals Make and Unmake Persons.* Princeton: Princeton University Press, 2013.

Deloria, Jr., Vine. "Minorities and the Social Contract." *Georgia Law Review* 20 (1986): 917–33.

Derrida, Jacques. "Economimesis." Translated by R. Klein. *Diacritics* 11, no. 2 (1981): 3–25. DOI: 10.2307/464726.

———. *Specters of Marx: The State of the Debt, the Work of Mourning and the New International.* Translated by Peggy Kamuf. New York: Routledge, 2011.

———. *The Truth in Painting.* Translated by Geoff Bennington and Ian McLeod. Chicago: University of Chicago Press, 2001.

DiAngelo, Robin. "White Fragility." *The International Journal of Critical Pedagogy* 3, no. 3 (2011): 54–70. https://libjournal. uncg.edu/index.php/ijcp/article/view/249.

Dingo, Rebecca Ann. *Networking Arguments: Rhetoric, Transnational Feminism, and Public Policy Writing.* Pittsburgh: University of Pittsburgh Press, 2012.

Dipiero, Thomas. *White Men Aren't.* Durham: Duke University Press, 2009.

Dormon, James H. "Ethnicity and Identity: Creoles of Color in Twentieth-Century South Louisiana." In *Creoles of Color of the Gulf South,* edited by James H. Dormon, 166–79. Knoxville: University of Tennessee Press, 1996.

———. "Preface." In *Creoles of Color of the Gulf South,* edited by James H. Dormon, 1–27. Knoxville: University of Tennessee Press, 1996.

Douglas, Ann. *The Feminization of American Culture.* New York: Farrar, Straus and Giroux, 1998.

Dray, Philip. *At the Hands of Persons Unknown: The Lynching of Black America.* Reprint edition. New York: Modern Library, 2003.

Du Bois, W.E.B. *Black Reconstruction in America: An Essay toward a History of the Part Which Black Folk Played in the Attempt to Reconstruct Democracy in America, 1860–1880.* New York: Atheneum, 1977.

———. "The Souls of White Folk." In *Writings: The Suppression of the African Slave-Trade; The Souls of Black*

Folk; Dusk of Dawn; Essays and Articles, 923–38. New York: Literary Classics of the United States, 1986.

Dubois, Sylvie, and Barbara M. Horvath. "Creoles and Cajuns: A Portrait in Black and White." *American Speech* 78, no. 2 (2003): 192–207. https://muse.jhu.edu/article/43882/pdf.

Dyer, Richard. *White: Essays on Race and Culture.* New York: Routledge, 2017.

Eastman, Julius. *Unjust Malaise.* New York: New World Records, 2005, 3 compact discs.

Ehrenberg, Alain. *The Weariness of the Self: Diagnosing the History of Depression in the Contemporary Age.* Montreal: McGill-Queen's University Press, 2010.

Ehret, Arnold. *Rational Fasting for Physical, Mental and Spiritual Rejuvenation.* Dobbs Ferry: Ehret Literature Pub. Co., 1987.

Ellison, Julie. *Cato's Tears and the Making of Anglo-American Emotion.* Chicago: University of Chicago Press, 1999.

Faigley, Lester. "Judging Writing, Judging Selves." *College Composition and Communication* 40, no. 4 (1989): 395–412. DOI: 10.2307/358238.

Fanon, Frantz. *Black Skin, White Masks.* Translated by Richard Philcox. Revised edition. New York: Grove Press, 2008.

Federici, Silvia. *Caliban and the Witch.* New York: Autonomedia, 2014.

Felman, Shoshana. *The Scandal of the Speaking Body: Don Juan with J.L. Austin, or Seduction in Two Languages.* Translated by Catherine Porter. Stanford: Stanford University Press, 2003.

Ferenczi, Sándor. "Confusion of Tongues between Adults and the Child." *Contemporary Psychoanalysis* 24, no. 2 (July 1, 1988): 196–206. DOI: 10.1080/00107530.1988.10746234.

Ferguson, Kathy E. *The Feminist Case against Bureaucracy.* Philadelphia: Temple University Press, 1984.

Ferguson, Roderick A. *Aberrations in Black: Toward a Queer of Color Critique.* Minneapolis: University of Minnesota Press, 2004.

Ferreira da Silva, Denise. "Hacking the Subject: Black Feminism and Refusal beyond the Limits of Critique." *PhiloSOPHIA* 8, no. 1 (2018): 19–41. DOI: 10.1353/phi.2018.0001.

———. *Toward a Global Idea of Race.* Minneapolis: University of Minnesota Press, 2007.

Fitzgerald, F. Scott. *The Crack-Up.* New York: New Directions, 2009.

Foucault, Michel. *The Archaeology of Knowledge: And the Discourse on Language.* Translated by A.M. Sheridan Smith. New York: Vintage, 1982.

Freud, Sigmund. "From the History of an Infantile Neurosis." In *The Standard Edition of the Complete Psychological Works of Sigmund Freud,* translated by James Strachey. New edition, vol. 17, 3–124. London: Vintage, 2001.

———. "The Ego and the Id." In *The Standard Edition of the Complete Psychological Works of Sigmund Freud,* translated by James Strachey, vol. 19, 3–68. London: Hogarth Press, 1961.

Fuentes, Marisa J. *Dispossessed Lives: Enslaved Women, Violence, and the Archive.* Philadelphia: University of Pennsylvania Press, 2016.

Gilmore, Ruth Wilson. *Golden Gulag: Prisons, Surplus, Crisis, and Opposition in Globalizing California.* Berkeley: University of California Press, 2007.

Gilroy, Paul. *The Black Atlantic: Modernity and Double Consciousness.* London: Verso, 2007.

Girard, René. *Deceit, Desire, and the Novel: Self and Other in Literary Structure.* Baltimore: Johns Hopkins University Press, 2010.

Glissant, Édouard. *Poetics of Relation.* Translated by Betsy Wing. Ann Arbor: University of Michigan Press, 1997.

Gordon, Lewis R. *Bad Faith and Antiblack Racism.* Amherst: Humanity Books, 1999.

Graeber, David. *The Utopia of Rules: On Technology, Stupidity, and the Secret Joys of Bureaucracy.* New York: Melville House, 2015.

Grande, Sandy. *Red Pedagogy: Native American Social and Political Thought.* Lanham: Rowman & Littlefield, 2004.

Grier, David Alan. *When Computers Were Human.* Princeton: Princeton University Press, 2013.

Guillaumin, Colette. *Racism, Sexism, Power and Ideology.* London: Routledge, 2005.

Gumbs, Alexis Pauline. *M Archive: After the End of the World.* Durham: Duke University Press, 2018.

———. "Nobody Mean More: Black Feminist Pedagogy and Solidarity." In *The Imperial University: Academic Repression and Scholarly Dissent,* edited by Piya Chatterjee and Sunaina Maira, 237–59. Minneapolis: University of Minnesota Press, 2014.

———. *Spill: Scenes of Black Feminist Fugitivity.* Durham: Duke University Press, 2016.

Halberstam, Jack. *The Queer Art of Failure.* Durham: Duke University Press, 2011.

Hammonds, Evelynn. "Black (W)Holes and the Geometry of Black Female Sexuality." *differences: A Journal of Feminist Cultural Studies* 6, nos. 2–3 (1994): 126–45.

Harney, Stefano, and Fred Moten. *The Undercommons: Fugitive Planning & Black Study.* Wivenhoe: Minor Compositions, 2013.

Harris, Cheryl I. "Whiteness as Property." *Harvard Law Review* 106, no. 8 (1993): 1707–91. DOI: 10.2307/1341787.

Harris, Joseph. *A Teaching Subject: Composition since 1966.* Upper Saddle River: Prentice Hall, 1997.

———. "Revision as a Critical Practice." *College English* 65, no. 6 (2003): 577–92.

Harris, Laura. "What Happened to the Motley Crew? C.L.R. James, Hélio Oiticica, and the Aesthetic Sociality of Blackness." *Social Text* 30, no. 3 (2012): 49–75. DOI: 10.1215/01642472-1597332.

Hartman, Saidiya V. *Scenes of Subjection: Terror, Slavery, and Self-Making in Nineteenth-Century America.* New York: Oxford University Press, 2010.

———. *Wayward Lives, Beautiful Experiments: Intimate Histories of Social Upheaval.* New York: W.W. Norton & Company, 2019.

Hickel, Jason. "The 'Girl Effect': Liberalism, Empowerment and the Contradictions of Development." *Third World Quarterly* 35, no. 8 (September 14, 2014): 1355–73. DOI: 10.1080/01436597.2014.946250.

Hisama, Ellie M. "'Diving into the Earth': The Musical Worlds of Julius Eastman." In *Rethinking Difference in Music Scholarship,* edited by Jeffrey Kallberg, Melanie Lowe, and Olivia Bloechl, 260–86. Cambridge: Cambridge University Press, 2015.

hooks, bell. *Ain't I a Woman: Black Women and Feminism.* 2nd edition. New York: Routledge, 2014.

Hopkins, Lightnin'. "Blues Is a Feeling." Recorded in 1962. *Mojo Hand: The Lightnin' Hopkins Anthology.* Rhino Records, 1993, 3 compact discs.

Horkheimer, Max, and Theodor W. Adorno. *Dialectic of Enlightenment: Philosophical Fragments.* Edited by Gunzelin Schmid Noerr. Translated by Edmund Jephcott. Stanford: Stanford University Press, 2002.

Hume, David. *A Treatise of Human Nature.* Edited by Ernest Campbell Mossner. Harmondsworth: Penguin Books, 1984.

Illouz, Eva. *Cold Intimacies: The Making of Emotional Capitalism.* Malden: Polity Press, 2016.

Inoue, Asao B. *Antiracist Writing Assessment Ecologies: Teaching and Assessing Writing for a Socially Just Future.* Fort Collins: The WAC Clearinghouse, 2015.

Ioanide, Paula. *The Emotional Politics of Racism: How Feelings Trump Facts in an Era of Colorblindness.* Stanford: Stanford University Press, 2015.

Jackson, Zakiyyah Iman. "'Theorizing in a Void': Sublimity, Matter, and Physics in Black Feminist Poetics." *South Atlantic Quarterly* 117, no. 3 (July 2018): 617–48. DOI: 10.1215/00382876-6942195.

James, Alison. *Constraining Chance: Georges Perec and the Oulipo.* Chicago: Northwestern University Press, 2009.

Johnson, Charles. "A Phenomenology of the Black Body." *Michigan Quarterly Review* 32, no. 4 (1993): 599–614. http://hdl.handle.net/2027/spo.act2080.0032.004:11.

Jung, Moon-Kie. *Beneath the Surface of White Supremacy Denaturalizing U.S. Racisms Past and Present.* Stanford: Stanford University Press, 2015.

Kant, Immanuel. *Critique of Pure Reason.* Translated by Paul Guyer and Allen W. Wood. Cambridge: Cambridge University Press, 1998.

———. *Critique of the Power of Judgment.* Translated by Paul Guyer and Eric Matthews. Cambridge: Cambridge University Press, 2009.

Kelly, Patty. *Lydia's Open Door: Inside Mexico's Most Modern Brothel.* Berkeley: University of California Press, 2008.

Kendi, Ibram X. *Stamped from the Beginning: The Definitive History of Racist Ideas in America.* New York: Nation Books, 2017.

Kernighan, Brian W., and Rob Pike. *The Practice of Programming.* Reading: Addison-Wesley, 1999.

Kierkegaard, Søren. *The Concept of Anxiety: A Simple Psychologically Orienting Deliberation on the Dogmatic Issue of Hereditary Sin.* Edited and translated by Reidar Thomte and Albert B. Anderson. Princeton: Princeton University Press, 1980.

———. *The Concept of Irony, with Continual Reference to Socrates.* Edited and translated by Howard V. Hong and Edna H. Hong. Princeton: Princeton University Press, 1989.

———. *The Sickness unto Death: A Christian Psychological Exposition for Upbuilding and Awakening.* Edited and translated by Edna H. Hong and Howard V. Hong. Princeton: Princeton University Press, 2006.

King, Mike. "Aggrieved Whiteness: White Identity Politics and Modern American Racial Formation." *Abolition,* May 4, 2017. https://abolitionjournal.org/aggrieved-whiteness-white-identity-politics-and-modern-american-racial-formation/.

Kristensen, Randi Gray. "From *Things Fall Apart* to *Freedom Dreams*: Black Studies and Cultural Studies in the Composition Classroom." In *Writing against the Curriculum: Anti-Disciplinarity in the Writing and Cultural Studies Classroom,* edited by Randi Gray Kristensen and Ryan M. Claycomb, 171–82. Lanham: Lexington Books, 2010.

Kuokkanen, Rauna. *Reshaping the University: Responsibility, Indigenous Epistemes, and the Logic of the Gift.* Vancouver: UBC Press, 2007.

Laymon, Kiese. *Heavy: An American Memoir.* New York: Scribner, 2018.

Le Menestrel, Sara. "The Color of Music: Social Boundaries and Stereotypes in Southwest Louisiana French Music." *Southern Cultures* 13, no. 3 (September 17, 2007): 87–105. DOI: 10.1353/scu.2007.0032.

Linebaugh, Peter. "All the Atlantic Mountains Shook." *Labour / Le Travail* 10 (1982): 87–121.

Lipsitz, George. *The Possessive Investment in Whiteness: How White People Profit from Identity Politics.* Revised and expanded edition. Philadelphia: Temple University Press, 2006.

Liu, Lydia H. *The Freudian Robot: Digital Media and the Future of the Unconscious.* Chicago: University of Chicago Press, 2010.

Lorde, Audre. *Sister Outsider: Essays and Speeches.* Reprint edition. Berkeley: Crossing Press, 2007.

Lowe, Lisa. *The Intimacies of Four Continents.* Durham: Duke University Press, 2015.

Lyons, Scott Richard. "Rhetorical Sovereignty: What Do American Indians Want from Writing?" *College Composition and Communication* 51, no. 3 (2000): 447–68.

MacPherson, C.B. *The Political Theory of Possessive Individualism: Hobbes to Locke.* Don Mills: Oxford University Press Canada, 2011.

Mahmood, Saba. *Politics of Piety: The Islamic Revival and the Feminist Subject.* Princeton: Princeton University Press, 2005.

Marks, Tony. "A Cultural Gumbo." *Evangeline Today,* July 9, 2018. https://www.villeplattetoday.com/news/cultural-gumbo.

Marriott, David. "Inventions of Existence: Sylvia Wynter, Frantz Fanon, Sociogeny, and 'the Damned.'" CR: *The New Centennial Review* 11, no. 3 (2012): 45–89. DOI: 10.1353/ncr.2012.0020.

———. "On Racial Fetishism." *Qui Parle: Critical Humanities and Social Sciences* 18, no. 2 (May 21, 2010): 215–48. DOI: 10.1353/qui.0.0012.

Marx, Karl. *Economic and Philosophic Manuscripts of 1844.* Translated by Martin Milligan. Moscow: Progress Publishers, 1932.

Marx, Karl, and Friedrich Engels. *Capital: A Critique of Political Economy.* Translated by Ben Fowkes and David Fernbach. 3 vols. London: Penguin Books, 1990.

Massenet, Jules. *Hérodiade.* Choeur et Orchestre du Capitole de Toulouse. Michel Plasson. Recorded November 19–27 and December 2 and 9–10, 1994. EMI Classics, 1995, 3 compact discs.

McKeon, Michael. *The Secret History of Domesticity: Public, Private, and the Division of Knowledge.* Baltimore: Johns Hopkins University Press, 2009.

McKittrick, Katherine. *Demonic Grounds: Black Women and the Cartographies of Struggle.* Minneapolis: University of Minnesota Press, 2006.

———, ed. *Sylvia Wynter: On Being Human as Praxis.* Durham: Duke University Press, 2015.

McRuer, Robert. *Crip Theory: Cultural Signs of Queerness and Disability.* New York: New York University Press, 2006.

Mee, Jon. *Romanticism, Enthusiasm, and Regulation: Poetics and the Policing of Culture in the Romantic Period.* Oxford: Oxford University Press, 2003.

Mehta, Uday Singh. *Liberalism and Empire: A Study in Nineteenth-Century British Liberal Thought.* Chicago: University of Chicago Press, 1999.

Merleau-Ponty, Maurice. *Phenomenology of Perception.* Translated by Donald A. Landes. Abingdon: Routledge, 2013.

Mohanty, Chandra. "Under Western Eyes: Feminist Scholarship and Colonial Discourses." *Feminist Review* 30 (1988): 61–88. DOI: 10.1057/fr.1988.42.

Moreton-Robinson, Aileen. *The White Possessive: Property, Power, and Indigenous Sovereignty.* Minneapolis: University of Minnesota Press, 2015.

Morris, Tracie. *handholding: 5 kinds.* Tucson: Kore Press, 2016.

Morrison, Toni. *Playing in the Dark: Whiteness and the Literary Imagination.* New York: Vintage Books, 1993.

Moten, Fred. *Black and Blur.* Durham: Duke University Press, 2017.

———. *In the Break: The Aesthetics of the Black Radical Tradition.* Minneapolis: University of Minnesota Press, 2003.

———. "Preface for a Solo by Miles Davis." *Women & Performance: A Journal of Feminist Theory* 17, no. 2 (July 2007): 217–46. DOI: 10.1080/07407700701387317.

Mullen, Harryette. "Optic White: Blackness and the Production of Whiteness." *Diacritics* 24, nos. 2–3 (1994): 71–89. DOI: 10.2307/465165.

Muñoz, José Esteban. *Cruising Utopia: The Then and There of Queer Futurity.* New York: New York University Press, 2009.

Nelson, Dana D. *National Manhood: Capitalist Citizenship and the Imagined Fraternity of White Men.* Durham: Duke University Press, 1998.

Ngai, Sianne. *Ugly Feelings.* Cambridge: Harvard University Press, 2007.

Nyong'o, Tavia. *The Amalgamation Waltz: Race, Performance, and the Ruses of Memory.* Minneapolis: University of Minnesota Press, 2009.

Omi, Michael, and Howard Winant. *Racial Formation in the United States.* 3rd edition. New York: Routledge, 2015.

Oza, Rupal. "The Entanglements of Transnational Feminism and Area Studies." *Environment and Planning D: Society and Space* 34, no. 5 (October 1, 2016): 836–42. DOI: 10.1177/0263775816656529.

Parham, Marisa. ".break .dance." *sx archipelagos* 3 (July 2019). http://smallaxe.net/sxarchipelagos/issue03/parham/parham.html.

———. "Sample | Signal | Strobe: Haunting, Social Media, and Black Digitality." In *Debates in the Digital Humanities 2019,* edited by Matthew K. Gold and Lauren F. Klein, chapter 11. Minneapolis: University of Minnesota Press, 2019. https://dhdebates.gc.cuny.edu/read/untitled-f2acf72c-a469-49d8-be35-67f9ac1e3a60/section/0fa03a28-d067-40b3-8ab1-b94d46bf00b6.

Pateman, Carole. *The Sexual Contract.* Stanford: Stanford University Press, 2009.

Philip, M. NourbeSe. *A Genealogy of Resistance: And Other Essays.* Toronto: Mercury Press, 1997.

Pinch, Adela. *Strange Fits of Passion: Epistemologies of Emotion, Hume to Austen.* Stanford: Stanford University Press, 1996.

Piper, Adrian. *Escape to Berlin: A Travel Memoir.* Berlin: Adrian Piper Research Archive Foundation Berlin, 2018.

Rancière, Jacques. *Disagreement: Politics and Philosophy.* Translated by Julie Rose. Minneapolis: University of Minnesota Press, 2008.

———. *The Ignorant Schoolmaster: Five Lessons in Intellectual Emancipation.* Translated by Kristin Ross. Stanford: Stanford University Press, 1999.

Rankine, Claudia. *Citizen: An American Lyric.* Minneapolis: Graywolf Press, 2014.

Rich, Adrienne. "Living in Sin." *The New Yorker,* January 23, 1954.

Richardson, Pete. "Doing Things with Wood: Builders, Managers and Wittgenstein in an Idaho Sawmill." *Critique of Anthropology* 29, no. 2 (June 1, 2009): 160–82. DOI: 10.1177/0308275X09104084.

Riley, Denise. *Impersonal Passion: Language as Affect.* Durham: Duke University Press, 2005.

Roach, Joseph. *Cities of the Dead: Circum-Atlantic Performance.* New York: Columbia University Press, 1996.

Robinson, Sally. *Marked Men: White Masculinity in Crisis.* New York: Columbia University Press, 2000.

Roediger, David R. *The Wages of Whiteness: Race and the Making of the American Working Class.* London: Verso, 2007.

———. *Towards the Abolition of Whiteness: Essays on Race, Politics, and Working Class History.* London: Verso, 2000.

Ryle, Gilbert. *The Concept of Mind.* Chicago: University of Chicago Press, 1984.

Schaefer, Donovan O. *Religious Affects: Animality, Evolution, and Power.* Durham: Duke University Press, 2015.

Sedgwick, Eve Kosofsky. *Between Men: English Literature and Male Homosocial Desire.* New York: Columbia University Press, 1985.

———. "Privilege of Unknowing." *Genders* 1 (Spring 1988): 102–24.

———. *Touching Feeling: Affect, Pedagogy, Performativity.* Durham: Duke University Press, 2003.

Shannon, C.E. "A Mathematical Theory of Communication." *The Bell System Technical Journal* 27, nos. 3–4 (July 1948): 379–423, 623–56. DOI: 10.1002/j.1538-7305.1948.tb01338.x.

Sharpe, Christina. *In the Wake: On Blackness and Being.* Durham: Duke University Press, 2016.

———. *Monstrous Intimacies: Making Post-Slavery Subjects.* Durham: Duke University Press, 2010.

Shotwell, Alexis. *Knowing Otherwise: Race, Gender, and Implicit Understanding.* University Park: Pennsylvania State University Press, 2011.

Silverman, Kaja. *Male Subjectivity at the Margins.* New York: Routledge, 2016.

Smith, Adam. *The Theory of Moral Sentiments.* Indianapolis: Liberty Classics, 1982.

Smith, Andrea. "Queer Theory and Native Studies: The Heteronormativity of Settler Colonialism." *GLQ: A Journal of Lesbian and Gay Studies* 16, nos. 1–2 (2010): 41–68. https://muse.jhu.edu/article/372444/pdf.

Smith, Valerie. "Black Feminist Theory and the Representation of the 'Other.'" In *Changing Our Own Words: Essays on Criticism, Theory, and Writing by Black Women,* edited by Cheryl A. Wall, 38–57. New Brunswick: Rutgers University Press, 1989.

Spade, Dean. *Normal Life: Administrative Violence, Critical Trans Politics, and the Limits of Law.* Brooklyn: South End Press, 2011.

Spillers, Hortense J. "'All the Things You Could Be by Now, If Sigmund Freud's Wife Was Your Mother': Psychoanalysis and Race." In *Black, White, and in Color: Essays on American Literature and Culture,* 376–427. Chicago: University of Chicago Press, 2003.

———. "Interstices: A Small Drama of Words." In *Black, White, and in Color: Essays on American Literature and Culture,* 152–75. Chicago: University of Chicago Press, 2003.

———. "Mama's Baby, Papa's Maybe: An American Grammar Book." In *Black, White, and in Color: Essays on American Literature and Culture,* 203–29. Chicago: University of Chicago Press, 2003.

———. "The Idea of Black Culture." *CR: The New Centennial Review* 6, no. 3 (2007): 7–28. DOI: 10.1353/ncr.2007.0022.

Spivak, Gayatri Chakravorty. *A Critique of Postcolonial Reason: Toward a History of the Vanishing Present.* Cambridge: Harvard University Press, 2003.

———. "Terror: A Speech after 9–11." *boundary 2* 31, no. 2 (Summer 2004): 81–111. https://muse.jhu.edu/article/171420.

Sprengnether, Madelon. *The Spectral Mother: Freud, Feminism, and Psychoanalysis.* Ithaca: Cornell University Press, 1990.

Stewart, Kathleen. *Ordinary Affects.* Durham: Duke University Press, 2008.

Stokes, Mason. *The Color of Sex: Whiteness, Heterosexuality, and the Fictions of White Supremacy.* Durham: Duke University Press, 2001.

Sullivan, Shannon. *Good White People: The Problem with Middle-Class White Anti-Racism.* Albany: State University of New York Press, 2014.

———. *Revealing Whiteness: The Unconscious Habits of Racial Privilege.* Bloomington: Indiana University Press, 2006.

Takaki, Ronald T. *Iron Cages: Race and Culture in 19th-Century America.* Revised edition. New York: Oxford University Press, 2000.

Tanesini, Alessandra. *Wittgenstein: A Feminist Interpretation.* Cambridge: Polity Press, 2004.

Tate, Claudia. *Domestic Allegories of Political Desire: The Black Heroine's Text at the Turn of the Century.* New York: Oxford University Press, 1992.

Taylor, Charles. *A Secular Age.* Cambridge: Belknap Press of Harvard University, 2007.

Taylor, Keeanga-Yamahtta, ed. *How We Get Free: Black Feminism and the Combahee River Collective.* Chicago: Haymarket Books, 2017.

Thandeka. *Learning to Be White: Money, Race, and God in America.* New York: Bloomsbury, 2013.

Tomkins, Silvan S. *Affect Imagery Consciousness: The Complete Edition.* 2 vols. New York: Springer, 2008.

———. *Shame and Its Sisters: A Silvan Tomkins Reader.* Edited by Eve Kosofsky Sedgwick and Adam Frank. Durham: Duke University Press, 1996.

Tomlinson, Barbara. "Wicked Problems and Intersectionality Telephone." In *Antiracism, Inc.: Why the Way We Talk about Racial Justice Matters,* edited by Felice Blake, Paula Ioanide, and Alison Reed, 161–87. Earth: punctum books, 2019.

Trilling, Lionel. *Sincerity and Authenticity.* Cambridge: Harvard University Press, 1997.

Trudy. "Explanation of Misogynoir." *Gradient Lair,* April 28, 2014. https://www.gradientlair.com/post/84107309247/

define-misogynoir-anti-black-misogyny-moya-bailey-coined.

Turing, Alan M. "Computing Machinery and Intelligence." In *The Essential Turing: Seminal Writings in Computing, Logic, Philosophy, Artificial Intelligence, and Artificial Life: Plus the Secrets of Enigma,* edited by B. Jack Copeland, 441–64. New York: Oxford University Press, 2004.

———. "On Computable Numbers, with an Application to the *Entscheidungsproblem*." In *The Essential Turing: Seminal Writings in Computing, Logic, Philosophy, Artificial Intelligence, and Artificial Life: Plus the Secrets of Enigma,* edited by B. Jack Copeland, 58–90. New York: Oxford University Press, 2004.

UWaterlooEnglish. *Hortense Spillers: The Idea of Black Culture,* 2013. https://www.youtube.com/watch?v=P1PTHFCN4Gc.

Walcott, Rinaldo. *Queer Returns: Essays on Multiculturalism, Diaspora, and Black Studies.* London: Insomniac Press, 2016.

Walker, David. *Walker's Appeal, in Four Articles: Together with a Preamble, to the Coloured Citizens of the World, but in Particular, and Very Expressly, to Those of the United States of America.* Chapel Hill: University of North Carolina Press, 2011.

Weber, Max. *Economy and Society: An Outline of Interpretive Sociology.* Edited by Guenther Roth and Claus Wittich. 2 vols. Berkeley: University of California Press, 1978.

Weheliye, Alexander G. *Habeas Viscus: Racializing Assemblages, Biopolitics, and Black Feminist Theories of the Human.* Durham: Duke University Press, 2014.

———. *Phonographies: Grooves in Sonic Afro-Modernity.* Durham: Duke University Press, 2005.

Weinberg, Justin. "Internet Abuse of Philosophers (2 Updates)." *Daily Nous,* January 15, 2016. http://dailynous.com/2016/01/15/internet-abuse-of-philosophers/.

Welch, Nancy, and Tony Scott. "Introduction." In *Composition in the Age of Austerity,* edited by Nancy Welch and Tony Scott, 3–17. Logan: Utah State University Press, 2016.

Wells, Ida B. *The Light of Truth: Writings of an Anti-Lynching Crusader.* Edited by Mia Bay and Henry Louis Gates, Jr. New York: Penguin Books, 2014.

Whitehead, Alfred North. *Process and Reality: An Essay in Cosmology.* Corrected edition. New York: Free Press, 1978.

Wiegman, Robyn. *American Anatomies: Theorizing Race and Gender.* Durham: Duke University Press, 2002.

Williams, Jr., Robert A. *Like a Loaded Weapon: The Rehnquist Court, Indian Rights, and the Legal History of Racism in America.* Minneapolis: University of Minnesota Press, 2005.

Williams, Patricia J. *The Alchemy of Race and Rights.* Cambridge: Harvard University Press, 1991.

Wittgenstein, Ludwig. *Philosophical Investigations.* Translated by G.E.M. Anscombe, 3rd edition. Malden: Wiley-Blackwell, 1991.

Woods, Clyde. *Development Arrested: The Blues and Plantation Power in the Mississippi Delta.* New York: Verso, 2017.

Wright, Michelle M. *Becoming Black: Creating Identity in the African Diaspora.* Durham: Duke University Press, 2004.

Wynter, Sylvia. "1492: A New World View." In *Race, Discourse, and the Origin of the Americas: A New World View,* edited by Vera Lawrence Hyatt and Rex Nettleford, 5–57. Washington: Smithsonian Institution Press, 1995.

———. "Beyond Miranda's Meanings: Un/Silencing the 'Demonic Ground' of Caliban's 'Woman.'" In *Out of the Kumbla: Caribbean Women and Literature,* edited by Carole Boyce Davies and Elaine Savory Fido, 355–72. Trenton: Africa World Press, 1990.

———. "Beyond the Word of Man: Glissant and the New Discourse of the Antilles." *World Literature Today* 63, no. 4 (1989): 637–48. DOI: 10.2307/40145557.

———. "The Ceremony Must Be Found: After Humanism." *boundary 2* 12/13, nos. 3–1 (1984): 19–70.

———. "Towards the Sociogenic Principle: Fanon, Identity, the Puzzle of Conscious Experience, and What It Is Like to Be 'Black.'" In *National Identities and Sociopolitical Changes in Latin America,* edited by Mercedes F. Durán-Cogan and

Antonio Gómez-Moriana, 30–66. New York: Routledge, 2001.

———. "Unsettling the Coloniality of Being/Power/ Truth/Freedom: Towards the Human, After Man, Its Overrepresentation—An Argument." *CR: The New Centennial Review* 3, no. 3 (2003): 257–337. DOI: 10.1353/ncr.2004.0015.

Yancy, George. *Black Bodies, White Gazes: The Continuing Significance of Race in America.* 2nd edition. Lanham: Rowman & Littlefield, 2016.

———. "Dear White America." *The Stone* (*The New York Times*), December 24, 2015. http://opinionator.blogs.nytimes.com/2015/12/24/dear-white-america/.

———. *Look, a White! Philosophical Essays on Whiteness.* Philadelphia: Temple University Press, 2012.

Yancy, George, and Brad Evans. "The Perils of Being a Black Philosopher." *The Stone* (*The New York Times*), April 18, 2016. https://opinionator.blogs.nytimes.com/2016/04/18/the-perils-of-being-a-black-philosopher/.

Yates, JoAnne. *Control through Communication: The Rise of System in American Management.* Baltimore: Johns Hopkins University Press, 1989.

Zuboff, Shoshana. *In the Age of the Smart Machine: The Future of Work and Power.* New York: Basic Books, 1996.